ATLA Monograph Series
edited by Dr. Kenneth E. Rowe

NO FOOT OF LAND:

Folklore of American

Methodist Itinerants

by

DONALD E. BYRNE, JR.

with a Foreword by

Stuart C. Henry

ATLA Monograph Series, No. 6

The Scarecrow Press, Inc., Metuchen, N. J.
and
The American Theological Library Association
1975

Library of Congress Cataloging in Publication Data

Byrne, Donald E
  No foot of land.

  (ATLA monograph series ; no. 6)
  A revision of the author's thesis, Duke University.
  Bibliography: p.
  Includes index.
    1. Methodist Church--Clergy. 2. Folk-lore--United
States. 3. United States--Religion--19th century.
I. Title. II. Series: American Theological Library
Association. ATLA monograph series ; no. 6)
BX8237.B93 1975   287'.0973   75-1097
ISBN 0-8108-0798-X

FOREWORD

Ecclesiastics have not always had the wit to perceive or the grace to admit the full significance of the relation between religion and folklore. To the sad loss of religion, the tendency to separate the two has frequently resulted in a provincial view of folklore. It may appear as a collection of stories or sayings which intrude, rather than illustrate, history; or as a persistence of meaningless, though quaint, practices which co-exist with religion, operating often in the same arena but bearing no more radical connection to each other than the clowns and aerialists who only chance to be confined in the same ring. When the stories, sayings, and rituals of folklore have succeeded, not simply in invading the sphere of formal religion but in gaining a foothold, then these phenomena and their stubbornly virile forms have achieved more than baptism: they have experienced (rather than won) redemption. They have actually been changed and become something different.

Thus it comes about, therefore, that the study of folklore can help, for example, to explain why, at a jocular level, laughter may defensibly be an appropriate expression of faith in its acknowledgement of the incongruity of life, and the futility of settling for anything less than orientation to transcendent value. Again, the legend of a miraculous resolution of difficulty or interruption of the world order does more than illustrate the faith: it enforces commitment. Folk wisdom is protean in form, though constant in essence --constant and vital. Wherever it has domiciled it has effected changes in the very forces which seem to overcome it.

Theologians operating in isolation always risk religious sterility, confusing truth with its propositional forms. And, worse than lifelessness, they risk more error than they need to, because (although ultimate truth is admittedly beyond the capacity of any mortal) the approximation of truth is more nearly possible when it is seen in the reflected light of folklore, than when it is pursued in the limits of pure reason

iii

alone. God is both what he is and what men understand him to be. The choice between humanism and revelation is not only artificial, it is unnecessary as well. The history of missions cannot be recorded in statistics, or even as the story of the power of logical conclusions. Rather it is the account of how people--nourished in one tradition--discover within another a resonance sympathetic to the deepest needs of their consciousness, with the result that they are affected by, and affect a new faith. The force of evidence of such double metamorphosis to be found in the study of folklore is abundant.

When, therefore, a scholar offers, as Donald Byrne does, a careful and lively study in folklore, he serves us well. Professor Byrne has done more. Together with the contribution to understanding of religion in general (which we should expect), he affords us three additional insights: he has gathered fugitive materials relating to insignificant chapters in social history and arranged them so that they both explain and describe distinctive elements in the American story. He has written of a peculiar dimension of American Methodism in such a way as to make possible not simply the recognition of the difference between the native and British phenomenon, but a partial understanding of why and how the difference came into existence. And as a sensitive and intelligent Christian whose personal commitment happens to be within the Roman Catholic communion, he has brought a fresh objectivity to the study of Protestantism which, coupled with his focus upon the discipline of folklore, demonstrates the strength of a tradition which transcends any restriction of creed.

Stuart C. Henry
Duke University

iv

EDITOR'S FOREWORD

Since 1972 the American Theological Library Association has undertaken responsibility for a modest dissertation publishing program in the field of religious studies. Our aim in this monograph series is to publish in serviceable format and at reasonable cost two dissertations of quality each year. Titles are selected from studies in the several religious and theological disciplines nominated by graduate school deans or directors of graduate studies in religion.

Professor Donald E. Byrne, Jr. has studied at St. Paul Seminary and Marquette University and received the doctorate from Duke University. He currently serves as Assistant Professor of Religion in Lebanon Valley College, Annville, Pennsylvania. We are pleased to publish his study of American Methodist itinerant folklore as number six in our series.

A special word of appreciation goes to Professor Stuart Henry of Duke University for the fine foreword.

Kenneth E. Rowe, Editor

Drew University Library
Madison, New Jersey

CONTENTS

PREFACE

> When, in my early teens, I became a traveling min-
> ister, sixty years ago, I listened to the folk-lore of
> the elder Methodists in my charges about the move-
> ments of the earlier leaders of the Methodist Epis-
> copal Church. [1]

The statement of an aging but still committed Methodist minister--to say nothing of the focus and perspective of
his recollection--provides at once a window through which to
observe a new dimension of American church history and a
summary of this volume, which attempts to "listen" to the
folklore of nineteenth century American Methodism.

The idea of using folklore as a tool by which to elu-
cidate history is not original with the author of this work.
Cultural anthropologists have had to formulate guidelines by
which to cull factual history from the oral traditions of non-
literate societies. [2] The American folklorist Richard Dorson
has suggested the uses of folklore for American historiography. [3]

Among scholars of religion, Mircea Eliade has discussed the importance of folklore for history of religions. [4]
George Pullen Jackson, noted for his studies of the shape-
note singing subculture in America, [5] remarked the folk character of popular religion. [6] Don Yoder, an American church
historian who is chairman of the Folklore and Folklife Department at the University of Pennsylvania, has noted the tensions between institutional religion and folk religion. [7] The
violent and tragic surfacing of folk belief in the Salem witchcraft trials of the late seventeenth century has, of course,
received substantial attention from students both of religion
and of history. [8]

In addition, numerous studies of folk religion by folklorists not directly concerned with the relationship of folklore

and the history of American religion have confirmed the widespread existence of such phenomena and have impressed upon my mind the importance of incorporating folk religion into wider syntheses of American religious life. 9

The possibilities suggested by such studies have prompted this work, which has gleaned folklore from the autobiographies, biographies, and reminiscences of nineteenth century Methodist itinerant ministers and which has attempted to suggest implications of such data for American religious history.

Inasmuch as, by the nature of the material, the evidence is cumulative rather than consecutive, I have summarized briefly at the end of each chapter and have drawn conclusions at the end of each part. The conclusion of the study recapitulates these summaries and conclusions. It is hoped that this procedure will enable the reader to keep a perspective on data which all too readily blur into a potpourri of motifs.

Punctuation and diction of the original sources have been retained throughout the study. Thus, the same items from different sources may appear different in the text of this study. Similarly, erratic use of quotation marks indicates inconsistencies in the sources, not in the preparation of the material.

This study approaches the history of American religion from an unusual perspective--that of the discipline of folklore. 10 Therefore I thought it was necessary to introduce the study with remarks on the nature of folklore and on the relationship of folklore to history and to religion. Needless to say, such remarks are not exhaustive (especially for specialists in each area) but indicative.

Furthermore, although the study suggests that folklore in written documents can be considered per se an historical source, the present task has been simply to assemble the data and to document its traditional nature. While documentation of traditional cultural structures in a given period is itself a contribution to the history of that period, elucidation of the inner meaning of such material may await the historian trained in anthropology, sociology, or psychology. In a particular way, therefore, this study is introductory, pointing out a direction along which further investigation must yet be made, rather than announcing arrival at a destination.

I am deeply grateful to the many who have assisted

me in the completion of this study: to Duke University, which
provided me with a Summer Scholarship for study at Indiana
University's Folklore Institute in the summer of 1970; to the
National Endowment for the Humanities which granted me a
Summer Stipend in 1973 to study remarkable providences; to
the library staffs of Duke University, Duke Divinity School,
Indiana University, Yale University, University of Pennsylvan-
ia, Drew University, and Lebanon Valley College; to Mrs.
Glenn Anglin, who typed the first draft, and to Mrs. Helen
Geib, who graciously assisted with revisions.

Special thanks to Dr. Ken Rowe of Drew University,
whose assistance facilitated not only revisions of this work
but also the location of appropriate illustrations.

I am also indebted to Dr. Don Yoder of the University
of Pennsylvania, who provided me with initial support and encouragement; to Dr. Richard Dorson, who helped me begin
my studies in folklore; to Dr. Dan Ben-Amos of the University of Pennsylvania, who, while visiting professor at the
Folklore Institute, offered much counsel and guidance; and to
Dr. Warren Roberts, who guided me through my first course
in the discipline of folklore.

The humanity, learning, and dedication of my professors at Duke University have continued to sustain me in my
scholarship and teaching. Although I did not take courses
from Dr. Ray Petry, I learned much from his sense of the
past. Dr. William Poteat both turned my philosophical head
and gave me a new appreciation of the art of teaching. Dr.
Egil Grislis renewed my respect for primary sources in the
study of history and offered wise counsel. Dr. I. B. Holley,
of the history department, disciplined my thinking, broadened
my perspectives, and provided encouragement and advice
throughout the second year of my graduate study.

I owe special thanks to Dr. Stuart C. Henry, my dissertation director, and continuing mentor and friend. His
appreciation of the incarnational aspects of religion and his
respect for the interests of his students created an atmosphere in which I was free to choose the subject of this study.
At every step of the work he knew how to encourage by speaking and by keeping silent; in the final stages he was unstint-
ing of his time and attention. I shall remember with great
relish long conversations over lunch, which allowed me to
sample not only his skill as a folk raconteur but also his
considerable culinary expertise. For his patience, respect,
and wise counsel I am deeply grateful.

The Tietjen and the Byrne families have sustained me by their confidence and encouragement. Julie, Donald III, and Clare have kept stories, songs, and laughter from becoming simply academic matters. Finally, Mary Anne has borne with me from the beginning to the completion of the work, proofreading, criticizing, above all giving love, friendship and peace. To her this study is dedicated.

D. E. B. Jr.
Lebanon Valley College

1. Thomas H. Pearne, Sixty-One Years of Itinerant Christian Life in Church and State (Cincinnati: Curts and Jennings, 1898), p. 64.
2. Jan Vansina, Oral Tradition, tr. by H. M. Wright (Chicago: University of Chicago Press, 1965).
3. "Historical Method and American Folklore," Indiana History Bulletin, XXIII (1946), 84-99. See also Dorson's American Folklore and the Historian (Chicago: University of Chicago Press, 1971).
4. Mircea Popescu, "Eliade and Folklore," Myths and Symbols: Studies in Honor of Mircea Eliade, ed. by Joseph Kitagawa and Charles Long (Chicago: University of Chicago Press, 1969), pp. 81-90.
5. White Spirituals in the Southern Uplands (Chapel Hill, N.C.: University of North Carolina Press, 1933).
6. "The Old Time Religion as a Folk Religion," Tennessee Folklore Society Bulletin, VII (1941), 30-39.
7. "Organized Religion versus Folk Religion," Pennsylvania Folklife, XV (1965), 36-52.
8. George Lyman Kittredge, Witchcraft in Old and New England (Cambridge, Mass.: Harvard University Press, 1929); Stuart C. Henry, "Puritan Character in the Witchcraft Episode of Salem," in A Miscellany of American Christianity; Essays in Honor of H. Shelton Smith, ed. by Stuart C. Henry (Durham, N.C.: Duke University Press, 1963), pp. 138-67; Chadwick Hansen, Witchcraft at Salem (New York: G. Braziller, 1969).
9. To mention a selection of these studies: Higini Angles, "Relations of Spanish Folk Song to Gregorian Chant," Journal of the International Folk Music Council, XVI (1964), 54-56; Wilfred Bonser, "The Cult of Relics in the Middle Ages," Folklore, LXXIII (1962), 234-57; Wilhelm Bousset, The AntiChrist Legend: A Chapter in Christian and Jewish Folklore (London: Hutchinson and Co., 1896); Wolfgang Brückner, "Popular

Piety in Central Europe," Journal of the Folklore Institute, V (1968), 158-74; idem, "Rulle und der marianische Umkreis der Bienenlegende," Rheinisch-Westfälische Zeitschrift für Volkskunde, IX (1962), 28-39; Josef Dietz, "Vom Brot im kirchlichen Brauch des Bonner Landes," Rheinisch-Westfälische Zeitschrift für Volkskunde, IX (1962), 18-27; Alfred E. Dowling, "A Study in the Flora of the Holy Church," American Catholic Quarterly Review, XXVII (1902), 452-75; James C. Downey, "Revivalism, the Gospel Songs, and Social Reform," Ethnomusicology, VIII (1965), 115-25; John E. Englekirk, "The Passion Play in New Mexico," Western Folklore, XXV (1966), 17-33, 105-21; Ellen Ettlinger, "Folklore in Oxfordshire Churches," Folk-Lore, LXXIII (1962), 160-78; Austin E. Fife, "Christian Swarm Charms from the Ninth to the Nineteenth Centuries," Journal of American Folklore, LXXVII (1964), 154-59; Jerome Field, "Folk Tales from North Dakota," Western Folklore, XVII (1958), 29-33; Nathan L. Gerrard, "The Serpent-Handling Religions of West Virginia," Trans-Action, V (1968), 22-28; Adrian de Groot, Saint Nicholas: A Psychoanalytic Study of His History and Myth (The Hague: Mouton and Co., 1965); Frederick W. Hackwood, Christ Lore, Being the Legends, Traditions, Myths, Symbols, Customs, and Superstitions of the Christian Church (London: Elliot Stock, 1902); Charles A. Huguenin, "A Prayer for Examinations," New York Folklore Quarterly, XVIII (1962), 145-48; Francis L. K. Hsu, "A Neglected Aspect of Witchcraft Studies," Journal of American Folklore, LXXIII (1960), 35-38; Marie-Louise Lagarde, "A South Louisiana Negro Baptizing," Louisiana Folklore Quarterly, II (1968), 45-55; J. Frank Lee, "The Informal Organization at White Southern Protestant Funerals: The Role of the Arranger," Tennessee Folklore Society Bulletin, XXXIII (1967), 36-40; Cosette Chavez Lowe, "A Lash for the Grace of God," New Mexico Folklore Record, XI (1963-64), 18-20; George Monteiro, "Parodies of Scripture, Prayer and Hymn," Journal of American Folklore, LXXVII (1964), 45-52; Julia Neal, "Shaker Festival," Kentucky Folklore Record, VIII (1962), 127-35; R. Patai and F. L. Utley, Studies in Biblical and Jewish Folklore (Indiana University Folklore Series No. 13; Bloomington, Indiana: Indiana University Press, 1960); N. N. Puckett, "Religious Folk Beliefs of Whites and Negroes," Journal of Negro History, XVI (1931), 9-35;

Patricia Rickels, "The Folklore of Sacraments and Sacramentals in South Louisiana," Louisiana Folklore Miscellany, II (1965), 27-44; Irmgard Simon, Die Gemeinschaft der Siebenten-Tags Adventisten in volkskundliches Sicht (Münster: Ascendorf, 1965); Ellen Stekert, "The Snake Handling Sect of Harlan County, Kentucky: Its Influence on Folk Tradition," Southern Folklore Quarterly, XXVII (1963), 316-22; Redding Sugg, "Heaven Bound," Southern Folklore Quarterly, XXVII (1963), 249-66; George Swetnam, "The Church Hymn as a Folklore Form," Keystone Folklore Quarterly, IX (1964), 144-53; Joseph Szoverfty, "Some Notes on Medieval Studies and Folklore," Journal of American Folklore, LXXIII (1960), 239-43; William Tallmadge, "The Responsorial and Antiphonal Practice in Gospel Song," Ethnomusicology, XII (1968), 219-38; Stephen Whitney, "The Church with the Hand on Top," Yankee, XXX (1966), 48-50; Mitchell A. Wilder, "Santos (Religious Folk Art of New Mexico)," American West, II (1965), 37-46; Marian Wenzel, " Graveside Feasts and Dances in Yugoslavia," Folk-Lore, LXXVIII (1962), 1-13. See also James T. Bratcher, "Religion-Centered Anecdotes of Fort Sill," Western Folklore, XXIII (1964), 265-67; Julia Hull Winner, "Some Religious Humor from the Past," New York Folklore Quarterly, XXI (1965), 58-62; Bruce Rosenberg, The Art of the American Folk Preacher (New York: Oxford University Press, 1970); Dorothy Horn, Sing to Me of Heaven; A Study of Folk and Early American Materials in Three Old Harp Books (Gainesville: University of Florida Press, 1970); Tony Heilbut, The Gospel Sound: Good News and Bad Times (New York: Simon and Schuster, 1971); Ross Phares, Bible in Pocket, Gun in Hand; The Story of Frontier Religion (Lincoln: University of Nebraska Press, 1971); Don Yoder, Pennsylvania Spirituals (Lancaster: Pennsylvania Folklife Society, 1961); Hilda A. Kring, The Harmonists; A Folk Cultural Approach (Metuchen, N.J.: Scarecrow Press, 1973).

10. The approach is unusual but not original. Dr. Don Yoder has pioneered the perspective in his many books and articles on Pennsylvania Dutch religious history.

PART I

INTRODUCTION

To facilitate understanding of the methodology of this study, first, the scope and content of the discipline of folklore are defined; second, theoretical possibilities advanced for the relationship of folklore and history are surveyed; and third, the relationship of folklore and religion as it pertains to the sources examined here is discussed.

Folklore

Throughout this discussion the term folklore will refer both to the content of the discipline and to the discipline itself. [1]

Folklore is a relative newcomer to the circle of sciences. The word "folklore" was coined in 1846 by W. J. Thoms, a British scholar, as an Anglo-Saxon replacement for the Latinate term "popular antiquities, " which designated "the loving study of old customs, usages, and superstitions. "[2] Darwinian theories of evolution spurred a creeping antiquarianism to new purpose: the reconstruction of the prehistory of mankind from survivals in peasant and savage traditions. By 1878 scholars had banded together in London, forming the Folk-Lore Society, which published a journal, Folk-Lore, still published today.

American enthusiasts, taking their cue from the British, founded the American Folklore Society in 1888 and began publishing the Journal of American Folklore. The initial burst of enthusiasm waned, and folklore became the avocation of cultural anthropologists, literary scholars, and collectors. Within the last three decades, however, American folklore has become the vocation of numerous avid students; several master's programs and two doctoral programs, one at the Folklore Institute of Indiana University (Bloomington, Indiana) and the other at the University of Pennsylvania, mark the gradual rise of the science to scholarly autonomy.

Folklore's ascent to a place in the pantheon of American academic disciplines has not been marked by unanimity among folklorists as to the nature and scope of their discipline. While in Britain and on the Continent the task of defining the folklore and folklife of a people has been facilitated by the relative stability and homogeneity of lower-class culture, in America the chore of definition has been vastly complicated by the fluidity and diversity of traditions and cultures attributable in part to ethnic and racial heterogeneity and in part to the brevity of U.S. national history. At issue are both halves of Thoms' neologism, "folklore." In America, who are the folk, and what is the lore?

To consider the latter question first: the predominant school of thought in America, influenced by a long apprenticeship at the hands of English and cultural anthropology, has tended to define folklore as "oral tradition." Hence, in the first half of the century, American folklorists paid overweening attention to ballad texts and folktales.[3]

Recently, however, certain scholars have tended to define the discipline after Continental, and especially German and Finnish, models. Preferring the term "folklife" (after the German "Volkskunde" and Swedish "Volkliv") to "folklore," this school of thought concentrates on the total traditional life of a society, including the physical objects used and manufactured by folk artisans.[4]

From such divergent emphases a tertium quid conception of folklore, embracing both schools of thought, has arisen. According to Jan Brunvand, therefore, there exist three kinds of lore: verbal, partly verbal, and non-verbal. Verbal folklore includes folk speech (dialect and place-naming), proverbs, riddles, rhymes, narratives, and folksongs. Partly verbal folklore includes beliefs and superstitions in which gestures accompany statements, games, dramas, dances, customs, and festivals. Non-verbal folklore includes folk architecture, arts, crafts, customs, costumes, food, gestures, and music.[5]

The common denominator of all definitions of the lore, even of the twenty-one definitions collected in the Standard Dictionary of Folklore, Mythology, and Legend, is tradition.[6] Transmission orally or by customary example differentiates folk items from other traditional cultural data. Verbal folklore

that has found its way into print must have been at some
time or other in oral circulation, in order to qualify as folklore. [7] Partly verbal and non-verbal folklore, to qualify as
true lore, must have been at some time transmitted informally
by demonstration and imitation rather than deliberately and
formally, as for example by educational agencies such as
schools. [8]

Three other marks distinguish the lore that is the subject of folklore. First, inasmuch as oral transmission tends
to foster different versions of the same item, variations or
versions verify the true folk datum. [9] Second, anonymity as
to authorship, time and place of origin is characteristic of
true lore. Thus, for example, the saga of Paul Bunyan is
anathematized by folklorists as "fakelore"[10] because the giant
of the Northland and his blue ox "Babe" are the product of
an advertising agent for the Red River Lumber Company of
Minnesota rather than the tradition of a folk group. [11] Third,
folklore tends to become formularized, that is, expressed at
least in part in cliches. Such cliches may be simple phrases,
narrative structures, or even whole narratives, as well as
standard gestures, patterns, styles and designs. [12]

Less controversy is apparent in contemporary scholars'
answers to the question, who are the folk?, although popular
understanding of the term burdens it with fallacious connota-
tions derived in part from early folklorists' conception of the
term. According to one fallacy, the folk are to be identified
with peasant society or with rural groups. Acceptance of
this narrow definition would mean that city dwellers were not
folk and could not, by definition, possess folklore. Another
fallacy holds

> that folklore was produced by a folk in the hoary
> past and the folklore still extant today consists
> solely of fragmentary survivals. According to this
> incorrect view, the folk of today produce no new
> folklore; rather, contemporary folk are forgetting
> more and more folklore, and soon folklore will
> have died out completely. [13]

Contemporary folklorists, such as Dundes, Brunvand, and
Dorson, are prone to define the folk, in Dundes' words, as
"any group whatsoever who share at least one common factor"
(italics in text). The linking factor can be occupation, language, religion, geographical proximity, even family. [14] The
final chapter of Dorson's _American Folklore_, for example,

discusses urban folklore (including traveling salesman stories, department store lore, the famous "Death Car" story, Detroit's "haunted street"), college student lore (stories about the sexual prowess of certain students, the quirks of odd professors, marking procedures, dumb athletes, examination superstitions, fatal fraternity initiations, college songs, sexual and alcoholic games), GI folklore (talismans against death, stories about classic military "snafus," jokes about green trainees and goldbrickers, songs). Other unexplored possibilities mentioned by Dorson include the folklore of labor unions, white-collar occupations, and sports and entertainment. [15]

The changing configuration of folk groups and the shifting forms of their lore does not necessarily mean that new lore is continually invented. On the contrary, surprising continuity is discernible from one generation to the next and from one group to the next. Peter Opie mentions a belief current among the Bantu tribe of Africa as an example. According to the Bantus, women may not drink milk since it is widely believed that milk causes sterility. Opie remembers hearing a similar belief current during the Second World War, when large numbers of women were involved in defense production and maintenance. Proximity to radar installations as well as prolonged use of welding equipment was said to cause sterility. Recently, the same belief, says Opie, has appeared vis-à-vis airline stewardesses (which this writer has also heard): repeated high altitude flights make stewardesses sterile. Opie comments:

> Such fears and rumours may not appear to be traditional to those who are open to them; but the folklorist should be as sceptical when told that a belief is new, as he is when informed that it is of timeless origin, and has been preserved without change. The majority of secret 'facts' which pass by word of mouth behind closed doors, about, for instance, conception, contraception, menstruation, and sex-determination, turn out to be traditional, and sometimes to have antecedents that go back to the time of Pliny. And is this really surprising? For most of the history of mankind most of the knowledge of mankind has been conveyed by the spoken word.... [16]

The continuity of folk themes amid changing circumstances is evident in joke cycles, such as the "Polish" jokes recently

fashionable, which have been told of the Irish, Italians, and
Swedes as well, and in Negro "freedom" songs, which adapt
traditional spirituals to present circumstances.

Anyone pointing out to a stewardess the folk nature of
her belief that continued high level flights would cause sterility would probably meet with a surly reaction. Members
of a folk group are characteristically indisposed to regard
their folklore with any objectivity, for objectivity, like logic,
is inimical to tradition, which receives its power from anony-
mous authority. Therefore other people have superstitions,
but we have beliefs. Others are credulous, but we "know."
"Primitive" people have folklore; modern people do not. 17
Such ethnocentrism diverts the popular understanding of folklore from the true sense of oral and customary tradition to
a bogus taste for the charming habits of local or distant
primitives whose backwardness appeals to middle-class ro-
manticism. Folklorists themselves have until recently done
little to correct this distortion: for example, much folklore
has to do with sexual matters and is quite obscene; yet until
recently little such lore has found its way into professional
journals or books. 18   Such bowdlerization has discouraged examination of a vast and unacknowledged portion of modern cultural life, and has encouraged, instead, the delicate examination of "popular antiquities."

To return to the definition of the "folk": when the
folk have been defined as any group whatsoever which pos-
sesses traditions circulated orally or by customary example,
further qualification must be made. Popular understandings
of the folk of history, influenced perhaps by survival theories
of folklore and by cultural masochism, tend to regard every
man of the past as a conduit of the tradition. Opie comments:

> I am quite certain that we delude ourselves if we
> look back at the historic past and think of the days
> as being filled with melody, with every yokel pos-
> sessed of a treasure of songs behind his honest
> brow and a silver tongue with which to sing them.
> Indeed, it is not biologically possible. When indi-
> viduals criticise our Television Age as one in which
> people spend their time watching rather than per-
> forming, they are comparing it with an idyllic past
> which I suspect has existed only in imagination. It
> is a recurring experience among collectors of folk
> songs and story that one or two people in a com-
> munity will have a wonderful repertoire, but that,

far from being typical, the rest of the community
will acknowledge these persons to be the custodians
of their traditions, and will cheerfully refer one to
them. [19]

The comment may overstate the case but it makes the point.
Not every person in a folk group transmits the tradition.
One man may have "pet" superstitions about planting, how to
remove warts, and what to do when someone dies in the
house, that may differ from the "pet" superstitions of his
neighbor. Some people are gifted with song, and others with
story. Thus, while the tradition is not entrusted exclusively
to one or two persons in a group, as Opie would have it, it
is true that few persons transmit more than a portion of the
given tradition. This does not imply that the traditions are
private. They are emphatically social. But it is important
to remember, in examining the lore of the Methodist itinerants, that not all itinerants express all of the tradition.

In summary: folklore may be defined, in Brunvand's
words, as "those materials in culture that circulate traditionally among members of any group in different versions,
whether in oral form or by means of customary example"
(italics in text). [20]

Folklore and History

American historians have long been aware of the need
for broad cultural syntheses to supplement the social and political history in vogue in the early years of the twentieth
century. [21] Thirty years ago Caroline Ware, editing and introducing a volume entitled The Cultural Approach to History
at the behest of the American Historical Association, commented:

> The cultural approach has much to offer to the
> modern historian. It deals with whole societies
> and all aspects of life; it recognizes the uniqueness
> of a particular group in time and place; it provides
> new terms in which to approach the problem of
> change.... In the hands of the sophisticated his-
> torian, the concept of culture makes possible an
> awareness of assumptions that are deeper than the
> biases which the older historian has learned to ac-
> knowledge. [22]

Theodore Blegen, the dean of Minnesota historians, rejoiced in 1947 at the turn towards cultural history, calling the old historiography, in terms reminiscent of Emerson's essay "Self-Reliance, " "'inverted provincialism'":

> This inverted provincialism considered itself urbane and cosmopolitan. It was little interested in the values of folk culture. It rejected the near-at-hand as local and insignificant. It cultivated the faraway, without fully understanding it because it did not understand the near-at-hand, without sensing, too, that the faraway may in its inner meaning be near-at-hand. Imitative because it lacked self-confidence, inverted provincialism in many instances established molds and patterns for our educational and institutional development that have been hard to break. 23

Yet Donald McCoy, writing in the Journal of American History in 1967, chided American historians for concentrating on political history and for utilizing only "quality sources" for their data. 24 Evidently, in spite of the growth in popularity of American Studies programs, cultural history has made only halting progress vis-à-vis traditional historiography.

One difficulty, as McCoy implies, is that historians are only too willing to content themselves with research from familiar sources. 25 Another problem is that cultural data, ephemeral, difficult to locate, and unfamiliar when discovered, are not hard "facts" in the same way that political and social data are facts. Hence political and social history stand a better chance of being history if history is defined as analysis of the past "as it really was. " A third difficulty may arise from the necessity for a "'multi-disciplinary approach'"--a phrase "big and impressive, " says Blegen, "like 'that blessed word Mesopotamia, '" but simple in meaning: "Our interest in American culture is shared by scholars in many other disciplines, and they all have contributions to make. "26

The urgency that Blegen and others convey of the need for cultural history cannot hide the difficulties inherent in such an enterprise. Granted that cultural historians need to draw upon the findings of sociology, psychology, anthropology, English, demography, geography, and related sciences in order to sketch in unfilled portions of the canvas entitled "American Civilization, " the cross-disciplinary approach involves intensive study of, if not mastery of, the formal approach of

the disciplines involved. Thus the question of competence
may discourage many historians from delving extensively into the lairs of other disciplines.

The effort, once made, however, can be extremely rewarding. While each of the academic fields mentioned above
presents its own theoretical problems when asked to work
with history, perhaps none is more problematic than folklore.
Yet the mere appreciation of what folklore is opens up whole
new areas not only of contemporary but of past cultural experience.

The most obvious question about folklore and history
has to do with the very definition of folklore. If folklore is
defined as oral tradition, how can the historian have access
to any folklore except that which has been collected aurally
in the field and recorded either in writing or on record or
tape? Such collections in America, however, date at the
earliest from the first decades of the twentieth century, when
John Lomax began scribbling down cowboy songs as he heard
them from range riders. Folklore would therefore be useless, for historical purposes, before aural collecting began.

Few would deny that texts recorded in the field and
carefully annotated as to date, performance, and circumstances are superior to folklore culled from written sources.
This is especially true for a younger generation of folklorists,
who are much more interested in the context and function of
a folk item than in the raw datum itself.[27] Older folklorists,
perhaps unduly swayed by the idea that folklore was going out
of existence and had to be collected before it did, were content to concentrate on collection and classification. Some
old collectors transcribed stories and songs by hand and
memory, others by crude recording devices. Frequently,
collectors tampered with the material, arranging it to suit
their own tastes rather than that of their informants. The
contemporary folklorist, on the other hand, regards the un-
varnished text as only the starting point of his field work;
even the most sophisticated recording devices cannot capture
the gestures, facial expressions, audience reaction, proxi-
mate and remote setting so essential to oral performance.
In short, the modern folklorist is more likely to follow the
leads of cultural anthropology than to indulge in "library"
folklore.

It must be granted, however, that folklore does exist
willy-nilly in historical documents of many kinds. Folklorists

may derive some benefit from studying their subject in contexts utterly unselfconscious rather than in situations where the act of observation may subtly influence the performance. The main benefit of "library" folklore, however, may accrue to the historian, for whom the admission that folklore of precollecting days does not meet contemporary exigencies of folklore is no more than the acknowledgment of the problem of history: only a minute portion of what has meaning for a given era finds its way to permanence and hence history must, with whatever kind of sources, be written from fragments. If, therefore, folklore exists in historical records, as it does, it must be recognized as an historical fact in the same way that any other datum is an historical fact, even if the folk item cannot be observed <u>as</u> <u>oral.</u>

Recognition of folklore in written sources depends, of course, on the characteristics of folklore already noted in the section on definition: traditionality, formularization, variation, and anonymity. "Oral" and "customary example" cannot be criteria except indirectly, when texts explicitly refer to such transmission, and presumptively, when texts explicitly discuss situations in which lore is likely to have circulated.

First of all, discernment of traditionality depends upon broad familiarity with collections of folklore already in existence,[28] as well as use of various classificatory tools by which narrative elements (called motifs), stories, proverbs, riddles, superstitions, song texts, folksongs and customs may be identified.[29] Such devices can aid the non-professional folklorist to perceive the analogies between the apparent uniqueness of the material he is dealing with and the tradition out of which the material arises.

Second, recurrence of themes, narratives, or structures in formularized cliches aids recognition of folk material. Obviously, only a wide sampling of data will allow this criterion to emerge.

Third, variation, which establishes that a particular story has been in oral circulation and has been modified at the hands of various storytellers to fit the exigencies of different times, places and characters, tips the hand of traditional material. Again, formularization aids recognition here.

Finally, anonymity, revealed by phrases such as "They say," or "It is reported," or "I have received this on good

authority from a certain minister ... " indicates the source-
vagueness characteristic of much folklore. Anonymity lends
an impressive authoritarian tone to tradition, for tied to a
specific source, folklore would lose its air of being general
and unquestionable cultural knowledge.

Armed with such rules, the "library" historian-folk-
lorist must avoid pitfalls in his use of data. One tempting
possibility, based upon the perception that oral traditions
are enduring and conservative, is to extrapolate backwards
from twentieth century folk collections to nineteenth and
eighteenth century generalizations. [30] Surely, the historian
might presume, a superstition garnered in North Carolina in
the twentieth century must have been prevalent there in the
nineteenth. Therefore, he might conclude, superstitious fatalism characterized the nineteenth century mindset as well
as that of the twentieth. Several factors make such hindsight
at best risky. For one thing, immigration and emigration
insure the likelihood of the introduction of new oral traditions
into an area where they did not exist before. For another,
the movement of oral tradition into the mass media--news-
papers, books, phonograph recordings, radio, and television
--and back into oral circulation (as well as the possible orig-
ination of oral tradition in historical events which would in-
tervene between the present collected item and the projected
generalization) makes backward extrapolation too problematic
to be trustworthy. Thirdly, questions of context and function
so important to contemporary folklorists do not invite such
hindsight; for example, a superstition characteristic of rural
North Carolinians in the nineteenth century could be collected
in a California hippie commune, or Negro spirituals could
(and have) become protest songs. In both cases the generalization to be drawn from the folk piece is substantially altered by the circumstances in which it is collected.

Such caveats notwithstanding, awareness of the recal-
citrance of folklore's basic patterns inevitably colors the mind
of the historian. Warned against projecting particular beliefs
into past eras, the scholar of contemporary folk collections
cannot help believing that present patterns, at least, reach
into the past. [31]

Besides being chary of such historicism, the historian
must carefully distinguish folklore from other forms of cultural analysis. Folklore is not, as its definition clearly implies, equivalent to popular culture. "Pop" culture, though
worthy of study in the opinion of some, is but transient and

faddish, whereas folklore is permanent and conservative, even if adaptable. Furthermore, folklore is not mass culture, although the masses may possess a lore. Folklore, rather, cuts across all cultural distinctions based upon education or lack thereof. Any group whatsoever in a given society may possess folklore, from the most intellectual or scientific elite to the uneducated mountain sharecropper, from rich man to poor man, from aristocracy to masses, from Methodist to Jew and from city dweller to farmer. Each group may be a folk group in terms of the culture endemic to that group circulating orally or by customary example. Thus, in this volume, nineteenth century Methodist preachers will be shown to constitute a folk group, without the slightest hint that the term "folk" connotes an implicit slur as to the mental capabilities or social standing of the folk group, and without implying that a "folklore" is unique to Methodists alone among nineteenth century religious groups.

A third clarification that the historian using folk data must understand is that folklore analysis is not equivalent to symbolical analysis--such as is found, for example, in Marvin Meyers' treatment of the "money" issue in The Jacksonian Persuasion: Politics and Belief[32]--or mythical analysis, as found in Arthur Moore's treatment of Kentucky in The Frontier Mind: A Cultural Analysis of the Kentucky Frontiersman.[33] A popular symbol is not necessarily a folk symbol; for example, the American eagle may be a popular cultural symbol, but it is not folk. The same holds true of myths: not all myths de facto meet the requirements of true folklore. The myth that Kentucky was a new Eden, in Moore's work, finds foundation primarily in literary, not folk sources. The point is that folklore considers historical sources not necessarily covered by cultural historians who analyze the "popular mind" either symbolically or by means of rhetorical myths.[34]

In summary: rules for discerning folklore and pitfalls notwithstanding, history can profit from folklore in several ways:

1) The historian, especially in cultures where all history is transmitted orally, may be able to learn "the facts" from ballads, myths, and stories. Jan Vansina has formulated guidelines for such a procedure vis-à-vis African cultures; the recent oral history movement in America has demonstrated the usefulness of such techniques even in literate cultures.[35]

2) Folklore can assist the social historian in discovering traditional customs, traits, and manners; and it can aid
the cultural historian in understanding group attitudes, preju-
dices and stereotypes as well as in assessing the relevance
of mythical and symbolical interpretations. [36]

3) The ability to recognize folk traditions can be of
immense help to the biographical historian. In researching
political figures (such as Washington and Lincoln), local heroes, frontiersmen, and industrial barons, for example, the
historian can more readily discern fact from fancy and can
achieve greater insight into the protagonist of his biography
by attempting to understand what forces propelled this figure
into the elusive stream of oral tradition. In the Methodist
lore to be examined in this paper, for example, the Autobiography of Peter Cartwright is filled with traditional lore
which the author has told of himself! [37]

4) The study of group and regional folklore can aid
and correct more synthetic treatments of American history
by insisting on heterogeneity rather than homogeneity. [38]

5) Considered as itself, and not simply as a source
of illustration for social, cultural, and biographical history,
folklore discloses the mind of a tenacious, perdurable, conservative counter-culture. For example, historians who
recognized the fatalism of American ballads and the theurgic
leanings of much superstition would be much more open to
acknowledging a basic continuity of attitude from Salem to
the Scopes trial and would be much less willing to generalize
about the transition in American thought from supernatural
to scientific paradigms in the eighteenth century.

Moreover, folklore provides the historian with a different kind of "fact" than usual historical research furnishes;
folklore unearths the ritual fact (traditionally patterned behavior) which can be properly interpreted only insofar as its
formal structure as well as its material content is remarked.
The interpretation that follows such recognition may well have
to depend explicitly upon disciplines which have as their formal object recognition and interpretation of ritual behavior.
In the history of American religion, for example, social psychology may help the historian to understand why visions recorded in nineteenth century autobiographies reduplicate visions recorded in medieval hagiography which in turn resemble biblical visions. For another example, cultural anthropology might help historians understand the implications

of the ritual behavior of enthusiasts during the camp meetings
of the Second Great Awakening. 39 In short, the interdisciplinary approach of folklore-and-history calls the historian
(and indeed the folklorist) to even broader approaches than
those suggested by the two disciplines themselves.

Folklore and Religion

        The relationships between folklore and religion are
tremendously complex. Religion, where possible, has traditionally baptized folk customs, rituals, myths, and beliefs
and has incorporated them into its liturgy and theology. A
prime example of such procedure is the Bible itself, which
is full of miracles, night visions, trances, revenants, and
cures. Furthermore, associational religious life provides a
common experiential bond which spawns a rich harvest of
oral traditions and customs. The folk, in turn, have recip-
rocated by baptizing their folk beliefs with the authority of
religion: hence, apocrypha, hagiography, legends, romances,
relics, feasts, festivals and apparitions which are more or
less unrecognized by the institutional church but which are
irrepressible and thus tolerated. 40

        Between the subsumption of folklore by religion--the
product of which in this book is termed "religious folklore"--
and the transfer of religious authority back to the folk--the
product of which is here termed "folk religion"--lies a hazy
"no man's land" wherein official religious culture of keryg-
mas, creeds, and theologies meets and mingles with the folk
counter-culture of folktale, superstition, and legend. Thus,
for example, the hypothetical folk Christian wanders between
resignation and divination, and his Christ between identity as
suffering servant and culture hero. The doctrine of providence vacillates between divine sovereignty and fatalism; redemption between free grace and magic.

        The study of folklore can therefore be of benefit to
religion in three ways: 1) An appreciation of "religious
folklore" can help the historian of religion understand the
radical incarnationalism of Christian theology and liturgy.
Moreover, study of the humor and legend generated by associational Christian life can help the historian understand the
dynamics of institutional life, especially the ways in which
people deal with the tensions arising from internal disagree-
ment and external competition. 2) The scrutiny of "folk

religion" can point up enduring tendencies of cultural man to
lapse into primitivism under the aegis of religion. 3) Study
of the "no man's land" between religious folklore and folk
religion indicates, perhaps more authentically than study of
creeds and theologies, the actual, lived experience of the
ordinary Christian, who apparently can, against all the canons
of logic, live with dual and often mutually contradictory belief-systems. 41

The distinctions between religious folklore, folk religion, and the phantasmagorical land between them undercut
and underlie the categorizations of Parts II and III of this
book. Most of the lore presented here belongs to the category of religious folklore; some stories, however, especially
in Part II (such as those dealing with divination) fall under
the aegis of folk religion.

Undoubtedly Methodist orthodoxy tacitly controlled what
could or could not find its way into autobiography, biography,
and reminiscence. Such silent censorship exercises itself
through the protagonists themselves, itinerant preachers,
who learned, if nothing else, to think with the church (sentire
cum ecclesia) from their associations and readings. Moreover, the publishing houses and official periodicals could certainly sense what was and was not appropriate to the traditions of Methodism.

Tantalizing snatches of superstitions and supernatural
legends in such sources, however, lead one to think that they
reveal only the surface of a pervasive, powerful folk religion.
If a few such beliefs escaped deletion, surely many more did
not. Moreover, "if the priests, what of the people?"; that
is, it is altogether reasonable to suppose that if religious
leaders participated in folk religion, their people did as well,
to a greater extent.

For the most part, such "folk religion" would have to
be culled from sources other than the more or less official
sources examined for this work. Yet, occasionally one does
encounter a biography published in orthodoxy's hinterlands
which gives full play to the tenets of folk religion. Such,
for example, is the biography of Robert Sayers Sheffey (1820-
1902), a circuit rider of the southwestern Virginia mountains. 42

The volume is, in reality, not a biography, but a collection of folk stories about Sheffey: "oral testimony, " says
the introduction, "has necessarily been the author's chief

Rev. W. H. Simpkins holding Brother Sheffey's
saddle bags and sheepskin

Robert Sayers Sheffey

reliance." Gathered from the lips of laity as well as fellow
preachers, the anecdotes reveal the extent of the Sheffey tradition. In the front of the book is a picture of the sheepskin on which Sheffey knelt to pour out prayers that struck
fear into men's hearts; the skin was valued as a relic by one
family[43]--and another of the authentic skins was reverenced
elsewhere.[44] Many homes at which he stopped prized relics
of his visit.[45] The legendary power of his prayer inspired
"literally thousands of stories";[46] for example, there are at
least twenty-five accounts of how Sheffey's prayers led to the
immediate destruction of whiskey stills and distilleries.
Many of the stories appear to be versions of the same episode. Widely credited with the power to effect cures and to
foresee the future, Sheffey was also remembered for his peculiarities. For example, so neurotically fastidious was he
about cleanliness that, according to one story, he would wash
his hostess' fingerprints off the saucer before drinking the
coffee she had served him.[47] Another idiosyncrasy was his
fondness for sweets: honey, sugar, blackberry or huckleber-
ry jam served his purpose. At the end of a meal he would
ladle his mouth full of the substance and go out to pray in
the yard, frequently climbing a tree and shouting until the
sweet was gone.[48] (The stories do not explain how he shouted
and consumed his mouthful at the same time.) If there was
no honey available at a certain house, he would pray for the
bees to swarm, and soon enough there was honey for all.[49]
Such stories, gathered almost a hundred years after the protagonist flourished, indicate the tenacity of the folk memory
as well as its appropriation of what orthodoxy would regard
as unedifying, if not heretical.[50]

Methodist Folklore

1. The sources. Nineteenth century Methodist
preachers' autobiographies, biographies, and reminiscences
constitute the primary sources examined for this study. Although most of the material was written in the second half
of the nineteenth century about early nineteenth century
preachers, some of the works were penned after the turn of
the nineteenth century, and some of the protagonists belong
to the eighteenth century. The majority, however, of those
ministers who are the subjects or authors of the material
considered flourished in rough coincidence with the frontier
period of American Methodism. The chronological terminus
quo of this study, therefore, is around 1800, and the terminus

ad quem slides toward the latter third of the century with the
westward-expanding frontier. Forays into the literature of
Methodism's major competitors on the American Frontier--
Baptists, Presbyterians, and Cumberland Presbyterians--con-
firmed the suspicion that Methodist preachers were not unique
as a folk group united by common religious and vocational
bonds and possessing a lively oral tradition. Such parallels
are noted in subsequent footnotes.

2. Oral traditions in the Methodist sources. The
sources incorporate several kinds of folklore, recognizable
by the criteria mentioned above: traditionality, variation,
formularization, and anonymity. This section of the study
seeks to establish the vitality of the folk tradition among
Methodist preachers by indicating the extent of "secular" folklore among them, and by noting instances where the sources
explicitly refer to oral transmission of certain data and to
situations in which lore was likely to have been shared.

In the first place, the unwitting inclusion of much
"secular" folklore in the literature argues toward the conclusion that Methodist preachers breathed an atmosphere in
which both the mode of communication and the content of folklore were natural and assumed.

Lurid story-telling around the blazing fires in frontier
cabins, according to many reminiscences, inflamed the imag-
inations and emotions of youth destined for the ministry.
Vivid accounts of Indian barbarities, heroic war exploits, and
narrow escapes from wilderness beasts vied with narratives
of malevolent witches, haunted houses and graveyards, ghosts,
premonitions and conjurations, fortune tellings and tall tales
for the attention of wide-eyed children and not-so-incredulous
adults:

> And around that weird fireplace in the long winter
> nights, when the cold winds were blowing with
> mournful sounds against the trembling doors and
> rattling windows--there they [the children] sat in
> breathless silence and listened with mute wonder
> to the long ghost stories and startling Indian war
> tales which entered so largely into the social en-
> tertainments peculiar to those times. [51]

Such storytelling lasted deep into the night, sometimes
"until the morning broke. "[52] Small wonder that, as the narrations grew in detail and horror with the shadows of night,

little listeners would edge toward the light and warmth of the
fire:

> And while the spook stories went around (a baneful
> thing to allow among children), I always stole from
> the outer edge of the fireside to the inside edge of
> the circle, despite the burning heat of the fire, and
> the danger of being roasted alive. For hours the
> sweat would pour off me, but I dared not stir. 53

Rev. Brantley York remembered the fear that such marathon
story-swapping incidents inspired:

> Often have I sat and listened to these stories till it
> seemed to me that each hair upon my head resem-
> bled a quill of a porcupine. I was afraid to go out
> of doors, afraid to go to bed alone, and almost
> afraid of my own shadow. 54

The lineage of the stories was diverse. One itinerant
remembered hearing terrifying stories from old Aunt Dinny,
a Negro servant in his youthful home. So formative were her
relations (which the itinerant, G. C. Rankin, calls "Negro
folklore stories") that, although he avowed "I am not superstitious, " yet

> when I start on a journey and a rabbit crosses the
> road in front of me my first impulse is to turn
> around, make a cross in the road and spit over
> my left shoulder at it, because Aunt Dinny always
> told me it was bad luck not to do it. 55

A preacher who grew up during the Second Great
Awakening of the early 1800's remembered the influence of
his mother's Celtic storytelling:

> Upon such scenes of frontier life, Rebecca Smith
> shed the influence of a strong but untutored mind,
> well stored with useful facts and Irish legends....
> She had been brought up by a Celtic grandmother,
> and had learned all the wild and beautiful legends
> of her native land. The stories and ballads that
> had touched her own heart when a child, became
> now, in the absence of books, the literature of her
> cabin--her children's poetry and faith. 56

Stories of religious conversions during the revival, the nar-

rator asserts, differed in content but not in tone from his
mother's fantastic legends:

> The stories of conversion that went round the neigh-
> borhood, were always full of marvelous incident and
> spiritual adventure; and he listened to these narra-
> tions as he listened to his mother's legends of the
> weird Banshee--with simple wonder and a childish
> faith. [57]

Those narrators who mention storytelling aver that the
folklore was received with general credulity. [58] Some saw
such belief as the province of the ignorant, [59] while others insisted that superstitions waned with the advent of schools. [60]
Many reminiscences assert, however, that no matter how
skeptical they may have become about such childhood experiences, they were unable to free themselves from residual
superstitions and fears. [61]

Thus, while Methodist preachers may have denounced
superstitious practices of groups such as the Roman Catholics
and the Mormons, and while they sometimes took pains to
debunk ghost stories, [62] it is clear that they were privy to
the influence of various traditions and customs which, being
"their own, " were therefore "true. "

For example, three accounts record haunted parson-
ages. One preacher's family was disturbed nightly by the
noise of a rocking cradle, [63] another's by the sound of a man
upstairs opening and shutting doors, [64] and another's by the
heavy wheezing of a man's breath. [65] The latter account,
laboring for an explanation of the phenomenon, recalled "the
mysterious noises in the Wesley family. " Quoting Samuel
Wesley's reply to his mother, who wrote to him asking for
an explanation, the narrator concludes, "'I cannot think at
all of any interpretation. Wit, I fancy, might find many, but
wisdom none. '"[66]

No "interpretation" other than traditionality needed invocation for the explanation of other "secular" folk items in
the sources. Local legends, folk customs, tall tales, folksongs, hymn parodies, proverbs, folk medicine, jokes and
jests, children's games, and folk songs permeate the Methodist literature. For example, two separate accounts record
a story about lovers, who, separated by fate shortly after
marriage and despairing of finding each other, marry and
raise families; in old age, when each is bereaved of spouse,

they meet by chance and find their love still warm enough to
join them for a few years of earthly bliss. [67] J. E.
Godbey tells the tale of Sam, the miller's son, who did amazing som-
nambulistic feats such as going down to the mill at night,
when it was his turn, crossing a log tiptoe and letting down
the gate, and returning to bed without waking. [68] Other accounts recorded customs such as "turning out the schoolmas-
ter" on the day before Christmas--a sort of schoolboy's feast
of fools during which the hapless teacher was barred from
his classroom until he served up beverages (often intoxicating)
and apples to the rampaging students. Should any master refuse, according to the custom he was dunked in the local
creek. [69]

        Another itinerant, John Burgess, recalls a recreation
of olden times which was "innocent and unsophisticated" but
which would be considered, in "exquisite and suspicious times, "
"out of place. " The "bundling party, " to which Burgess refers, was a sort of mixed pajama party: the hostess made
up ä large, temporary bed; then

>   six or more couple [sic], as the bed is large or
>   small, sit for awhile on the edge or front, say for
>   an hour or so, then throw themselves back, and
>   all lie there and talk and laugh, or sing in royal
>   merriment, until one sings out to rise, when other
>   couples take the position; and thus the night of
>   romp is spent, until departure for home. [70]

        J. K. Peck remembers the incredible strength of his
blacksmith father Luther: the man could lift ten men and a
boy, and always held up alone the first side of the building
when the second was being lifted during barn raisings. [71] One
itinerant recalled seeing Johnny Appleseed pass through his
town;[72] while another recorded stories and boasts of the legendary Mike Fink and his keelboatmen. [73] Charles Giles told
of mysterious "ringing goblets" he had seen during his
youth, [74] while John Scarlett remembered frozen fish that
revived when he put them into a bucket of water. [75] Snakes
charm their victims, according to one account, [76] and a tobacco leaf poultice proved the best cure for rattlesnake bite,
according to another. [77] W. Lee Spottswood recalled a street
song sung of the traitor Benedict Arnold during Revolutionary
War days, [78] and William Milburn noted various anecdotes
told of national political figures, such as Lincoln and Stephen
Douglas, John Randolph and John Calhoun, Daniel Webster,
Henry Clay, and others. [79]

In addition to such miscellaneous folk traditions, the
Methodist preachers record numerous proverbs and proverbial phrases in their narratives: for example, O. P. Fitzgerald, discussing what effect a formal, classical education
might have had on the subject of his biography, John B. Mc-
Ferrin, summarized: "Where the blade is thin and of poor
metal much whetting destroys it; where it is heavy and of
fine quality the whetstone need not be feared."[80] Referring
to a successful young minister, Andrew Manship commented:
"He had an old man's head on a young man's shoulders."[81]
Commenting on boisterous, noisy preaching, Tobias Spicer observed: "Empty wagons often make more noise than loaded
ones, and shallow waters sometimes make more foam than
deep waters."[82] Speaking of Bishop Waters, one itinerant
recalled:

> He was always ready, and always good; so that it
> was commonly said of him, 'He is real bacon and
> cabbage,' a dish well known, and not lightly es-
> teemed, in the South, and one always in season and
> at hand.[83]

"'Didn't he squat like a pheasant?'" Rev. Samuel Clawson
laughed, after excoriating a brash young preacher who kept
interrupting the older ministers' discourses at Conference.[84]

In short, the literature indicates that Methodist preachers were well aware of certain "secular" storytelling traditions and their lasting effect upon them. Unreflectingly, however, they channeled many other folk traditions, beliefs, and
mannerisms to posterity.

Secondly, the existence of a lively oral tradition a-
mong Methodist preachers is marked by explicit references
to exchange of oral tradition.

Such exchange depended upon a sense of intimate fellowship born of the realization that only brother preachers
shared the incredible difficulty of itinerant life and that only
fellow circuit riders could appreciate the full meaning of
that unique experience. As a result, relations of setbacks,
disappointments, and joys among the brotherhood released the
tension that each man felt between the burden of his call and
his actual performance in commiseration and laughter which
in turn strengthened the bonds of communion. As the following quotation illustrates, one of the greatest hardships for
itinerants, who plied their vocation alone on frontier trails,

was the inability to share their experiences with anyone:

> One of the 'lights,' or joyful circumstances of
> 'itinerancy,' is the meeting together, and mutual
> comforts of the preachers. One of the 'shadows,'
> or sorrowful circumstances, is, the separation,
> and solitary sufferings. [85]

Invariably, therefore, ecclesiastical convocations such
as conferences became important social occasions as well,
during which ministers played tricks on one another, [86] told
stories about themselves and others, shared information and
experience, and in general, made business tolerable, if not
pleasurable. One old Methodist minister, interviewed in 1967
by Elizabeth Tokar, divulged numerous stories and humorous
anecdotes he had collected during conferences. "'When the
preachers first got up to speak,'" A. L. Steinfeldt reported,
"'before a dry report and to attract attention and break the
monotony, they would give a joke. It kept them from getting
bored. Preachers got awfully tired listening to reports.'"[87]
Stories were traded, however, not only during business hours,
but before and after official work was done. Enoch Marvin
provided the following vignette of the camaraderie as conference began:

> What occasions our Conferences were.... Late in
> the afternoon of Tuesday there is the bustle of much
> coming and going about the Methodist church. Men
> come in buggies, on horseback, from the depot on
> foot, all making their way to the church. One
> squad is no sooner disposed of than another comes.
> Each one is assigned to a "home" for the session.
> After a little the first comers, having been duly in-
> stalled in their homes, return to greet the fresh
> arrivals. Caples comes leisurely along from his
> boarding-house in company with two or three others.
> I can see the sunshine in his face now. They are
> in earnest conversation. Caples stops and halts the
> others. I know from his very attitude that he is
> telling an anecdote--an uncommonly rich one. Pres-
> ently he bends forward and laughs one of his laughs.
> They all join, not boisterously, but convulsively--
> laugh until the tears run down their faces. They
> move on and meet others. Caples quickens his
> pace. 'Why,' says he, there's Billy--God bless you,
> old fellow! Why, they have fed you high up there
> on Grand river. 'Why, Ben., bless your soul, is

this you?' Then the shaking of hands! Commend
me to a Methodist preacher when I am to shake
hands. It is not an art with them, but a natural
gift. 88

Spottswood records the raillery that took place at a hotel
where preachers were staying between two humorists, "T. M. "
and "W. D. Ryan. " Each was telling good-natured stories on
the other, attempting to "come a topper. " According to
Spottswood, the two humorists had a large and appreciative
audience: "They unbent, and there was pleasantry. "89 It is
no wonder that William Milburn asserted: "To know what
the pleasures of conference are, a man must have been a
western Methodist preacher. "90

Another occasion for sharing anecdotes and experiences, especially during frontier days when travel was tedi-
ous, was the journey to and from conference:

The seat of the Tennessee Conference for the session of 1842 was Athens, Alabama.... McFerrin
made the journey from Nashville on horseback, in
company with the Rev. John Hanner and eight others. That was a lively party that thus rode together through that beautiful region in its autumnal glory. The long miles were made short by the relation of itinerant experience, anecdote, snatches of
spiritual songs, and sallies of wit and humor within the bounds of ministerial decorum. 91

Everyone liked to ride, "'cheek by jowl,'" with Robert Corson, because he had such a lively sense of humor. 92

Occasions such as Conference and the long journeys
to and from stimulated and perpetuated folk traditions. Itinerants, says Milburn, "were usually the best story-tellers
on their long circuits...."93 Some preachers, such as J.
DeVilbiss and W. Caples, became renowned for their anecdotal abilities. 94 The embroidery of facts for which Caples
was famous may have prompted remarks such as that reported of the staid Rev. Dr. Stephen Olin: to wit, "that he
had never known a man who could tell a good story, who did
not lie. "95

Other preachers became the butt of the storytellers,
who realized that the use of certain names lent plausibility
to stories. According to Plyler, hundreds of stories without

the slightest authenticity attached themselves to the name of
Lorenzo Dow, who was noted for eccentricity. [96] Peter Cartwright felt compelled to deny that he had "whupped" Mike
Fink, the legendary ruffian of midwestern keelboatmen.
"Thousands of the thrilling incidents that have gained publi-
city, and have been attributed to me, " says Cartwright in his
introduction, "will create disappointment" when not found in
his Autobiography. [97] William Closs, an eccentric of the
same stripe as Dow and Cartwright, besought a colleague to
keep his anecdotal tradition authentic:

> 'When I am dead, the people will tell a great many
> anecdotes on me, and make it appear that I was an
> eccentric old man. I have told you all the stories
> that are told on me. I do not object to any of
> them being told, if they are told truly. Do me the
> kindness when you hear these stories, perverted,
> to give the true version of them. '[98]

Biographers sometimes tidied the anecdotal record; for example, John F. Marlay, noting that the numerous stories
told of Bishop Thomas Morris were "pointless and unprofit-
able, " and were "not the things, however innocent and proper,
for which Bishop Morris would wish to be remembered, "
bowdlerized his narrative of such material. [99]

Such expurgations, in the name of edification, must
have been frequent enough for literary purposes, but not pervasive enough to dam the flow of oral tradition.

A third context for the circulation of traditional materials, besides travel and Conference, was didactic, that is,
preaching, teaching, and mutual instruction.

The revivalistic orientation of frontier Methodism
meant that preachers had to express themselves in terms
vivid enough to shake people from their lethargy and plain
enough to be understood. Sermons and exhortations, therefore, were spiced with frontier idiom and heavily laced with
exempla as startling as Biblical precedent allowed. Moreover, preaching had to be spontaneous. No itinerant could
expect to hold the attention of fatigued, preoccupied frontiersmen by reading from text or notes. Rather, he had to rear
back, let the Word ferment within him under the power of
the Spirit, and shout God's saving message in such a way that
no man, woman, or child could ignore its urgency and im-
mediacy. [100]

A Typical Frontier Preaching Situation

   In many respects, the pastoral milieu of the Methodist
itinerants resembles that of the thirteenth century mendicants.
Both mendicants and Methodists were reformers who sought
to bring religion to the people by itinerant preaching. Both
found themselves in a "frontier" situation--the mendicants insofar as clerical and scholarly hegemony over religion had
rendered the medieval countryside a religious wilderness,
and the itinerants insofar as the American wilderness had reduced their potential converts to religious vacuity. [101] Both
mendicants and itinerants ransacked traditional culture and
contemporary experience for narratives which would concre-
tize the doctrinal and moral ideals of Christianity for their
people. [102] And finally, both saw their favorite narratives
gathered into collections which not only aided subsequent
preachers but also transmitted the fruits of folk and popular
imagination from one generation to the next. [103]

   Inasmuch as the primary sources of this study are not
sermon collections, there is no direct evidence of the kind
of exempla used in sermons. But there is indirect evidence.
For one thing, certainly exempla that were used in sermons
were also used in other didactic situations. Thus we might
expect that exempla would find their way into popular devotional and instructional literature--literature such as pious
autobiography and biography. [104] Secondly, there is the testimony of such inimitable preachers as Peter Cartwright, who
relates how he gained the attention of a vast, noisy crowd at
a camp meeting by relating anecdotes "well-calculated to excite their risibilities." When he had them "all eyes and
ears," he launched into the serious portion of his sermon,
utilizing, no doubt, more serious stories. [105] Many of the
stories noted in this study, therefore, were originally used
in the context of preaching.

   Many of the stories, too, functioned as didactic devices in other teaching situations. Elizabeth Tokar's interview of Rev. A. L. Steinfeldt points up such contexts:

> These "preacher tales" (stories that concerned the
> preacher or the church, but were not suitable in
> Rev. Steinfeldt's estimation for use in sermons)
> were told mainly from memory for this collection
> .... They are largely humor turned back on the
> preacher and were told to help make contact with
> the 'ordinary' non-religious man when he, as other
> preachers, went 'calling, ' standing on street corn-
> ers or waiting in line at the store. He also enter-

tained at young peoples' socials and group meetings by telling stories.[106]

Undoubtedly, many such stories and exempla could be lifted by the assiduous itinerant from standard collections of sermons and religious biographies which he pored over on horseback and at night in dimly lighted frontier cabins.[107] Another source, however, was the brotherhood of preachers. According to one anecdote, Bishop Francis Asbury posed a question during a sermon: " 'How do you preachers know so much?' "   Answering his own query, he said, " 'We tell one another.' "[108]   The same reply reportedly was given by the Rev. Andrew Monroe to a Presbyterian clergyman who expressed surprise that

> without the training of the Seminary and under the disadvantages of their itinerant life Methodist preachers, as a class, were such good theologians as well as effective preachers....[109]

"Whenever an older preacher was met," tells Samuel Ayres, "the younger one would ask questions and receive instruction and advice."[110]

"We tell one another"; on such occasions, certainly, traditional exempla were handed from one generation to another.   In addition, itinerants could refurbish their store of narratives at camp meetings or at conferences by listening to their fellows preach.

Finally, many of the narratives circulated as polemical knowledge.   Proselytizing on the frontier was often violently competitive, and confrontations between Methodists and their opponents were resolved on the side of the man of quick wit and ready slogan rather than on the side of the reasoned theologian.   The Reverend Dan Young, an old New England itinerant, includes in his Autobiography "a short and easy method with error, being the substance of conversations which I have had with various persons at different times."[111]   The "method" lists hypothetical, stereotyped arguments for use with atheists, deists, universalists, and others whose theological opinions were at variance with those of Methodism.[112] Perhaps an even better example of polemical narrative are the various anti-Baptist and anti-Campbellite slurs and jokes recorded in part three, chapter eleven, of this work.

In short, then, preaching, teaching and polemics provided contexts in which traditional and contemporary narratives circulated among American Methodist itinerant preachers.

To summarize: the involvement of Methodist preachers in a folk tradition is indicated by "secular" folklore in the sources, by explicit reference to the oral communication of stories and anecdotes, and by evidence of situations such as travel, Conference, preaching, teaching, and mutual instruction in which folk traditions circulated.

In the following sections, Methodist lore has been arranged functionally. Part II notes "Remarkable Providences, " that is, lore primarily didactic in intent. Part III gathers together the folk narratives of itinerant Methodism, that is, stories which have as their intent entertainment, concretization of ideals, celebrations of events and/or persons. The remarkable providences in Part II will be shown to connect Methodism with an ancient Christian heritage, whereas the folk narratives of Part III have much in common with folk traditions colored by the American experience.

Notes

1. See Richard Dorson, Folklore and Folklife: An Introduction (Chicago: University of Chicago Press, 1972), pp. 1-2. For discussion of the nature and purpose of folklore, see the following: William Bascom, "Folklore and Anthropology, " Journal of American Folklore (Hereafter abbreviated JAF), LXVI (1953), 283-90; idem, "Four Functions of Folklore, " JAF, LXVII (1954), 333-49; idem, "Verbal Art, " JAF, LXVIII (1955), 245-52; Richard Baumann, "Towards a Behavioral Theory of Folklore. A Reply to Roger Welsch, " JAF, LXXXII (1969), 167-70; Samuel P. Bayard, "The Materials of Folklore, " JAF, LXVI (1953), 1-17; Tristram Coffin, "Folklore in the American Twentieth Century, " American Quarterly, XIII (1961), 526-33; "Conference on the Character and State of Studies in Folklore, " JAF, LIX (1946), 495-527; Richard Dorson, "The American Folklore Scene, 1963, " Folk-Lore, LXXIV (1963), 433-49; idem, "Current Folklore Theories, " Current Anthropology, IV (1963), 93-112; idem, Folklore: Selected Essays (Bloomington, Ind. : Indiana University Press, 1972); Alan Dundes, "The American Concept of Folk-

lore," Journal of the Folklore Institute, III (1966),
226-49; idem, The Study of Folklore (Englewood
Cliffs, N. J.:   Prentice Hall, Inc., 1965); "Folklore
Research in North America," JAF, LX (1947), 350-
416; Herbert Halpert, "Folklore: Breadth vs. Depth, "
JAF, LXXI (1958), 97-103; Wayland Hand, "American Folklore after Seventy Years: Survey and Prospect," JAF, LXXIII (1960), 1-11; Melville Herskovits, "Folklore after a Hundred Years: A Problem
in Redefinition," JAF, LIX (1946), 89-100; W. W.
Newell, "Review," JAF, XI (1898), 302-4; Stith
Thompson (ed.), Four Symposia on Folklore (Bloomington, Ind.:   Indiana University Press, 1953);
Roger Welsch, "A Note on Definitions," JAF, LXXXI
(1969), 262-64; Don Yoder, "The Folklife Studies
Movement," Pennsylvania Folklife, XIII (1963), 43-
56; Jules Zanger, "A Report of the Eleventh Newberry Library Conference on American Studies," Newberry Library Bulletin, V (1961), 227-39.
       For a basic bibliography, see Charles Haywood,
A Bibliography of North American Folklore and Folksong (New York: Greenburg, 1951); this work was
reprinted by Dover Press in two volumes, 1961, without correction of numerous factual errors.

2.   Richard M. Dorson, American Folklore (Chicago: Uni-
     versity of Chicago Press, 1959), p. 1.

3.   See Herskovits, "Redefinition. "

4.   See Yoder, "Folklife Studies. "

5.   Jan Harold Brunvand, The Study of American Folklore
     (New York: W. W. Norton and Co., 1968), pp. 2-
     3.   See also Dundes, Study, for a more exhaustive
     list of folk genres, with examples.

6.   Edited by Maria Leach and Jerome Fried (2 vols.; New
     York: Funk and Wagnalls Co., 1949-50, I, 398-403.

7.   See Brunvand, American Folklore, pp. 133-34.

8.   Ibid., p. 4.

9.   Ibid., p. 5: "Folklorists often speak of individual pieces
     of folklore as either 'texts' or 'versions,' reserving
     the term 'variants' for texts that deviate more widely
     from the common standard. "

10. Richard Dorson introduced the term "fakelore" as a
     description of bogus folklore in an article in The
     American Mercury, LXX (1950), 335-43.

11. Dorson, American Folklore, pp. 216-23. This is not
     to say that a literary creation may not become a
     folk item by entering into the oral tradition of a
     group; it is simply to point out that it is misrepre-

sentation to say that Paul Bunyan belongs to the folklore of the lumberjacks of the Northwest when in fact
he did not. Presumably exploiters hope that romantic associations connected with the term "folklore" in
the popular mind will make the deception profitable.

12. Brunvand, American Folklore, p. 6.
13. Dundes, Study, p. 2. According to Peter Opie, "The
     history of folk-lore collecting has, from the beginning,
     contained a contradiction. It has consisted of anti-
     quarians fretting about the disappearance of charming
     customs and amusements; and of young men, long
     after those antiquarians have themselves passed away,
     walking out into the English or Scottish countryside
     and collecting material as beautiful as ever their
     predecessors found." "The Tentacles of Tradition, "
     Folk-Lore, LXXIV (1963), 509.
14. For studies based on occupation, see Mody C. Boatright,
     Folklore of the Oil Industry (Dallas: Southern Metho-
     dist University Press, 1963); George Korson, Black
     Rock: Mining Folklore of the Pennsylvania Dutch
     (Baltimore: The Johns Hopkins Press, 1960); for a
     study based on ethnic background, see Phyllis H.
     Williams, South Italian Folkways in Europe and
     America (New Haven: Yale University Press, 1938);
     for a study based on religion, see Austin E. and Alta
     S. Fife, Saints of Sage and Saddle (Bloomington, In-
     diana: Indiana University Press, 1956)--a study of
     Mormon folk traditions; for a study based on geo-
     graphical unity, see Emelyn Gardner, Folklore from
     the Schoharie Hills, New York (Ann Arbor: Univer-
     sity of Michigan Press, 1937)--essentially rural folk-
     lore--and Roger Abrahams, Deep Down in the Jungle
     ... Negro Narrative Folklore from the Streets of
     Philadelphia (Hatboro, Pa., Folklore Associates,
     1964)--an urban study.
15. Pp. 224-76.
16. Opie, "Tentacles, " p. 519.
17. Ibid., pp. 518-19.
18. See, however, Gershon Legman, Rationale of the Dirty
     Joke (New York: Grove Press, 1968).
19. "Tentacles, " p. 513.
20. Brunvand, American Folklore, p. 5. For a discussion
     of various formal approaches to the subject, see
     Dorson, "Current Folklore Theories, " pp. 93-112.
     Inasmuch as folk traditions vary from country to
     country, definitions of subject matter and hence for-
     mal approach follow suit. Brunvand's definition

reflects the main thrust of American folklorists' understanding of their discipline.

21.   For studies dealing with the relationship of folklore and history, see Theodore Blegen, Grass Roots History (Minneapolis: University of Minnesota Press, 1947); Arthur L. Campa, "Folklore and History," Western Folklore, XXIV (1965), 1-5; Signe Carlson, "An Interdisciplinary Approach to Folklore Study," Journal of the Ohio Folklore Society, II (1967), 149-65; H. R. Ellis Davidson, "Folklore and Man's Past," Folk-Lore, LXXIV (1963), 527-44; Levette Davidson, "Folklore as a Supplement to Western History," Nebraska History, XXIX (1948), 3-15; Richard Dorson, "Ethnohistory and Ethnic Folklore," Ethnohistory, VIII (1961), 12-27; idem, "Folklore and Cultural History," in Research Opportunities in American Cultural History, edited by John F. McDermott (Lexington, Ky.: University of Kentucky Press, 1961); idem, "Folklore in Relation to American Studies," in Frontiers of American Culture, edited by Ray Browne (West Lafayette, Ind.: Purdue University Studies, 1968); idem, "Oral Tradition and Written History: The Case for the United States," Journal of the Folklore Institute, I (1964), 220-34; idem, "A Theory for American Folklore," JAF, LXXII (1959), 197-215; idem, "A Theory for American Folklore Reviewed," JAF, LXXXII (1969), 226-44; John Elliot, "Folksong and Its Use as Evidence in the Humanities," issued as an insert in English Song and Dance, XXX (1968); Austin Fife, "Folklore and Local History," Utah Historical Quarterly, XXXI (1963), 315-23; Richard Hurst, "History and Folklore," New York Folklore Quarterly, XXV (1969), 243-61; idem, "On the Relationship of Folklore and History," Journal of the Ohio Folklore Society, I (1966), 63-74; Louis Jones, "Folk Culture and the Historical Society," Minnesota History, XXXI (1950), 11-17; idem, "Three Eyes on the Past: A New Triangulation for Local Studies," New York Folklore Quarterly, XII (1956), 3-13, 143-49; Philip Jordan, "History and Folklore," Missouri Historical Review, XLIV (1950), 119-29; Frank Kramer, Voices in the Valley: Myth-Making and Folk Beliefs in the Shaping of the Middle West (Madison: University of Wisconsin Press, 1964); Donald McCoy, "Underdeveloped Sources of Understanding in American History," Journal of American History, LIV (1967), 255-70; Mario de Pilis, "Folklore and the American West," Arizona

and the West, IV (1963), 291-314; Stith Thompson,
"Folklore and Minnesota History, " Minnesota History,
XXVI (1945), 97-105; Merle W. Wells, "History and
Folklore: A Suggestion for Cooperation, " Journal of
the West, IV (1965), 95-97.

22. (New York: Columbia University Press, 1940), pp. 11,
12. In the same volume, see two articles which discuss the relationship of folklore and history: B. A.
Botkin, "Folklore as a Neglected Source of Social
History, " pp. 308-15; Charles Seeger, "Folk Music
as a Source of Social History, " pp. 316-23.
Recurring symposia echo the plea for cultural
history; see McDermott, Research Opportunities
(1961), and Browne, Frontiers (1968).

23. Grass Roots, p. 5.

24. "Underdeveloped Sources, " pp. 256-57, 262.

25. Ibid., p. 262.

26. Grass Roots, pp. 254-55.

27. Abrahams, Jungle, p. 3. See also Opie, "Tentacles, "
p. 515.

28. See The Frank C. Brown Collection of North Carolina
Folklore, edited by Newman Ivey White, et al. (7
vols.; Durham, N.C.: Duke University Press, 1952-
64), for the most extensive American folk collection
from a single area. See Brunvand, American Folklore, Dorson, American Folklore, and Dundes, Study,
passim, for further bibliography of collections.

29. For motifs, see Stith Thompson, Motif-Index of Folk
Literature: A Classification of Narrative Elements
in Folktales, Ballads, Myths, Fables, Medieval Romances, Exempla, Fabliaux, Jest-Books, and Local
Legends (6 vols.; revised and enlarged edition;
Bloomington, Indiana: Indiana University Press, 1955-
1958); for the folktale, see Antti A. Aarne, The
Types of the Folktale: A Classification and Bibliography, tr. and enl. by Stith Thompson (2nd revision; Folklore Fellows Communications, V. 75, no.
184; Helsinki: Suomalainen Tiedeakatemia, 1961);
for proverbs see Archer Taylor and Bartlett J. Whiting, A Dictionary of American Proverbs and Proverbial Phrases, 1820-1880 (Cambridge, Mass.:
Harvard University Press, 1958); for riddles see
Archer Taylor, English Riddles from Oral Tradition
(Berkeley, Calif.: University of California Press,
1951); for superstitions, see Wayland D. Hand, "Introduction, " Frank C. Brown Collection, VI, xix-
xlvii, as well as the classification in the table of

contents (xii-xvii) and bibliography (xlix-lxxi); for
ballads, see Tristram Coffin, The British Traditional Ballad in America (rev. ed.; Philadelphia: American Folklore Society, 1963); G. Malcom Laws, Native American Balladry: A Descriptive Study and Bibliographical Syllabus (rev. ed.; Philadelphia: American Folklore Society, 1964); for folk music, see
Bruno Nettl, Folk and Traditional Music of the Western Continents (Englewood Cliffs, N. J.: Prentice
Hall, Inc., 1965). For classifications of numerous
other folk genres, see Dorson, American Folklore,
Brunvand, American Folklore, Dundes, Study, and
Haywood, Bibliography.

30. This practice is enjoined by McCoy, "Underdeveloped
Sources," p. 264, and questioned by Dorson, "Folklore in Relation to American Studies," p. 189.

31. According to H. Davidson: "Such indeed is the nature
of continuity in folklore; details change and so do the
accepted reasons for the practice, but fundamentally
the basic principle remains and falls into a definite
and discernible pattern. In following up such patterns, we shall find that folklore has much to teach
us concerning man's approach to the supernatural and
his feeling towards myths, rites, and symbols. What
the conscious mind ignores or denies, a deeper in-
stinct recognizes and welcomes." "Man's Past," p.
540.

32. Palo Alto, Calif.: Stanford University Press, 1957.

33. Lexington, Ky.: University of Kentucky Press, 1957.

34. The issue is one aspect of an exchange between folk-
lorist Richard Dorson and historian Mario de Pilis;
Dorson's "Theory for American Folklore" (1959) was
attacked by de Pilis' "Folklore and the American
West" (1963); rebuttal was provided in Dorson's
"Theory for American Folklore Revisited" (1969).

35. See Vansina's Oral Tradition. For an example of the
use of oral history in America, see William L.
Montell, The Saga of Coe Ridge: A Study in Oral
History (Knoxville: University of Tennessee Press,
1970.

36. Dorson, "Historical Method," p. 88.

37. Edited by Charles L. Wallis (New York: Abingdon
Press, 1956). See Dorson, "Historical Method,"
p. 87; Hurst, "History," p. 244.

38. Dorson, "Historical Method," p. 94.

39. See Dickson D. Bruce, And They All Sang Hallelujah:
Plain-folk Camp-Meeting Religion, 1800-1845 (Univer-

sity of Pennsylvania: Unpublished Doctoral Dissertation, 1971).

40. C. Grant Loomis, White Magic: An Introduction to the
Folklore of Christian Legend (Cambridge, Mass.:
Harvard University Press, 1948); idem, "The American Tall Tale and the Miraculous," California Folklore Quarterly, IV (1945), 109-28; idem, "Legend
and Folklore," California Folklore Quarterly, II
(1943), 279-97; Francis Lee Utley, "The Bible of the
Folk," California Folklore Quarterly, IV (1945), 1-
17.

41. For an anthropological study of such syncretism, see
Charles Hudson, "The Structure of a Fundamentalist
Christian Belief-System," in Religion and the Solid
South, edited by Samuel S. Hill, Jr., pp. 122-42.

42. Willard Sanders Barbery, Story of the Life of Robert
Sayers Sheffey: A Courier of the Long Trail--God's
Gentleman--a Man of Prayer and Unshaken Faith
(Bluefield, Va.: n.p., n.d.).

43. Ibid., p. 54.

44. Ibid., p. 116.

45. Ibid., p. 16.

46. Ibid., p. 60.

47. Ibid., p. 31.

48. Ibid., pp. 89-90.

49. Ibid., p. 68.

50. Another such volume is the biography (again a collection of oral traditions) of Rev. John Hersey: F. E.
Marine, Sketch of Rev. John Hersey, Minister of the
Gospel of the M. E. Church (Baltimore: Hoffman
and Co., 1879).

51. Green P. Jackson, Sunshine and Shade in a Happy Itinerant's Life (Nashville: Publishing House of the
M. E. Church, South, 1904), pp. 4-5.
    For further documentation see John Carroll,
My Boy Life, Presented in a Succession of True
Stories (Toronto: William Briggs, 1882), pp. 95-
100, 109-15. According to Carroll, in his youth
there was "a great deal more talking than reading.
Most persons were dependent on conversations or
oral communications for learning and mental entertainment ..." (p. 95). Carroll also mentions song-
singing as a recreation second only to storytelling
in importance, and gives several examples of the
kinds of songs sung.
    See also Elnathan C. Gavitt, Crumbs from My
Saddle Bags or, Reminiscences of Pioneer Life and

Biographical Sketches (Toledo: Blade Printing and
Paper Co., 1884), p. 4: "Supper being ended, they
spent an hour or two in recounting the incidents of
pioneer life, their adventures with bears, wolves, or
Indian depredations; or some marvelous tale as to the
large hollow sycamore tree which they had discovered
during their hunting expeditions, so full of bears,
coons, and other wild animals that every time they
breathed the tree would open and shut...."

52. John Burgess, Pleasant Recollections of Characters and
Works of Noble Men, with Old Scenes and Merry
Times of Long, Long, Ago (Cincinnati: Cranston and
Stowe, 1887), p. 108.

53. Carroll, Boy Life, p. 113.

54. From York's Autobiography, quoted, without page reference, in Marion T. Plyler and Alva W. Plyler, Men
of the Burning Heart: Ivey--Dow--Doub (Raleigh,
N. C.: Commercial Printing Co., 1918), p. 31.

55. G. C. Rankin, The Story of My Life, or More Than a
Half Century as I Have Lived It and Seen It Lived
(Nashville: Smith and Lamar, 1912), p. 21.

56. John A. Williams, Life of Elder John Smith: With Some
Account of the Rise and Progress of the Current
Reformation (Cincinnati: R. W. Carroll and Co.,
1870), p. 21.

57. Ibid., p. 27. While the biography contains elements of
a polemic against Methodist belief in experienced
conversion as the hallmark of true religion, it is
doubtless true that the supernatural morphology of
many religious stories followed that of much current
folklore. Moreover, structural similarity of numerous conversion accounts as well as the formularized
descriptions of camp meeting exercises such as "jerks"
may point to oral circulation.

58. Carroll, Boy Life, p. 115.

59. William E. Hatcher, Life of J. B. Jeter, D. D. (Baltimore: H. M. Wharton and Co., 1887), p. 35.
Jeter was a Presbyterian.

60. W. S. Blackman, The Boy of Battle Ford and the Man
(Marion, Ill.: The Egyptian Press Printing Co.,
1906), p. 20. Blackman was a Baptist.

61. William M. Green, Life and Papers of A. L. P. Green,
D. D., ed. by Thomas O. Summers (Nashville: Southern Methodist Publishing House, 1877), pp. 559-62.
The account includes an extensive list of superstitions
believed current by the author.

62. Susannah Johnson, Recollections of the Rev. John John-

son and His Home: An Autobiography, ed. by Adam
C. Johnson (Nashville: Southern Methodist Publishing House, 1869), pp. 261-62.

63. O. P. Fitzgerald, Sunset Views, in Three Parts (Nashville: Publishing House of the M. E. Church, South,
1906), p. 42.

64. Brother Mason, the Circuit Rider; or, Ten Years a
Methodist Preacher (Cincinnati: H. M. Rulison,
Queen City Publishing House, 1856), pp. 123-39.

65. W. Lee Spottswood, Brief Annals (Harrisburg, Pa.:
Publishing Department M. E. Book Room, 1888),
pp. 65-68.

66. Ibid., p. 68.

67. O. P. Fitzgerald, John B. McFerrin: A Biography
(Nashville: Publishing House of the M. E. Church,
South, 1888), pp. 60-1; Green, Life, pp. 358-65.
The same story is told on a grave marker in Beau-
fort, N. C., of the lady who lies beneath it. (Ob-
served by this writer.)

68. Lights and Shadows of Seventy Years (St. Louis, Mo.:
Nixon-Jones Printing Co., 1913), p. 8.

69. Ibid., pp. 10-11. See also, J. M. Peck, "Father
Clark," or, The Pioneer Preacher (New York: Shel-
don, Lamport, and Blakeman, 1855), pp. 166-71;
Landon Taylor, The Battlefield Reviewed (Chicago:
Published for the Author, 1881), pp. 6-8; John Ma-
son Peck, Forty Years of Pioneer Life: Memoir of
John Mason Peck, edited by Rufus Babcock (Phila-
delphia: American Baptist Society, 1864), p. 123.
The custom has its roots in English tradition; see
John Brand, Observations on the Popular Antiquities
of Great Britain, rev. by Henry Ellis (London:
H. G. Bohn, 1853), pp. 441-454.

70. Pleasant Recollections, pp. 325-26.

71. Luther Peck and His Five Sons (New York: Eaton and
Mains, 1897), pp. 51-62.

72. Burgess, Pleasant Recollections, pp. 110-11.

73. William Henry Milburn, Ten Years of Preacher-Life:
Chapters from an Autobiography (New York: Derby
and Jackson, 1859), pp. 216-22.

74. Charles Giles, Pioneer: A Narrative of the Nativity,
Experience, Travels, and Ministerial Labours of
Rev. Charles Giles, Author of the "Triumph of
Truth," etc., with Incidents, Observations, and Re-
flections (New York: G. Lane and P. P. Sandford,
1844), pp. 31-33.

75. The Itinerant on Foot; or, Life-Scenes Recalled (New

York: W. C. Palmer, 1882), pp. 153-54.
76. Blackman, Boy, p. 16.
77. Lorenzo Waugh, Autobiography of Lorenzo Waugh (San
    Francisco: Methodist Book Concern, 1896), p. 136.
78. Spottswood, Brief Annals, p. 53.
79. Ten Years, pp. 137-8, 172-74, 181-84, 192-93.
80. Fitzgerald, McFerrin, p. 72.
81. Thirteen Years' Experience in the Itinerancy; with Ob-
    servations on the Old Country (Philadelphia: Metho-
    dist Episcopal Book and Publishing House, 1881),
    p. 169.
82. Autobiography of Rev. Tobias Spicer: Containing Inci-
    dents and Observations: also, Some Account of His
    Visit to England (New York: Lane and Scott, 1852),
    p. 311.
83. John Ellis Edwards, Life of Rev. John Wesley Childs:
    for Twenty-Three Years an Itinerant Methodist Minis-
    ter (Richmond, Va.: John Early, 1852), p. 28.
84. James Robison, Recollections of Rev. Samuel Clawson
    (Pittsburgh: Charles A. Scott, 1883), p. 69.
85. Elijah Woolsey, The Supernumerary; or, Lights and
    Shadows of Itinerancy, compiled by George Coles
    (New York: Lane and Scott, 1852), p. 37.
86. Spottswood, Brief Annals, pp. 336-37.
87. Elizabeth Tokar, "Humorous Anecdotes Collected From
    a Methodist Minister," Western Folklore, XXVI
    (1967), 93.
88. E. M. Marvin, The Life of Rev. William Goff Caples,
    of the Missouri Conference of the Methodist Episco-
    pal Church, South (St. Louis: Southwestern Book
    and Publishing Co., 1871), pp. 166-67.
89. Brief Annals, pp. 76-77.
90. Ten Years, p. 74.
91. Fitzgerald, McFerrin, p. 129. See also Milburn, Ten
    Years, pp. 70-74, for examples of the sort of hu-
    morous anecdote told while riding; also Frank Rich-
    ardson, From Sunrise to Sunset (Bristol, Tenn.:
    The King Printing Co., 1910), p. 196.
92. Carroll, "Father Corson," p. 54.
93. Ten Years, p. 360.
94. H. A. Graves, Reminiscences and Events in the Minis-
    terial Life of Rev. John Wesley DeVilbiss (Galveston:
    W. A. Shaw and Co., 1886), p. 114; Marvin, Caples,
    p. 71.
95. Thomas M. Finney, The Life and Labors of Enoch
    Mather Marvin, Late Bishop of the Methodist Epis-
    copal Church, South (St. Louis: James H. Chambers,

1881), p. 682.
96. Plyler and Plyler, Men, p. 181.
97. Pp. 206, 12.
98. L. L. Nash, Recollections and Observations During a
    Ministry in the North Carolina Conference, Metho-
    dist Episcopal Church, South, of Forty-Three Years
    (Raleigh: Mutual Publishing Co., 1916), p. 17.
99. The Life of Rev. Thomas A. Morris, D.D., Late
    Senior Bishop of the Methodist Episcopal Church
    (Cincinnati: Hitchcock and Walden, 1875), p. 402.
100. See Mody Boatright, "Comic Exempla of the Pioneer
    Pulpit," in Coyote Wisdom, ed. by J. Frank Dobie,
    Mody Boatright, Harry H. Ransom (Texas Folklore
    Society Publications, No. XIV; Austin: Texas Folk-
    lore Society, 1938), pp. 155-68.
101. See Thomas Crane (ed.), The Exempla or Illustrative
    Stories from the Sermones Vulgares of Jacques de
    Vitry (London: The Folklore Society, 1890), xix;
    J. A. Mosher, The Exemplum in the Early Reli-
    gious and Didactic Literature of England (New York:
    Columbia University Press, 1911), pp. 84-86;
    G. R. Owst, Preaching in Medieval England; An
    Introduction to Sermon Manuscripts of the Period
    c. 1350-1450 (New York: Russell and Russell,
    1965), pp. 299-300.
102. See Thomas Wright (ed.), A Selection of Latin Stories,
    from Manuscripts of the Thirteenth and Fourteenth
    Centuries: A Contribution to the History of Fiction
    During the Middle Ages (London, 1842), vi-vii; see
    also J. B. Wakeley (ed.), Anecdotes of the Wes-
    leys: Illustrations of their Character and Personal
    History (New York: Carlton and Lanahan, 1869),
    pp. 3-4, and idem, Anecdotes of the Rev. George
    Whitefield, M.A., with Biographical Sketch, 3rd ed.
    (London: Hodder and Stoughton, 1875), pp. 61-62,
    196-97, 376-77, for remarks on the importance of
    exempla for the archetypal Methodist itinerants.
103. For collections of mendicant exempla, see Crane, The
    Exempla, Wright, Latin Stories, and Charles Swan
    and Wynnard Hooper (eds.), Gesta Romanorum, or
    Entertaining Moral Stories, Invented by the Monks
    as a Fireside Recreation, and Commonly Applied in
    their Discourses from the Pulpit.... (London:
    George Bell & Sons, 1877).
        For collections of itinerant exempla, see Sam
    Jones' Anecdotes and Illustrations, Related by Him
    in His Revival Work (Chicago: Rhodes and McClure

Publishing House, 1889); William L. Stidger, Sermon Nuggets in Stories (New York: Abingdon-Cokesbury Press, 1946); George R. Stuart, Stories and Parables to Illustrate Gospel Truths (Nashville: Publishing House of the Methodist Episcopal Church South, 1920); J. G. Vaughan, The Gem Cyclopedia of Illustrations (Cincinnati: Cranston & Stowe, 1889); and finally, Wakeley, Anecdotes of Wesley, and Anecdotes of Whitefield.

    G. R. Owst has argued the importance of the mendicant transmission of traditional folk and popular culture for the rise of literature in England; Literature and Pulpit in Medieval England; A Neglected Chapter in the History of English Letters and of the English People (Oxford: Basil Blackwell, 1966), p. 207.

104. See Mosher, The Exemplum, p. 115.
105. Autobiography, pp. 149-50. A similar episode, perhaps referring to a performance by Cartwright, is recorded in James B. Finley, Autobiography of Rev. James B. Finley, or Pioneer Life in the West, edited by W. P. Strickland (Cincinnati: Jennings and Pye, 1853), pp. 322-24.
106. Tokar, "Humorous Anecdotes," p. 96.
107. Johnson, Recollections, p. 90, for a list of one itinerant's books. See also James Erwin, Reminiscences of Early Circuit Life (Toledo: Spear, Johnson, and Co., 1884), pp. 48-49, for another list and for an account of reading on horseback. Such reading lists were geared to uplifting the general educational and theological background of the itinerants (see Kenneth E. Rowe, "New Light on Early Methodist Theological Education," Methodist History, X (1971), 58-62); cursory examination of the suggested books reveals precious few of the kind of exempla that appear in the autobiographies and biographies as well as in the collections of exempla noted above. For exempla the itinerants must have relied heavily on other, perhaps oral, sources.
108. John F. Wright, Sketches of the Life and Labors of James Quinn, Who Was Nearly Half a Century a Minister of the Gospel in the Methodist Episcopal Church (Cincinnati: Printed at the Methodist Book Concern, 1851), p. 275.
109. Finney, Marvin, p. 177.
110. Methodist Heroes of Other Days (New York: The Methodist Book Concern, 1916), p. 9.

111. Autobiography of Dan Young, A New England Preacher
of the Olden Time, edited by W. P. Strickland
(New York: Carlton and Porter, 1860), p. 363.
112. Young, Autobiography, pp. 368-80. See also Cartwright, Autobiography, pp. 329ff. for a formulaic
argument against an "infidel Doctor."

PART II

REMARKABLE PROVIDENCES

One thing is certain: there is little space between
us and the unknown world, and we sometimes receive impressions from that mystic land. 1

At a revival meeting on the Canton circuit, Central
New York Conference, in 1833, the Rev. James Erwin told
the story of a young lady who had visited her uncle in Hartford, Connecticut, during the time of a great revival. The
girl attended one revival meeting, but after initial seriousness, she lost all interest in the state of her soul. Cousins
and friends prayed for her and admonished her, but to no
avail. The night before she left the city, she replied to repeated entreaties: "'I would rather take my seat in hell.'"

On the train-ride home, the young lady caught a cold
which soon developed into a critical illness. The attending
doctor pronounced her case hopeless. To the minister who
came to pray with her she confessed: "'It will do no good;
it is too late!'" "She died," Erwin reported, "in great agony,
crying: 'I have sealed my damnation and am lost.'"

At the conclusion of the story an old Universalist
preacher, a "bold, hardened opposer" who "arrayed himself
against the success of the meeting," rose up and asked Erwin for the "name of a responsible party to whom he might
write, to learn the truth of these statements." Erwin had a
ready answer:

> I replied most certainly, and without any hesitancy
> gave him the name of Dr. Smyth, president of the
> Wesleyan University of Middletown, Ct., who was
> familiar with the case, and could give him all the
> particulars, or if more convenient for him he might
> address Rev. Mr. Elsworth, of Lowville, Lewis
> county, N.Y., who was an intimate friend of the

young lady and her family, who would take a melan-
choly pleasure in giving him the facts.[2]

Erwin was neither a charlatan nor a fool. He was,
rather, a traditionalist, and his verbal duel with the cynical
old Universalist provides a scenario of the nineteenth century
tension between the seventeenth century supernaturalist mindset and the rationalistic mindset that emerged in the eighteenth century. That Erwin could adduce "facts" to verify his
story indicates his desire to reconcile the two mindsets. But
the story of the young woman places him squarely in a tradition whose roots reach back in time through the Puritan
Mathers into an Old World tangle of folk religion.

The bare bones of this tradition, to shift the metaphor,
stem from the ancient Christian belief in God's providential
direction of the universe. According to such belief, God directly controls and guides all that happens in the material
universe, so that not only the ordinary course of nature but
also the extraordinary exceptions to that course disclose his
purposes. Moreover, invisible reality so permeates visible
reality that man's moral or immoral choices incarnate themselves beautifully or hideously, either in the ordinary course
of events or in an extraordinary fashion allowed by Divine
Providence in order to illustrate strikingly the tangible consequences of moral action. Stories which recount extraordinary exceptions to known natural sequences and extraordinary
manifestations of the results of human actions are commonly
denoted in the tradition as remarkable providences.

The flesh and sinew, on the other hand, of the remarkable providence tradition come from innumerable legends
and exempla told again and again of various personages and
in varying circumstances. For example, Erwin's story of
the young lady's rash wish providentially fulfilled is told by
Cotton Mather more than a hundred years earlier of an im-
pudent young man:

A lewd young man, being dissatisfied, with the service wherein he lived, at the house of an honest
man, in a neighbouring town, when they told him,
that his bad courses would bring him to hell at the
last, he wickedly said, He had rather be in hell
than in his master's house. Immediately after this,
he was in a very strange manner drowned off a little bank in the river.[3]

The story of a man who denied a theft of which he was accused, told in C. Grant Loomis' White Magic, indicates the hagiographic Old World lineage of the motif. The man swore, "'May Edburga never let me leave this place alive, if I committed the theft!'" He immediately fell dead. 4

The motif of Erwin's story is not only ancient but widespread. One indication of its universality is its inclusion in Stith Thompson's massive Motif-Index of Folk-Literature. 5 Another indication of the diffusion of a given story is the location of variants or versions. Several parallels to the Erwin story occur in the Methodist literature itself. One autobiography, for example, tells the story of a man who had been a practicing Methodist but became "an awful backslider." When his father-in-law admonished him to mend his ways, he asserted: "'I would sooner be damned than be a Methodist.'" A short time afterward he went out to his field to work, and although his health had been perfect, he sickened and died on the spot. 6 Another man, notes a Cumberland Presbyterian biographer, left a religious meeting in a rage, saying "he would as leave be among a pack of wolves, as at such a meeting." A few days later "he was a corpse."7 Another account attributes the remark, without the usual dire consequences, to the acerbic John Randolph of Roanoke, who lost his temper on his sick bed, one day after listening to repeated mispronunciations of a word by an attending Methodist minister. Said Randolph: "'I had rather die and go to hell than to hear that word called that way anymore.'"8

The concern of this chapter, therefore, is with the mindset of Methodist preachers like Erwin, indicated by stories of remarkable providences whose traditional nature is verified by scrutiny of folk sources in Thompson's Motif-Index, of hagiographic legends in Loomis' White Magic, of Old and New Testament miracle traditions in E. Cobham Brewer's Dictionary of Miracles, 9 and by location of versions and variants in the Methodist literature itself.

Old World traditions found the New World ready soil for vigorous growth. Three factors help explain the transplant: 1) the early settlers' providential view of history; 2) the settlers' image of the New World as howling wilderness; 3) their image of the New World as Eden. 10

1) New England Puritans, whose providential historiography impelled them to see the finger of God not only in the general course of events but also most emphatically in

their own hegira to the New World, 11 were particularly susceptible to noticing unusual events and to regarding them as
the special stirring of divine providence.   In fact, as Cotton
Mather wrote, those who looked for providences were likely
to find them:

> To regard the illustrious displays of that PROVI-
> DENCE wherewith our Lord Christ governs the
> world, is a work, than which there is none more
> needful or useful for a Christian: to record them
> is a work, than which, none more proper for a
> minister: and perhaps the Great Governour of the
> world will ordinarily do the most notable things for
> those who are most ready to take a wise notice of
> what he does. 12

2)   The susceptibility of "those who are most ready
to take a wise notice of what he [God] does" was fanned and
fired by the dangers of the New World.   Not only did harsh
weather and poor crops (such as those which brought the Virginia colony to its "starving time") seem to hint at the divine
disposition, but also bloodthirsty Indians, whom the providentially sent elect were prone to regard as the demonic op-
posers of their mission, lurked in the black forest at the
fringes of the settlements, waiting for chances to rape and
plunder unsuspecting villages.   Frequently Indians carried
off captives, and the stories of those who escaped from their
savage captors excited the horror and wonder of listeners
around flickering fires in dim wilderness cabins. 13   Credulous settlers easily transformed such threatening experiences
into providential terms which reinforced their conviction that
they were a new Israel confronting the opposition of a wilderness Canaan.   Moreover, the activities of Indian medicine
men and conjurers, who were widely believed to ply their
trade with demonic connivance, seemed proof positive to
curious colonials of the unfolding moral drama in which they
were involved.   As an example of the fascination with which
settlers viewed evil Indian sorcery, John Lawson, the sur-
veyor-general of North Carolina, records in his History how
a conjurer calmed a wind:

> At Night, as we lay in our Beds, there arose the
> most violent N. W. Wind I ever knew.   The first
> Puff blew down all the Palisadoes that fortified the
> Town; and I thought it would have blown us all into
> the River, together with the Houses.   Our one-
> eyed King, who pretends much to the Art of Conjura-

tion, ran out in the most violent Hurry, and in the
Middle of the Town, fell to his Necromantik Practice; though I thought he would have been blown
away or killed, before the Devil and he could have
exchanged half a dozen Words; but in two Minutes,
the Wind was ceased, and it became as great a
Calm as ever I knew in my Life. As I much ad-
mired at that sudden Alteration, the old Man told
me the Devil was very angry, and had done thus
because they had not put the Sinnagers to Death. [14]

3)   If the settlers experienced the full force of the
New World as wilderness, travelers experienced it as an
earthly Eden.   To credulous audiences in the capitals of the
Old World they sent glowing accounts of the new land, com-
bining misinformation, exaggeration, and sometimes outright
lies into fabulous accounts of New World conditions. [15]   Lawson, for example, describing the fecundity of the land, mentions cornstalks in Indian fields "as thick as the Small of a
Man's Leg...."[16]   He reports a "Tulip-Tree" so large that
a "lusty Man" moved in his "Bed and Household Furniture,"[17]
and flocks of pigeons whose flight blotted out the sun. [18]   The
fecundity of the land affected persons as well: childless women, he records, come to North Carolina and "become joyful
Mothers, " seldom miscarrying and having "very easy Travail
in their Childbearing."[19]

The predilection for providences, therefore, found
ready material in the terrors of the wilderness and the wonders of an earthly Eden.   Apparitions and visions, spectres
and ghosts, strange deformations and sudden deaths, lightning
bolts and comets, unexpected cures and sickenings, witches
and warlocks made the scrutiny of providences rewarding
business for Puritan divines.   While the divine intent was not
always patent, as for example when Cotton Mather's own
house was blasted by lightning while he was preaching a sermon entitled "Brontologia Sacra,"[20] nevertheless Puritans believed that God punished the impious and rewarded the pious,
and in general providentially confirmed the progress of their
errand into the wilderness.

But the tradition of remarkable providences belongs
not alone to New England Puritans.   The English Jesuits of
Maryland colony recorded divine confirmations of their work,
as well.   One letter to the Provincial in Europe, contrasting
the fortunes of two prospective converts, related how a man
about to embrace religion suffered a fire in his cabin.   Instead

of taking the blaze as an evil omen, he saw it as a confirmation of his intent:

> for his house being almost uninjured, he thence drew the conclusion that God was propitious to him and approved his design by a manifest token. [21]

The other man, after briefly entertaining thoughts of conversion, "determined to cast aside all such thoughts, and go back to the customary paths of his earlier life." As an impious gesture he ground up his Rosary beads and smoked them with tobacco in his pipe, "often boasting that he was eating up his 'Ave Marias....'" A year to the day after this action, he was attacked while swimming by a large fish which tore away part of his thigh and precipitated his demise. It was an act of divine justice, comments the correspondent, "that he, who a little while before boasted that he had eaten up his 'Ave Maria beads,' should see his own flesh devoured, even while he was yet living."[22]

Jasper Danckaerts, an agent for the pietistic Dutch Labadist sect, recorded providences in his journal of a visit to America. A wicked man who suffered innumerable personal and domestic tragedies finally recognized his chastisement as divine and embraced religion. [23] In another instance, Danckaerts recounts in good faith the story that a converted Indian told him about a hunting trip during which God sent a deer before his rifle in order to confute a blasphemous fellow hunter. [24]

In summary, the recording of providences, such as Erwin's story of God's visitation upon the girl who refused religion, has an eminent heritage, both from the Old World, which provided the incentive and the themes, and from the New World, which furnished the stimulation and the context.

The pages that follow document the extension of that tradition into the nineteenth century among Methodist preachers.

Some accounts written by Methodist preachers who followed the New World into the interior of the continent, that is, who moved with the frontier, seem to reflect the same credulity noted in the colonial traveller's accounts. George F. Pierce, writing home about his experiences in Texas, told of oak trees giving wheat, an eighteen pound turnip, a three-year-old cabbage stalk with one hundred and sixty-three heads,

and of a hen who laid an egg "with a handle five inches and
a half long." The same traveller tells of remarkable births
at a place he visited:

> First, a mule brought forth a colt; a ram had a
> horn upon his ear; and a sow had a litter of pigs,
> each having the ear mark which mine host's wife
> had adopted to distinguish her stock. This beats
> Jacob and Laban, with the brown sheep and the ring-
> streaked, spotted and speckled goats. [25]

Another Texas traveller told of horse-flies so numerous on
the prairie that horses who made for the timber died before
they could reach it, and of mosquitoes on the same prairie
so large they could penetrate a buckskin glove. [26] One itinerant, in an account reminiscent of Lawson's story, spoke of
flights of millions of pigeons that blackened the sun, and that
broke branches by their weight when they roosted:

> Their numbers and weight broke down hundreds, yea,
> acres of large trees, and stripped others of their
> limbs, equal to the sweeping hurricane in its mad-
> dened march. [27]

In another account Bishop Capers tells how, as a youth, he
shattered a glass snake with a stick, and how "the pieces,
when broken square off, wormed themselves about as if a-
live." [28] Bee swarms, recalls a preacher, were so plentiful
in his youthful days on the frontier that "it was no unusual
thing to find ten swarms in a day," and that some trees
yielded up to thirty-six gallons of honey. [29]

Other Methodist accounts continued the tradition of
narrating Indian captivities and remarkable escapes there-
from.

In short, if the New World nurtured Old World beliefs
in God's providence by appearing as wilderness and Eden, the
New Frontier of the New World did the same, after indepen-
dence from England had been won, for the adventurous pioneers. Stories of natural wonders and Indian captivities on
the western frontier provided the mysterious and fabulous
backdrop for stories indicating Methodism's providential role
in spreading the gospel.

This Part studies the sources to illustrate the vigor
and nature of a traditional mindset among Methodist itinerants.

HE DISCOVERED NUMEROUS GUNS SET AGAINST THE HOUSE, WITH STRINGS OF SQUIRRELS, A FEW OPOSSUMS, AND ANY QUANTITY OF PARTRIDGES, DISTRIBUTED SO AS TO READILY SHOW THEIR PROPER OWNERSHIP.

An Appointment at a Wilderness Eden

Anecdotes relating providentially ordained dreams, judgments, conversions, deliverances, encounters and omens not only provided categories by which preachers could organize their own experience but also didactic devices by which they could help their people interpret the inscrutabilities of life under divine providence. Various preaching and teaching contexts, therefore, provided the occasion for relation of such lore.

Where possible, the traditionality of story motifs has been established by indication of folk, hagiographic, and biblical precedents. No attempt has been made to pronounce upon the facticity of various narratives. Whether a particular event as described in the following anecdotes was an historical event, the belief that it so occurred or the recorded anecdote relating its occurrence are historical, datable facts.

Notes

1. Henry Clay Morrison, Autobiography of Bishop Henry Clay Morrison, edited by George Means (Nashville: Publishing House of the M. E. Church, South, 1917), p. 28.
2. Erwin, Reminiscences, pp. 165-66.
3. Cotton Mather, Magnalia Christi Americana: or, The Ecclesiastical History of New England, From its First Planting, in the Year 1620, Unto the Year of our Lord 1698 (2 vols.; Hartford, Conn.: Silas Andrus and Son, 1852), II, 393. (Hereafter cited as Mather, MCA; all references from volume II unless otherwise noted.) Mather gives seven other examples of rash wishes, careless oaths, or curses providentially punished, pp. 393-394.
    Collecting and publishing stories of remarkable providences was a serious business for seventeenth and sixteenth century English apologists. See John Aubrey, Miscellanies (London, 1696); Thomas Beard, The Theatre of Gods Iudgements: or, A Collection of Histories out of Sacred, Ecclesiasticall, and Prophane Authors, Concerning the Admirable Iudgements of God Upon the Transgressions of His Commandements (London, 1597); L. Brinckmair, The Warnings of Germany, by Wonderfull Signes, and Strange Prodigies Seene in Divers Parts of that Countrey of Germany, Between the Yeare 1618 and 1638 (London, 1638); Henry Burton, A Divine Tragedie Lately Acted, or, A Collection of Sundry Memorable Examples of

Gods Judgments upon Sabbath-Breakers, and Other
Libertines, in their Unlawfull Spirits.... (1636);
Henry Jessey, The Lords Loud Call to England:
Being a true Relation of Some Late, Various, and
Wonderful Judgments, or Handy-works of God, by
Earthquake, Lightening, Whirlewind, Great Multitudes
of Toads and Flyes; and also the Striking of Divers
Persons with Sudden Death, in Several Places....
(London, 1660); Henry Spelman, The History and Fate
of Sacrilege, Discovered by Examples of Scripture, of
Heathens and of Christians; from the Beginning of the
World Continually to this Day (London, 1698); Wil-
liam Turner, A Compleat History of the Most Re-
markable Providences, Both of Judgments and Mercy,
Which Have Happened in this Present Age (London:
J. Dunton, 1697); Nathaniel Wanley, The Wonders of
the Little World: or, A General History of Man in
Six Books (London, 1678); Robert Woodrow, Analecta;
or, Materials for a History of Remarkable Providences; Mostly Relating to Scotch Ministers and
Christians (4 vols.; Edinburgh: Printed for the Maitland Club, 1842-43); Thomas Wright, The Glory of
Gods Revenge Against the Bloody and Detestable Sins
of Murther and Adultery, Expressed in Thirty Modern Tragical Histories (London, 1685).
    These collections draw upon a tradition trans-
mitted in part by innumerable English and Continental
hagiographies, martyrologies, collections of exempla,
and ecclesiastical histories.

4.   Loomis, White Magic, p. 100. Loomis delicately allows the original Latin describe the man's death:
"'ecce protinus intestinorum viscera per anum effu-
dit, et, ut voce petuit, vivus a loco non surrexit.'"

5.   The term "motif," the author explains, is loosely defined as "any of the elements of narrative structure."
Thompson, Motif-Index, p. 19. Motifs are arranged
alphabetically into twenty-three genera, then numer-
ically within each broad genus. The use of decimal
points in numerical classification allows for detailed
sub-classification within the genera. For example,
Erwin's story falls under section "Q." "Rewards
and Punishments." Within section "Q" it corresponds
to a specific motif, Q221.4.2: "Man vows to recover
loose boat or go to hell trying."
    A given story, legend, or anecdote may ex-
emplify several motifs. Thompson notes: "There is
much common matter in the folk-literature of the

world. The similarities consist not so often in complete tales as in single motifs ... these elements ...
can form a common basis for a systematic arrange-
ment of the whole body of traditional literature, "
ibid., p. 10. Hence the Erwin story also exempli-
fies two other traditional motifs: K2312: "Oath literally obeyed"; C94. 2: "Tabu: false and profane
swearing of oath. "
    The basis for inclusion of a given narrative
element in the Motif-Index is traditionality: "Most
of the items are found worthy of note because of
something out of the ordinary, something of sufficient-
ly striking character to become part of tradition,
oral or literary, " ibid., p. 19.
    For a full explanation of the purpose and scope
of the Motif-Index see Thompson's "Introduction, "
volume I, 9-27. See also Brunvand, American Folklore, pp. 80-83, for further explanation.
    As is the practice in scholarly folklore, refer-
ences to the Motif-Index will be by motif-number and
motif. Dorson, American Folklore, pp. 301-6.

6.   George Coles, My First Seven Years in America, edited
    by D. P. Kidder (New York: Carlton and Phillips,
    1852), pp. 221-22.

7.   David Lowry, Life and Labors of the Late Rev. Robert
    Donnell, of Alabama, Minister of the Gospel in the
    Cumberland Presbyterian Church (Alton, Ill. : S. V.
    Crossman, 1867), p. 224.

8.   Graves, DeVilbiss, p. 165.

9.   E. Cobham Brewer, A Dictionary of Miracles; Imita-
    tive Realistic, and Dogmatic With Illustrations (Phila-
    delphia: J. B. Lippincott Company, n. d., repub-
    lished by Detroit: Gale Research Company, 1966).
    The inevitable overlapping among the three tools is
    offset by the fact that Thompson's Motif-Index ex-
    cludes religious beliefs (p. 11), and that Brewer's
    work assumes that the miracle legends of Christian
    tradition all derive ultimately from the Scriptures
    (p. xvii), thus excluding the Celtic and Oriental
    derivations which Loomis includes.

10.   For the following analysis (pp. 58-64), I am indebted
    to Dorson, American Folklore, pp. 7-23.

11.   Perry Miller, Errand Into the Wilderness (Cambridge,
    Mass.: Harvard University Press, 1956), pp. 1-15;
    the belief that they were instruments of divine intent
    was true of the Virginia colonizers and their spon-
    sors as well as of the New England Puritans; idem,

"The Religious Impulse in the Founding of Virginia: Religion and Society in the Early Literature," William and Mary Quarterly, 3rd series, V (1948), 492-522.

12. Mather, MCA, p. 341.

13. Cotton Mather includes as an example of Heaven's remarkable deliverances the narrative of one Hannah Swarton, captured and finally freed by the Indians: MCA, pp. 357-61. See Harold H. Peckham, Captured by Indians: True Tales of Pioneer Survivors (New Brunswick, N.J.: Rutgers University Press, 1954).

For an anthology of early American writings on wonders, providences, captivities, witchcrafts, and wars, see America Begins: Early American Writing, ed. by Richard M. Dorson (New York: Pantheon Books, Inc., 1950).

14. John Lawson, Lawson's History of North Carolina, Containing the Exact Description and Natural History of that Country, Together with the Present State Thereof and a Journal of a Thousand Miles Traveled Through Several Nations of Indians, Giving a Particular Account of Their Customs, Manners, Etc. Etc. (London, 1714; republished Richmond, Va.: Garret and Massie, 1951), p. 47; see pp. 19-20, 229-33, for other accounts of the feats of Indian conjurers. Also, Robert Beverley, The History and Present State of Virginia, edited with an introduction by Louis B. Wright (Chapel Hill, N.C.: University of North Carolina Press, 1947), pp. 204-5, for the account of an Indian conjurer making rain for Colonel Byrd.

15. James R. Masterson, "Traveler's Tales of Colonial Natural History," Journal of American Folklore, LIX (1946), 51-67. Percy G. Adams, Travelers and Travel Liars 1660-1800 (Berkeley, Calif.: University of California Press, 1962).

16. Lawson, History, p. 37.

17. Ibid., p. 95.

18. Ibid., p. 42.

19. Ibid., pp. 85-86.

20. "The Sacred Lessons of the Thunder," MCA, p. 363.

21. Clayton C. Hall, Narratives of Early Maryland 1633-1684 (New York: Charles Scribner's Sons, 1910), p. 133.

22. Ibid., p. 134. For further remarkable providences in Maryland, see pp. 42, 120-21, 122, 125-26, 126, 139.

23. Jasper Danckaerts, The Journal of Jasper Danckaerts
     1679-1680, edited by Bartlett B. James and J.
     Franklin Jamison (New York: Charles Scribner's
     Sons, 1913), pp. 190-95.
24. Ibid., pp. 206-7.
25. George C. Smith, The Life and Times of George Foster
     Pierce, D. D., LL. D. (Sparta, Ga.: Hancock Pub-
     lishing Co., 1888), pp. 356-57; also, pp. 368-69,
     for an account of Texas paradoxes; p. 372, for a
     Texas rabbit that measured eighteen inches between
     the ears.
26. Graves, DeVilbiss, p. 35.
27. Burgess, Pleasant Recollections, pp. 322-33.
28. William Wightman, Life of William Capers, D. D., One
     of the Bishops of the Methodist Episcopal Church,
     South; Including an Autobiography (Nashville, Tenn.:
     Southern Methodist Publishing House, 1859), pp. 29-
     30.
29. Chauncey Hobart, Recollections of My Life (Red Wing,
     Minn.: Red Wing Printing Co., 1885), p. 51.

Chapter 1

DREAMS, VISIONS, VOICES, OMENS

Elihu said to Job:

'For God speaketh once,
Yea twice, though man regardeth it not.
In a dream, in a vision of the night,
When deep sleep falleth upon men,
In slumberings upon the bed:
Then he openeth the ears of men,
And sealeth their instruction.'[1]

In Christian tradition, dreams have been valued "as a sign of contact with religious reality." Dreams "gave purpose and meaning, warning where spiritual disaster impended," and the interpretation of dreams was valued as a religious gift.[2] Visions occur so frequently in hagiographic lore that Loomis declines to include them in his study, noting only that "visions of heaven and hell are very common."[3]

That the Methodist itinerants and their biographers felt uneasy in assuming the divine origin of dreams is evidenced by the anecdote in which a Swedenborgian dreamed that his head fell off and, when restored to its original location, was turned backwards. When asked for an interpretation of the dream by the Swedenborgian, a Methodist preacher said:

> Your head has got wrong side foremost, sure enough, else how could you gulp down the fantastic dreams and imaginary visions of Swedenborg.[4]

Despite their emphasis on emotional conversion, Methodist preachers had little time for visionaries, ecstatics or spiritualists.[5] One itinerant asserted that omens of death were the result of fatigue, and that hard-working Methodist preachers should not pay attention to such presentiments.[6]

As a hedge, therefore, against what they regarded as dangerous enthusiasm, Methodist preachers often introduced accounts of their dreams with a caveat. One man wrote: "I am no enthusiast, in the general sense of the word, nor do I view myself as a visionary ...," and then related his dream.[7] "In general, I put no confidence in dreams ...," began another.[8] Peter Cartwright prefaced his relation of a dream by noting: "Although I have never laid much stress on dreams, yet on Monday night ... I had a dream that made some impression on my mind."[9] Itinerant James Quinn, after relating a dream in which he was covered with golden stars in heaven, protected himself by remarking:

> Whatever opinions may be entertained of dreams in general or of this one in particular, it is supposed all will agree that this was a very pleasant one; and while it may be interesting to some, it will injure no one to read it.[10]

Hedging notwithstanding, the fact remains that Methodist preachers did tell their own and others' dreams and cited Scripture as a basis for doing so. After recounting the story of a doctor who died on the exact day predicted in a dream, the narrator comments:

> Thus his dream was literally fulfilled. Is it unreasonable? If it is, still it is in perfect accord with the teaching of the Scriptures.[11]

Another author asserts:

> If any shall say that it is inconsistent that dreams should have any influence on us, I answer, the Bible is full of testimony to the point that dreams often have a significant import.[12]

A third author cites Job 4.12-17 as the authority for his belief that "dreams do sometimes come from God."[13] Rev. Johnson Olive declares, as authority for telling dreams, that "the Bible authorizes him who has a dream to tell a dream."[14]

On such authority, therefore, itinerants cautiously related their dreams, visions, presentiments and omens. Among believers, such relations could furnish ample evidence of the transparency of the human person to divine intent and of the ever-present prompting of providence for God's chosen ones.

For purposes of clarity, the dreams have been divided
into five major sections, with subsections: the other world,
otherworldly visitors, revenants, future events, and cosmic
omens.

The Other World

1. <u>Dreamer visits heaven</u>. Benjamin Abbott recounts
a dream he experienced at age thirty-three. After dreaming
about hell several weeks previously, one night he dreamed
that he died and was carried into "one of the most beautiful
places I ever saw, " that his guide directed him into "one of
the most elegant buildings I ever beheld, " the gates of which
"opened to us of their own accord, " and that inside "we were
met by a company of the heavenly host, arrayed in white rai-
ment down to their feet. " Then he saw the "Ancient of Days
sitting upon his throne";

> I stood amazed at the sight; one stepped forward to
> me arrayed in white, which I knew to be my wife's
> mother, and said to me, 'Benjamin, this place is
> not for you yet'; so I returned, and my guide
> brought me back.

Abbott's spiritual flight prompted, in the days following, a
short-lived repentance. Soon, Abbott recalls, "I went to my
old practices. " But the dream functioned as a catalyst, sev-
en years later, when he heard a sermon on the afterlife and
experienced a conversion which proved life-long in its effect. [15]

2. <u>Soul separates from body and travels to heaven</u>.
In each of the accounts of this experience the subject had
been given up for dead. One man, a Deist, heard his wife
exclaim: "'Isaac is dying--call father!' " He lost consciousness, and when he recovered, "he appeared to himself to be
out of his body. " Then he rose through the ceiling and roof,
into the sky until earth disappeared. While he was still
ascending, a hand appeared above him "that seemed to make
a motion for him to go back. " Immediately he descended
back through the roof into his body.

The chronicler of the occurrence, Rev. Tobias Spicer,
notes that the man soon recovered from his fatal sickness,
and that the memory of the experience gave him no rest until

he converted.   Notwithstanding these benefits, Spicer remained
noncommittal:

> I can make no comment on this strange account.   I
> have no doubt that it seemed all real to him.   And
> who can say it was not?   There may be something
> like this in the departure of human souls. [16]

In another account, a critically ill man had the experience of conversing with his disembodied soul as well as with
Jesus before being restored to physical wholeness.   The protagonist explicitly likened his experience to that of St. Paul
in the desert: " 'Whether I was in the body or out of the
body, I cannot tell.' "[17]

3.   Swooning woman voices spiritual utterances.   A
woman whose husband forbade her to attend a Methodist meeting disobeyed him, and while listening to a sermon, as if in
divine confirmation of her courage, sank "slowly and softly
to the floor, and fell away into the sweet visions of a divine
swoon."   The next morning at ten o'clock she awoke from
her trance and told assembled people what she had seen.   "If
she had been a fine classical and thorough biblical scholar, "
notes the narrator

> she could not have given a more accurate account
> or grander description of Tartarus with its dismal
> woe for the sinner and paradise with its exhaustless
> weal for the saint than she gave on that hot, sultry
> summer morning. [18]

Among those who sought religion, after her account, was her
husband, who had been summoned during the night and had
listened to her morning relation.

A Presbyterian narrator of a similar swooning incident
judges, after recounting in great detail the lady's experiences,
that "this was no doubt a case of epilepsy...."   The story becomes the opportunity for a slur upon Methodists: "This [in-
cident] was considered miraculous by many, and the Methodists preached about Susannah, and related her sayings in
their sermons."[19]

In another example of denominational slurring, the
Methodist preacher Peter Vannest recalls with relish hearing
an entranced Baptist minister's daughter "in conversation with
her father tear his Calvinistic system to pieces...."[20]

4. <u>Dreamer participates in his own judgment.</u> Shortly
after his conversion experience, a young man who feared that
his new-found religion was an illusion dreamed that Satan appeared to him and urged him to write his name in a "large
black book." When the young man had resisted the temptation,
he saw "the Savior" appear with "the book described by John
in the Apocalypse, in these words 'There is another book,
which is the book of life.'" Jesus opened the book and showed
him his name recorded therein. 21

In another account, a man, Brother Gould, who was
ridiculing Methodism, dreamed one night that the Judgment
trumpets sounded and that he was summoned before the great
Judge. Books figure in this version as well as the last; in
this case the Judge consulted the books of Providence, Scripture, God's remembrance, and life before making his decision.
Not finding the ridiculer's name anywhere, the Judge sent him
to hell. Gould awoke screaming and shortly thereafter found
religious peace. 22

5. <u>Dreamer visits hell.</u> A young lady, attempting to
banish religious thoughts from her mind, allied herself with
Universalist opinion: "I had heard something of Universalism,
and the more I felt myself in danger of hell, the harder I
strove to doubt its existence." The conflict emerged in a
dream in which the subject stood on a platform of logs, from
which she could see below "a boundless sea of fire."

> Gazing intently, I could distinguish the points of the
> wavering flames, and ever and anon an arm and
> clenched fist extruded above the surface, with here
> and there a head and face peering out for a mo-
> ment, and sinking back with a terrific groan. 23

She asked a "devoutly pious" neighbor standing with her on
the platform "what this was." He replied, "'It is hell.'"
The dream precipitated a spiritual agony which terminated in
the girl's conversion.

6. <u>Vision of the "'Valley of the shadow.'"</u> In this
account a critically ill circuit rider had a vision, he believed,
of the valley through which man passes from life to death.
Standing at the brink of the valley, the itinerant saw grada-
tions of beauty and light along its length, and realized "that
every man enters the valley of the shadow at the point he
has earned by the life he has lived."24

Otherworldly Visitors

1. <u>Dreamer encounters heavenly visitor.</u> One itinerant tells how as a young man, while he was struggling against Methodism, he dreamed that he fell through a trap door "into a very deep cellar." The trap door far above him was the only exit, and so he concluded that he "should there starve to death." Then he heard a voice saying, "'Come here and I will help you out.'" Above him he saw a man, who "reached down his hand, and his arm became elongated, so that he took me by the shoulder, raised me up, and set me on the floor." Suddenly the savior's "garments became as white as light, and his countenance like the sun." The luminous visitor spoke:

> 'I am Christ, and I have come to help you out of this cellar, and warn you of your danger. This trap-door on which you stepped, where all appeared safe, is to represent to you the doctrine of universal salvation, in which you are trusting; and as it gave way, and dropped you into despair, so if you continue to trust in that doctrine it will lead you to utter ruin.'

After the Christ-figure vanished, the dreamer awoke and reviewed his beliefs in Universalism. The dream, he recalls, "has probably had a great bearing on the course of my life."[2]

2. <u>Dreamer encounters hellish visitor.</u> A Methodist circuit rider dreamed that, as he was standing on the precise location of his first experience of God's pardon, he heard "a horrid noise, like that of a whirlwind, carrying everything before it," approaching him. He cried out, "'it is the devil,'" and suddenly the arms of a man, "holding a large auger at my left breast," appeared and began screwing into his heart.

> The auger was turned two or three times, when I seemed to hear the bones and sinews crack, and it gave me terrible pain. I cried out, 'Lord, help!' Immediately the motion ceased; I cried again, and the auger began to unscrew, and my pain was much abated. I repeated the cry the third time, 'Lord, help!' and all disappeared, and I awoke.

The dream occurred at a time in the itinerant's life when he was traveling reluctantly to an undesirable appointment. He comments: "I felt as though I had learned where to look for help in case I should get into trouble in Albany. "26

In other dreams diabolical visitants appear as vicious dogs, 27 as snakes, 28 as a hideous beast, or as a giant, ragged, and filthy Negro with a chain. 29

Revenants

1. Dreamer sees departed wife. One itinerant, after the death of his wife, fell into a doze and dreamed of his departed companion:

> My dear wife appeared to me, accompanied by two other females, dressed in white, and all extremely happy. My beloved Elizabeth looked at me, smiled, and then disappeared with her companions.

A "verbal testimony of her future hopes" would have afforded much consolation, the preacher reflected,

> but her unspotted and religious life, her heavenly looks after death, are sufficient evidence of her happy exit from this vale of tears to the paradise of God. 30

Another minister was able to extract "verbal testimony" from a spouse who appeared in a dream. He told her, "'I want to ask you some questions about the other world.'" The revenant said, "'There are many questions that might be asked about that world, which might be very improper for me to answer.'" The astute dreamer then asked a question she could not refuse to answer: "'I want to ask a question about yourself: is it well with you?' She said, 'It is well.'"

His spouse then described heaven, glory, and the New Jerusalem in language "not for mortals." Finally the itinerant turned to leave, and had walked only a few paces when he thought of another question.

> 'My dear, I want you to answer me one more question, if it will not be offensive to God.' I thought her countenance looked forbidding. I mentioned the name of a woman who was dead, and said, 'Is she in heaven?' After a short pause, she said, 'I did not see her there.'

Uxorial testiness notwithstanding, the dreamer, when he awoke,
felt a "pleasant sensation" because he knew that his wife "had
entered on her eternal rest. "[31]

        2. <u>Dreamer sees departed daughter</u>. James Quinn,
a Methodist itinerant, dreamed after his daughter's death that
he himself died and "passed to the heavenly world. " At the
entrance of that world

> six beautiful young females met him, all dressed in
> snow white robes, and one of them was his de-
> ceased daughter. They all came forward and re-
> joiced at his arrival, and then placed golden stars,
> of indescribable luster, upon him, which adhered
> to and remained on his raiment, forming the most
> brilliant and magnificent ornaments he ever beheld.

Then, from a point above his head, a shower of the same
kind of stars covered him from head to foot. His elation
caused him to begin "shouting the praise of God aloud in his
sleep. " His startled wife awoke him, and the dream faded.
But Quinn, "having a well-grounded hope of possessing many
stars of rejoicing when really called to his reward in heaven, "
was happy for many days. [32]

        3. <u>Dreamer sees departed mother</u>. A discouraged
Oregon circuit rider, mulling over his difficulties, had "a
dream or a vision. " His mother appeared and

> spoke the words that the Angel said to Elijah as he
> lay sleeping under the juniper tree, 'Arise and eat
> because the journey is too great for thee. '

Revivified by the advice, the preacher arose the next morning feeling "like another man. "[33]

        4. <u>Methodist itinerant dreams of departed colleague</u>.
Jonathan Stamper dreamed that he visited the house of John
P. Finley after the latter's death. The dead man met him
at the door, and after an exchange of pleasantries, showed
him to a chair by the fire. Stamper recounts, "'I was at
once filled with curiosity to learn something from him re-
specting the world of spirits. '" Finley advised him that he
would answer any questions "'so far as I can consistently
with the laws of the country where I live. '"

        Stamper asked if Finley was happy, if he had entered

heaven immediately, whether heaven was as glorious as the
Scriptures said it was, if the saints of heaven knew each
other, and if the saints knew what transpired on earth. When
Finley had answered these questions, he asked Stamper if
Methodists paid their preachers better than formerly. When
Stamper replied in the negative, the dead man exclaimed:

> 'O ... what a pity--what a pity! The itinerant plan
> is the plan of God. He designs it to take the world,
> and nothing will prevent it but a want of liberality
> in our people. But ... you must never locate.
> God has called you to this work. He will support
> you....'

Finley repeated this admonition, then

> reached up to the chimney-piece, and took down a
> considerable roll of bank-notes of the most singular
> and beautiful appearance I had ever seen, and, hand-
> ing them to me, he said 'Here, these are for you.'

Stamper protested, saying the money ought to be given to Finley's own needy family. The revenant replied,

> 'No, it is for you. There is a bank in heaven for
> the support of itinerant preachers, and this is for
> you.'

Stamper took the money, and after praying with Finley and
parting, he awoke.[34]

    A. E. Phelps, it is reported, had substantially the
same dream. His biographer says that he received the account of the dream in a letter from Rev. Francis Smith who
heard it personally from Phelps.

    In this account Phelps met the deceased Rev. Jesse
Haile on the former's way to Conference. After the usual
caveat that the revenant could not tell everything about heav-
en, Phelps asked Haile how the various denominations stood
"'in the estimation of the inhabitants of heaven?'" After
answering this question in favor of Methodism, and volun-
teering information about the heavenly activities of various
deceased itinerants, Haile asked Phelps, "'Do you have as
hard times in the itinerancy as formerly?'" Phelps replied
that there was little improvement. Haile asked if preachers'
pay had improved. Phelps said that there was some better-

ment in that matter. The revenant commented:

> 'The Church has driven many good and useful men
> from the work, crippled others by her penurious-
> ness, and thereby greatly circumscribed the work.
> Do you think of locating?'

When Phelps said that sometimes he was tempted to, Haile
responded:

> 'Never locate, brother Phelps, but preach the Word
> with all its point and energy, Endure unto the end,
> and there is a crown of many stars for you.'[35]

The relevance of the dream to the agonizing problem
of remuneration within the ministry suggests that the dream
may have been "dreamed up" as a polemical device before it
was dreamed. A clearly literary account of a similar dream
in which Francis Asbury returns to console an embittered
superannuate, likewise suggests a source external to the
dreaming psyche of individual preachers.[36] The variation of
details within the two dreams cited may suggest, however,
oral circulation.

Dreams of Future Events

    1. Dream as a factor in conversion. One man, strug-
gling to find grace, dreamed that he was attacked by a large
dog, which he understood was the devil. He beat off the dog,
then dreamed that he was walking on "slippery and dangerous
rocks" in a river. He awoke when he reached safety, and
believed

> that this was intended as encouragement for me to
> persevere, and by so doing I would be enabled to
> conquer my spiritual foes, and obtain the favour of
> God, which I thought was the only thing that could
> give me satisfaction.[37]

In other accounts, conversion occurs in a vision. A
man named Scarlett, under conviction of sin but unable to find
forgiveness, almost yielded to suicidal tendencies. Then, in
a vision, he "was lifted up out of all sorrow, instantly."
Guilt and heaviness of spirit vanished as well. He prayed,
and "instantly a communication from God was received, filling

me with unutterable ecstasy ... it was from a <u>new</u> <u>source,</u>"
and was "' of a new creation.' "38   In yet another account
the vision encourages perseverance after conversion. A man
saw the "Angel of the Covenant" coming to him and saying:
"'Doubt no more!'"   The vision, said the man, "confirmed
me in the belief that I was in the kingdom of grace."39

Other folk are said to have heard voices telling them
to convert. A young man who had returned from a camp
meeting without being converted heard a voice "apparently
proceeding from the barn," crying "'Frederick! Frederick!!
Frederick!!! go back, and seek religion this night.'"40   A
young boy, standing at a well at home, just after conversion
at a camp meeting, heard his mother's voice singing an old
camp meeting song, as if in confirmation of his experience.41
A troubled old lady, about to hang herself in the barn, heard
a "voice, or inward impression" which said to her: "'What
you now suffer is nothing compared to Hell!'"   She later
found peace with the Lord.42

2.   <u>Dream as factor in vocation to ministry.</u>   William
Taylor dreamed that, while he was attending a religious service, the preacher looked at him and said:

> 'William, God has a special work for you to do.
> If you will follow His Spirit, confer not with flesh
> and blood, turn neither to the right nor to the left,
> your wisdom will be like the continual dropping in-
> to a bucket.'

Taylor saw a "large empty bucket, with the rapid dropping
of the purest water," in confirmation of the words. Shortly
thereafter, a preacher addressed him directly from the pulpit, and he became a Methodist itinerant.43

3.   <u>Dream as a factor of perseverance in ministry.</u>
Nathan Bangs, perceiving that his work was bearing little
fruit, determined to leave the ministry. He began his ride
home from a frontier circuit, but a January thaw in a large
river "'providentially arrested'" him and forced him to return to his post.   There he dreamed that he "'was working
with a pickax on the top of a basaltic rock.'"   After hours
of fruitless labor, he resolved to quit.

> Suddenly a stranger of dignified mien stood by his
> side and spoke to him. 'You will pick no more?'
> 'No.' 'Were you not set to this task?' 'Yes.'

'And why abandon it?' 'My work is vain; I make
no impression on the rock.' Solemnly the stranger
replied, 'What is that to you? Your duty is to pick,
whether the rock yields or not. Your work is in
your own hands; the result is not. Work on!'

Bangs shouldered the pickax again, and his first blow, "'giv-
en with almost superhuman force,'" shattered the rock "'into a thousand pieces.'"

The introduction of the story in the text witnesses to
widespread oral circulation: "The story has been so often
and so variously related that we give it here as it was told
by one who had it direct from his [Nathan Bangs'] lips."44

Another dejected itinerant heard a voice which told
him that not he, but his Master, was rejected by the people. 45   A discouraged pastor was told by a voice to continue
preaching;46 still another itinerant was spared from a falling
tree limb by a voice instructing him to move. 47

4.   Itinerant dreams of next appointment.   In this account a man dreamed that he would be assigned to a particular district.   Later, his dream was not only confirmed but
he was made presiding elder of that district. 48

5.   Preacher dreams of financial catastrophe for dere-
liction of duty.   One Brother Ketchum entered the ministry
as an itinerant but soon yielded to financial needs and located.   His time was always divided between his business
and his preaching.   Once he dreamed that, at the time that
a service was to begin, two loads of wheat arrived in his
store.   He decided to weigh them before going to church;
but when he got to the church, he discovered that the people
had gone home.   He returned to his store to find that rats
had gnawed holes in his bin and let the grain into the river.

The dream proved correct in essence; for, "after all
his endeavors to accumulate something for old age, he did
not succeed."   The polemical intent of the account emerges
in the narrator's next statement: "Probably he would have
succeeded just as well in getting his family through, if he
had continued in the regular work."49

6.   Dream reveals event at conference.   A general
conference was hotly debating the question of whether or not
the office of presiding elder should be made elective by

annual conferences. On the night before the ordination of
bishop-elect Joshua Soule at the conference, James Quinn, who
had been asked to deliver the ordination sermon, dreamed
that he saw people building a church "somewhere in the western country. " The builders asked for his assistance in laying the fourth foundation stone. Before setting to work, they
prayed for God's blessing; but when they took up the stone,
they found that it had turned to a block of wood. Quinn
turned to the people and said: " 'Brethren, this will never
do for a foundation, ' " and then awoke. The next morning
Quinn told an associate, " 'There will be no bishop ordained
today, ' " and related his dream as evidence.

The same day Soule, who believed that election of
presiding elders by annual conferences improperly impinged
on the prerogatives of the episcopacy, resigned his election
and so fulfilled the prediction that Quinn made. 50

7. Stranger in dream appears in reality. A "very
wicked" man who "professed to be a deist" dreamed that the
day of judgment was coming, and that three strangers had
been sent from the East to warn him. Shortly thereafter he
saw James Gwin, William McKendree, and Brother Goddard
pass by his house on their way to a camp meeting. The sinner "followed them to the camp-meeting, and they ... warned
him of his danger sure enough. " After a tumultuous struggle
with his sinfulness, the man "was happily and powerfully converted to God. "51

In variations of this dream a lonely, hungry preacher
finds lodging at the cabin of a woman who had dreamed of
his coming, 52 an insane woman finds mental and spiritual
help when she sees the preacher of her dreams, 53 or a Connecticut woman dreams that a preacher will come and the
next day Jesse Lee arrives. In one account of the Lee dream,
Lee regards the incident as confirmation "that he was providentially designated for the work upon which he had entered
in Connecticut. "54

8. Dream of revival of religion. Rev. Joseph Travis
dreamed that a "huge and raging bull" kept him from entering
his church. People who stood nearby refused to help him,
so he cried, " 'In the name of God, I seize you!' " and taking
the bull by the horns, "twisted his neck entirely around. "
The bull ran away and hid under the church. A short time
later, Travis, preaching in fashionable Georgetown near the
nation's capital, "was strangely led off from the thread" of

his sermon and began to address sinners earnestly. A great revival followed.[55]

In another version of the dream, a lady dreamed of seeing a beautiful garden belonging to the young minister. Her prediction that he would precipitate a revival in the town proved correct.[56]

In a third account, a brother and sister dreamed concurrently of a revival. The brother saw a spring of water bubbling from a rock, and fire from heaven igniting stones. The sister dreamed "that she received a letter from heaven in letters of gold, the contents of which were, that there was coming a ship-load of love divine from heaven."[57]

9. __Dreamer dreams his own death.__ In one account a narration begins with the observation that the dream and its fulfillment were "a most marvelous occurrence ... deeply tinged with the supernatural and mysterious." A robust, healthy doctor dreamed that an angel appeared to him in a cedar grove. Suddenly a rich green vine laden with beautiful flowers "sprang up" and covered a dead stump nearby. The angelic messenger instructed him to cut the vine at the roots. When he did as he was told, "a strange fascinating voice came forth from it, announcing the exact date of his death." On that day, as the dream had foretold, he died.[58]

Sometimes dreams of death were mistaken. A young girl who dreamed that she would die three years from the date of the dream lived in fatalistic expectation until that day. The appointed day, however, brought only "one of the most terrific storms I ever saw...." She remarks: "it was almost a disappointment, when the day was gone, that my-- long-cherished, shall I say?--expectation had not been realized."[59] Another man, who dreamed of the exact date of his death, was providentially prevented from traveling on that day and so, many thought, was spared.[60]

In other versions of the dream, a Cumberland Presbyterian minister plead for continuation of life with an angel of doom,[61] a Methodist itinerant dreamed of ascending a ladder to heaven to a banquet with Wesley,[62] and a circuit rider met in a dream a colleague who had just died and was damned, he avowed, for not preaching the gospel.[63]

Sometimes a premonition of death was fulfilled by the death of another person. Rev. Billy Hibbard, who had re-

ceived a revelation when he was twelve years old that he
would die at age thirty-six, lost his son instead when the
time arrived.[64]

Many of the accounts record omens or premonitions
of death. Men going into battle[65] and travelers foretold their
deaths.[66] In another relation, a dead father appeared to a
young man in a dream and told him of impending death.[67]

Cosmic Omens

Unusual weather and meteorological phenomena are
quite arbitrarily included as an appendage to the section on
dreams. Quite obviously, cosmic phenomena are not pro-
ductions of the psyche but are rather events to which the
wondering spirit reacts. However, cosmic manifestations
resemble certain dreams functionally, in that they are sometimes thought to portend a future event and are regarded as
some sort of providential interposition. They could just as
properly, however, be included in the following section, under remarkable judgments.[68]

1. Unusual snowfalls. An upstate New York itinerant remembers the " 'cold summer' " of 1816. A school-
teacher at the time, the preacher

> 'looked out of my schoolhouse window in June, and
> saw the snow falling as in midwinter; and it struck
> me that God was visiting the earth with judgments. '69

Two separate accounts remember the great March
snowfall of 1843. Neither ties it to divine intervention explicitly, however. For one man, a hunter, the snowfall was
the occasion for catching "more than one hundred birds. "70
A Methodist preacher recalls that the "remarkable snow ...
was covered with a thick, slick, shield of ice which rendered
travel surpassingly difficult and dangerous. "71

2. Earthquakes. One biographer, recalling the earthquakes of the winter of 1811 and the spring of 1812, notes
that

> strange convulsions and violent shakings of the
> earth have been considered, in all ages of the
> Christian world, as the precursors of the wrath of

> a justly-incensed God. 'Then the earth shook and
> trembled; the foundation of the hills moved and
> were shaken, because he was wroth.' (Psalm xviii,
> 7)

George Walker, the subject of the biography, and his family
regarded the earthquakes "as tokens of coming vengeance and
wrath." Many people, in fact, were disturbed by the tremors,
because '''wars, and rumors of wars, and earthquakes in divers places,' filled many with great fear and dread." In
such unsettling times men turned to religion:

> These successive concussions of the earth had a
> salutary influence upon the minds of many, who,
> at the time, were 'living without hope and without
> God in the world.'72

Parallel Baptist and Cumberland Presbyterian accounts
record the same widespread terror resulting from the 1811-
1812 earthquakes. In the Cumberland Presbyterian account,
one sleeping family was roused from bed by the shaking.
The woman of the house sat up in bed and exclaimed: " 'Judgment, the judgments of God upon our world for its wickedness!'" Then, "they got the Bible, and turned it over from
passage, to passage, and came to the conclusion that it was
an earthquake."73 The Baptist, Elijah Hanks, converted because of the tremors.74

3. Meteor showers. Two separate accounts record
the great meteor shower of autumn, 1833. In one relation
the phenomenon inspires the fear that the last days had
come.

> Early in the morning, before the day broke in the
> country where I lived, the family arose affrighted
> and dismayed. We saw the stars flying, shooting
> and apparently falling in every direction. There
> were none in the family versed in astronomy, and
> we could not assign a cause for it. But there were
> a number of poor sinners in the family, greatly
> terrified; for we supposed 'the great day of wrath
> had come, and we were not able to stand.' ...
> And all with whom I was associated, were terrified
> awfully; because we knew we were not prepared for
> 'the day of vengeance of our God.'75

Another account records the humor that an educated

preacher, John B. McFerrin, saw in the concern of the common folk over the shower:

> 'Several laughable scenes took place among those
> who thought the world was coming to an end. Men
> prayed who were not in the habit of calling on God,
> but their piety was meteoric.'

But McFerrin's biographer had to admit that the scene "ex-
ceeded in its awful splendor every thing witnessed by him
[the biographer] on earth, he expects to see nothing to equal
it until the trump of God shall announce the judgment of the
last day. "76

Still another account lists diverse responses, some
ludicrous, to the cosmic display:

> People were generally much alarmed.   Horns were
> blown here and there to arouse the people.   Many
> thought the day of Judgement had come, and the
> end of all things was at hand.   Others took this
> wonderful phenomenon as obtusely as a neighbor of
> mine who said, he thought that was the way the
> stars went out every morning. 77

4.   Comets.   Jesse Lee's biographer narrates Lee's
reaction to a 1783 comet that moved through the skies for
many minutes in broad daylight, finally disappearing with a
thunder over the horizon: "The matter had no other effect
upon his mind than to excite his wonder, and raise his
thoughts to Him who is the Maker and preserver of all. "78

Without elaboration, another itinerant mentions the appearance of a comet in 1842:   "This has been a distinguished
winter for its coldness, for the comet, and for Millerism. "79
An 1819 comet excited comment from a Missouri Baptist:
"On the 15th, at night, we saw a comet plainly visible, which
not a few regarded as the forerunner of another Indian war."80

5.   Solar phenomena.   An itinerant saw a "spot" on
the sun (it is not clear whether the black spot is an eclipse
or a sunspot).   At first he "was not a little astonished";
then he prayed:

> 'Lord, what weak creatures are we to be so agi-
> tated at any uncommon appearance, and yet to be-
> hold thy wondrous works from day to day without

the least marks of astonishment or admiration!
O Lord, let me ever behold the light and glory of
this thrice glorious Sun, and may I always consider
every intervening spot as a fatal omen!'[81]

Another account records that, during a total eclipse, a "number of scoffers" asserted: "'If the world is coming to an
end, we would like to be among people who pray.'" But when
the eclipse was over "they went out to scoff again."[82]

Summary

The data indicate that dreams played an important role
in the lives of those who recounted them, and that many
preachers felt that certain dreams ought to be told. The
dreams served a two-fold function: revelation and prediction.
At critical points in the religious life of the subject--when he
was fleeing religion, struggling with conversion, or doubting
commitment--dreams offered warning, confirmation and assurance. And at periods of uncertainty concerning his spiritual future, dreams provided windows by which to see what
was next, even allowing glimpses of the afterlife. Relations
of such dreams, therefore, reinforced the belief in God's
providential care and reasserted a worldview according to
which invisible reality was decisive. As one narrator commented, after telling a dream:

> This incident is no less striking as an exhibition of
> ministerial fidelity and perseverance, than it is re-
> markable as another instance of that supernatural
> agency which has presided over the progress of the
> gospel from the beginning. Let the fact as to the
> dream be admitted, and it does not challenge a rea-
> sonable doubt, and it cannot be accounted for ex-
> cept by a recurrence to the truly spiritual dispensa-
> tion under which we live. In all the essential par-
> ticulars, there is no real difference between this
> case and that of St. Paul, when he was invited to
> 'come over into Macedonia.' In both, 'God spoke
> in a dream, in a vision of the night, when deep
> sleep falleth upon man.'[83]

The literature says nothing about how often Methodist
itinerants dreamed, but one may safely assume that they
dreamed as often as anyone else did. The dreams they considered

significant, however, were those that reinforced convictions
they already held: the importance of fidelity to primitive
itinerant ideals, the centrality of conversion in Christian life,
the superiority of Methodism to competing religions. Structurally, their dreams fell into patterns that can be collated
with biblical, hagiographical, and folk traditions. It is difficult to escape the conclusion (bracketing for a moment the
question of other sources of their dreams) that Methodist
itinerants dreamed thematically and structurally the way their
tradition told them they should dream, and that the remembered and related dream, in a reciprocal fashion, validated
that tradition. To put it another way, tradition, by being
enacted, became true.

Dreams, then, had a role to play in expressing and
extending Methodism, and were considered important enough
to tell, retell, and finally to write down. Evidence on the
previous pages witnesses to the literary preservation. Many
dreams, however, appear to have circulated orally as well.
Frequently accounts of dreams are prefaced by statements to
the effect that the dream was told to a person who wrote it
down and gave it to or who told it to the biographer.[84] Furthermore, the existence of variants of the same dream argues to oral circulation: as the account passed around the
circuit or conference by word of mouth, details changed while
the essence remained the same.

Notes

1. Job xxxiii. 14-16. Verse and citation in Jackson, Sun-
    shine, p. 122.
2. Morton Kelsey, Dreams: The Dark Speech of the Spirit;
    A Christian Interpretation (Garden City, N. Y.:
    Doubleday, 1968), p. 10. Dreams and visions are
    of a piece, asserts Kelsey: "it is not possible to
    discuss dreams without considering the thought pro-
    cess that goes on in sleep, the true vision, and fan-
    tasy as well. The four experiences are basically
    the same in nature. They are intrusions into con-
    sciousness of activities over which we have little if
    any conscious control." See also Joseph Campbell
    (ed.), Myths, Dreams, and Religion (New York:
    E. P. Dutton & Co., Inc., 1970).
3. White Magic, p. 52. Brewer, Dictionary, pp. 117ff.,
    "Dreams, Warning and prophetic"; p. 308, "Trance,
    Ecstasy"; p. 321, "Visions and Revelations"; p. 326,

"Voice from Heaven, " for the correlation between biblical dreams and hagiographical dreams.

4. Wright, Quinn, p. 39. The story utilizes a common folk theme, E12. 2.: "Head of decapitated person is replaced backwards. "

5. Cartwright, Autobiography, pp. 46-47; W. W. Pinson, George R. Stuart: Life and Work (Nashville, Tenn.: Cokesbury Press, 1927), pp. 52-55.

6. George Peck, Sketches and Incidents: or, A Budget From the Saddle-Bags of a Superannuated Itinerant (2 vols.; Cincinnati: Swormstedt and Mitchell, 1848), I, 59.

7. Joseph Travis, Autobiography of the Rev. Joseph Travis, A. M., A Member of the Memphis Annual Conference, edited by Thomas O. Summers (Nashville: E. Stevenson and F. A. Owen, 1856), p. 30.

8. George Brown, Recollections of Itinerant Life: Including Early Reminiscences (Cincinnati: R. W. Carroll and Co., 1868), p. 269.

9. Autobiography, p. 104.

10. Wright, Quinn, p. 183.

11. Jackson, Sunshine, p. 122.

12. D. Young, Autobiography, p. 28.

13. Scarlett, Itinerant, p. 132.

14. Johnson Olive, One of the Wonders of the Age; or, The Life and Times of Rev. Johnson Olive, Wake County, North Carolina, Written by Himself, at the Solicitation of Friends, and for the Benefit of All Who Read it (Raleigh: Edwards, Broughton, and Co., 1886), p. 109.

15. John Ffirth, Experience and Gospel Labours of the Rev. Benjamin Abbott; to Which is Annexed a Narrative of His Life and Death (New York: B. Waugh and T. Mason, 1833), pp. 8-10. Motifs F1.: "Journey to otherworld as dream or vision"; V511. 1.: "Visions of heaven. " For parallel accounts in the Methodist literature see J. P. Rogers, Life of Rev. James Needham, The Oldest Methodist Preacher (Pilot Mountain, N. C.: The Surry Printing House, 1899), p. 30; James B. Finley, Autobiography, pp. 375-76: critically ill man is led from the room by a heavenly visitor on a tour of paradise and jumps from his bed shouting the glory of God when he awakes.

16. Spicer, Autobiography, pp. 52-54. Motif E721. 7.: "Soul leaves body to visit hell (heaven). "

17. B. Hibbard, Memoirs of the Life and Travels of B. Hibbard, Minister of the Gospel, Containing an Account

of His Experience of Religion; and of His Call to and Labours in the Ministry, for Nearly Fifty Years: in Which are Recorded Many Important, Curious, and Interesting Events, Illustrative of the Providence and Grace of God (New York: Printed for and Published by the Author, 1843), pp. 224-25. See also Brewer, Dictionary, pp. 308ff., for trances paralleling the Pauline account in II Corinthians xii. 2-4.

18. Jackson, Sunshine, pp. 78-81. Motif F11.1.: "Journey to heaven in a trance."

19. James W. Alexander, The Life of Archibald Alexander (New York: Charles Scribner, 1854), pp. 102-4.

20. The New Jersey Conference Memorial, Containing Biographical Sketches of All Its Deceased Members, Including Those Who Have Died in the Newark Conference (Philadelphia: Perkinpine and Higgins, 1865), p. 199.

In one humorous account, a sagacious old German lady exposes the sham of an entranced girl: "And a German sister, who believed that she [Beckie, the girl] was a deceiver all the time ... leaned over her, as if to turn her in bed; and she said, afterwards: 'I shust put my hands under her und dickled her ribs, und she shust come out of her spell alaughing.'" Spottswood, Brief Annals, pp. 253-54.

21. Jacob Young, Autobiography of a Pioneer; or, The Nativity, Experience, Travels, and Ministerial Labors of Rev. Jacob Young, with Incidents, Observations and Reflections (Cincinnati: Cranston and Curts, 1857), pp. 46-47. Motif V512.: "Vision of judgment."

22. Erwin, Reminiscences, pp. 73-74. Motif V522. is exemplified here and in several of the preceding accounts: "Sinner reformed after visit to heaven and hell." For parallel accounts in the Methodist literature see Olive, One of the Wonders, p. 48: Judge searches the Book of Life and the dreamer's name is not there; Charles Giles, Pioneer, pp. 29-30: a vision of Judgment Day after reading Bunyan's Pilgrim's Progress. Cotton Mather tells the story of a man converted after dreaming of his final judgment: MCA, p. 377.

23. Johnson, Recollections, pp. 34-35. Motifs F81.: "Descent to lower world of dead"; V511.2.2.: "Vision of fires of hell." Also, Benjamin Abbott's account of a hell dream, in which he is tortured in a vise, stung with scorpions; Ffirth, Abbott, p. 7. Motif

A671. 2. 9. : "Scorpions in hell. "

24. John L. Leming, Experiences of The Circuit Rider (New
York: Methodist Book Concern, 1932), pp. 131-35.
Motif F151. 1. 1. : "Perilous valley." The description
of the valley given here resembles somewhat the val-
ley through which Christian passed in John Bunyan's
The Pilgrim's Progress From This World to That
Which is to Come (New York: Rae D. Henkle Co.,
Inc., n. d.), pp. 64ff.

25. D. Young, Autobiography, pp. 28-29. Motifs V510. 1. :
"God speaks in vision to devotee"; D1814. 3. : "Advice from God (or gods)." See also Scarlett, Itinerant, pp. 132-34, for a vision of the Son of Man
giving an itinerant a piece of burning bush on Mount
Tabor; Ffirth, Abbott, pp. 17-18, for the dream of
wrestling with an angel (Motif H1598. 1. : "Contest
between man and angel"); ibid., p. 60, for a woman's vision of Moses, Elias, and Jesus during a
conversion experience.

         See also Peck, Sketches, pp. 28-35, for a
vision of the pilgrim church marching to the eschaton.
Compare with Brewer, Dictionary, p. 353: "St.
Francisca sees in a vision the different orders of
the heavenly host. "

26. Spicer, Autobiography, pp. 78-79. Motifs G303. 9. 6. 2. :
"Satan attacks saints"; G303. 6. 3. 2. : "Devil comes
in the whirlwind"; G303. 16. 2. : "Devil's power over
one avoided by prayer. "

27. Olive, One of the Wonders, p. 47; Peter Howell, The
Life and Travels of Peter Howell, Written by Himself;
in Which Will Be Seen Some Marvelous Instances of
the Gracious Providence of God (New Bern, N. C. :
Published by W. H. Mayhew, for the Author, 1849),
p. 6. Motif G303. 3. 3. 1. 1. : "Devil in form of dog. "

28. Rogers, Needham, p. 29. Motif G303. 3. 1. 6. : "Devil
in form of snake. "

29. Olive, One of the Wonders, pp. 47, 46. Motif G303. 3.
1. 6. : "The devil as a black man. " See also Brewer,
Dictionary, p. 321: "St. Aldegundis's vision of the
devil. "

30. Travis, Autobiography, p. 175. Motif E322. : "Dead
wife's friendly return. "

31. Woolsey, Supernumerary, pp. 96-98. Motif E361. 2. :
"Return from dead to give consoling message. " See
also Brewer, Dictionary, pp. 15-16; apparitions by
dead persons, comforting grieving relatives, are common.

32. Wright, Quinn, pp. 182-183. Motif E324.: "Dead
     child's friendly return to parents." Brewer, Dic-
     tionary, p. 16: "Apparition of St. Agnes to her
     mother," admonishing her not to weep.
33. A. J. McNemee, "Brother Mack" The Frontier Preacher:
     A Brief Record of the Difficulties and Hardships of a
     Pioneer Itinerant (Portland, Ore.; T. G. Robison,
     1924), p. 40. Motif E323.4.: "Advice from dead
     mother."
34. Finley, Autobiography, pp. 426-29. Motifs E374.:
     "Dead returns to life and tells of journey to land of
     dead"; F1068.1.: "Advice and information given in
     dream"; E365.6.: "Dead provide material aid to
     living."
35. J. J. Fleharty, Glimpses of the Life of Rev. A. E.
     Phelps and His Co-Laborers; or, Twenty-Five Years
     in the Methodist Itinerancy (Cincinnati: Hitchcock
     and Walden, 1878), pp. 164-66.
          The idea of payment in crowns of glory may
     have given rise to the following jest among the chron-
     ically underpaid itinerants: "When a gentleman, with
     great simplicity, inquired, 'Mr. Cook, what do you
     get for your preaching?' the reply was, 'Only a
     crown, sir.' 'A crown!' 'Yes sir, and I trust for
     that till the day of judgment.'" Henry Smith, Recol-
     lections and Reflections of an Old Itinerant, edited by
     George Peck (New York: Carlton and Phillips, 1854),
     pp. 267-68.
36. Jay Benson Hamilton, From the Pulpit to the Poor-House
     and Other Romances of the Methodist Itinerancy (New
     York: Hunt and Eaton, 1892), pp. 79-102.
37. Howell, Life and Travels, p. 6.
38. Scarlett, Itinerant, pp. 89-90.
39. Giles, Pioneer, pp. 72-73. Motif V235.0.1.: "Mortal
     visited by angel in vision."
40. Manship, Thirteen Years', pp. 56-57.
41. Morrison, Autobiography, pp. 14-15.
42. E. F. Newell, Life and Observations of Rev. E. F.
     Newell, Who Has Been More Than Forty Years an
     Itinerant Minister in the Methodist Episcopal Church;
     New England Conference (Worcester, Mass.: C. W.
     Ainsworth, 1847), p. 153.
          For further parallels: Spottswood, Brief An-
     nals, p. 4; Smith, Recollections, p. 251; Ffirth,
     Abbott, pp. 31-32; for a parallel Baptist account:
     Jesse J. Goben, Writings of Jesse J. Goben, To
     Which Are Added the Letters of Willis E. Moore

and William H. Darnall (Middletown, N. Y. : G.
Beebe's Sons, n. d.), pp. 30-31; for a parallel Cumberland Presbyterian account: Lowry, Donnell, pp.
22-23.

43.   William Taylor, William Taylor of California, Bishop of
Africa: An Autobiography, revised, with a preface
by C. G. Moore (London: Hodder and Stoughton,
1897), pp. 14-15.   Motif 1812. 3. 3. : "Future revealed in dream."
        For parallel accounts see Travis, Autobiogra-
phy, pp. 30-31; McNemee, "Brother Mack," p. 9;
A. H. Tuttle, Nathan Bangs (New York: Eaton and
Mains, 1909), pp. 41-42; Burgess, Pleasant Recollections, pp. 91-93; Newell, Life, p. 87; for a
Baptist account see Goben, Writings, pp. 40-41; for
a Presbyterian account see Alexander, Life, p. 138.
The famous eighteenth century Methodist itinerant,
George Whitefield, reportedly received his call by
means of a dream; see Wakeley, Whitefield, pp. 65-
66.

44.   Tuttle, Bangs, pp. 52-53.   Motif H1116. ; "Task:
breaking huge rock to pieces"; H975. : "Deity per-
forms task."

45.   McNemee, "Brother Mack," p. 36.   Brewer, Dictionary, p. 446: "Reviled and Persecuted."

46.   Smith, Recollections, pp. 21-22.   Brewer, Dictionary,
p. 328: "St. Henry of Northumberland strengthened
in the right way by a voice from heaven."

47.   Rogers, Needham, p. 28.   Motif V542. : "Man hears
voice telling him to leave danger spot in mine."
        For further parallels: Brown, Recollections,
p. 269;• Hibbard, Memoirs, pp. 350-52.   Emotional
concern, leading to dreams about ministerial vocation, could have been prompted by stories such as
the one concerning a man who decided not to become
a Methodist itinerant and was thereupon afflicted
with a stutter.   D. Young, Autobiography, pp. 186-
87.   Motif Q451. 3. : "Loss of speech as punishment."

48.   Giles, Pioneer, pp. 203-4, 208.   Motif D1812. 3. 3. :
"Future revealed in a dream."

49.   Spicer, Autobiography, pp. 114-15.   Motif Q223. 13. :
"Neglect of clerical duties punished."

50.   Wright, Quinn, pp. 128-30.   Motif D452. 1. : "Trans-
formation: rock (stone) to other object"; D1812. 3. 3. :
"Future revealed in dream."

51.   Thomas O. Summers (ed.), Biographical Sketches of
Eminent Itinerant Ministers, Distinguished, for the

Most Part, as Pioneers of Methodism Within the
Bounds of the Methodist Episcopal Church, South
(Nashville, Tenn.: Southern Methodist Publishing
House, 1859), p. 52. Motif D1812.3.3.: "Future
revealed in a dream." Brewer, Dictionary, p. 340:
"Wise Men of the East."

52. Summers, Biographical Sketches, pp. 197-98.

53. William Ryder, The Superannuate: or Anecdotes, Incidents, and Sketches of the Life and Experience of
William Ryder, a "Worn-out" Preacher of the Troy
Conference of the M. E. Church, edited by George
Peck (New York: G. Lane and B. Tippett, 1845),
pp. 94-97; also Goben, Writings, pp. 49-53. In both
instances the dreamer sends someone out to search
for the man who can cure. Motif D2161.5.1.: "Cure
by holy man."

54. Leroy M. Lee, The Life and Times of The Rev. Jesse
Lee (Charleston, S. C.: Published by John Early,
for the Methodist Episcopal Church, South, 1848),
p. 235. Details differ widely between this account
and that in George Coles, Heroines of Methodism; or
Pen and Ink Sketches of the Mothers and Daughters
of the Church (New York: Carlton and Porter, 1857),
pp. 136-37.

55. Travis, Autobiography, pp. 54-55. Motif F682.1.2.2.:
"Man swings wild steer by horns round and round
till it is stunned, casts it to ground." Also Brewer,
Dictionary, p. 97: "The devil, in the guise of a bull,
tries to kill Catherine of Sweden"; p. 119: "Bruno
(Leo IX.), by a dream, is shown the ill condition of
the Church, and its reform."

56. Z. Paddock, Memoir of Rev. Benjamin Paddock, With
Brief Notices of Early Ministerial Associates (New
York: Nelson and Phillips, 1875), pp. 147-49.

57. Woolsey, Supernumerary, pp. 16-17. Motif F933.:
"Extraordinary occurrences connected with springs";
A285.1.: "Lightning weapon of the gods"; F962.12.4.:
"Written scroll (letter) received from heaven"; V211.
10.: "Letter (message) of Christ." Also Brewer,
Dictionary, p. 436: "St. Vincent Ferrier receives
from heaven a paper containing the writing of God."
The "letter from heaven" is a common article
of popular piety. For further information see James
Marchand, "A Note on the Sunday Letter," Tennes-
see Folklore Society Bulletin, XXIX (1963), 4-9.
Among Pennsylvania miners, the letter from heaven
is written in gold letters and [is believed to be] sent

by God himself.   Circulated as a broadside, it was
either hung on the wall or preserved in the family
Bible. George Korson, Black Rock, p. 273.
        See McNemee, "Brother Mack, " p. 37, for
the account of a revival promised by a mysterious
voice.

58. Jackson, Sunshine, pp. 120-22.   Motif D1812.0.1.:
     "Foreknowledge of hour of death." According to
     Loomis, the saints commonly predicted the hour of
     their death: White Magic, p. 71.   See also Mather,
     MCA, p. 468, for the account of a doctor whose
     dreamed premonition of death was fulfilled.

59. Johnson, Recollections, pp. 35, 39.

60. Spottswood, Brief Annals, pp. 18-19, 31-32.

61. Milton Bird, The Life of Rev. Alexander Chapman
     (Nashville, Tenn.: W. E. Dunaway, 1872), pp. 238-
     39.

62. Spicer, Autobiography, pp. 63-65.   The dream was in-
     terpreted as an indication that the man would, in
     fact, join the heavenly company before long, which
     he did.   Brewer, Dictionary, p. 205: "Jacob's Lad-
     der." See Wakeley, Wesleys, pp. 181-82, for an
     account of John Wesley's own "ladder" dream.

63. Manship, Thirteen Years', pp. 111-13.   Later checking
     corroborated that the "damned" preacher had died at
     the time he indicated in the dream.   Motif D1812.3.3.
     11.: "Death of another revealed in dream." Cotton
     Mather records the case of a man in Boston who ex-
     perienced a bloody apparition of a brother (who was
     then in London) at the moment of the latter's vio-
     lent death; MCA, pp. 468-69).

64. Hibbard, Memoirs, pp. 224, 264-66.

65. Morrison, Autobiography, pp. 27-28.   Motif D1812.0.1.:
     "Foreknowledge of hour of death"; M341.2.18.:
     "Prophecy: death in battle. "

66. Nash, Recollections, pp. 27-28.

67. Smith, Recollections, pp. 66-67.   See also a Cumber-
     land Presbyterian account of a fulfilled premonition
     of death; Richard Beard, Brief Biographical Sketches
     of Some of the Early Ministers of the Cumberland
     Presbyterian Church (Nashville, Tenn.: Southern
     Methodist Publishing House, 1867), p. 216.   In a
     Baptist account, a boy recalls how his father, hunt-
     ing one day, shot a squirrel, which turned black as
     it fell from the tree into bushes.   Loud groans came
     from the underbrush, but the squirrel's carcass could
     not be found.   A few months later the father died,

groaning exactly after the fashion of the groaning in
the bushes. Goben, Writings, pp. 7-8. Motif B147.
3.1.2.: "Other animals furnish bad omens."

68. According to Loomis, "Portents, signs, and symbols of
various nature, such as crosses in the sky, comets,
bloody moons, day-stars, and similar phenomena are
numerous" in the hagiographical tradition. White
Magic, p. 52. For the role of portents in Elizabethan England, see L. H. Buell, "Elizabethan Portents:
Superstition or Doctrine?" in Essays Critical and Historical Dedicated to Lily B. Campbell (Berkeley:
University of California Press, 1950), pp. 27-41.
For accounts of prodigies in New England Puritan
literature, see Dorson, America Begins, pp. 149-61.
In general, the attitude of nineteenth century American itinerants toward cosmic phenomena was considerably more restrained than that of their Puritan
and Elizabethan forebears.

69. P. Douglass Gorrie, The Black River Conference Memorial: Containing Sketches of the Life and Character
of the Deceased Members of the Black River Conference of the M. E. Church (New York: Carlton and
Phillips, 1852), p. 311. Motif F962.11.: "Extraordinary snowfall."

70. Joseph H. Borum, Biographical Sketches of Tennessee
Baptist Ministers (Memphis: Rodgers and Co., 1880),
p. 102.

71. Jackson, Sunshine, p. 8.

72. Maxwell Pierson Gaddis, Brief Recollections of the Late
Rev. George Walker (Cincinnati: Swormstedt and
Poe, for the Author, 1857), pp. 48-49, 53. Motif
F969.4.: "Extraordinary earthquake."

73. Richard Beard, Brief Biographical Sketches of Some of
the Early Ministers of the Cumberland Presbyterian
Church, Second Series (Nashville: Cumberland Presbyterian Board of Publication, 1874), pp. 359-60.

74. Borum, Sketches, p. 317.

75. Manship, Thirteen Years', pp. 17-18.

76. Fitzgerald, McFerrin, p. 99.

77. Hobart, Recollections, p. 86. In folk tradition, shooting stars are good omens: D1812.5.2.6.: "Shooting
star as good omen."

78. Lee, Life, p. 115.

79. Andrew Carroll, Moral and Religious Sketches and Collections, with Incidents of Ten Years' Itinerancy in
the West (Cincinnati: Methodist Book Concern, 1857),
p. 136.

80. Peck, Forty Years, p. 149.
81. Joseph Holdich, The Wesleyan Student; or, Memoirs of
     Aaron Haynes Hurd, Late a Member of the Wesleyan
     University, Middletown, Conn. (New York: Published
     by George Lane for the Methodist Episcopal Church,
     1841), p. 57.
82. Erwin, Reminiscences, pp. 268-69.   Motif D1812.5.1.4.:
     "Eclipse as evil phenomenon."
83. Lee, Life, p. 236.   See also Paddock, Memoir, p. 149.
84. Tuttle, Bangs, p. 52.

Chapter 2

REMARKABLE JUDGMENTS

> 'Opposition, of course, came from various quarters;
> the vicious and immoral of all classes arrayed
> themselves with all their energies against the ser-
> vants and work of God. But although they took
> counsel together, and set themselves against the
> Lord and his people, yet Jehovah of hosts was with
> his servants; and as the God of Jacob was their de-
> fense, many of the stout-hearted enemies of God
> and his Christ, his Church and his ministers, were
> made to lick the dust; they were taken, they were
> killed with the two-edged sword, they were healed
> and made alive by an application of Gilead's heal-
> ing balm.'[1]

The structure of many stories illustrating providential
judgments is similar to the structure of anecdotes recounting
providential conversions. In the former genre of relations,
however, the two-edged sword of God's grace finds the hardened heart impervious to the divine initiative and cuts it off
by death, blindness, paralysis, loss of property or a similar
terrible punishment, whereas in the conversion stories grace,
often after spiritual or material punishment, softens the heart
into an acceptance of religion. As an example, many anecdotes record the opposition of a husband to his wife's conversion to Methodism. Sometimes Providence smites the cruel
spouse for his opposition; most often, however, he himself
converts at the display of uxorial courage. The intention of
the stories, despite their similar structure, is different; in
the former case, the story shows that God punishes those
who oppose pious persons; in the latter case, the narrative
illustrates the belief that the example of believing Christians
is often a means by which grace works.

The stories that follow are divided into three categories: judgments upon impiety; judgments upon those who oppose

religion; judgments upon those who scoff at religion. Within
these categories many sub-classifications are included. In
stories with more than one theme, as for example the account
of the impious man who died horribly after cursing a minister (see page 85), classification has proceeded on the basis
of what seems to be the predominant intent of the story. The
story just noted, however, could illustrate judgment for impiety or judgment for opposition to a holy person. In such
cases classification of intent comes close to arbitrary assign-
ment. Most of the anecdotes, however, are less ambiguous.

Judgments upon Impiety

The conviction that impious men receive their just
desserts in this life is at least as old as Flavius Josephus'
account of King Herod's miserable end.[2] In Methodist lore,
the most striking punishments of divine wrath fall upon those
who refuse to give God his due, as prescribed in the first
commandments of the Decalogue. The impious man, commonly called an "Infidel" in the literature, is frequently a
professional, such as a doctor, lawyer, judge, or military
man. Outright atheism is never mentioned as an occasion
for the judgment of God; rather, "rationalistic" religions such
as Deism or Universalism, which have little to do with the
experienced conversion considered essential to true religion
by the Methodist itinerants, bring down the wrath of God, in
the literature, upon educated professionals.

1. Impious man punished by death. A Dr. Conklin,
an "avowed Deist," whose "grown-up children were active
participants in the work of persecution [of a certain Methodist
congregation]," struck his head on a beam while visiting his
ashery and fell into a kettle of boiling lye. After lingering
but thirty hours, he died without regaining consciousness.
His children immediately stopped their persecution. The narrator terms the incident "a joint action of God's providence
and God's grace."[3]

Frequently the death scene is made more vivid by the
sinner's despair. Rev. John Wesley Childs tells of a man
he met, who, although known as a gentleman, was an "avowed
infidel," "engaged in a traffic well adapted to blunt and destroy all the finer sensibilities of the human heart." When
he admonished the man, Childs was roundly cursed. The
"gentleman" went home and was seized with remorse. He

told his wife that he had sworn at a man of God:

> I cursed the preacher to-day--I did wrong. He is
> a good man, I doubt not, and I should not have
> treated him as I did; and now I am going to die,
> and I shall go to hell. I ought not to have cursed
> that man.

The next morning he lay in bed mortally ill. His remorse
and despair increased together; from his bedside he told all
who would listen to seek pardon for their sins. But for himself, "despair--utter despair was depicted in his face."[4]

The hopelessness of the infidel is often corroborated
at his death by a vision of the fate that awaits him. As one
doomed soul screamed at the last moment that devils were
around his bed,[5] so another, the president of a club of deists
who "burned all the Bibles they could get," died with the
consciousness of hellfire bright around him:

> 'And just as his soul was leaving the tenement of
> clay, it seemed to have a glance at the horrid
> abyss into which it was just to make its final
> plunge. He uttered a frightful scream; his face
> was distorted, and his eyes looked wild and terrific,
> and nearly started from their sockets, and we all
> stood in silent horror as his last groans died away
> upon our ears.'[6]

In some accounts the story of the damned infidel dying
horribly is juxtaposed with the record of a converted man ex-
piring in peace and confidence.[7] It is axiomatic throughout
the literature that Methodists die well, or that Methodist
preachers die well.[8] Even a condemned criminal who converts to Methodism before hanging dies more neatly than his
Roman Catholic counterpart, who takes twenty minutes of
swinging on the rope before he dies.[9] The morphology of
this belief corresponds to the folk opinion that the manner of
death reveals the ultimate destiny of the dying person.

2. Impious group dies unnatural deaths. God's terrible judgment not only visits the individual infidel with death,
but also falls upon the group of faithless--denominated variously as "Infidel Club,"[10] "Temple of Reason Club,"[11] or in
Ireland, "Hellfire Club"[12]--who gather to discuss deism and
to defame Christianity. The Temple of Reason Club, according to one author, published a newspaper and republished

"infidel works" of writers such as "Tindal, Paine, and Lack-
ington, " for the "avowed purpose of destroying Christianity. "
Many stories were told about them, some perhaps exaggerated,
the author admits, but it was generally believed that they "ad-
ministered what they called the sacrament to a dog!" Shortly
after this sacrilegious act, the man who had acted as priest
died in a "very awful manner, " and was followed to the grave
by many of his cohorts. In the course of time most of the
members of the club met unnatural ends:

> two of them starved to death; seven were drowned;
> eight were shot; five committed suicide; three were
> killed by accidents; and ... seven have died on the
> gallows.

Of those who died naturally, "in every instance their dying
hour presented an unusually awful scene. "13

A variation of the story has to do with the fates of
officials involved in a sincere, but mistaken condemnation of
a local Methodist preacher in Georgia for the murder of a
little girl. After the innocent preacher, Mr. Johnson, died
on the gallows, the real criminal confessed his guilt. The
judge, upon hearing the news, "blew his brains out with a
pistol. " In addition, "nearly all of the jury came to an unnatural death. " A member of the legislature who had refused
clemency and had "added some hard epithets about Methodist
preachers" was "killed at the tree by his runaway horse."
Although he is not positive, says the author, "memory inti-
mates that the fiery bolt of retribution fell upon others of
that body. "14

3. <u>Impious man punished by death of child</u>. One infidel told a preacher that religion was a farce and a humbug.
The profane man, a few months later, had to sit in the
church and listen to the minister preach his daughter's funeral sermon. 15 In a variation of this anecdote, parents left
home to harass a revival, and returned to find their children
dead in a cabin fire. 16 Still another variation is recorded
in the biography of Leonidas L. Hamline, a distinguished
bishop of the Methodist Church. Hamline believed he was
being punished for resisting the grace of God. His daughter
became ill, and when his wife proposed to call the doctor,
he said:

> I have no objection; but I assure you there is no
> hope. I believe that the child will die, and I have

felt so from the beginning. It is a deeply-wrought impression in my bosom that she will be taken from us on my account.

Shortly thereafter she died, and the lesson was not lost on Hamline. He said to himself: "'Heaven can strike one heavier blow, and it will come unless I turn. There is no way of escape but by repentance.'"17

4. **Impious man, confronted by death, acknowledges that his principles are unlivable.** In this story, an unbelieving Doctor (or in one version a "gentleman") and his deeply religious wife were about to lose their only daughter to the grave. Just before death, the girl took her father's hand in her own, looked into his eyes, and said: "'Pa, I am at the point of death; and now tell me which I am to believe--you or ma.'" The Doctor was a man "of great decision of character," and this decision "was a fair test of principles." He replied to his dying daughter: "'My daughter, it is the safest to believe your mother.'"18

A variation of the theme has a distinguished infidel writing a devastating attack against Christianity, then falling sick before he could publish it. His extreme condition led him to abandon his belief, says the narrator, "as infidels generally do when they see death near." Quoting a proverb, the author concludes: "'Fools men may live, but fools they cannot die.'"19

5. **Impious man procrastinates and dies.** Manship tells the following story as a "most solemn circumstance." A man attended a revival, was moved by the Spirit, but "supposed another time would suffice." His night was restless, and he expressed regret to a friend that he had not heeded the invitation of love. Unfortunately, "it was his very last call!" The next morning he died suddenly on his way to work, "in sight of the place of prayer where he had the preceding evening been entreated to be reconciled to God."20 Some men had even less time to reconsider. One fellow, urged at a Friday night meeting "to arise and come to his Father," thought "some other time would do as well, and declined." Upon reaching home that night he fell lifeless to the floor.21

When the procrastination story is directed to the edification of the young, plausibility is increased by making the death violent as well as sudden. Thus, one young man who

told the preacher "he had not quite done sowing his wild oats
yet" was stricken with cholera before the preacher was out of
sight of his house. The youth died with despairing words on
his lips. 22 W. G. Miller provides a variant case in which
the boy dies during a cholera epidemic, praying and cursing
with the same breath after having refused religion. 23

A variant punishment for procrastination is noted in
the case of a young man to whom the preacher made a direct
appeal during the sermon, and who rode off on his horse "at
rapid speed"; the horse "lost his footing and fell sprawling
on the side of the road and pitched his unfortunate rider head-
long against a strong, rough stone wall.... "24

Another variant punishment occurs in the story of a
young lady who decided to take her chances after being urged
by her friends to seek salvation. Shortly after her refusal,
a flood struck the village in which she lived. Her friends
saw her floating by on driftwood, her cries for mercy being
heard "above the wailing of the wind, and noise of the rushing
flood. "25

Punishment by dissolution constitutes a final variant
punishment. A procrastinator, turned drunkard and gambler,
"under the influence of ardent spirits, with a weapon of
death, murdered one of his fellow men!" He died on the gallows. 26

The irony of the procrastinator's position, as the itinerants depicted it, is perfectly expressed in the anecdote of
an old North Carolina preacher:

Any one who once heard 'Uncle Ivey' tell of the
man so pressed for time that God and religious
duties had not place could not forget.... 'What do
you think happened, ' said Uncle Ivey, with a startled look of surprise and unexpected astonishment,
'before six months, that man actually took time on
a pretty day, the first of the week, in the busiest
time of the year, when he was behind with his work,
yes, he actually took time, (would you have thought
it?) to lie down and die. '27

6. Relapse of piety (backsliding) punished by death.
God's judgment fell upon those who lost religion, once having
had it, as well as upon those who delayed. For example, the
converted daughter of a former dance-hall owner "fell away,

I used to be a Methodist myself,' said Pete with a sort of choking in his throat."

A Backslider Comes to His Senses

and being led by some young persons, took a pleasure trip on
the Christiana. " The boat went down, the girl drowned, and
was "brought home to her distressed mother a corpse. "[28]
Another backslider died within a day after being reproved by
his father-in-law. [29]

7.   Pride punished. One man, Captain Ebenezer Witt
of Brookline, Massachusetts, reportedly purchased a fine
horse and ordered a stylish bridle and saddle, so that he
could "make a show in the world. " But before the bridle and
saddle were finished, the "splendid horse was struck by lightning and killed on the spot. " Witt apparently took the lesson
to heart, for the narrator comments: "This touching providence led him to see the uncertainty of all sublunary things
and to seek the substantial joys of pure, undefiled Religion. "[30]

8.   Use of intoxicating drinks punished. An intoxi-
cated actor, enjoying a cotillion, "at midnight's hour fell head-
long down stairs, and broke his neck.... "[31] Drink was also
the downfall of a wedding party crossing the ice of the frozen
Delaware River after the ceremony. In the middle of the
river, as they paused to toast the bride and groom, the
treacherous ice gave way, and "the whole company perished
in the chilling stream. "[32]

9.   Avarice punished. A lawyer, who remarked to a
friend, " 'I am in perfect health, ' " went to his office and
found a poor man waiting for him. The latter desired to set-
tle a debt out of court, but the lawyer demanded the same
fee as if he had actually argued the case in court. As the
pauper handed over the money, he said, " 'Squire, can you
take this from me and go up the hill to your dinner?' " The
greedy lawyer replied, " 'I will try. ' " The barrister then
left his office, walked halfway up the hill to his house, and
fell dead. [33]

10.   Cruelty punished. Andrew Carroll quotes a
story from Taylor's Life of Cowper, in which a young cock-
fighter roasted alive his favorite gamecock for losing a fight
on which he had wagered heavily. Some gentlemen attempted
to interfere; the young man picked up a poker and swore that
he would kill the first man who intervened; but "in the midst
of his passionate asseverations, awful to relate, he fell down
dead upon the spot. "[34]

Judgments upon Those Who Oppose Religion

The itinerant biographies and autobiographies convey the strong impressions that Methodism met violent opposition both in society and in individual families. As a subsequent chapter will describe, every camp meeting had "lewd fellows of a baser sort"[35] lurking at its edges, drinking, swearing, and seeking opportunities for disruption. Most of these situations were met by equivalent frontier toughness and belong more to the heroic <u>gesta</u> of various itinerants rather than directly to providential interposition. But in some cases the dispersion of those who would hinder God's work was traditional, direct, and striking.

1. <u>Disruption of religious services punished.</u> Divine operation is assumed in the stories already noted of the couple who returned from disruption of a meeting and found their children had perished in a cabin fire, and of the young man thrown from his horse for mocking the services at a camp meeting.[36]

Youth could take warning not only from this last example but also from the story of the young people who disrupted a service at which the minister was discoursing on the parable of the Wise and Foolish Virgins. By the "midnight cry," the preacher insisted

> death was also comprehended, and at midnight literally, the cry would be made, and some one present would have to go. And who knows ... but it may be one of those who are inclined to annoy the meeting?

Shortly thereafter, one of these young disrupters fell sick unto death:

> as the town clock dolefully struck twelve; we were all upon our knees, calling upon a merciful God in his behalf. Before the last stroke of the clock was heard, we saw plainly death had struck the fatal blow.[37]

Another story, labelled "A FEARFUL VISITATION UPON INCORRIGIBLE SINNERS," chronicles the fate of a family of three young men and one young woman, who, during a revival, threatened and cajoled all who professed to be saved. One night of the revival "they brought nuts to the place of worship, and, sitting with their hats on in time of prayer, busied themselves in cracking and eating them!" For these grave offenses, one brother crushed in a sawmill and two died of sickness, the latter full of both remorse and despair. 38

Lorenzo Waugh recounts variant punishment in the story of a wicked man who came, with "some of his special associates near him," into the church to break up the meeting. The bully walked boldly up to the altar rail, stopped and leaned on it, saying nothing. In a short time he paled and began trembling, "and soon fell over the rail down into the altar, and was for a time as a dead man. "39

In Wisconsin, a Mr. Foster opposed the introduction of Methodism into the area by announcing that a dance would be held the same night as a scheduled revival meeting. The preacher cancelled the meeting, and the dance was a great success. Two weeks later, Mr. Foster had a dream in which an angel visited him and informed him that within three days his body would be burned to death and his soul sent to hell. Just three days later he was missed at his breakfast, and a search was undertaken. The conclusion of the story is remarkable, indeed:

> His store in which he slept remaining closed, was during the day forcibly opened; and he was found on the floor burned to death. 40

Stories, replete with bizarre detail and fearful outcome, such as that of the two drunken Indians who, after disturbing a camp meeting, engaged in a fatal knife-fight, are duplicated many times. 41 Perhaps none is more striking or amusing than that of the man who set fire to the Methodist church. The people gathered to watch their "beloved old temple" fall into charred ruins. As the ridgepole of the church slowly sank down, Rev. Andrew Dixon, an aged pastor,

> lifted his hand for silence and offered a fervent prayer. He prayed that the man who had fired their church should some day be bowed over as their roof-tree was then bending. I was assured by aged men there that, inside a year, this suspected villain began to fail in health and soon became bowed. This affliction grew upon him till at last he moved along like an animal on all fours. Explain it if you will. I don't pretend to. 42

2. Opposition to holy person punished. The conversion of an individual often stirred up violent familial objec-
tion. The majority of the stories dealing with such opposition
center around a husband beating his wife or driving her out
into inclement weather. There are many variations of the
theme: fathers whip daughters or sons, brothers beat brothers, or wives harass husbands.

The stories are usually intended, however, to illustrate remarkable conversions, rather than terrifying judgments, and will be included in a later chapter. Sometimes,
however, the tales recount how Providence deals directly
with those who attempt to obstruct divine grace.

Death is a rare punishment for hindering the work of
conversion. One father, who fruitlessly whipped his daughter
with cowhide for attending a Methodist service, finally dis-
owned her. A year later he died, nursed by the child he had
persecuted. The story is, however, an example of the "trials through which both the preachers and the people of early
Methodism were called to pass."[43]

More frequently, the enraged husband or father is
rendered powerless by God in the act of beating. One husband hauled his wife home from a meeting and insisted that
she live by his rules or die. She told him that she would
rather die, whereupon he began to beat her. Saved and taken
away by some passing Methodists, she later returned to her
husband. When he saw her, he shouted that he would " 'wash
his hands in her heart's blood.' " She fell to her knees and
prayed to God for deliverance:

> God heard her cries, and smote him to the floor
> by his almighty power alone; and there he remained,
> helpless and speechless, for three hours.[44]

Another reprobate, who whipped his sons for going to
a Methodist meeting, threw himself on his bed and howled
when they came in to pray for him. When they left, he was
unable to arise; "Something rendered him helpless, insomuch
that he was not able to whip his boys any more for worship-
ping God." The impotent state, notes the informant, continued
for eight years.[45]

Wives sometimes obstructed their husband's salvation.
One woman fell into a rage when her husband came home converted, and died cursing Methodism.[46] Another harridan

nagged her spouse to death for his conversion. [47] A Roman
Catholic woman hid her husband's clothing to keep him from
attending meeting. [48]

Consequences more heartbreaking than any of these attended the obstruction of children's salvation by well-meaning
parents. One wealthy man would not allow his well-educated
son and daughter to go to Methodist services, with the result
that "the son became a wretched sot, and the daughter became an exceedingly vicious woman."[49] Another young girl,
desirous of joining the Methodists, was taken instead by her
parents to New York City and thrust into its gay social life.
Within a short time she caught consumption and died in great
despair. [50]

Frequently the Methodist itinerant himself, instead of
the convert, received the opprobrium of those resisting Methodism. One old man, for example, after his daughters were
converted by a Methodist preacher said: " 'I will buy the
rope if any one will hang him!' " The old man "did not live
long thereafter."[51]

A gentleman told a slanderous story about a Methodist
minister. When a delegation of persons who had investigated
and disproved the story confronted him in his field, "he appeared agitated and made an effort to speak, but fell instantly dead on the ground."[52]

Other stories having to do with intimidation of ministers, however, illustrate ministerial heroism in the face of
personal threat and the power of Christian conviction as a
means of conversion. Hence, these stories belong, along
with accounts of heroic individuals who resist bullying to convert their relatives, to the section on remarkable conversions.

Judgments upon Those Who Scoff at Religion

The violent, unnatural deaths of the Temple of Reason
Club noted above were precipitated at least as much by their
mockery of the Lord's Supper as by their virulent infidelity.
Special and remarkable providences visited those who attempted to strip away the sacredness of those things connected with the worship of the Lord.

1. Sacrilege punished. A young man who held mock

worship in a saloon, and who attempted to give the sacrament
to his fellow drunkards, was told by the preacher: "'Brother
Tommy, I am afraid you will come to some bad end.'" A
short time later the man cut his throat with a razor. 53

2. Scoffing at religious practices punished. A man,
"notorious for his opposition to the Methodists," visited a
camp meeting ground with his wife and a friend after a revival had closed. He told his wife and friend, "'I will show
you how the mourners, as they called them, acted.'" He began to burlesque the frenzy of those under conviction; in a
short while his companions asked him to stop, declaring the
charade was becoming unpleasant. But "it became evident
that he could not stop, and he continued it until stopped by
death."54

Another "mocking" story is preceded by remarks
which give a key to the significance of such stories in the
Methodist mind. The source of the story (who is the author's
brother) regarded the tale as being in the category of "terrible providential afflictions." He regarded it as "substantially truthful," although the author himself comments: "As
to the abstract possibility of the occurrence, the reader
must judge for himself." He himself, however, took the
trouble to verify the account from people other than his informant who witnessed it.

The protagonist was a schoolboy. One of his peers
asked him who was teaching school in the next district. The
boy replied: "'It is Paddock, a Methodist.'" His questioner
exclaimed, "'A Methodist! ... what is that? Is he a black
man?'" The protagonist replied in the negative and continued:

> 'I will tell you who the Methodists are. They hold
> prayer meetings, get on their knees when they pray,
> halloo, shout, and say Amen. Come.... I'll
> show you how they do it, if you'll get down on your
> knees by this bench.' Some of them did so, when
> in the most grotesque style, he essayed to mimic
> and show off the Methodists. In the midst of this
> profane exercise the chief actor was struck blind,
> and cried out with fear and trembling. 55

Blindness also struck a young lady who mocked a
friend's conversion. When she heard that her friend had
embraced religion, she "'came to get something to laugh at

Boys' Prayer Meeting

and tell of.'" But upon hearing her friend pray, she began to run. As she stepped out of the door, "she was struck blind, and screamed out for someone to take her by the hand .... "56

3. Profanation of Sabbath punished. A businessman, building a new factory, continued construction of a smoke-stack on Sunday. As dinner was served, a "little cloud" passed over, and a "sharp clap of thunder" was heard. The businessman said to his wife: "'Will you look out and see if my smoke-stack is all right.'" A moment later she returned and said: "'There is nothing left of it!'" The man vowed never again to have his work done on the Sabbath. "How true it is that nothing is gained by slighting the commands of God," the author observed. 57

One could lose one's life as well as one's smoke-stack. A young indentured servant decided, one Sabbath, to go cherry-picking rather than to go to church. As he stood in the top of the tree, gathering the cherries, the limb on which he was standing broke; he fell, and "came in direct contact with a sharp fence stake, that pierced him through in a vital part." He died instantly; if he had remembered the command, explains the author, "'Remember the Sabbath day to keep it holy,'" he might yet be living and useful. 58

A woman, Mrs. Carter, was killed by Indians, thought one itinerant, because she stayed at home on Sunday to make sugar rather than go to meeting. At her funeral, the next day the preacher asserted:

> I do not mean to insinuate that her death was a judicial punishment ... and yet we trace a provi-dence in her death. God, who numbers the hairs of our heads, did not see cause to interpose a spe-cial providence to save her ... at the same time God did much to draw her from the place of danger.

In short, he said, the woman's fault was to put herself out-side of ordinary providences, such as a nearby meeting when savages were prowling around her cabin, by which God in-tended to deliver her. Therefore she was left to her own devices. 59

Proper Sabbath behavior is indicated by the anecdote of the devil-sent deer and the God-sent deer. According to the story, a man opened his door one Sunday morning to get

fire-wood. Through the partially open door he saw a deer.
His family was hungry, and the meat would be welcome. As
he went for his rifle, he remembered that it was the Sabbath; turning around, he went out to get the wood, "leaving
the deer to do as he pleased." All day he was troubled, but
by nightfall he thanked God for sustenance in the hour of his
temptation. But virtue's reward was amplified. The next
morning, as he again went for fire-wood, he saw "a noble
buck standing within convenient range!" This time he was
able to use his rifle to the advantage of his family's larder.
The moral, comments the narrator, is " 'that godliness is
profitable unto all things, having promise of the life that now
is, as well as of that which is to come.' "60

4. Profane swearing punished. A final kind of profanation is the careless oath or rash wish. In such cases the
profanation seems to involve denial, either through anger or
calculation, of the adequacy of God's providences. The person who so swears is allowed, in many cases, to have his
way, and the wish becomes the fact. The lesson is that it
is much better to be under God's guidance than to be left to
one's own devices.

The introduction to this chapter noted the fulfillment,
in various situations, of rash wishes such as " 'I would rather
be damned than to be a Methodist.' "

In another story, a rash wish involves the death of
members of the family. A stonemason, it is reported, was
at work with his two sons in a quarry. They pestered him
for a meat-pie for the imminent Christmas holiday. He became impatient with them, and "swore that he wished they
were both dead that he might make a meat-pie out of them."
No sooner had he uttered these words when a flash of lightning killed them both. 61

Summary

Methodist stories of remarkable judgments taught people, as did their traditional precedents, that a providential
God would not forever brook opposition to his purposes. In
Methodist hands, however, the stories acquired an added significance: they identified God's purposes with those of Methodism. Therefore impiety was, by definition, opposition to
Methodist religious ideals. Such usage of remarkable judg-

ments was nothing new; in earlier times Puritans and Roman Catholics had used the stories for similar purposes. What is significant, however, is that in each instance the transcendent God of the Judaeo-Christian tradition had been partially transformed into the lares and penates of a particular expression of that tradition: God, in effect, had become a Roman Catholic, or a Puritan, or a Methodist. Such domestication of the divinity into an avenging clan god indicates an important dynamic of reform-minded movements such as Methodism: external opposition--persecution, ridicule, competitive religions--leads the movement to shift its emphasis from cultivation of the religious ideal to combat against the opposing element. Thus nineteenth century itinerants, competing with rationalists, Universalists, Deists, Baptists, Presbyterians and others for frontier souls, drafted God to their side and boldly marched to the fray, intent at least as much upon winning as upon reforming. 62

Notes

1. Quinn, Wright, pp. 213-14.
2. Flavius Josephus, The Genuine Works of Flavius Josephus, translated by William Whiston, M. A. (6 vols.; Edinburgh: Printed for Thomas Brown, 1793), V, 135-40. Motif Q220.: "Impiety punished." Brewer, Dictionary, p. 385; "Death terrors." Loomis notes that contempt, blasphemy, perjury, breaking the Sabbath are routinely punished, in hagiographical records, by paralysis, death and blindness: White Magic, pp. 98-100. Mather records many instances of providential judgments in MCA, pp. 394-405.
3. Paddock, Memoir, pp. 71-73. Motif Q220.: "Impiety punished"; Q411.3.: "Death of father (son, etc.) as punishment."
4. Edwards, Childs, pp. 88-91. Motif Q265.4.: "Punishment for undeserved curse"; Q558.13.: "Mysterious death as punishment for opposition to holy person."
5. Edwards, Childs, p. 91. Motif R11.2.1.: "Devil carries off wicked people."
6. D. Young, Autobiography, p. 114. Newell, Life, p. 23. Tom Paine, the noted deist, was said to have died in despair. One itinerant told of an interview with Paine, whose bestial habits indicated the consequences of his beliefs: Paine was "filthy in his person and habits, as well as drunken, and most repulsive in his manners, going about with his coat tied around

him with a piece of rope; and thrusting his hands at
table into the sausage dish instead of using a fork--
characteristics which in no wise recommend infidelity
to us for this life, while it leaves us without hope
for the life to come." John Carroll, Case and His
Contemporaries; or, The Canadian Itinerants' Memorial: Constituting a Biographical History of Methodism in Canada, from its Introduction into the Province Till the Death of the Rev. William Case, in
1855 (5 vols.; Toronto: Published at the Wesleyan
Conference Office, 1867-1877), I (1867), 123. See
Hobart, Recollections, pp. 285-86, for an account of
a seance with Tom Paine.

7.   Travis, Autobiography, pp. 18-20. Motif Q147.: "Su-
     pernatural manifestations at death of holy person."
8.   Manship, Thirteen Years', pp. 393-97; Life and Times
     of William Patton (n.p., n.d.), p. 226.
9.   Green, Life, p. 224. In another account, the spirit of
     a saintly Methodist itinerant, James Moore, is heard
     being carried away by angels who sing with a "soft,
     sweet, and celestial" sound. New Jersey Conference
     Memorial, p. 78. Motif V234.1.: "Angels sing over
     saint's body"; F63.2.: "Mortals taken to heaven by
     angel." Brewer, Dictionary, p. 7: "Angels carry
     Souls to Paradise"; ibid., p. 433: "Music heard at
     Death," ibid., p. 434: "Celestial music heard at
     the death of St. Servasius."
10. Brother Mason, p. 103.
11. Spicer, Autobiography, p. 72.
12. New Jersey Conference Memorial, p. 338.
13. Spicer, Autobiography, pp. 72-73. Motif Q222.1.:
     "Punishment for desecration of the host." This
     writer recalls hearing a similar tale about a group
     of greedy executives or millionaires who died un-
     natural deaths.
14. George M. Yarbrough, Boyhood and Other Days in
     Georgia, edited by H. M. DuBose (Nashville: Pub-
     lishing House of the M. E. Church, South, 1917),
     p. 142.
15. Burgess, Pleasant Recollections, p. 258.
16. Paddock, Memoir, p. 71.
17. Walter C. Palmer, Life and Letters of Leonidas L.
     Hamline, D.D. (New York: Nelson and Phillips,
     1877), pp. 44-45. F. G. Hibbard, Biography of
     Rev. Leonidas L. Hamline, D.D. (Cincinnati: Wal-
     den and Stowe, 1881), pp. 42-43. Motif Q402.:
     "Punishment of children for parents' offenses";

Q553. 4. 1. : "Child taken from parents because they
have ceased to think of God. " Cotton Mather tells
the story of an obstinate, impious Indian who converted after he lost his home and three children in
a fire; MCA, pp. 443-44.
18. J. Anderson and S. B. Howard, Memoirs of Rev. Laban
Jones and Rev. John H. Irvine, Late Ministers in
the Cumberland Presbyterian Church and Members of
the Kentucky Presbytery (Louisville: Morton and
Griswold, 1850), pp. 245-47. The Cumberland Presbyterian version is more detailed than a Methodist
version in Manship, Thirteen Years', pp. 229-31.
The story is very old; a version appears in the medieval collection of exempla of Jacques de Vitry. See
Crane, Exempla, pp. 121-22.
19. D. Young, Autobiography, pp. 115-16. Motif V331. 1. 3. :
"Conversion to Christianity because the heathen gods
prove to be less powerful. "
20. Thirteen Years', pp. 204-5.
21. Ibid., p. 110. Motif Q221. 6. : "Lack of trust in God
punished. "
22. Anderson and Howard, Memoirs, pp. 248-49.
23. Thirty Years in the Itinerancy (Milwaukee: I. L. Hauser
and Co., 1875), p. 123. Motif Q552. 10. : "Plague
as punishment. "
24. Jackson, Sunshine, pp. 177-78. The errant horse as a
vehicle of judgment is a common motif in English
Puritan and Methodist remarkable providence stories.
In other American versions of this story the same
fate punishes a young man not for procrastination but
for mocking a meeting; Landon Taylor, Battlefield,
p. 303; Cartwright, Autobiography, p. 292. Motif
E501. 18. 1. 1. : "Wild hunt harmful to mockers. "
25. Spicer, Autobiography, pp. 106-7. Motif Q428. : "Punishment by drowning. "
26. Manship, Thirteen Years', pp. 59-60.
27. Plyler and Plyler, Men, p. 39.
28. Manship, Thirteen Years', p. 207. Motif Q428. : "Punishment by drowning. "
29. Coles, My First Seven Years, pp. 221-22.
30. Newell, Life, pp. 22-23. Motif A285. 1. : "Lightning as
a weapon of the gods"; Q552. 1. 0. 1. : "Destruction of
property by thunderbolt as punishment. " As Cotton
Mather noted, lightning was a quixotic supernatural
agency, sometimes in the employ of God and sometimes the devil; MCA, pp. 361-62. Just as lightning
blasted preachers' houses in old New England (MCA,

p. 362) so it killed a preacher in Methodist lore;
Manship, Thirteen Years', pp. 218-19. Another account records that two unsuspecting lovers were sent
into oblivion by lightning while a minister preached
judgment; D. Sullins, Recollections of an Old Man:
Seventy Years in Dixie, 1827-1897 (Bristol, Tenn.:
The King Printing Co., 1910), pp. 124-25.

31.   Manship, Thirteen Years', p. 142.   Motif Q386.2.:
      "Drunken dancers punished. "

32.   Coles, My First Seven Years, p. 237.   Motif Q428.:
      "Punishment by drowning. "   Green, Life, p. 39, for
      the account of a drunkard igniting spontaneously not
      far from a church; Mather records cases of inebri-
      ates falling into fires and from there into everlasting
      fire, MCA, pp. 394-95.

33.   Newell, Life, p. 136.   Motif Q272.:   "Avarice punished. "

34.   Sketches, pp. 56-57.   Motif Q285.1.:   "Cruelty to ani-
      mals punished. "

35.   Green, Life, p. 390.

36.   Paddock, Memoir, p. 71; Taylor, Battlefield, p. 303.
      See Mather, MCA, pp. 396-97, for tales of provi-
      dential deaths of schismatics.

37.   Manship, Thirteen Years', p. 164.   Motif Q411.11.:
      "Death as punishment for desecration of holy places. "

38.   Green, Life, pp. 19-23.   Motif Q411.11.:   "Death as
      punishment for desecration of holy places. "   The cor-
      respondence of the one brother's punishment (crush-
      ing in a sawmill) to his offense (cracking nuts) re-
      flects the grim glee of earlier English and continental
      remarkable judgment stories.   According to these
      stories, judgment often resembles the impious act:
      thus, blasphemers' tongues rot, drunkards die of
      thirst or spontaneously ignite, Royalist conformists
      die with blue spots on them, judges who burn saints
      burn up with a fever, etc.   Such correspondences
      have overtones of sympathetic magic.

39.   Waugh, Autobiography, p. 73.   Motif Q551.7.:   "Magic
      paralysis as punishment. "

40.   Hobart, Recollections, pp. 293-94.   Motif Q552.13.1.1.:
      "Death by fire from heaven as punishment for oppo-
      sition to holy person. "

41.   E. J. Stanley, Life of Rev. L. B. Stateler: A Story
      of Life on the Old Frontier, Containing Incidents,
      Anecdotes, and Sketches of Methodist History in the
      West and Northwest, revised ed. (Nashville: Publish-
      ing House of the M. E. Church, South, 1916), pp.
      84-85.

42. George Cleaton Wilding, Memories of a Mountain Cir-
    cuit (Richwood, W. Va.: Published by the Nicholas
    News Company, n.d.), p. 44. Motif Q551.3.2.:
    "Punishment: transformation into animal." Cf. foot-
    note 38.
43. Marlay, Morris, pp. 46-47. Motif S11.6.: "Father
    flogs child." Brewer, Dictionary, p. 416: "House-
    holds set at Variance by the Gospel."
44. Coles, Heroines, pp. 163-64. Motif Q551.7.1.: "Mag-
    ic paralysis as punishment for opposition to holy per-
    son"; S62.: "Cruel husband"; S411.: "Wife banished."
    Brewer, Dictionary, p. 321: "Eldebod lifted up his
    arm to strike St. Maximus, and it was paralyzed."
45. Hibbard, Memoirs, p. 160. Motif S11.6.: "Father
    flogs child"; Q551.7.: "Magic paralysis as punish-
    ment."
46. William M. Green, Life and Papers of A. L. P. Green,
    D.D., edited by T. O. Summers (Nashville: South-
    ern Methodist Publishing House, 1877), pp. 61-62.
47. Newell, Life, pp. 71-72.
48. Manship, Thirteen Years', pp. 297-98.
49. D. Young, Autobiography, p. 27. Also Ffirth, Abbott,
    p. 51. Motif Q553.4.1.: "Child taken from parents
    because they have ceased to think of God."
50. D. Young, Autobiography, pp. 127-32.
51. Manship, Thirteen Years', pp. 72-73. Motif Q227.:
    "Punishment for opposition to holy person." Brewer,
    Dictionary, p. 176: "Honour God's Saints"; ibid.:
    "Nizon, bishop of Freisingen, struck dead for threat-
    ening Leo IX."
52. D. Young, Autobiography, p. 133. Motif Q297.: "Slan-
    der punished"; Q558.13.: "Mysterious death as pun-
    ishment for opposition to holy person."
53. Fleharty, Phelps, p. 129. Motif Q222.1.: "Punish-
    ment for desecration of the host."
54. D. Young, Autobiography, pp. 132-33. Motif Q591.:
    "Lie becomes truth"; Q222.: "Punishment for dese-
    cration of holy places (images, etc.)."
55. Paddock, Memoir, pp. 74-75. Motif Q451.7.0.2.1.:
    "Miraculous blindness as punishment for opposition
    to holy person." Brewer, Dictionary, p. 247: "Paul
    puts blindness on mocker."
56. Woolsey, Supernumerary, p. 83.
57. Taylor, Battlefield, pp. 281-82. Motif Q223.6.: "Fail-
    ure to observe holiness of Sabbath punished"; Q552.
    13.: "Fire from heaven as punishment"; Q552.1.0.1.:
    "Destruction of property by thunderbolt as punish-

ment. " Brewer, Dictionary, p. 280: "Sabbatic rest. "
Breaking of the Sabbath is commonly punished by ex-
traordinary means in hagiographic lore, according to
Loomis, White Magic, p. 99.

58. Manship, Thirteen Years', p. 59.
59. [Thomas Ware], Memoir of Thomas Ware (n. p., n. d.),
     pp. 138-42.
60. Paddock, Memoir, pp. 131-32. In another text, a doe
     comes on the Sabbath, and is spared. She returns
     on Monday with her mate, so that the reward for
     virtue is doubled. Gavitt, Crumbs, pp. 177-79.
     Motif Q141. 2.: "Plentiful game animals as reward";
     Q20.: "Piety rewarded. "
61. D. Young, Autobiography, pp. 133-34. The author notes
     that this account first appeared in Wesley's Arminian
     magazine. Motif K23. 2.: "Oath literally obeyed";
     C94. 2.: "Tabu: false and profane swearing of oath";
     N699. 6.: "Overheard wish is realized. " Also Loomis,
     White Magic, p. 100; Mather, MCA, pp. 393-94.
          In a parallel account, a woman often expressed
     the wish when her husband went to Methodist ser-
     vices, that he be brought home a corpse. Her wish
     was partly granted, for he struck his head at a house-
     raising and was brought home to die. Newell, Life,
     pp. 71-72.
62. The combative aspect will become more clear in Chap-
     ter III, part III, of this study. For a discussion of
     the dynamics of reform movements from an anthro-
     pological viewpoint, see A. F. C. Wallace, "Revi-
     talization Movements, " in Reader in Comparative Re-
     ligion (3rd ed.), ed. by W. A. Lessa and Evon Z.
     Vogt (New York: Harper and Row, 1972), pp. 504-
     12.

Chapter 3

REMARKABLE CONVERSIONS

If the previous genre of stories illustrated the invincibility of divine judgment upon those who stood in grace's way, the following stories indicate the irresistibility of that grace. The "means" by which grace worked were various and sometimes devious, as the following pages illustrate. But rarely was the Lord's touch so insistent as to pluck a brand from the burning, as in the case of Mofford, "one of the most wicked sinners in the settlement." Although Mofford's wife was at the point of giving birth to his child, he left home with a sneer and went to the tavern. There, while imbibing "with two of his bottle companions, the power of the Lord arrested them, and the arrows of the Almighty pierced them, and they screamed out as if just dropping into hell."[1]

More frequently, the media of providential conversions were tangible persons (although the agency of a ghost, in one instance, might force the sense of tangibility to its limits), or events. In general, the structure of the conversion stories is always the same: a person belligerent toward the cause of religion is overcome by the example of a believer or by an unusual or startling event.

Conversion by Personal Example

According to this theme, a belligerent inflicts suffering upon someone and is converted by their example. The suffering agent is usually a wife, less often a son or daughter, and rarely a husband.[2] Rarely, too, is the afflicted one a Methodist minister.[3] The latter, who did suffer from every other circumstance of their vocation, usually met belligerence with wit, equivalent intimidation, and even physical force.

1. _Cruel husband converted._ In one variation of this theme, the wife went to a meeting against her husband's

105

An Irishman Experiences Conversion
at a Camp Meeting

wishes. When he found out, he "lifted his fist" and demanded
her to promise never to attend a Methodist service again, or
to leave the house immediately. Even though it was snowing,
the nearest house half a mile away, and the woman but "thinly clad with poor shoes, " she said to him, "'Painful as it is
I must leave your house.'" He thrust her out and slammed
the door with a fury behind her. She made her way through
the snow to a log barn on the property, and crawled into the
hay, "blessing and praising God for his mercy to me"--the
mercy, that is, of allowing her to sleep in a stable as did
the child Jesus. Meanwhile, the thought of his wife's suffering preyed on the husband's mind. Finally he took the lan-
tern, followed her footsteps to the log barn and begged her
forgiveness. He promised to let her go to meetings and to
attend himself, and was later converted. 4

   A second variation of this theme is the blistering
story, which appears with great detail in W. H. Withrow's
Makers of Methodism. According to the account, a Dr.
Hinde, who was General Wolfe's military physician, settled
in Kentucky after the French war. His wife and daughter
joined the Methodists, for which offense the doctor banished
the latter and put the former under his own care for insanity.
The remedy was a "blister plaster extending the whole length
of the back." His wife's patience under this suffering brought
the doctor to his senses. He later converted and became
"one of Asbury's best friends." The latter is said to have
remarked: "'He will never again put a blister on his wife's
head to draw the Methodism out of her heart.'"5

   In a third variation of the theme, the wife literally
disarms her husband. A Mrs. Jones went to a meeting
against her husband's orders and over the threat of being
shot upon her return. When she came home, she encountered
her armed husband at the door and said to him mildly: "'My
dear, if you take my life, you must obtain leave of my heavenly spouse.'" Then she took the gun from his hands without any resistance; he later converted. 6 A twist is given
the story by the account of the lawyer who threatened to shoot
himself because his wife joined the Methodist Episcopal rather
than the Protestant Episcopal Church. He raged: "'You will
have every ragamuffin in this town calling you sister.'"
Thereupon he took up a gun and said, "'I had as well die at
once.'" But his wife took him in her arms, saying, "'My
dear husband, do thyself no harm.'" He fell on his knees,
went to meeting with her that day, and was converted. 7

A fourth variation portrays the Methodist wife patiently enduring the abuse of a drunken husband, who realizes at last her worth and joins the religion that furnishes her with such courage. [8]

2. Cruel master converted. In this story, a young slave and the master's son were converted together, and the slave began to hold meetings among "the colored people." The old master heard about it and was angry, "especially because his son had become pious." He ordered the slave, Jack, to hold no further meetings under pain of whipping. In spite of the threat, Jack held meetings regularly on Sundays, and just as regularly on Mondays, the old master tied him up and cut his back to pieces with cowhide. The conflict went on for a year and a half. One Monday morning, just before the regular whipping, the old master asked Jack why he persisted in his behavior. The slave replied:

> 'Why, master, in the morning of the resurrection, when my poor body shall rise from the grave, I intend to show these scars to my heavenly Father, as so many witnesses of my faithfulness in his cause.'

The old man ordered the slave untied, and sent him out to work in the field. Later that day the master approached him and asked him to pray for him. They fell to their knees in the dirt, and prayed together until the master found peace. [9]

3. Praying old lady converts hidden listeners. One account of the story remarks its providential character:

> The faith and perseverance of a few individuals have sometimes been blessed in bringing about gracious revivals; and, many times, means the most unlikely have been used to bring about events the most extraordinary, when ordinary means had utterly failed.

A small Methodist society was formed in a frontier location. The people began to build a church, but for various reasons the society disintegrated, and the church was left unfinished. Soon, of the original group, only one old woman remained. She continued to go off to the unfinished church in the woods every Sunday, by herself, to worship. The rumor spread that she was a witch, and two young men went out to the church and hid themselves upstairs to see if the rumor were true. They watched the woman come in, and as she prayed,

their hearts were melted. Climbing down from their perch,
they knelt and prayed with the old lady, and when they had
finished, agreed to hold a meeting the following Sunday.
Word of the incident, in the intervening week, brought hundreds to the little church. "Soon, " the story concludes, "a
revival followed, and a good Methodist society was raised up
in the place, and the long deserted house was finished. "[10]

4. Belligerent man converted by minister. The
would-be persecutor, in stories of this kind, is usually a
doctor, lawyer, or crusty, retired military man whose status leads him to assume that he can threaten the preacher,
whom he regards as a weakling or a fop. In every case the
insouciance of the threatened itinerant makes the braggart
back down, and often precipitates his conversion.

In one account, a "good-natured" man (not a professional) determined to flog the preacher for converting his
wife. When he came to the meeting, and saw the preacher,
Valentine Cook, he said to himself, "'He looks stout, but I
can manage him. However, I'll hear him preach first.'"
The sermon, as it happened, eroded his anger, and he soon
joined the Methodist church. [11]

Conversion by Unusual Means

1. Dead daughter of preacher revives and is converted. According to Travis, the following "almost miraculous account of faith and prayer" came to him from "a very
responsible minister of the gospel. " The daughter of Ashley
Hewitt, an eminent and respected minister of the South Carolina Conference, fell victim to a fever at the same time as
her father did. Both lay dying in adjoining rooms; Hewitt's
concern, however, was not for himself, but for his daughter,
who remained unconverted. He had long prayed for her, and
would not give up hope. When word was brought to him that
his daughter was dead, he asked if she had professed religion
before she died. The answer was no. He exclaimed, "'She
is not dead. God will not permit her to die until she is converted.'" His faith appeared to be misplaced, however, for
"she was laid out, shroud made, eyes closed, etc. " To
everyone's astonishment, however, after about an hour, her
eyes opened and "she said distinctly: 'Glory to God, my sins
are forgiven, and I am going safe to heaven.'" Then she
closed her eyes for the final time; shortly afterwards, her

father followed her, as another account of the story says,
"so soon after the daughter that there was no need to close
the gate after the triumphant entrance of one till the other
was there."[12]

Travis gives the lesson of this anecdote: "Parents,
never cease to pray for your children! Don't give them up!
--don't give them up!!" This exhortation is footnoted by the
editor of the Travis autobiography:

> It must not be supposed that God will work miracles
> to control irresistibly the free agency of sinners in
> answer to the prayers of their pious friends--God
> compels no one to be religious. We are sure that
> the author would deprecate such an inference from
> this singular anecdote.[13]

Interestingly enough, the point of Thomas Summers' footnote
is not that God cannot work miracles to produce religious conversion but that he does not work them to the detriment of
free agency.

2. <u>Conversion by hymn.</u> This episode appears in
Smith's <u>Recollections</u> and again in Charles Buoy's <u>Representa-
tive Women of Methodism</u> with only slightly different details.
The relationship, therefore, may be literary rather than oral,
although the motif is traditional.[14]

The story is that Sophia, the only daughter of Harry
and Prudence Gough (owners of Perry Hall in Maryland, site
of the historic 1784 Christmas Conference), became deeply
convicted of her sinfulness, and "sought the Lord earnestly
in the use of all the means of grace, but found no relief."
One day she sat down at the piano and played and sang a
hymn: "'Come thou Fount of every blessing.'" While she
was singing "the Holy Comforter descended, brought peace to
her troubled soul, and wrote pardon upon her heart." She
ran to her parents with her news, and the household was
blanketed with joy.[15]

3. <u>Conversion by trick.</u> a) <u>By imitated sermon.</u>
According to this story, James Vansant, a Methodist preacher, had "remarkable powers of imitation." On one occasion,
"while in his backslidden state," he was working on a boat
with his cousin. Vansant recited to his relative a sermon
that he had heard delivered by "that prince of pathetic and
stirring preachers," Thomas G. Stewart. The imitation was

so impressive that an "unconverted man near by, over hearing it, was seized with conviction and became converted. "
Years later it was announced in this man's home town that
James Vansant would preach. He mentioned that he had already heard Vansant. When reminded that at the time he
named, Vansant was not a minister, he replied, "'I don't believe it, for no man could preach as he did without being a
converted man. '"16

b) By trick voice. Young introduces this episode by
noting that thoughtlessness is a great cause of irreligion, and
therefore that "whatever will wake up the mind to the subject
will be likely to produce a good result. "

A couple in Vermont, he continues, lived "in jar and
contention. " A shrewd but irreligious young man decided to
try an "experiment" on them. One morning before they had
risen from bed, he approached their house, hid behind a
stump, and said in a loud, guttural voice: "'Awake thou
that sleepest, and arise from the dead, and Christ shall give
thee light. '" The startled couple jumped out of bed and hurried to the window, but, seeing no one, "came to the conclusion that it was a supernatural voice. " As a result of the
trick they became converted and, "like Zachariah and Elizabeth, " lived happily ever after. Noting the happy results of
his experiment, the irreligious trickster also later converted
--himself in a way, the dupe of a trick. 17

c) By trick inscription. A couple who refused to
contribute from their abundance to the maintenance of their
preacher were warned by a trick message on an egg. The
morning after they had pointedly rejected the preacher's appeal for financial aid, they found an egg in a nest in the
barn with the inscription: / "'Woe, woe to the covetous. '"
The next day another egg was found bearing the inscription:
"'Covetousness which is idolatry. '" Naturally the family was
frightened, and regarded it as "a solemn warning from heav-
en. " They sought advice from a neighbor, who told them
that it was time to reform "lest a worse thing should befall
them. " They made their contribution and the messages
ceased. A few weeks later, the narrator notes, he met the
neighbor who had given the advice, and asked him "how much
vitriol and tallow it took to give heaven's warning by an egg?"
The man's reaction convinced the narrator "that I had rightly guessed the human instrumentality. "18

d) By hiring a girl to pray. The following story is

told of Henry O. Sheldon, of the North Ohio Conference.
Once, while visiting a Christian family, Sheldon noticed that
a servant girl did not kneel down for prayers. In the course
of a lengthy dialogue with her he discovered that not only did
she not know how to pray but did not want to pray. He
asked her: "'Now, could you be hired to pray?'" She responded affirmatively, and so the bargain was struck. Every
morning for four weeks she agreed to go into her room at
ten o'clock and recite the prayer, "'Lord, be merciful to me,
a sinner.'" In return, she would receive five dollars from
the preacher.

The first day she went into her room, said her prayer, and came out laughing. The next day she went into her
room for prayer, and came out serious. The third day,
while she was on her knees, "deep conviction fell upon her,"
and she came out weeping. Soon she was converted, and
when Sheldon returned, he "found her happy, praising and
loving Jesus." It is not recorded whether or not Sheldon
paid her. [19]

e) <u>Unconverted husband, taking sermon notes for
wife, is converted</u>. The story concerns a husband whose
zealous Methodist wife was too ill to attend a revival. Although he was not a believer, he decided to go and take notes
of the sermon for his wife. At first he could keep up with
the preacher

> but as Brother Clawson grew warmer, his utterance
> became more rapid, until it became a perfect tor-
> rent, and the man got confused, and put up his pen-
> cil and paper, and listened attentively till the ser-
> mon was over, and went home in a very serious
> mood.

At bed-time that night he was uneasy and close to tears, and
told his wife he could not retire without praying first. She
was overjoyed, and knelt with him until he found peace. [20]

f) <u>Man hiding behind door during sermon is converted</u>.
Here a belligerent but curious sinner who comes to a meeting hides behind a door so that he will not be noticed by his
friends. He feels that the sermon is directed to him, and,
after initial anger, converts.

In one version of the story, a farmer named Armstrong came to a meeting one night and found the preaching

so close to his own sinfulness that he felt sure the preacher
meant to expose him. He left in a rage, and tried to find
out who had told the minister about him. The next night he
came back and hid behind the door to avoid further exposure.
The preacher's sermon this night catalogued new areas of sinfulness, and again Armstrong felt he was singled out. He
remembers: "I got awfully angry there behind the door, but
I was cornered, and could do nothing but bite my lips and
swear to myself...." But he recalled, as he listened, that
the preacher had said that all would be able to see themselves in the "Gospel glass" that was held before them. Soon
Armstrong felt convicted of his guilt, and rushed to the mourner's bench to seek the Lord.[21]

In another version of the story a saloon keeper was
induced by his wife to attend church on a Sunday evening,
but hid behind the door. The preacher discoursed on hiding
from God, and called out, "'Come out of your hiding place!'"
When the man got home he unbraided his wife for telling the
minister that he was hiding behind the door.[22]

A variation of this story is said to have occurred in
Wexford, Ireland. Methodists were persecuted by the "Pap-
ists" and therefore held their meetings in secret. One of
the Roman persecutors hid himself in a sack by the door so
that he might open the door to his fellows after the meeting
had begun. Before he could get out of the sack, he was convicted of sinfulness by the sermon and converted.[23]

Another "hiding" story has to do with a tavern keeper
who came to a meeting to hear the excellent music. He was
afraid of the preaching, so he sat with his fingers in his
ears. At length a fly lit upon his nose, and as he brushed
it away, the preacher cried out, "'He that has ears to hear,
let him hear.'" He was convicted of sin and later converted.[24]

4. Lady converted by apparition. Ghosts make rare
appearances in the literature examined, and seemingly (save
in dreams) never for religious purposes.

The protagonist of the story was an intelligent lady
who was having intellectual difficulties with religion. An
uncle, who had led a careless, irreligious life, had just died
without reconciling himself to God. One night she went to
bed, extinguished the lamp, and, while "musing" on her
couch, saw a "dismal light." She recounts:

> 'Without feeling any dread, I gazed at it, wondering,
> and distinctly saw, in the centre of the light, the
> exact figure and dress of my deceased uncle. While
> the pale horrid light flitted around, the ghastly fig-
> ure moved slowly along toward me, and stopped by
> the side of my bed, where it stood, motionless,
> with a gloomy countenance, looking wishfully on me!

Still not fearful, she decided to see if the apparition were
"spirit" or "substance."

> 'Resolved to know, by actual experiment, I stretched
> my arm from the bed, and drew it slowly till it
> passed through the figure, separating it as easily as
> if it had been a column of smoke.'

The apparition instantly disappeared, whereupon she felt a
terror that made her shriek aloud. If she could doubt the
truths of Christianity, notes the narrator, she could not doubt
the apparition: "The scene ... was so convincing that her
doubts were overpowered by the force of evidence...."25

    5. <u>Man converted by remarkable deliverance</u>. One
story, says Young, was told to him by a man named Morris,
of New Hampshire, who was "elderly and very intelligent" and
"had long been engaged in seafaring life." According to the
story, a sailor was guarding the boat while a watering party
searched a small tropical island for water. To pass the time,
the man went swimming. When he was some distance from
the shore, he "was suddenly alarmed by seeing a crocodile
approaching him." He swam furiously for shore,

> but as he neared it his terror was increased by
> seeing a tiger rush from the thicket, and come
> bounding at him; but the danger behind pursued him
> so closely that he still pushed for the shore. The
> tiger made a leap for him, but just missed him;
> the crocodile caught the tiger, who made a des-
> perate struggle for a moment, but the monster of
> the deep drew him under water, and bore him off
> as his lawful prey.

The astonished sailor, finding himself alone, fell to his knees
and thanked God for his "wonderful deliverance," and "made
a covenant to serve him forever."16

    6. <u>Man rendered helpless by preaching converts</u>.

The nexus between traditional conversion accounts and the expectations of working preachers is illustrated by the following
story. William Taylor introduces his account by saying that
he had read narratives of the effect of Benjamin Abbott's
preaching. 27 According to Ffirth's account, catatonic seizures were normal, not only for individuals but groups, as
the result of Abbott's rhetoric. Taylor "became greatly ex-
ercised on the subject, " and prayed that if this way would be
more effective that God would use him to produce similar effects. Shortly thereafter, during one of his sermons, a
"man fell down in a state of insensibility. "

The fellow was carried out, taken home, and visited
by a doctor. By this time "he was nearly as cold as death,
and his limbs were as still as a poker. " The doctor covered
the man's trunk with a huge mustard plaster, then began to
rub his limbs to promote circulation. Shortly the man revived, told the doctor that nothing was wrong with him but
sin, and ordered that the preacher, Mr. Taylor, be brought
to his bedside. Taylor talked to him, prayed with him, and
in about fifteen minutes the man "surrendered to God and received Jesus Christ. " He "sprang out of bed rejoicing. " In
reaction to the "cure, " Taylor wrote:

> I said to myself, 'Well, thank the Lord, my prayer
> is answered. That is a regular knock-down case,
> such as I have been reading about. '

The real test of a conversion, according to Taylor, is
not the mode by which it is achieved, however. [Inasmuch
as the validity/of highly emotional conversions was a concern
for many itinerants, a brief excursus, with illustrative stories,
is in order here.] Taylor juxtaposes this conversion story
with that of a man converted humbly and unobtrusively. Then
he says, "I will watch these two cases and see which will
pan out the better. " In other words, the fruit of conversion
is the real test of its worth. Taylor noticed that the man
converted by being knocked out was "an easy-going" brother
who "did not backslide, " but whose life bore no positive religious fruit. The man converted by ordinary means, on the
other hand, "in the Church at large became a very useful
man. " Taylor concludes from the "experiment":

> So if the Lord can't get a certain class of sinners
> down in any other way we shall be glad to have Him
> knock them down, as He did Saul of Tarsus and the
> man Curry; but to receive the truth, count the cost,

and deliberately say, like the prodigal, 'I will arise
and go to my father,' and do it, is the rule; the
other, the exception.

In short, Taylor is not as credulous as he appears in
his desire to imitate the old-time preacher's results. It
would not be difficult, in fact, to read the narration as a
repudiation of the kind of expectation that Abbott's account
engenders. Without denying the possibility of such conversions, Taylor clearly favors the ordinary means of conversion over the extraordinary. 28

In a more humorous fashion, two other stories illustrate Taylor's point that conversions are proved by their
fruits rather than by any circumstances, however remarkable,
attending them.

One of the stories concerns the conversion of a young
woman whose son was destined to become a Methodist circuit
rider. Shortly after her conversion, she overheard her
daughters talking about the event:

> 'Well,' said one, 'mother is born again.' 'What is
> that?' said another. 'Why, she is now holy, and
> she will always do right, and not give way to her
> temper any more.' Another said, 'We will know
> more about that in the evening, when mother goes
> to milk <u>that</u> cow.'

The narrator explains that the cow was a stubborn and rebel-
lious beast. When the mother heard this conversation, she
went to her closet and prayed that she would not do anything
"that might lessen the opinion her children had of religion."
When time came for her to milk the cow, she approached the
animal "in the kindest manner," and spoke pleasant words
while stroking its back.

> The cow looked amazed, and stood still in her
> tracks, through the whole process, even to the
> 'strippings.' 'And I verily thought at the time,'
> said Mrs. Walker in the love-feast, 'that the cow
> was also converted.'

"Gentle men," concludes the narrator, "have gentle horses."29

For full enjoyment, this story must be contrasted with
another which slurs the fruits of Baptist conversion. The fol-

lowing story, says the Methodist narrator, "is a very fair specimen of the ignorance and superstitution of those who hold to immersion as a saving ordinance." Furthermore, the account "is by no means a fable."

The protagonist of the narrative is Uncle Micha Manuel. One Sabbath Uncle Micha put on his old pants, went to the "protracted meeting up on Crab Run," and was baptized by immersion. When he returned home, full of grace and enthusiasm, he immediately began organizing his unsuspecting family into patterns of religiosity. The narrator lampoons his ignorance at great length; one excerpt will illustrate the manner. After supper, Uncle Micha called everyone together for family prayers:

> All having assembled and order being restored, Uncle Micha opened his large family Bible, and commenced reading, but not being accustomed to that kind of work, he started in as follows: Abraham begat Isaac, Isaac begat Jacob, and Jacob begat Judas, and now becoming somewhat embarrassed, and not knowing where this begetting might end, catching his breath he paused and now added, 'And God only knows when they quit. But it must be remembered that the Jews were a numerous people and very superstitious, and we should be thankful that it is not now as it was once. If a beggar came along, slap went his hide to cover the binnacle of a ship.'
>
> 'No, father,' said his wife, 'you don't mean that. The Bible says: Badger skins to cover the tabernacle.'
>
> 'I know that,' said Uncle Micha, 'but it must be remembered that the Bible was written by Martin Luther after he was converted, and he being an ignorant Dutchman, did not know the difference between beggar and badger.'

This sort of familial edification was outdone the next morning, when Uncle Micha went out to do the chores. His wife, having prepared breakfast, waited for his return.

> At length he entered, cursing and swearing, a hole in the knee of his pants, his wide-brimmed hat all mashed in and he well covered with mud and milk. Taking his place at the table, he commenced by saying:

'You may all go to eating, as there will be
no more prayers or blessings in this house until
there is a better state of things. That devilish
young heifer presumes too much on my piety, and
I will let her know that there is a God in Israel if
she don't do better.'

That night Uncle Micha's sons went out and tormented the
heifer with sharp pointed sticks. When they came into the
house, they told their mother:

If dad thinks of selling that red heifer don't you
consent. As long as we can keep the devil in her
we won't have any more of dad's awful religion.30

Baptists had a similarly jaundiced view of the effectiveness of Methodist conversions. One sarcastic Baptist
preacher, known as the "Arminian Skinner" for his invective
skill, said of Methodist conversion:

'The only way to save Methodist converts is to cut
off their heads and send them straight to heaven, before they have an opportunity of falling from grace.'31

Occasionally, the fruit of a conversion was proved
miraculously, as in the case of William Ryder, whose baptism was the occasion for much merriment among local ne'er-
do-wells. As a test of his sincerity, they thrust a willow
riding switch into the ground, and it grew into a large tree.32

7. Woman rendered helpless by preaching, revived and
converted by singing of hymn: medicine and religion. This
story is clearly a variation of the preceding one in which the
stricken man revives at the praying of the preacher. In this
account, a young society lady was felled at an exuberant camp
meeting. When the minister and a Dr. Curtis examined her,
they found her "warm, but pulseless and breathless." The
doctor took the preacher aside and told him that it was "a
very dangerous case of catalepsy," and that the girl must be
kept quiet, lest her mind "go off like a match."

A group of young ladies guarded her all night. The
next morning, she was still entranced. The minister, meanwhile, recalled reading of a similar case in an old Methodist
magazine: a girl, apparently dead, was revived by an Irish
crone who came into the sick room with her hymn book and
sang, "Alas, and did my Savior bleed?" The girl had arisen
and "embraced the old saint."

The minister determined to try the same device, inasmuch as the doctor could do nothing for the girl. He told the young ladies guarding the fallen one to sing "Alas, and did my Savior bleed?" During the last verse the girl opened her eyes, and when they sang the hymn again, "she rose up shouting." Her face was "heavenly-looking."[33]

The same story, with different principals and in greater detail, is told by Dan Young. In this narrative, the ineptitude and consequent embarrassment of the doctor is emphasized. "Poor fellow!... All the display of his medical sagacity about Mary's dangerous fit was blown up to the moon." Young cites as the source of his story a "talented preacher."[34]

While resentment at the ineptitude of the medical profession recurs again and again throughout the literature, the intent of the hymn story is not primarily to illustrate medical incompetence per se but to indicate that science has no grasp whatever of the means by which spiritual transactions are effected. Hence professional medicine has no power whatsoever to cure the "catalepsies" caused by conviction of sinfulness.

The implication of such stories, that is, that physical sickness is often merely a manifestation of spiritual malaise, gives rise to a correlative belief that the man of God may cure the physical as well as the spiritual ailment. In one story the presence of an itinerant causes a girl's fever to subside;[35] in another instance an insane woman with a knife calms at the sight of the holy man.[36] A North Carolina itinerant, George W. Ivey, was called in by a woman to heal her cow which "showed every appearance of having the hollow-horn or having been subjected to the wiles of witches."[37] The curative power could transfer to religious events; for example, a sick child brought against all advice to a camp meeting recovers.[38]

Summary

Stories of remarkable conversions, whether by personal example or by unusual means, fall into traditional patterns of the remarkable providence tradition. The impression that emerges from reading these stories is that Methodist itinerants believed in the disruptive nature of the divine initiative, which called for immediate and total acceptance or rejection. Correlative to this conviction is the idea that God, while he can use ordinary means, has the power and inclination to employ extraordinary means or to dispense with means altogether. Underlying the latter opinion is a skepticism that demands perseverance as the real proof of validity.

Like the dream accounts, stories of remarkable conversions not only expressed the Methodist belief in immediate divine grace, but also extended such belief. Those who heard how God had worked in the past could expect him to work similarly in the future. In short, conversion stories offered a paradigm to prospective converts whose conversion stories, in turn, would validate the paradigm.

Moreover, like remarkable judgments, remarkable conversions vindicated a Methodist God. Who could doubt that God was on his side if his deity proved merciful as well as vengeful?

Notes

1. Smith, Recollections, pp. 82-83. Motif Q552.13.0.1.: "Punishment by arrows of fire from heaven."
2. For examples of children as suffering agents, see Hibbard, Memoirs, pp. 154ff. Sometimes, stories told of fathers shamed into religion by the question of an innocent child. In Travis, Autobiography, pp. 226-27, a little boy asks/his father, "'Pa, where is that God you used to be talking to?'" In a story told by Cotton Mather, a dying child says on the Sabbath: "'This is the day on which my father used to go to prayer.'" MCA, p. 272. See also A. C. Morehouse, Autobiography of A. C. Morehouse: An Itinerant Minister of the New York and New York East Conferences of the Methodist Episcopal Church (New York: Tibbals Book Company, 1895), pp. 97-98.
3. Simon Peter Richardson, The Lights and Shadows of Itinerant Life: An Autobiography (Nashville: Publishing House of the Methodist Episcopal Church, South, 1901), pp. 11-12.
4. Newell, Life, pp. 47-49; repeated verbatim in Coles, Heroines, pp. 161-63, with acknowledgment of Newell as source. Motif S466.: "Practice of one's religion forbidden"; S411.: "Wife banished"; S62.: "Cruel husband"; V331.10.: "Conversion to Christianity

because of admiration for Christian virtue. "
For versions see D. Young, Autobiography,
p. 26; Erwin, Reminiscences, pp. 90-92: the man
beats his wife and she stays with friends. A few
days later he chases her into the meeting with homi-
cidal intent, hears her testimony and is converted.
He later buys a broad-brimmed white hat for the
preacher, whom he had threatened to kill. Also
Smith, Recollections, p. 107, for the same story in
the setting of a camp meeting; Borum, Sketches, pp.
119-20, for the story in Baptist biography: the husband pushed his wife off a horse into mud because
of her conversion. She stays with friends, testifies
later at a meeting, and her listening husband is converted.

5. (New York: Eaton and Mains, 1898), pp. 271-72. See
   D. Young, Autobiography, pp. 121-22, for the same
   story with less detail. In this version, only the wife
   is mentioned. The physician used various means to
   prevent her from attending Methodist worship; finally,
   at the approach of a quarterly meeting, he told her
   she was in danger of becoming sick and applied a
   large blister to her chest. Her patient submission
   effected his conversion.

6. Ware, Memoir, pp. 168-69.
7. Manship, Thirteen Years', pp. 300-1.
8. D. Young, Autobiography, pp. 122-23.
9. Peck, Sketches, pp. 151-54. Motif V331. 10.: "Conversion to Christianity because of admiration for
   Christian virtue. "
   See N. N. Puckett, Folk Beliefs of the Southern Negro (Chapel Hill, N. C.: University of North
   Carolina Press, 1926), p. 529, for a similar account. An informant of Puckett's "tells of the master whipping one old slave, who prayed for the master all the time he was being whipped. His master
   was touched and allowed him to preach to the men
   on the plantation with the result that hundreds were
   converted. "
   Despite religious dressing, both stories clearly resemble the Old Marster--Slave John stories
   noted in Dorson, American Folklore, pp. 186-88.
   In this cycle of stories, which utilize traditional
   trickster folk motifs as a protest against racism,
   John often outwits the Marster.
   See Green, A. L. P. Green, pp. 537-38,
   "Jim and his Master, " for an account in which de-

nominational difference adds to the humor of the situation. In this story Jim, a black Methodist preacher outwits old Master, a white Baptist preacher.

In another account the story is told of the slave who attended camp meetings and regularly got the "jerks." The jerks made him so sore that he could not do his work, whereupon his blacksmith master forbade him to go to meetings, under pain of a flogging. The slave went anyhow, and came home disabled. The enraged master seized his cowhide, and had just raised his arm to strike the first blow when the whip flew out of his hand and he himself caught the "jerks." John Mathews, Peeps into Life (Published by Request of The Tennessee Annual Conference of the Methodist Episcopal Church, South, 1904), p. 28.

10. Spicer, Autobiography, pp. 234-35. See also a version in Daniel Wise, Sketches and Anecdotes of American Methodists of "The Days That Are No More" (New York: Phillips and Hunt, 1866), pp. 91-94. The location is specified as Holland Purchase, in this account.

11. Smith, Recollections, p. 32. For parallel accounts: Richardson, Autobiography, pp. 164-65; A. D. Field, Worthies and Workers, Both Ministers and Laymen, of the Rock River Conference (Cincinnati: Cranston and Curts, 1896), p. 141, p. 199; Summers, Biographical Sketches, p. 284; Woolsey, Supernumerary, pp. 104-5.

12. Summers, Biographical Sketches, p. 236. The main narration is taken from Travis, Autobiography, pp. 214-15. The Summers account includes pulse arrest as an indication of death.

Motif V23.1.: "Unshriven man restored to life in order to confess." See Brewer, Dictionary, pp. 83-85, for hagiographic and biblical examples of resuscitation, especially p. 85: "St. Severus raised to life a dead man, in order to confess and absolve him." Also Loomis, White Magic, p. 83: "Cronan gave life again to the occupant of an ancient sepulchre. When he had baptized the fellow, he permitted him to die again."

13. Travis, Autobiography, p. 215.

14. Smith, Recollections, pp. 192-93; Buoy, Representative Women of Methodism (New York: Hunt and Eaton, 1893), p. 272. See Travis, Autobiography, pp. 231-32, for the story of a girl who converts others sing-

ing a hymn at a "conversation party. "
15. Motif: D1588. : "Magic hymn assures heaven for per-
     son who sings it"; D1766. 9. : "Magic results from
     singing hymn. "
16. Nicholas Vansant, Sunset Memories (New York: Eaton
     and Mains, 1896), pp. 40-41.
         A variation of this story has a group of jovial
     sots betting who could preach the best sermon. One
     John Thorpe mounted the table "full of hilarity. "
     But when he opened the Bible to the text, " 'Except
     ye repent ye shall all likewise perish, ' " he became
     so terrified that "his hair stood on end, and he
     preached in earnest. " Later he became a bona fide
     minister. Peck, Sketches, pp. 168-69. The same
     story is recounted in Wakeley, Whitefield, pp. 158-
     60.
17. D. Young, Autobiography, pp. 111-13. Motif F966. :
     "Voices from Heaven (or from the air). "
18. Erwin, Reminiscences, pp. 136-37.
19. Burgess, Pleasant Recollections, pp. 437-38. Similar
     to this story is the one about the Infidel Club whose
     members agreed to read the Bible and pray daily.
     Although they did not fulfill their part of the bargain,
     they were converted when they arrived at the minis-
     ter's house. Taylor, Battlefield, pp. 241-43. See
     Gaddis, Walker, pp. 126-28.
20. Robison, Clawson, pp. 26-27.
21. Taylor, Autobiography, p. 45. Motif J1738. 8. : "Men
     hide so that God will not see their sin. "
22. Mathews, Peeps, p. 33.
23. Peck, Sketches, p. 168.
24. Ibid., p. 169. The same story is told of an English
     innkeeper in Edwin Paxton Hood (ed.), The World of
     Anecdote (Philadelphia: J. B. Lippincott Company,
     1887), p. 308. Hood cites as his source the Life
     and Times of the Countess of Huntingdon.
25. Giles, Pioneer, p. 70. Motif E363. 3. : "Ghost warns
     living. "
26. D. Young, Autobiography, pp. 258-59. Motif F1088. :
     "Extraordinary escapes. " The same tall tale is told
     in Hood, World of Anecdote, p. 341, citing Bagley's
     Family Biblical Instructor as a source.
27. Probably Ffirth's life of Abbott, published in 1833 and
     frequently mentioned as a source of edification by
     Methodist writers.
28. Taylor, Autobiography, pp. 54-56. Throughout the lit-
     erature various narrators line up on one side or the

other on the question of the value of the various emotional excesses usually associated with the camp
meeting--jerks, laughs, barks, seizures, marrying
exercises, and shouts. Some were disgusted with
them; Williams, Smith, pp. 46-47. Others thought
meetings were unsuccessful without emotional demon-
strations: Taylor, Battlefield, p. 249. In the middle were those who, like William Taylor, felt that
true conversion, and not the phenomena which accompany it, is the criterion of success: Smith, Recollections, pp. 60-61.

29. Gaddis, Walker, pp. 447-48. Motif H1155.2.: "Milking unruly cow."

30. Gavitt, Crumbs, pp. 250-54. Motif H1155.2.: "Task:
milking unruly cow"; J1823.: "Misunderstanding of
church customs or ceremonies causes inappropriate
action"; J2495.: "Religious words or exercises interpreted with absurd literalness."

   See Richard Dorson, Buying the Wind (Chicago
and London: University of Chicago Press, 1964), pp.
513-14, for a similar story told of a Mormon elder,
who gets all dressed up for church but has to feed
the calf before leaving. He takes a bucket of warm
sudsy milk to the animal, who thrusts in her nose
and then shakes milk froth all over the elder. He
shouts: "If I wasn't a member of the Church, if I
wasn't trying to foreswear swearing, if I wasn't a
good brother in the priesthood, if I couldn't control
my temper, I'd take your goddamn head and push it
through the bottom of this bucket."

31. Hatcher, Jeter, p. 29.

32. Ryder, Superannuate, pp. 41-43. Motif F971.1.: "Dry
rod blossoms"; also related to motif H331.3.:
"Suitor contest: prize to one whose staff blooms";
H432.4.: "Blooming staff as chastity index"; D1673.:
"Magic staff blossoms." Loomis, White Magic, p.
94, notes that a characteristic of flowering staff
stories in hagiographic lore is that the staff continues
to grow until a mature tree, as did Ryder's staff.

33. Richardson, Autobiography, pp. 89-90. Motif D1766.9.:
"Magic results from singing hymn." Cotton Mather
recounts the story of a dying Indian revived by the
singing of a Psalm, MCA, pp. 442-43.

34. Autobiography, pp. 262-64. Some itinerants, however,
distinguished natural from supernatural seizures.
Hibbard, Memoirs, pp. 162-65, for the account of
a lady rendered helpless by preaching during a thun-

Remarkable Conversions   125

derstorm. Hibbard, the preacher, noted that when
her shoes and stockings were removed, her feet were
swollen. He concluded that "her complaint was natural" not supernatural. Lest she die, however, and
give scandal, Hibbard and others chafed her wrists
and legs for nearly two hours before she revived.
Referring to her reviviscence, Hibbard writes: "I
did not consider this as a miracle, though I could
not account it anything less than the power of God."
Some cataleptics did not revive. See Cartwright, Autobiography, pp. 68-69.
35. Smith, Recollections, pp. 318-19. Motif D2161.5.1.:
"Cure by holy man."
36. P. Douglass Gorrie, The Lives of Eminent Methodist
Ministers; Containing Biographical Sketches, Incidents, Anecdotes, Records of Travel, Reflections,
&c., &c. (New York: R. Worthington, 1881), pp.
367-368. Motif V221.4.: "Saint subdues madman."
37. Plyler and Plyler, Men, pp. 60-61. Motif M471.1.1.:
"Curse: milk will not turn to butter."
38. Burgess, Pleasant Recollections, pp. 118-19.

Chapter 4

REMARKABLE DELIVERANCES

Confronted by the physical dangers of the wilderness and persecution, and dependent for the necessities of life upon fickle and often stingy people, Methodist preachers lived between faith and practicality. Stories of remarkable deliverances from danger and financial necessity, drawing upon traditional motifs, illustrate the old time preacher's trust in God's providential care at the same time as they point to the dire circumstances which that trust often incurred.

Deliverances in the Wilderness

Methodist circuit riders moved with the fringe of the moving frontier, sometimes following fresh wagon tracks in lieu of trails. A story told of the itinerant Richmond Nolley illustrates old time Methodist speed:

> He visited all parts of his extensive parishes. It is said that on one occasion he followed a wagon track and found a settler about to camp. He was asked if he was a Methodist minister, and when the settler learned the fact he said: "I quit Virginia to get out of the way of them, and went to a new settlement in Georgia, where I thought that I should be quite beyond their reach, but they got my wife and daughter into the church. Then in the late purchase--Choctaw Corner--I found a piece of good land, and was sure that I would have some peace of the preachers; but here is one of them before my wagon is unloaded."[1]

Early circuit riders traveled by compass and carried hatchets to blaze the trail. Bold turks among them, such as Jesse Lee, aspired to "break the first bush, " that is, to be pioneers of Methodism in an area.[2]

126

Thus Methodism became synonymous with zeal on the frontier, even in the estimation of its rivals. An old "Ironside" Baptist preacher allegedly remarked that "the Methodists beat any set of folk that he ever saw." They

> 'would put up a brush arbor, roll a few logs together for seats, nail a bookboard between two trees, go to singing and preaching, and have half a dozen folk converted before even the Lord knew what they were doing.'3

But frontier cabins were few and far between, and the dictum of the Discipline never to be late for an appointment kept the circuit riders stretching their luck (or providences) to arrive on time. Frequently they lost their way on dark, lonely trails.

1. **Itinerant gives horse loose rein and finds path.** Chandley Lambert's diary recalls an episode in which darkness obscured a forest path "and it seemed necessary we must pass the night in the wilderness." The hungry, fatigued preacher knelt down and "asked God to protect me from harm, and direct me in the right way." Lambert then mounted his weary horse, gave him the reins, and the faithful beast carried him to a cabin.4

2. **Lost itinerant finds help by singing hymn in woods.** Rev. John Johnson lost his way on a dark April night, and he and his horse tumbled into a ravine. The horse fled, and Johnson, after stumbling into a cold stream several times, managed to scramble out of the ravine and to recover his frightened steed. "Wet, cold, hungry, weary, and confused," he remounted, and asked himself, "'Well, where am I?'" The response came to him as of an audible voice.

> 'I'm marching through Immanuel's ground,
>   To fairer world on high!'
> He began and sung this triumphant old hymn entirely through, when his heart became so filled with 'peace and joy in the Holy Ghost,' that he made the gloomy old forest reverberate with shouts of 'Glory to God!'

Then Johnson heard a voice asking "'Who's that?'" He replied, "'A poor traveler, who has lost his way.'" Soon he found himself in the warmth and light of some hunters' campfire. Not one to miss an opportunity for proselytizing,

Johnson began to pour out his soul, "and the unlooked-for
encounter was converted into a prayer-meeting, which lasted
till long after midnight, and resulted in the conversion of
three precious souls."5

3. Lost folk protected and guided. Anson Green narrates the story of Brother Belton who "took a wrong path one
stormy day." Near nightfall he met an acquaintance who
asked him: "'Sure, and is this you, your riverence; pray,
where are you going?'" Belton replied, "'Oh, to hunt up
the lost sheep.'" Said the inquirer, "'Indade, well, I am
afraid the sheep stand a poor chance of being found to-night,
since the shepherd himself is lost!'"6

Biographers noted deliverances bestowed upon people
other than Methodist itinerants when they demonstrated the
overreaching influence of Providence.

In one account, a four year old boy wandered from
his family when they stopped for a rest on a Great Lakes boat
journey. When he discerned that he was lost, the lad trekked
along the lakeshore for four days and nights, subsisting on
grapes during the day and covering himself with sand at night.
Finally, after trudging more than forty miles, he rejoined
his overjoyed family in Niagara. The episode, remarks the
narrator, displays "an extraordinary interposition of divine
Providence," for "herein was that scripture fulfilled, 'When
my father and mother forsake me, then the Lord shall take
me up.'"

In a footnote, the narrator notes the reason for the
Providence. Years later, on a steamer, he met the little
boy, now a grown man, who had "embraced religion" and who
had become a circuit steward. 7

Another account tells the story of a woman who, captured by Indians, escaped from them and ran for hours along
the bank of a river until she was nearly exhausted. At a
point in the bank she came to an inland path and followed it
a short distance. Suddenly the path forked, one trail leading into the wilderness and one to the settlements. Ignorant
of the right direction, she was about to speed down the wrong
trail when "a little bird, of a dove color, flew close by her
face, and fluttered along into the other path." The woman
stopped and watched the bird repeat its performance. Then,
"taking this to be a providential interference," she followed
the other trail to the settlement. 8

Deliverance from Dangerous Beasts

In the hierarchy of terrors which beset frontier folk, few were more fearsome than the wild panthers that lurked in the trees overhead, the wolves that trotted the night trails behind solitary travelers, the bears that loomed like unexpected trees in the path ahead, or the snakes that curled under sleepers' blankets.

Stories told around campfires or in dark cabins undoubtedly magnified the real danger, so that stumps became bears at twilight and the screams of hoot owls became cries of a springing panther to the credulous itinerant. One itinerant noted: "Wolves were very common, but instances of their attacking a man on horseback were considered exceedingly apocryphal. "9

A young itinerant, in a blacksmith shop on his first circuit, heard terrifying stories of bears, catamounts, and rattlesnakes from a swarthy disciple of Vulcan. The latter then asked him: " 'Don't you scare at b'ar and painter (panther) tales?' " More wise than his years, the young preacher replied:

'Not just at the tails. If there are real, live, animals hitched to the business ends of the tails, I might be scared, but not at the mere tails. '10

Nevertheless, even the imagined dangers created real fears, and the real dangers were dreadful enough. Heroic though they were, the Methodist itinerants shared the fears of frontier folk, especially their terror of wild beasts such as the panther.

1. _Preacher saved from panther._ In one version of the story, Henry Bascom, later a Bishop of the Methodist Episcopal Church, South, decided, one day on his circuit, to read under a tree in the forest. He sat down and opened the book, and immediately became uneasy. Try as he might, he could not feel comfortable under the tree, so he got up and walked from underneath it. Just then a friend who was with him spotted a panther in the branches above Bascom's vacated resting place. He raised up his rifle and fired, and the "huge ferocious panther" fell to the very spot on which Bascom had been sitting. "The mysterious and apparently causeless inquietude which drove him from beneath the tree, " the biographer notes, "perhaps at the moment when the fero-

cious beast was about to pounce upon him, was the work of
a special providence of God. "11

    Other panther encounters occurred along trails at
night.   One itinerant, chased by a large beast while returning home on a wilderness path with his wife and child, lin-
gered behind and threw a piece of meat to distract the animal, then ran to his cabin behind his family.   When the beast
appeared at the door, he felled it with a handspike.   The narrator regarded this preservation as a providence which enabled him "to take part in the great and glorious Temperance
enterprise. "12

    Another courageous circuit rider, seeing a beast ahead
of his sleigh, increased his speed and ran him off into the
woods; the next day hunters told him the animal was a large
panther. 13

    2.   <u>Preacher saved from wolves</u>.   One itinerant, treed
by wolves and lacking sufficient ammunition to kill them all,
shot one, which the others rent to pieces.   He asked God for
deliverance, and even as he prayed, "the wolves got into a
general fight among themselves, and scampered off. "14

    Another "wolf" story makes clear how lack of experi-
ence and the evening hour induced frightened circuit riders
to exaggerate their dangers.   While riding through the woods
at dusk, a preacher heard a "tumultuous yell" nearby, as if
"a score of demons had determined to try their most fright-
ful strains. "   After a wild flight through brambles and thick-
ets, he arrived at a house and told the people "from what a
<u>congregation</u> of enemies" he had just made his escape.

        They smiled at my notions of the number, alleging
        that three or four wolves would be all the congre-
        gation necessary to make any amount of music of
        the sort I had just described. 15

    In another story, a providentially placed mountain
cabin rescued the pursued itinerant.   The ubiquitous Henry
Bascom, one dark night, raced ahead of a pack of howling
wolves on a rugged trail.   With the wolves nipping at the
heels of his horse, he spied the cabin of a "rude mountain-
eer" and found safety therein. 16

    3.   <u>Preacher saved from bears</u>.   The following stories
fall in this section only because they illustrate one of the

An Itinerant Treed by a Bear

wilderness dangers faced by itinerants. The manner of dis-
posal of bruin, however, clearly indicates that the tales belong primarily to the genre of tall tales rather than to that
of remarkable deliverances.

An Oregon itinerant remembered, in a bear fight, "how
we used to kill the salmon with a club by hitting them on the
nose just below the eyes." Wading into a tangle of dogs and
bear, he "hit him on the nose just below the eyes and he
died instantly."17

Another itinerant spoke softly and dispensed with the
big stick. Meeting a bear that "must have been as large as
a good-sized yearling steer," the preacher determined "to
try mild and pleasant words." Therefore, speaking "tender-
ly," the itinerant addressed the beast:

> 'Mr. Bruin, I do not wish to trespass upon your
> rights; but really I want to go just where you are
> now sitting. If you can make it quite convenient to
> get out of my way, I shall be much obliged to you;
> but if you cannot, or will not, why then I must give
> you the path, and get out of the way myself.'

The bear ruminated this discourse for a while, then turned
and went quietly into the woods. The persuasive itinerant
gave the moral: "'A soft answer turneth away wrath,' whether in man or beast."18

4. <u>Man saved from rattlesnake, wild bull.</u> In this
story, the remarkable providence occurs as an answer to a
man's doubts about his vocation. The episode represents
divination by providence, in fact, in that a man makes his
decision dependent upon a divine sign.

John Smith, doubting his call to preach, began to
watch

> every phase of ordinary Providence without, and
> every change of feeling within, in hope, that in
> some incident of experience, he might find the en-
> couragement that he sought.

One day, resting on a large log from his work in the fields,
he looked down and saw a rattlesnake coiled between his feet.

He sprang aside unharmed; for the reptile seemed

restrained, as if some spell was on it. As he
went back to his plowing, he thought of Gideon and
his fleece, and he wondered whether the Lord had
not sent this charmed snake as a sign that he, too,
should help to deliver Israel.

If special providences were needed to assure one's
vocation, one had only to look for them: "Having begun to
interpret such incidents in this way, it seemed to him that
... the Lord was multiplying his special providences around
him. "

For example, a short time later a vicious ox he had
purchased pursued him across a field, "and actually pushed
him as he ran. " He thought, even as the bull breathed on
his neck:

> 'If the Lord should be with me in this extremity,
> and deliver me out of this trouble, I will know as-
> suredly that he wants me to preach, and I will no
> longer scruple to be ordained. '

Immediately, one of the horns caught his clothing and tossed
him aside, saving him from the onrushing beast. 19

5. <u>Preacher saved from runaway horse.</u> Horses, although not wild beasts, could be dangerous enough when
frightened or startled. As a later chapter will indicate,
memory often invested the itinerant's horse with heroic qual-
ities, but stumbling or skittish horses must frequently have
endangered the ever-traveling itinerants.

One itinerant tells of borrowing a "wild and very furi-
ous" horse from a friend. The saddle was old, and the
stirrup buckles "had become deeply bedded in the leather
straps. " While riding along the summit of a hill the preacher was thrown from the horse so that one foot stuck in the
stirrup. As the frightened steed began to run, "the stirrup
leather was unbuckled, and the strap drawn out from the saddle, leaving it hanging to the stirrup-iron which was round
my ankle. " Nothing but providence could have effected this
rescue, reasoned the itinerant:

> If the strap had not been unbuckled, and drawn out
> by an invisible hand, (it evidently was not unbuck-
> led when I mounted, or it would have drawn out
> then) I should have been dragged by the ankle over

> the rugged road.... It may appear to some quite
> enthusiastical, still I have no doubt that an invisi-
> ble agent, with the quickness of lightning, extricated
> me in a miraculous manner from my perilous situa-
> tion, and so permitted me to go on and finish my
> work.

Such providences, he asserts, occur not for individual
preservation or edification but for the church:

> The event laid me under new obligations to be true
> to my sacred trust, and labour more faithfully in
> my holy vocation. [20]

Deliverances from Dangerous Men

1. <u>Preacher saves himself from robbers by showing
them his Bible.</u> One itinerant, traveling through the town of
Chillicothe at night, was startled by a large man who jumped
out of an alley, seized his horse by the bridle, and demanded
his money. The circuit rider replied to the man that he
could have all his money, inasmuch as he had only fifty cents,
that he was a Methodist minister and that if the robber entertained doubts about his profession he "would show him my
Bible and hymn book, as there was a bright star light and
he could see for himself." The thief surmised that he had
apprehended the wrong man, and sent him on his way. The
frightened itinerant was

> more than thankful for my Bible, which had served
> me better than a revolver. This was a new kind
> of weapon, the merits of which he appeared to have
> no desire to contest. [21]

2. <u>Preacher saved from Indians.</u> Although the Methodist itinerants did not equate Indians, as did Cotton Mather,
with demonic forces, [22] they did, with the Puritan divine, regard escapes from Indians as providentially directed. [23] Itinerants were frequently accosted by Indians on their circuits,
sometimes for money[24] and sometimes for darker purposes,
as in the case of the Indian who waylaid the Rev. George
Washington Densmore on a lonely trail and said, "'You be
Yankee ... you be good to eat.'"[25]

Itinerants regarded their escape from such encounters

as a manifestation of special providence. One itinerant,
Thomas Ware, traveling on the Kentucky-Tennessee border
in 1787, escaped because his horse snorted and wheeled from
a hidden Indian. "I had been told," he notes, "that some
horses were singularly afraid of an Indian." But the reaction of his horse, he continues, "was the means, under God,
of saving me from death or captivity."26

      Another itinerant, during the Spirit Lake Indian mas-
sacre (Iowa, 1857), saw a movement in the willows along a
road he was riding. "At the time," he recounts, "I was
thinking about something else, when one (Indian) appeared in
that vacancy so plainly that not a place for a doubt remained."
He whipped his horse up a ravine to another road and escaped. "Never since then," he concludes, "have I doubted
divine interposition in discovering those Indians."27

      3. Preacher saved from hostile mob. Billy Hibbard,
a famous New England itinerant, tells his story in the context of a jeremiad over the wickedness of New Englanders:
"I went mourning for the unhappy state of delusion that seemed
to triumph in New England over thousands." The unabated
scorn, opposition, and persecution, Hibbard believes, was
the work of Satan:

            if it (persecution) declined in one place, it would
            increase in another; for wherever the Lord poured
            out his Spirit, there Satan would rage, until he
            was overpowered by faith and prayer.

People threw stones, and set their dogs upon him, as he
rode from one appointment to the next. But such attacks
were a trifle, he says, for God "was with us, and enabled
us to endure." No stone ever struck him, nor did any dogs
bite him. Threatened whippings never materialized. On one
occasion, a mob was waiting in a swamp along the road from
Springfield to Westfield. As he approached the swamp, a
lady called to him from a house that someone was sick and
needed spiritual assistance. He turned his horse across
country, visited the sick man, and went to Westfield by another road. His friends at that town, who by then had
heard of the mob's intent, expected to see him badly mauled,
but rejoiced when he arrived unharmed that a "good providence" had saved him.28

Deliverance from Sickness

Relations of providential cures occur frequently in the literature. Usually, however, such incidents illustrate the belief that God providentially answers prayers or that bodily sickness is a sign of sinfulness and can be cured only by spiritual means. The following episodes illustrate a belief in physical cures providentially effected without prayer.

A tumor (graphically described in the text) on Rev. E. F. Newell's throat defied treatment. While riding on his horse, with "solemn thoughts of death" running through his mind, he entertained a dialogue in his mind:

> Q. What do you want to live for? A. To labor in the vineyard of the Lord. Q. If he has need of you can he not heal you with or without means? A. Yes. 'Then go on,' something seemed to say, 'and do your work, and give your case up to God and wait the event.'

Immediately, Newell felt divine peace, "like a river," along with "relief from the burning, prickling pains...." Newell notes that the cure has lasted even to the writing of his autobiography:

> Often the disease has stirred in my system from that time to the present; but, when I come to the same place, or state of mind, viz; resignation and unreserved consecration, which I felt when it was first checked, I feel the same power stop its working!

"God has done it," he exclaims, "and I adore!" One could only wish to be spared his final suggestion for public confirmation of the deliverances: "O that this account and the scar may be seen at my funeral."[29]

Deliverance from Financial Concern

Methodist preachers were allowed ample opportunity to test the Gospel dictum, "Give and it shall be given to you."[30] The itinerancy demanded both spiritual and material giving; besides preaching the gospel, the itinerant was called to sacrifice land, income, domestic ease, and even life itself for the sake of the Word, and to eke out subsistence on a meagre salary frequently unpaid. Some circuit riders were more disposed to provide for themselves than to wait upon providence for their reward, especially when they beheld the old retired supernumeraries, after years of service, dying in penury. [31]

The early itinerants, like the people to whom they ministered, had fresh in their memories the established churches and forced tithing of colonial days, [32] and readily accepted poverty as a way of life. Ideally, reaction to involuntary contribution should have been balanced by the Gospel theme that laborers are worthy of their hire. Unfortunately for the itinerants, however, hard-pressed frontier folk had little money to contribute, if not inclination to do so. [33] One destitute circuit rider, told that he should be satisfied to live off the Gospel, said he would try but asked how his horse could manage it. [34]

Second and third generation Methodist ministers, by way of reaction, asserted that voluntary poverty was a practice mistakenly elevated to a principle, as indeed they protested that much of the early ethical rigor had become formalism. [35]

Against this background, stories of remarkable financial deliverances function not only to illustrate beliefs and to exhort but to ward off the accusation that the early men were mere formalists. Unfortunately for those who held such beliefs, changing times within and without the church rendered the providential mindset increasingly at odds with practicality.

1. <u>Poor preacher unexpectedly receives compensation.</u>
One itinerant narrates how, in reduced financial circumstances, "I gritted my teeth and almost murmured at the providence that had sent me to such a hard service." Returning to his room he found "a letter containing for me a five-dollar bank note from a kind-hearted old lady." [36]

Another itinerant, on the trail with but twenty cents in his pocket and prospects of having to stay at a Baptist inn where lodging cost a dollar, was spared humiliation by the steward of his church, who met him on the road and gave him a five-dollar advance on his salary. [37]

Billy Hibbard, arriving at a new appointment, sick and without money, was informed by his wife that she had

food enough for only three meals. He sat in the corner and
pondered his situation. Asking credit of strangers, he thought,
"would be a disgrace to the Methodist Church, " and begging

> would sink the dignity of a minister, that ought to
> put his trust in that God that fed the prophet Elijah
> by ravens, that brought him bread and flesh in the
> morning, and bread and flesh in the evening.

Resolving "if I starve and die, I will not do anything that
would disgrace the cause, or the Church I serve, " he decided
to put his trust in God's providence. Three hours later
Brother Suckley visited, but the Hibbards "said nothing to
him of our poverty. " When Suckley left, he gave the preacher a five-dollar bill. In the next few days came a deluge of
supplies to reward, as Hibbard saw it, his happy resolution
of the crisis of faith. Concludes the itinerant: "O! the good
of religion in time of trouble. "[38]

Sometimes the reward for trust took the shape of
goods or services. Thomas Ware, in a "destitute condition, "
received from a gentleman he met a credit for twenty-five
dollars' worth of goods in the man's store. [39] Bishop Morris
approached a toll-bridge across the Muskingum river, penniless and rifling his pockets "for a knife, comb, or something
that would be accepted as a pledge until his next round!... "
The female toll-keeper eyed him closely for a moment, and
then remarked, "'I believe you go free.'" Morris said afterwards that he "never saw that lady before or after that day, "
and that although he had many following occasions to cross
that bridge this was the only time he passed free. [40]

Another "service" was provided to William McKendree
by a providential snowfall. McKendree was not a freeloader;
he characteristically relied on God but "took care not to expect Providence to do for him what he could and ought to do
for himself. " With one exception, relates his biographer,
McKendree always had money enough for his bills.

Just a day's journey from his headquarters, where he
had money, the Bishop paid all of his cash to a greedy tavern-
keeper. When he saddled his horse for the last leg of the
journey, he found that the animal had lost a shoe. Without
any money he could not have the beast shod. Just as he was
pondering the dilemma, "it commenced snowing, and snowed
rapidly until a beautiful soft carpet covered his way, and
made the travelling more pleasant both to himself and horse
than if there had been a shoe on his foot. "[41]

Providential care could extend to the itinerant's family as well. The wife of one circuit rider delayed by a snowstorm several days from returning home, "with a trembling hand ... gave the last piece of bread to her hungry children, and retired supperless, herself, feeling confident, however, that he who sent the ravens to Elijah, would not forget her." That same night a member of the church had a troubling dream about the preacher's family, and came by the next morning with provisions to inquire about their well being.

On another occasion the same woman was sick, in the absence of her husband. A nurse she had hired asked for money for provisions. Fearing that her helper would quit if she knew there was no money to buy provisions, much less pay wages, the preacher's wife asked for the Bible, "intending to seek comfort from its holy counsels." When she opened the book she found a five-dollar bill nestled in the page. [42]

2. __Man who gives away object receives immediate compensation in kind.__ This cycle of stories sharpened the belief that God providentially aids his servants by adding the idea that objects given will be literally, not metaphorically or in the future, given back.

In one story an itinerant met a beggar in the market place and gave the man his last ten dollars. On the way home the preacher stopped at the post office and found waiting for him a letter containing checks worth one hundred and twenty-five dollars.

The narrator recounts the incident for the edification of his colleagues. "As a general thing," he remarks, "I don't believe there is a more liberal set of men in the world," yet, "perhaps the devil will tempt us that we should come to want, and lead us to inquire, who will take care of our wives and children when we are gone?" The answer is in the Word: "There is that scattereth, and yet increaseth; and there is that withholdeth more than is meet, but is tendeth to poverty."

An experience in which the narrator essayed to prove the theory follows in the account. He began with five dollars, gave it away, and received five dollars in return by providential means. The same sequence repeated itself five times in twenty-four hours, so that after beginning with five dollars and giving away twenty-five dollars he ended up with five dollars. [43]

The drama of another such story is heightened by a
cold Christmas Eve setting. The itinerant, Mr. Crouch,
took his last quarter to the store for provisions, but on the
way met a poor man and gave him the money. He returned
home, and at nine o'clock that evening a sleigh drew up and
a couple who wished to be married debarked. After the ceremony, the groom paid the preacher with a five-dollar gold
piece. More remarkable yet, according to the biographer,
the couple who were married had originally intended to be
married by another preacher, but changed their minds in
favor of Mr. Crouch at precisely the moment he gave his
last quarter to the poor man. [44]

According to another story the Methodist Bishop William Capers, one night at an inn, spent his last money out-
fitting a freezing postboy with warm clothing. The next night
Capers lodged with a Presbyterian gentleman who gave him
twenty dollars as an ecumenical gesture. [45]

Another cycle of stories uses the "Give, and it shall
be given to you" motif to encourage the hospitality of Methodist laity toward traveling preachers. On the vast circuits
of the early frontier days Methodist preachers, like all travelers, could expect lodging at any home. As the circuits
stabilized, some homes became known as Methodist preachers' homes, where exhausted itinerants could find congeniality
as well as physical comfort. Children, when grown, would
assert that they were raised to feed preachers, and many
humorous stories, to be recounted in another chapter, deal
with the behavior of the chickens when the preacher arrived.
But other people, as has been indicated, felt that Methodist
preachers "sponged" off their laity and would eat any char-
itable laymen out of house and home.

Perhaps as an antidote to such feelings, some narrators state that the very reverse happens, that is, that
those who give to preachers receive a hundredfold. One Mr.
Gage, whose "house was always open to God's servants,"
ended his life in opulence. By contrast, "others, who blamed
him for his liberality in entertaining ministers, contracted
bad habits and were miserable...." Such providential rewards were not uncommon, according to the narrator:

> I have known similar results in hundreds of cases
> through the country, where persons commenced
> poor, but, by the advantages arising from the gos-
> pel, and the visits of gospel ministers, have risen

preeminently above their stingy, worldly, and scoffing neighbours. [46]

The Mr. Gage mentioned above told the narrator that once he used a little plot of ground near his cabin for the sole purpose of growing oats for the itinerants' horses: "I harvested three times the quantity on that little piece which I have ever been able to raise from the same quantity of land since!"[47]

There were stories to illustrate what happened to those who were stingy with their wealth; one man who refused to contribute to Methodist missions lost a prize heifer a few days later by lightning. The next time the mission collector appeared the man asked to be pledged for five dollars. [48]

3. Preacher posses inexhaustible quarter. No one in the community knew that the preacher and his wife had only a quarter left and were hungry. Not even their little daughter Lucy, whom they sent to the store with the money to buy milk, knew their desperation. The lady at the store, not a Methodist, sent the milk and the quarter back with the girl, along with a note saying "she would take out her pay in preaching." Then Lucy went to the grocery store for coffee, and came back with bundles of groceries and the quarter, compliments of the French Catholic merchant. Again and again, Lucy went out with the quarter and returned with it "until we came to expect it."

> We lived off it, making no debts; and it never
> passed out of our possession till other money came
> into our hands! This was the case of Elijah, and
> was not ours as strange as his? 'So he went and
> did according to the word of the Lord: for he went
> and dwelt by the brook Cherith, that is before Jor-
> dan. And the ravens brought him bread and flesh
> in the morning, and bread and flesh in the evening;
> and he drank of the brook. '[49]

Miscellaneous Deliverances

1. Man late for doomed train. Green records a personal anecdote that occurred when he was visiting England. A blundering tailor botched a waistcoat he had made and

delivered to Green. The mistake caused a day's delay in
Green's schedule. When Green returned the vest to the tailor,
the latter "pronounced the blunder unaccountable." But the
next day Green understood the whole affair. His scheduled
train had wrecked, and two unidentified men were killed.
Friends at his next appointment assumed that Green was one
of the unfortunates. Told of the reason for his delay, they
exclaimed: "'What a mercy! God has evidently used that
tailor, whom you blamed, to keep you out of danger.'"
Green assessed the affair similarly: "Let those doubt a special providence who may, I cannot."50

    2. Man sings himself out of prison. One Benjamin
Bidlack was imprisoned in Pennsylvania, but was such a
"splendid singer, and a merry fellow" that in the evenings
a company of idlers, ex-soldiers and jesters would gather
to hear Bidlack perform on the front steps of the jail. One
night, when he had lulled his captors into carelessness, he
leaped from the stoop, over the fence and ran away into the
night. "The next day," concludes the narrative, "our hero
arrived safely at his father's house in Plymouth, a distance
of fifty miles, performed on foot, having sung himself out of
prison." Bidlack later became a Methodist preacher, "as
great a singer of the songs of Zion as he had been of the old
patriotic ballads."51

Summary

    In summary, stories of providential deliverances il-
lustrated and reinforced the belief that God's care included
the material as well as the spiritual welfare of his servants
and people in the wilderness. The precondition for such protection was an ironclad trust in God. Some folk, as in the
case of the man saved from the rattlesnake and bull, reversed
the process and made the protection a precondition for trust.
In any event, however, remarkable deliverances were granted
not for the glorification of the person involved but for the
furtherance of more comprehensive, if often unknown, designs
of the same providence.

Notes

1. Ayres, Methodist Heroes, p. 67. Substantially the
        same story is told in Summers, Biographical Sketches,

pp. 266-67.

2. "It was customary with the early Methodist Preachers,
   in their travels through the country, to break a bush
   at a fork of the road, or where they left it, to indicate their course to those who came after them. The
   side of the road on which the broken bush was found,
   pointed out the path to be followed." Lee, Life, p.
   267. For accounts of trail-blazing, see Marlay,
   Morris, pp. 64-65; for travel by compass, see Carroll, Case, II, 365.

3. Alva W. Plyler, The Iron Duke of the Methodist Itinerancy: an Account of the Life and Labors of Reverend John Tillett of North Carolina (Nashville: Cokesbury Press, 1925), p. 135.

4. Gorrie, Black River, p. 139. Motif B563.1.1.:
   "Horses carry lost riders to safety."
       For a parallel account see Lee, Life, p. 297;
   Jesse Lee gave his horse the reins: "Beside the
   Providence in which he trusted at all times with a
   joyous confidence, he had one other source of conso-
   lation--his horse had travelled the path before."
   Also Smith, Recollections, pp. 332-33; Fleharty,
   Phelps, p. 30.

5. Johnson, Recollections, pp. 55-57. Motif D1380.14.1.:
   "Magic hymn protects."

6. Green, Life, p. 51.
       The story occurs in many different settings.
   Korson, Black Rock, pp. 295-96, tells the story of
   a preacher lost on his way to a Pennsylvania Dutch
   funeral. He asks a boy for directions to Heckelschtedtle (the site of the burial) and the boy asks
   him how he can tell people to get to Heaven if he
   doesn't know the way to Heckelschtedtle.
       The story, in a different form, is told in
   Vance Randolph, Hot Springs and Hell and Other Folk
   Jests and Anecdotes From the Ozarks (Hatboro,
   Pennsylvania: Folklore Associates, 1965), p. 37; a
   preacher, in Joplin, Missouri, asked where he's
   bound, replies he's bound to the Promised Land.
   The questioner says, "'Well, if you ain't got no further than Joplin, you must be on the wrong road.'"
   Randolph lists nine other occurrences of the joke.
       A story which likewise capitalizes on alleged
   ministerial inexpertise is that of the preacher frightened of snakes who is told by the Negro cook:
   "'Preachers dat come into dese woods to bruise de
   head ob dat old sarpint, de debil, musn't be fright-

ened into a fit at de sigh ob a milk snake.'" J. V.
Watson, <u>Tales and Takings, Sketches and Incidents,</u>
<u>From the Itinerant and Editorial Budget of Rev.</u>
<u>J. V. Watson, D.D.</u>, Editor of the Northwestern
<u>Christian Advocate</u> (New York: Carlton and Porter,
1856), p. 21.

7. Woolsey, <u>Supernumerary,</u> pp. 44-48.
8. James B. Finley, <u>Sketches of Western Methodism: Bio-</u>
    <u>graphical, Historical, and Miscellaneous, Illustrative</u>
    <u>of Pioneer Life,</u> edited by W. P. Strickland (Cin-
    cinnati: Printed at the Methodist Book Concern, for
    the Author, 1855), p. 169. Motif B563.2.: "Birds
    point out road to hero."
9. Watson, <u>Tales and Takings,</u> p. 242.
10. Wilding, <u>Memories,</u> pp. 27-28.
11. M. M. Henkle, <u>The Life of Henry Biddleman Bascom,</u>
    <u>D.D., LL.D.,</u> Late Bishop of the Methodist Episco-
    pal Church (Louisville: Morton and Griswold, 1854),
    p. 68. See Gavitt, <u>Crumbs,</u> pp. 92-94, for a vari-
    ant: Mary, unrequited admirer of Henry (not Bas-
    com), at once saves his life and wins his attention
    by shooting a panther about to spring upon him.
    Bascom figures in a slightly different version of the
    story which is intended to demonstrate his frontier
    prowess rather than providential deliverance: he
    shoots a panther that has crawled down a tree and
    seized an infant: Buoy, <u>Representative Women,</u> p.
    297.
12. Cotton, <u>Cotton's Sketch-Book</u> (Portland, Maine: B.
    Thurston and Co., 1874), pp. 53-57. Motif R231.:
    "Obstacle flight--Atalanta type."
13. P. Douglass Gorrie, <u>Black River and Northern New</u>
    <u>York Conference Memorial, Second Series</u> (Water-
    town, N.Y.: Charles E. Holbrook, 1881), pp. 164-
    65. Summers, <u>Biographical Sketches,</u> p. 371, for
    itinerant W. Redman's unexplainable deliverance from
    a panther.
14. Erwin, <u>Reminiscences,</u> pp. 301-2.
15. Paddock, <u>Memoir,</u> p. 101. Motif W211.2.: "'I surely
    saw a hundred wolves.'"
16. Henkle, <u>Bascom,</u> pp. 78-79. More remarkable than
    Bascom's deliverance was his meeting with that
    same mountaineer several years later in a Charles-
    ton, West Virginia, church.
17. McNemee, "Brother Mack," pp. 8-9. See Peck, <u>Forty</u>
    <u>Years,</u> pp. 127-28; Cotton, <u>Cotton's Sketch-Book,</u> pp.
    48-49, for two thrilling bear fights, the former fin-

ished with a knife, the latter with a club. See also
Pearne, Sixty-One Years, pp. 215-23, for three ex-
citing Oregon grizzly stories.

18. Paddock, Memoir, p. 108.
19. Williams, Smith, pp. 80-81. The incident may exem-
plify Motif F1088. 2.: "Hero unharmed by serpent
which coils around his waist."
    The belief that providences occur for those
who look for them was voiced by Cotton Mather:
"perhaps the Great Governour of the world will ordinarily do the most notable things for those who are
most ready to take a wise notice of what he does."
The sentiment is echoed in Gaddis, Walker, p. 119.
    For the use of divination to resolve one's vo-
cation, using the Bible as a tool, see Ernest Ashton
Smith, Martin Ruter (New York, Cincinnati: The
Methodist Book Concern, 1915), pp. 12-13. Ruter
opened the Bible and the first passage that met his
eye was "'The Master is come and calleth for thee.'"
His agonized mother, unwilling for him to enter the
hardships of itinerant life, used the same device and
the first words she saw were "'Loose him and let
him go.'" For another divination by bible (biblio-
mancy) see Johnson, Recollection, pp. 130-32.
    Divination by use of the bible is common in
hagiographic legend: Loomis, White Magic, p. 73.
20. Giles, Pioneer, pp. 136-38. Motif D2165.: "Escapes
by magic." See Spottswood, Brief Annals, pp. 133-
34, for the providential arrest of an itinerant's runaway carriage.
21. Gavitt, Crumbs, pp. 204-5. Motif K218. 2.: "Devil
cheated of his victim by boy having a bible under
his arm." See Hood, World of Anecdote, pp. 57,
78-94, for other stories in which the Bible functions
as a charm. The motif is made clearer by a variant account in Cumberland Presbyterian biography,
in which the incident is seen as a thinly veiled manifestation of the conflict between Satanic malignancy
and divine Providence, Anderson and Howard, Memoirs, pp. 10-15.
    Armed banditti, to judge from the literature,
were not uncommon: see Williams, Smith, pp. 41-
44, for an etiological account of the naming of a valley in Kentucky "Harpes' Head" after enraged settlers caught, beheaded, and impaled on a stake the
head of the leader of a family of bandits. Also
Gavitt, Crumbs, pp. 219-36 for an account of the

desperadoes of northern Illinois.
22. Ware, Memoir, pp. 242-48, in fact, voices strong ob-
     jections to the treatment of Indians by white settlers
     and particularly Indian agents who sell alcohol to
     them.
23. See D. Young, Autobiography, pp. 38-44, for a repeat
     of Cotton Mather's escape narrative, MCA, pp. 357-
     61. The Young account identifies the woman as
     Hannah Dustin, the Mather account as Hannah Swar-
     ton. Similarity of the last names suggests oral
     transmission.
          See Peck, "Father Clark," pp. 181-89, for
     the story of the Gilham family's capture in Kentucky,
     1790; Beard, Sketches, pp. 218-27, for the account
     of the capture and murder of Rev. Joseph Brown,
     a Cumberland Presbyterian, and his family, at the
     hands of Indians; L. B. Gurley, Memoir of Rev. Wil-
     liam Gurley, Late of Milan Ohio, A Local Minister
     of the Methodist Episcopal Church: Including a
     Sketch of the Irish Insurrection and Martyrs of 1798
     (Cincinnati: Printed for the Author, at the Metho-
     dist Book Concern, 1858), pp. 233-38, for the mas-
     sacre of the Snow and Putnam families during the
     war of 1812. Also Peckham, Captured by Indians,
     for an anthology and bibliographic guide.
24. Carroll, "Father Corson," pp. 234-35.
25. Carroll, Case, I, 269-70.
26. Ware, Memoir, p. 136. Motif B521.: "Animal warns
     of fatal danger."
27. Taylor, Battlefield, pp. 177-79.
28. Hibbard, Memoirs, pp. 160, 175-76. A similar story,
     told of Jesse Lee in New England, illustrates Lee's
     cheek more than divine providence. Warned of a
     mob on a bridge, he went that way anyhow and made
     them think he was not the man they wanted. D.
     Young, Autobiography, pp. 108-9.
29. Newell, Life, pp. 105-7. Motif F950.: "Miraculous
     cures." For other accounts of providential deliver-
     ances from sickness: Smith, Recollections, p. 168;
     John T. James, Four Years of Methodist Ministry,
     1865-1869 (Staunton, Va.: Stoneburner and Prufer,
     Steam Printers, 1894), pp. 120-21; also Beard,
     Sketches, II, 138-39, for the account of a critically
     ill minister who receives mysterious assurance of
     his recovery at the same time as does his congrega-
     tion praying for him miles away.
30. Marlay, Morris, pp. 44-45: of all the difficulties at-

tending itinerant life, poor pay was the greatest.
31. Ware, Memoir, pp. 213-15, presents an earnest appeal
    for the support of elderly ministers. Fictionalized,
    melodramatic accounts portrayed the sorry circum-
    stances to which the old were driven by the neglect
    and unconcern of the young: Hamilton, Pulpit to
    Poorhouse, pp. 43-58.
32. Williams, Smith, p. 78.
33. Billy Hibbard divided Methodists into two financial
    classes: those who contribute out of sympathy and
    those who give out of principle. Unfortunately, he
    was aware, the former were more numerous. Hib-
    bard, Memoir, pp. 232-34.
        Old Father Clark characterized the parsimoni-
    ous laymen more graphically: "He was discoursing
    on the subject of beneficence, and urging Christians
    to do good with their property in their lifetime, in-
    stead of deferring the matter until death. ... He said
    he knew of but one kind of domestic animal that was
    wholly useless during lifetime. The horse and the
    ox perform very useful labor; the cow yields her
    milk, the sheep her fleece, and the fowls their eggs.
    But the swine is of no use while he lives; he can be
    turned to no account until he is dead!" B. M. Hall,
    The Life of Rev. John Clark (New York: Carlton
    and Porter, 1857), p. 236.
        Some laity called itinerants "spongers," com-
    plaining that they did not work like everyone else for
    their living: Johnson, Recollections, pp. 193-94;
    Woolsey, Supernumerary, p. 52.
        More hardy itinerants castigated the carping
    of their fellows about pay, saying that bad preachers
    deserve bad pay: Richardson, Autobiography, p. 15.
    One proud soul denounced preferential treatment given
    to clergy: "this idea of playing the dead beat be-
    cause I was a Methodist preacher was not pleasant
    to me." McNemee, "Brother Mack," pp. 17-18.
        Frontier itinerants of all denominations suf-
    fered the same poverty. One Cumberland Presby-
    terian rider, who received a new shirt collar from
    his charges as payment for six months' work, "shook
    the dust of the red hills of St. Charles from his feet,
    and never returned." R. C. Ewing, Historical Mem-
    oirs; containing a Brief History of the Cumberland
    Presbyterian Church in Missouri, and Biographical
    Sketches of a Number of Those Ministers Who Con-
    tributed to the Organization and the Establishment of

That Church, in the Country West of the Mississippi
River (Nashville: Cumberland Presbyterian Board of
Publication, 1874), pp. 118-19.
34. Williams, Smith, pp. 78-80.
35. Finney, Marvin, pp. 222-23; also Smith, Pierce, pp.
    90-91, 141-42.
36. Morrison, Autobiography, p. 41. Brewer, Dictionary,
    p. 398: "God will provide"; as an hagiographical in-
    stance: "St. Mayeul, abbot of Cluny, finds a purse
    of money when reduced to great extremities."
37. Sullins, Recollections, pp. 102-7. Another destitute cir-
    cuit rider, after receiving unexpectedly twenty dol-
    lars from an unknown widow, remarked: "That min-
    ister who cannot trust God is surely very unbeliev-
    ing." Summers, Biographical Sketches, p. 237.
38. Hibbard, Memoirs, pp. 220-21. Motif Q22.: "Reward
    for faith." The faithful were encouraged by such
    stories to trust God. One destitute widow found a
    "ball of wet, dirty paper on the pavement, which,
    when unrolled, was a five dollar bill." Spottswood,
    Brief Annals, pp. 5-6.
39. Ware, Memoir, pp. 162-63.
40. Marlay, Morris, pp. 51-52. Brewer, Dictionary, p.
    471: "Wants supplied"; for a hagiographical example:
    "St. Dominic, wanting to cross a ferry, finds the
    fare at his feet."
          See Taylor, Autobiography, p. 60, for a provi-
    dentially furnished berth on a California-bound clip-
    per.
41. Summers, Biographical Sketches, p. 61. Motif F962.
    11.: "Extraordinary snowfall."
42. New Jersey Conference Memorial, pp. 360-61. Brewer,
    Dictionary, p. 126; "Elijah fed by Ravens"; as an
    hagiographical instance: ibid., p. 127: "Brother
    Giles miraculously supplied with food."
43. Manship, Thirteen Years', pp. 190-92. Motif D1652.
    18.: "Inexhaustible article." Brewer, Dictionary,
    p. 418: "Lending to the Lord"; for an hagiographical
    instance, ibid.; "Putting the text to the test."
44. New Jersey Conference Memorial, pp. 232-33. Brew-
    er, Dictionary, p. 381: "Charity brings its own
    Reward."
45. Wightman, Capers, pp. 336-38. Brewer, Dictionary,
    p. 61: "Christ identifies Himself with His Disciples
    and with Objects of Charity"; for an hagiographical
    example, ibid., p. 62: "St. John of St. Facond
    gives the best of his coats to a beggar."

46. Green, Life, p. 94. Motif Q1.: "Hospitality rewarded --opposite punished"; Q42.3.: "Generosity to saint rewarded." Brewer, Dictionary, p. 8: "Angel entertained unawares."
47. Green, Life, p. 93. Motif D2157.2.1.: "Magic growth of saint's crops."
48. Burgess, Pleasant Recollections, pp. 336-37. Motif Q552.1.0.1.: "Destruction of property by thunderbolt as punishment." Cotton Mather tells the story of townspeople who, refusing to compensate their ministers adequately, lost their cattle as punishment: MCA, p. 392.
49. Spottswood, Brief Annals, pp. 107-8. Motif D1652.18.: "Inexhaustible article." Brewer, Dictionary, p. 67: "Consumed but not diminished"; also Loomis, White Magic, p. 87.
50. Green, Life, p. 347. Motif V541.: "Man is prevented from taking passage on ship which later sinks." See Hood, World of Anecdote, p. 323, for a story with the "sinking ship" motif. There are many other examples of the story in British Methodist biography.
51. New Jersey Conference Memorial, pp. 63-66. Motif K606.: "Escape by singing song."

Rev. J. B. McFerrin, M. D.
One of the stalwarts of the M. E. Church, South

Chapter 5

REMARKABLE ENCOUNTERS

The mobility of both preachers and people on the frontier diminished the possibilities for lasting spiritual relationships and at the same time heightened the opportunities for chance encounters. Biographers recognized these encounters as providentially arranged opportunities for a wandering, pilgrim church to gain a foretaste of heavenly communion. In addition, the revelation to a preacher that previous work in the vineyard had borne unexpected fruit afforded him powerful encouragement and reinforced his belief in the workings of providence, and as well allowing the beneficiary of that labor an occasion to relive the constitutive event of his spiritual life.

Preacher Meets Person He Converted Years Before

John B. McFerrin, a famous Tennessee Methodist preacher, met in his last year of life an old Methodist lady who told him she was converted while he was singing a hymn at a camp meeting fifty years before. "'I remember,' she said, 'the hour, the words of the song, and the tune.'" According to McFerrin's biographer, "it was a rare thing for him to preach anywhere in Tennessee without some occurrence of the kind." Many preachers, in fact, claimed him as their spiritual father. Such memories of the triumph of grace

> were grateful reminders along all the pathway of
> threescore years and more, and the echoes were
> like the notes of a prolonged strain of music. It
> is a blessed thing now in this life, and typical of
> the fuller blessedness of the life to come, that the
> discords drop out of the memory and only the music
> remains. From the unhindered operation of this
> law will come the perfect concord and unbroken
> blessedness of the heavenly world. [1]

Another touching narration recounts how McFerrin met
in Indian Territory a Cherokee woman he had converted in
Alabama. Bishop McTyeire, who witnessed the reunion, comments that the meeting " 'made one think of that day, and of
the joy with which a saved spirit will recognize a benefactor
long lost sight of, but not forgotten. ' "2

Preacher Meets Child He Unknowingly
Converted or Influenced

One itinerant advised his colleagues to write down the
names of the children in homes along the circuit and to call
the minors by their proper names, rather than " 'bud' " and
" 'sissy. ' " This helped him

> to get hold of the children, and get them to like me;
> and when I had got hold of the children, I always
> found that I had the parents too. 3

Another circuit rider indicates that attention to his
hosts' children was the rule rather than the exception: "it
was useless for the minister to expect the friendship and appreciation of the hostess, unless he paid some attention to
the children, and gave his opinion as to their future prospects. "4 To judge by stories of remarkable encounters, such
attentions by itinerants, whether learned or expected, sowed
a good crop for later reaping.

One account tells how a gentleman approached an itinerant on the train, and, after questioning, confirmed his suspicion that the preacher was the man who had influenced him
as a child:

> You use to lay your hand on my shoulder, and talk
> to me so kindly about being a good and useful boy,
> to grow up a good man, and about making my mark
> high in life. . . .

Thrilled with the revelation of his previous usefulness, the
minister exclaims as a commentary on the event: "Will not
Jesus place their salvation as stars in my crown of endless
rejoicing?"5

A variant recounts how the eminent British Methodist,
Thomas Coke, on one of his visits to America, stopped at a

frontier cabin for warmth and food, and left a religious tract
with the hospitable widow and her sons. Five years later, on
another visit, traveling to conference with a group of preachers, Coke met a young man who revealed to him that that
single tract had been the instrument of his own and others'
conversion, and that now he, too, was an itinerant with saddlebags full of tracts. Obviously an exhortation to preachers
toward a particular pastoral duty, the anecdote illustrates as
well the truth of the Scripture which introduces the narrative
in the text: "'Cast thy bread upon the waters, for thou shall
find it after many days.'"[6]

Preacher Meets Hospitable Person Years Later

A subsidiary lesson of remarkable encounter stories
was the duty of hospitality, a charity long enjoined in Christian tradition under the idea that supernatural beings sometimes visit as strangers to test the generosity of hosts.

Henry Bascom, in a story already noted, tells the
story of meeting years later a man whose cabin had once
saved him from a pursuing pack of wolves.[7] In another story,
Bascom, pursued by Indians and "mailed in ice" from a dip
in a stream, found lodging at a cabin on the Mad River.
After warming himself and eating, he sank into a deep sleep,
only to be aroused at the impending "accouchement" of the
woman of the house. Years later, a "genteel young lady"
approached him and apologized "for causing him the loss of
a night's rest when he needed it." She then introduced herself to the puzzled Bascom as the newborn infant who had
been the occasion for Bascom's displacement many years before.[8]

Notes

1. Fitzgerald, McFerrin, p. 322. Motif N710.: "Acciden-
   tal encounters."
2. Ibid., pp. 322, 335. Note also the mention of the incident in McFerrin's funeral sermon, p. 443. See also
   Taylor, Autobiography, pp. 66-67.
3. Nash, Recollections, p. 50.
4. Gavitt, Crumbs, pp. 65-66. Gavitt found this aspect of
   itinerant life "most embarrassing." To "examine their
   heads" and pronounce upon their future vocation, then

to kiss them before bed was more than he could com-
fortably manage when more often than not the children
were "fearfully dirty." Motif V223.6.: "Saint as
prognosticator."

5. Burgess, Pleasant Recollections, pp. 128-29.
6. Peck, Sketches, pp. 127-30. Brewer, Dictionary, p.
    380: "Cast thy bread on the waters."
            For parallels: Stanley, Stateler, pp. 101-3;
    Smith, Recollections, pp. 333-34; Robison, Clawson,
    pp. 31-33; Elbert Osborn, Autobiography of Elbert
    Osborn, An Itinerant Minister of the Methodist Epis-
    copal Church (New York: Published for the Author,
    1868), p. 75.
7. Henkle, Bascom, pp. 78-79.
8. Ibid., pp. 88-92. Motif Q1.1.: "Gods (saints) in dis-
    guise reward hospitality and punish inhospitality."
    Brewer, Dictionary, p. 8: "Angels entertained un-
    awares."

Chapter 6

REMARKABLE PROVIDENCES EFFECTED
BY PRAYER

Providences stimulated by the prayers of Methodist preachers include special intelligence, exorcisms, spiritual benefits, and deliverances from financial difficulty, sickness, danger, and the elements. The prayers themselves do not constitute a providence, according to the literature, but they are everywhere regarded as precipitants of divine intervention.

The vigor and effectiveness of Methodist preachers' prayers was legendary. One circuit rider who requested lodging at the home of an old Methodist layman had to pray in the parlor to establish his authenticity before the old man would accept him.[1] Another itinerant, "old Father Henry Bray," established a reputation "for having his prayers answered." Evil-doers feared him, because

> it is said, he would pray for the death of incorrigi-
> ble [sic] sinners who would not quit their sins,
> and come to Christ, and the Lord would answer his
> prayers, and take them away.[2]

Another preacher testified that, while praying with colleagues privately, "a light appeared above my head."[3]

Other anecdotes extolled the spontaneity of Methodist prayer as contrasted with the formalism of some other denominations' prayers. During a cholera epidemic at a frontier fort, the Episcopalian chaplain could find no prayer in his Book suited to the occasion, and had to send to his Bishop for one. By the time the authorized prayer arrived, the epidemic had passed and the prayer, "like a 'last year's almanac,' ... was out of date."[4]

155

Prayer Gives Preacher Special Intelligence

The newspapers reported the death of John B. McFerrin, who had long been critically ill.   When McFerrin's
friend, Bishop Pierce, heard the report, he asserted, "'There
must be some mistake....'"   Entering his study, he shut and
locked the door, and "knelt in prayer before God." When he
emerged, "his face wore the peculiar radiance that many have
seen upon it when he was fully under the divine afflatus in
the pulpit." His wife showed him the "particulars" of Mc-
Ferrin's death in the Atlanta newspaper.   But Pierce/was
adamant: "'There must be some mistake; he is not dead.
I have prayed and gotten the answer.'"

Subsequent reports proved his assertion correct.   Mc-
Ferrin's biographer comments that God does not always grant
"direct and literal bestowment of the thing asked for in inter-
cessory supplication," but that "it does come in conscious
benediction to the trusting soul." Those who live "close to
God" can expect experiences "like this of Bishop Pierce," if
their prayers "are the breathings of unselfish desire and unwavering faith."[5]

Prayer Brings Domestic Relief

A widow who divided her last loaf of bread among her
children and sent them to bed with no prospect of food for
breakfast prayed all night "that if the little sparrows 'were
not forgotten before him, that he would remember the widow
and the orphan in this the hour of their extremity.'"   At
sunrise an ordinarily "penurious" neighbor arrived, profess-
ing to have been troubled all night over her welfare.   When
he heard the family's want, he generously supplied all their
needs. [6]

During the war of 1812, a fisherman whose waters
were patrolled by British ships could not earn enough to satisfy his creditors.   He prayed to God for help, and soon found
a small whale stranded on the beach by the tide. [7]

In a third variant of the theme, a circuit rider's corn
needed plowing just as he was about to leave for a round of
appointments.   He prayed for help, and had just risen from
his knees when a man knocked at the door, desiring to buy
corn.   In exchange for the corn the man agreed to do the
preacher's plowing. [8]

Prayer Relieves Sickness

Solomon Sharp, a Methodist preacher otherwise known
as the "devil-driver" for his alleged powers of exorcism, had
a reputation for exerting awesome influence on the deity
through his prayers. Some thought "'he was so familiar with
the Almighty that he took great liberties with him.'" On one
occasion Sharp entered the room of a man "'given up to die'"
and prayed:

> 'Lord, thou canst do without him. Thou hast many
> about thy throne to do thee honor. We have too
> few such as we need. This is one of those that we
> want here for thy work.'

Then Sharp "'importuned,'" that is, he "'took hold of God's
strength.'" The man recovered, the people said, because
Sharp's prayers would not let him die. [9]

In other accounts, preachers' prayers reportedly cured
men dying of fever or "winter-fever"[10] as well as men or
women dying of unspecified illnesses. [11] One man's death
was delayed until morning by a preacher's prayer. [12] An old
woman, it is reported, was cured of crippling rheumatism by
the communal prayer of a congregation. [13] The prayers of
the attending doctor's mother, some distance away, reportedly cured a Methodist preacher of a severe sore throat. [14]

Usually, in these stories, the cure occurs after a doctor has pronounced the case hopeless. Anecdotes in which
the prayers of the doctor's mother does what the doctor himself cannot do, or in which a doctor himself is cured by
prayer, [15] exhibit not only antipathy to medical science (and,
by extension, rationalism) but also an insistence on the prim-
acy of spiritual reality over matter. [16] One prayer-healing
narrative admonishes people to call the preacher at the same
time as they call the doctor, rather than to fall upon the
minister only when the patient is in extremis. [17] The power
of prayer over sickness is emphasized by a Cumberland Presbyterian account:

> Perhaps our cold-hearted skepticism will revolt at
> these accounts. I have nothing to say in relation
> to them, except that they seem very well authenti-
> cated. I am writing history, and not attempting to
> explain all the methods of God's providence in his
> dealings with good men. But, in conflict with all

our skepticism, what does the apostle say: "Is any
sick among you?   Let him call for the elders of
the Church, and let them pray over him, anointing
him with oil in the name of the Lord; and the prayer
of faith shall save the sick, and the Lord shall
raise him up; and if he have committed sins, they
shall be forgiven him. 18

Prayer Saves Preacher from Danger

1.   Prayer helps preacher find path.   Bishop Henry
Clay Morrison tells of his deliverance in the woods by prayer
in order to teach Methodist ministers to "pray in the common affairs of life."   In this story Morrison, having lost the
trail on a dark night, knelt and prayed for deliverance, then
arose and found the path. 19

2.   Mother's prayer saves preacher crossing stream.
William Raper, according to this story, fell from his horse
into a cold stream he was crossing.   While struggling to
swim in heavy clothing, "the thought rushed upon him, 'My
mother is praying for me, and I shall be saved.'"   After he
had clambered onto the opposite bank and dried his clothing
and saddlebags, he went on his way.   Later conversations
revealed that, at the precise moment of his danger, his
mother awoke from her sleep, and "the thought rushed upon
her, 'William is in great danger....'"   When she had prayed
for him for some time, "in intense supplication for his safety," she "received a sweet assurance that all was well."20

3.   Preacher, threatened by toughs, prays for rain
to disperse them.   Rowdies, according to an account, threatened to disrupt the last day of a camp meeting.   Dr. Jacoby,
a German Methodist preacher, asked God to "send the rain
in such quantities that his enemies might be defeated," even
though, the narrator continues, no rain had fallen for weeks
and no sign of rain was visible on the horizon.   At six
o'clock a storm suddenly loomed in the sky, and moments
later dumped great quantities of rain on the camp-ground,
dispersing the rowdies.   So much rain fell, in fact, that an
old lady remarked, "'Rain was a very good thing, but these
Methodists are always overdoing matters.'"21

Preacher's Prayer Influences Elements

1. <u>Prayer brings needed rain.</u> During a drought, according to one account, the people met with Brother Needham to pray for rain. After the opening services concluded, Needham made "some remarks" about the subject, while the doubters mumbled that there were no signs of rain. The itinerant fell to his knees and prayed with great earnestness. While he prayed it thundered, and he arose to tell the people "to hurry to their homes, or they would be caught in the rain." "On that day," comments the biographers, "some who had been skeptical as to the efficacy of prayer learned to believe that God hears and answers prayer."22

A variation of this story in Cumberland Presbyterian biography has the Governor of Kentucky calling for a day of "fasting, humiliation, and prayer" to relieve a terrible drought. The appointed day coincided with a camp meeting held at Mt. Gilead, Montgomery County, Kentucky. "The people fasted and prayed, and in the forenoon of the day the rain began to fall." All felt that the rain answered their prayer; it was a "fine occasion" notes the biographer

> for showing off the folly of <u>the fool</u> who would pretend that such a coincidence as they had witnessed was a mere casualty, ignoring the interposition of a wise and good Providence who hears and answers prayer. 23

2. <u>Prayer delivers camp meeting from approaching thunderstorm.</u> In one variation of this story, after the preacher prays that the storm be stayed, the clouds split around the camp-meeting ground and pass by:

> It is said that during his eldership [John Berryman] on the Knoxville District, at a camp-meeting held near Canton, whilst William Clark was preaching with marked effect, a storm was about to break forth in wild fury. Some arose to go as the rain began to fall. Elder Berryman arose, walked to the front of the pulpit, threw his hands heavenward, and said, 'My Lord, stay the storm!' told the people to be seated, and the cloud parted and passed on each side of the encampment. 24

Another version of the story has the preacher delay the storm until the preaching was finished. On two separate

Rev. Charles Pitman

occasions Rev. Charles Pitman allegedly halted a storm, once
in Delaware and once in New Jersey, until his preaching was
finished. [25] In the account of the New Jersey miracle, the
biographer perceives the storm as symbolic of the baptismal
flood as well as an instrument of even more remarkable providence:

> the thunders were pent-up, and the word of the
> Lord had freed course and was glorified. And
> closing the services, he [Pitman] shouted: 'To your
> tents, O Israel! to your tents, O Israel! for the
> Lord's message having been delivered, and our
> prayers having been answered, the rain will now
> descend from the clouds!' And the people, obeying
> the voice of the preacher, fled to their tents for
> further worship, 'and the rain descended and the
> floods came, ' and a spiritual baptism of converting
> power came with them; and as an estimate of God's
> great power, over five hundred souls were con-
> verted. [26]

A third version of the story has the preacher mysteriously predicting that a threatening storm will not strike until
the camp meeting is concluded. In both examples of this version the people regard the power of the minister as responsible for the deliverance. [27]

In another version of the story the itinerant actually
calms the storm beating upon the roof of a tiny country
church: "The winds suddenly died away, till not a breath
stirred the leaves. "[28]

3.   Preacher stays rain until crops are gathered.
The narrator of the following story witnesses to old James
Moore's power over the elements when the farmer and his
workers were gathering hay in a field as a thunderstorm approached. They were struggling with the last load when they
saw the downpour advance to within a few hundred yards of
the wagon. Orders were given for a retreat into the barn,
but Moore, who had been watching from the farm house, came
out on the porch, lifted his hands to the sky and prayed that
the storm be delayed. His prayer was heard, and the workers secured the last load of hay. The narrator remembers
a peculiar circumstance of the deliverance:

> the rain came up even with the fence that bounded
> the field where they were at work, where it poured

in torrents, but over which it did not cross until
they had finished gathering the hay, and then, as
soon as they were all sheltered in the house or
barn, it came down over all the farm with tempes-
tuous fury. 29

4.   Preacher's prayer disperses gloomy weather.   In
this story rainy weather endangered the progress of three
preachers to a revival.   Father John Clark prayed that travel
conditions be improved for them.   Overnight the weather
changed to balmy sunshine.   God, says the narrator, not
nature, controls the world:

> We leave it to that class of speculatists, who fancy
> that the Almighty does not concern himself with hu-
> man affairs, to explain the philosophy of this sud-
> den and unexpected change.   Doubtless they can
> solve the mystery by referring to an occult female,
> without either intelligence, goodness or power,
> called NATURE, but whose LAWS every change is
> produced.   Their progenitors lived about 3, 680
> years ago, and in their superabundant wisdom ex-
> claimed, 'What is the Almighty we should serve
> him; and what profit should we have if we pray un-
> to him.' (Job xxi:15)30

5.   Preacher's prayer controls wind.   One biographer,
attempting to illustrate the power of prayer in the life of his
subject, asserts that "he who looks for answer to prayers,
will often have the pleasure of witnessing their striking fulfillment of accomplishment."   His own search for providential
answers to prayers leads him to a Wesley anecdote narrated
in the Life of Dr. Adam Clarke.   In this episode Wesley, on
a ship tacking unsuccessfully against unfavorable winds,
prayed with fellow ministers for a change in the wind.   Wesley, says the quoted author, was so used to such answer
"that he took for granted he was heard," and did not even
bother to go up on deck to see that the wind had actually
shifted.   But, continues the narrator, "Mr. Wesley was no
ordinary man ... and it is not to be wondered at that he
was favored, and, indeed, accredited with many very signal
interpositions of Divine providence."31

Prayer Brings Spiritual Benefits

1.   Prayer precipitates conversion of evildoer.   In

this story two drunkard brothers and their wives (who were
sisters) attended a meeting at which a minister preached
from the text: "'She hath done what she could' (Mark xiv,
8)." The gist of the sermon was that a good beginning is
not always a good ending, and that perseverance alone insures
a useful religious life. The brothers and their wives returned
home, and that night the two sisters

> concluded that they had not done all they could for
> the conversion of their husbands, and renewed their
> covenant that they would pray for them every day
> as long as they lived, and they would commence
> that very night, and plead with God as they had
> never before.

At midnight one of the brothers got up, prayed with his wife,
and "found peace in believing." The couple went to the other
pair's home, "with the hope of encouraging them," and met
them on the road, "coming with the same delightful intelligence," namely, that the other drunkard brother had been
converted around midnight. [32]

2. <u>Prayer brings preacher proof of his vocation.</u>
The prayer for a sign to validate a vocation resembles thematically a previously noted story in which a man attempts
divination by providence. In this case, however, the providence is granted not by chance but in response to a specific
request in prayer.

The Rev. George Walker, who was doubting his call
to the ministry, prayed that God would convert a soul at the
meeting of the "'band society'" over which he presided. Inasmuch as "no one was permitted to be present [at this meet-
ing] that did not enjoy religion" it was difficult to see how
God could respond to his request for a sign. Yet Walker
felt

> 'that it would be much more easy for the Lord to
> bring a sinner to the meeting-place of their little
> 'band,' and to convert him, also, than to make a
> minister out of such a poor worm as he felt him-
> self to be.'

The meeting had almost concluded, without any sign, and
Walker's discomfort grew. Then "there was a rap on the
church-door." Two young men entered, apologized for disturbing the meeting, and begged the assembled group to help

them find peace. Walker was overwhelmcd and regarded the
appearance of the two young men as the providentially granted
sign for which he had prayed.[33]

3. Prayer humbles evil-doer. At a meeting, according
to the story, a "wild and reckless young man" named Joe
Brouse "was attempting to turn into mockery and derision the
solemnities of divine worship." William Losee, the preacher,
"lifted his eyes and hands to heaven and called upon God to
"smite" Brouse. The young man " 'fell like a bullock under
the stroke of the butcher's ax and writhed on the floor in
agony until the Lord in mercy set his soul at liberty. ' "34

Exorcisms by Prayer

The sources reveal that many Methodist preachers saw
the devil really lurking at the fringes of religious experience,
just as many ordinary people, religious or not, believed in
the close presence of malevolent powers. The devil walked
in Methodist dreams,[35] possessed dogs,[36] tormented souls
in the throes of conversion,[37] and danced with expectant glee
at the beds of dying infidels.[38] Peter Cartwright scorned
Universalist opponents who would reduce the devil to an evil
disposition in man and hell to guilt.[39] In some extraordinary
circumstances, therefore, it was deemed necessary to employ
the power over demons accorded to God's servants in the Gospel accounts.

Solomon Sharp, known "all over the island and county
as 'Solomon Sharp, the devil driver,' " believed that he had
exorcised a young woman and had actually seen the devil walking out the door. Two independent witnesses confirmed the
incident but did not tell the biographer that they saw the devil.
Sharp's reputation rested on his own assertions that he saw
the devil, and the account, while it does not question the assertion, makes this point clear: "He never wavered in his
belief that this was a case of demoniacal possession, or that
God gave him power on that occasion to carry out the command, 'Cast out devils. ' "40

The invocation of Biblical authority for exorcism is
apparent in another incident:

> Yes, in that Tent meeting, the devil seemed to
> throw him [an old Captain] down and tear him, and

he foamed at the mouth, and speaking as one having authority, and not as the scribes, Rev. William
Connelly said, apparently addressing the devil, 'I
command you to come out of him. ' 'And devils
were subject to them. ' The devil was literally cast
out. '41

Summary

The stories above illustrate the belief that prayers are
answered not just metaphorically, but literally, if uttered in
faith and humility. Such dispositions, while theoretically ac-
cessible to all Christians, seem to be restricted, in the literature, to persons with reputations for holiness, often elderly persons. These persons seemingly are familiar enough
with God, as were Moses and hundreds of hagiographical
figures after him, to call upon God publicly with enough confidence to know that they will not be humiliated. Prayer
stories expressed and propagated the view that a providential
God, not scientifically deduced laws of medicine or nature,
controlled events, and that this providential God was susceptible to the holy desires of his saints.

The different versions of the prayer stories, especially those dealing with thunderstorms, indicate that such anecdotes must have been discussed and passed around among
preachers and people and that from this oral circulation they
passed into the biographies and autobiographies of holy figures.

Notes

1. Scarlett, Itinerant, pp. 233-35. Motif H1508. : "Test:
   long praying. "
2. Nash, Recollections, pp. 14-15.
3. Carroll, Case, II, 477-78. Motif V222. 1. : "Marvelous
   light accompanying saint. "
4. Hall, John Clark, pp. 73-74.
5. Fitzgerald, McFerrin, pp. 401-3. Motif V223. : "Saints
   have miraculous knowledge. "
6. Taylor, Battlefield, pp. 112-13. Motif D2105. 1. : "Provisions provided in answer to prayer"; D1030. 1. 1. :
   "Food supplied by means of prayers. " Brewer, Dictionary, p. 354: "Ask, and ye shall receive"; p. 126:

"Elijah fed by ravens. "

    The story above is similar in structure to the one in New Jersey Conference Memorial, pp. 360-61, in which the distress of the woman is relieved by a stingy neighbor troubled during the night.

7. Newell, Life, pp. 175-76. Motif V52.4.: "Objects supplied through prayer. "

8. Bird, Chapman, p. 171. Motif V52.: "Miraculous power of prayer. "

9. John Alexander Roche, Autobiography and Sermons Together with the Expressions Elicited by his Death, compiled by his children (n. p.: Printed by Eaton and Mains, n. d.), pp. 41-42. Motif E121.5.2.: "Resuscitation through prayers of holy man. " Mather gives an account of prayers saving a dying child's life, MCA, pp. 441-42.

10. Rogers, Needham, p. 19; Beard, Sketches, II, 138-39.

11. Summers, Biographical Sketches, pp. 194-95; Rogers, Needham, p. 19; Gavitt, Crumbs, pp. 173-74; Robison, Clawson, pp. 172-73.

12. Erwin, Reminiscences, pp. 344-45. See also Bird, Chapman, p. 186.

13. Robison, Clawson, pp. 146-47.

14. Spottswood, Brief Annals, pp. 68-69.

15. Ibid.; Robison, Clawson, p. 172.

16. Gavitt, Crumbs, pp. 173-74.

17. Erwin, Reminiscences, pp. 344-45.

18. Beard, Sketches, II, 139.

19. Morrison, Autobiography, pp. 89-90.

20. Coles, Heroines, p. 71.

21. Taylor, Battlefield, pp. 72-73. Motif D2143.1.3.: "Rain produced by prayer. "

22. Rogers, Needham, p. 20. Motif D2143.1.3.: "Rain produced by prayer. " Brewer, Dictionary, p. 129: "Elijah makes Rain to cease and to fall"; ibid.: "St. Bont, Bishop of Clermont, intercedes for rain. It comes so that the congregation cannot leave church. Also Loomis, White Magic, p. 39.

23. Beard, Sketches, II, 294. Another version of the same incident is found in Anderson and Howard, Memoirs, pp. 33-35.

24. Fleharty, Phelps, pp. 151-52. Motif D1841.4.4.: "Rain or snow avoids certain places according to the desire of a saint or monk. " D2147.: "Magic control of clouds. " See Brewer, Dictionary, p. 443: "Rain Etc., obedient to the Saints"; ibid.: "St. Antony of Padua, preaching, commanded the rain not

to molest his congregation. " Also Loomis, White
Magic, p. 39, for a similar incident recorded of St.
John of Capistrano.
      See Beard, Sketches, pp. 16-17, for the ac-
count of James McGready making the clouds separate
around a camp meeting.

25. C. A. Malmsbury, The Life, Labors, and Sermons of
    Rev. Charles Pitman, D. D., of the New Jersey Con-
    ference (Philadelphia: Methodist Episcopal Book
    Room, 1887), pp. 105-7, 203-4. These incidents
    are also recorded, with verification, in New Jersey
    Conference Memorial, pp. 255-61. Motif D2140.1.1.:
    "Saint has power to control winds and storms at will. "

26. Malmsbury, Pitman, p. 204. Similar powers were at-
    tributed to Cumberland Presbyterian ministers: Alex-
    ander Chapman allegedly stayed a storm until the
    end of the camp meeting: "The cloud stood still as
    with the roaring of a great cataract, from about 3
    o'clock P. M. until near sunset. " Bird, Chapman,
    pp. 190-1.

27. Ware, Memoir, p. 229; Cotton, Sketch-Book, pp. 17-18.
    Motif V223. 6. 1.: "Saint can foretell weather. "

28. Charles Sims, The Life of Rev. Thomas M. Eddy (New
    York: Phillips and Hunt, 1880), p. 165. Motif
    D2140. 1. 1.: "Saint has power to control winds and
    storms at will. " Brewer, Dictionary, p. 441: "St.
    Bont stills a tempest by prayer. "

29. New Jersey Conference Memorial, pp. 69-70. Motif
    D1841. 4. 4.: "Rain or snow avoids certain places
    according to the desire of a saint or monk. " Brew-
    er, Dictionary, p. 443: "Rain Etc., obedient to the
    Saints"; ibid., p. 444: "St. Genevieve commands
    rain not to fall on a field under reapers. "

30. Peck, "Father Clark, " pp. 275-78. Motif D2140. 1.:
    "Control of weather by saint's prayers. " See Loom-
    is, White Magic, p. 45, for a similar occurrence.

31. Gaddis, Walker, pp. 123-26.

32. Gavitt, Crumbs, pp. 101-2; also Vansant, Sunset, p.
    29; Gaddis, Walker, pp. 126-28.

33. Gaddis, Walker, pp. 121-22.

34. W. H. Withrow, Barbara Heck: A Tale of Early Meth-
    odism (Toronto: William Briggs, 1895), pp. 155-56.

35. J. Young, Autobiography, pp. 46-47.

36. Manship, Thirteen Years', pp. 32-33.

37. Cartwright, Autobiography, p. 37.

38. Ffirth, Abbott, p. 89.

39. Cartwright, Autobiography, pp. 258-59, 293ff.

40. Manship, Thirteen Years', pp. 50-51. Motif G303. 16.
     11. 4. : "Saint expels devil to hell. " Brewer, Dic-
     tionary, p. 100: "Devils cast out. "
41. Andrew Manship, History of Gospel Tents and Experi-
     ence (Philadelphia: Published by the Author, 1884),
     p. 16. Motif D2176. 3. 4. : "Devil cast out of man
     possessed. " See also Carroll, Case, I, 39, for the
     story of an itinerant exorcising a possessed woman
     spitting in his face. Taylor, Battlefield, pp. 152-53,
     for an account of an itinerant exorcising with a Bible
     the devils that a drunkard sees in his room.

Chapter 7

CLAIRVOYANCE

In certain narrations a person reportedly knows the occurrence of an event at a distance without any physical communication of the knowledge. Frequently, the providentially-inspired knowledge concerns the fate of a loved one.

Sometimes the knowledge concerns death. For instance, one young man told his mother that his father had drowned crossing the Ohio River. The next morning his statement was verified.[1] The wife of a preacher knew in North Carolina that her husband had died in St. Louis at Conference.[2]

Sometimes the awareness has to do with the sickness or danger of a loved one. William Raper's mother leapt from her bed and prayed for him at the moment he was foundering in a stream.[3] A Methodist itinerant believed that his sudden cure from a bad sore throat occurred just when the mother of the attending doctor prayed for him.[4] An itinerant who awoke at night with the feeling that he should hurry home arrived to find his father terminally ill.[5]

In another account, a brother and sister dreamt simultaneously, though not with the same imagery, that a revival would soon take place.[6] A Methodist preacher, in another narration, heard angels carrying away a saintly old itinerant's spirit just at the moment he died a few doors away.[7] In a Cumberland Presbyterian biography, Rev. William Harris, critically ill, received assurance that he would live at the same time as his congregation, praying for him miles away, received similar assurance.[8]

Notes

1. Smith, Recollections, pp. 66-67. Brewer, Dictionary, p. 253: "Post-prophetic intuition and second sight"; ibid., p. 254: "St. Hermeland knows of the death of

St. Maurontus, though it occurred sixty miles away. "
Cotton Mather records several instances of knowledge
of death at a distance, MCA, pp. 468-71.

2. Nash, Recollections, pp. 27-28.
3. Coles, Heroines, p. 71.
4. Spottswood, Brief Annals, pp. 68-69.
5. Morrison, Autobiography, p. 88.
6. Woolsey, Supernumerary, pp. 16-17.
7. New Jersey Conference Memorial, p. 234.
8. Beard, Sketches, II, 138-39.

Chapter 8

CONCLUSION TO PART II

Remarkable Providences, the Bible, and Folklore

Well into the nineteenth century in America, men such as the Methodist itinerants and their chroniclers believed that events were transparent to divine providence in such a way that God could interpose and alter the course of things. While such providential direction had to do with the moral life of man, the belief that providence could and often did manipulate or dispense with natural agencies suggests that it extended as well to the natural order. Such belief indicates that the light of the eighteenth century Enlightenment had not substantially affected the rank and file of Methodist preachers of the nineteenth century, and even less the people to whom they preached. The assessment of various religious revivals and of the spread of evangelical tradition in general may depend as much, therefore, upon an understanding of the beliefs represented in such stories as upon environmental, social, psychological, or other factors.

Ralph Henry Gabriel reinforces the point when he writes that "the twentieth century student is often astonished at the extent to which supernaturalism permeated American thought of the nineteenth century."[1] Such supernaturalism assumed not only esoteric forms, such as spiritualism, rapping, and phrenology,[2] but also recapitulated traditional forms such as those found in the Bible.

Perry Miller points to the permeation of early nineteenth century culture by the Old Testament:

> The Old Testament is so truly omnipresent in the American culture of 1800 or 1820 that historians have as much difficulty taking cognizance of it as of the air people breathed.[3]

While it is not the purpose here to assign the reason for the

171

extension of belief in remarkable providences into the nineteenth century, it is suggested that supernaturalism and the
permeation of the American mind by biblical categories may
be mutually related. The mass of the people, including many
Methodist preachers, were accustomed to accepting Scripture
at face value. Because the Bible said that dreams were
sometimes of divine origin, because it told how God smote
the wicked and aided the downtrodden, because scripture said
that prayers would be literally answered, because, ultimately,
God was concerned with every hair of man's head, the phenomena of this world were mere tools for his purposes. People could easily assimilate remarkable providence stories into the biblical frame of reference. Thus, while the new science may have forced Cotton Mather and other highly educated persons to plant a foot in the Age of Reason, it had
little effect on the people and their understanding of the Bible.

Moreover, biblical supernaturalism may have been
taken by people as a carte blanche for more esoteric forms
of supernaturalism, such as those suggested in Tyler (see
note 2). Mac E. Barrick, a folklorist, has suggested that
a similar validation occurs between the bible and folk superstition. The fundamentalist, argues Barrick, believing that
God is deeply concerned with the intimate affairs of daily
life, may believe that other supernatural forces as well may
be controlled or influenced. Often such a person seeks biblical foundations for his superstitious beliefs. The process
of transferring religious authority to folk belief is essentially the process which the Introduction of this work denotes as
"folk religion. "[4]

The fascinating possibility that the animistic, supernaturalistic, fatalistic cosmos tacitly assumed by folk beliefs, ballads, and legends prepared for religion can only be
suggested here. [5] Such a situation would reverse the procedure outlined above, in which biblical supernaturalism validates folk belief. Rather, in the latter case, folk belief
would be regarded as validating religion. Many commentators note the religious vacuum existent on the American
frontier before the Second Great Awakening. It may well be
that the wildfire spread of religious conviction found proxi-
mate preparation in folk belief, which could have prepared
for religion either positively, by accustoming people to think
in terms of a supernatural world close at hand, or negative-
ly, by enclosing them in a fatalistic universe from which
they were anxious to escape into the freedom of grace.

Finally, if reason must be assigned for the extension
of such belief in remarkable providences into the nineteenth
century, surely the facts that the stories were employed in
sermons and that, as Bruce Rosenberg has shown in The Art
of the American Folk Preacher, the preaching tradition is
tenaciously conservative of its themes and structures, must
be taken into account. In short, the belief did not die because it was an integral part of a living oral tradition.

Remarkable and Ordinary Providence
on the Frontier

Perry Miller notes the distinction, in the writings of
seventeenth century New England Puritans, between ordinary
and remarkable providence. "Ordinary providence" is manifest in the eternal and immutable order of nature, whereas
"remarkable providence" is manifest in exceptions to that
order. If the belief in ordinary providence provided a bas-
tion against superstition, according to Miller, the belief in
remarkable providence hedged against fatalism. [6] Theoretically, the mutually corrective beliefs should have balanced
each other. Miller notes, however, how even within the
seventeenth century the balance vacillated in response to
ideological expediencies:

> In the 1620's the danger was not that exceptions to
> the settled order would be underestimated, but that
> the order itself would not be sufficiently respected.
> By the time of Increase Mather's An Essay for the
> Recording of Illustrious Providences, peril lay in
> the other direction, and he, as well as others both
> in New England and England, felt that greater stress
> should now be placed upon the uncommon and the
> peculiar than upon the regular. The New England
> literature is part of a wider movement, inspired no
> doubt, as among the Cambridge Platonists and in
> the works of Joseph Glanvill, by apprehensions lest
> the all-conquering science result in a theory of
> blind mechanism or endorse the blasphemies of
> Thomas Hobbes. [7]

If Puritan divines felt that emphasis on remarkable
providences could redress the mechanistic implications of the
new science's cosmology, frontier preachers could have perceived, as well, the appeal of remarkable providences to folk

who had fled the stifling social and economic order of the
East. To elaborate: the recognition that theological arguments may support more than religious convictions is a com-
monplace. For example, elaborate theological defenses of
slavery supported an immoral social order in nineteenth century America. Similarly, the belief in ordinary providences
could reflect social, psychological and ideological positions.
Such belief glorified God by recognizing the order that he
built into his creation and the utter sufficiency of that order.
Discernment of such providence was habitual and <u>post factum</u>,
that is, whatever happened was assumed to have been the
ordination of divine will. Ordinary providence could easily
be reconciled with theories of historical (earned) rights, with
laissez-faire social and economic theories, with rationalism,
and with mechanistic cosmologies.

By contrast, the belief in remarkable providence glorified God by recognizing his sovereign power to dispense with
or to appropriate in unusual fashion the secondary causes of
the order he created. Radical interruptions of expected order
were occasional, mysterious, and unexplainable, and were
seen only with the eyes of faith. Such belief, at odds with
social and economic models that locked men to their places,
with rationalism, and with cosmologies that locked God to
his causes, were reconcilable with aggression rather than
submission and with freedom rather than fatalism.

Frontier folk, who left their Eastern homes looking
for "a place in the sun, " found the doctrine of remarkable
providence ideally suited to their expectations. The frontier
itself was a suspension of normal order. There, God could
work freely, spontaneously, unexpectedly, and mysteriously.
All were equal under a God whose grace was indifferent to
distinctions, and whose guidance could seem, at times, even
quixotic. This is not to say that frontier folk lived in a
chaotic world; as the following section will argue, the belief in providence assured the believer that the baffling am-
biguities of life had explanation, even if known only to God.
It is simply to remark that social and psychological conditions had much to do with the continuance of the traditions of
remarkable providences.

Stories of Remarkable Providence
as Religious Symbols

The social anthropologist Clifford Geertz, in an article

entitled "Religion as a Cultural System," notes how religious
symbols both shape an ethos and embody a world-view. Offering interpretations of bafflement, suffering, and the ethical
paradox by giving empirical regularity, emotional form, and
moral coherence, such symbols occasion mutual validation of
metaphysic and ethic, "the way things are" and "what to do, "
by being enacted. In Geertz's words, "men attain their faith
as they portray it."8 In other words, the enacted symbol
validates the world-view which explains the enacted symbol.
To put it more simply, when a man does what his world-
view tells him to do, what he has done makes his world-
view come true. The symbols themselves are accepted as
valid vehicles for such a function on the authority of tradition, not on evidence that suggests they are plausible.

The religious symbols of Protestantism belong to an
evangelical rather than to a sacramental order. Such a di-
chotomy is not intended to draw an a priori but simply a
descriptive distinction between foci of Protestant and Roman
Catholic approaches to symbolism; the symbols of the former
have focused on the preached Word; those of the latter, on
ritual objects and actions. The distinction should not be
overdrawn, however. Both symbolic foci tangibly depict
world-views: the sacramental order through rituals and actions and the evangelical through stories. For example, the
story of a Methodist hero is no less concrete than a Roman
Catholic statue of St. Joseph. Both appeal to the imagination through different sensory media.

If it is true, as has been argued in this section, that
the stories here presented were employed in sermons and
other teaching situations, then such stories are also religious
symbols. Without implying that the Methodist itinerant world-
view and ethos can be studied only, or even primarily, from
such data, it is argued that such symbols reveal a "reflex"
religion not readily visible in more obvious sources.

As has been noted, the Methodist itinerant world-view
focused upon a sovereign and providential God. "Providential"
does not mean animistic or pantheistic: God is distinct from
the visible world; he is sovereign. Yet every second of
every day reveals his intimate, immediate governance of
events. Moreover, for reasons known only to him, he can
dispense with ordinary providential guidance both in the natural and moral orders and demonstrate vividly and forcibly
his control. Reason, and especially science, by definition
can offer only inadequate explanations of the ultimate nature
of reality.

This sovereign, providential God offers his love and
grace to man. The offer of grace precipitates a crisis
wherein man must decide to accept or reject the offer.[9] If
he accepts he experiences "conversion." Conversion is, of
course, the ethos, the "what to do" suggested by the world-
view. If, however, man refuses grace, he suffers damnation. Inasmuch as the visible world is susceptible to invisible reality, even to human volition, a man's moral choices
will sooner or later manifest themselves visibly. Therefore
the converted are vindicated and the damned punished. The
providential God sometimes allows the visible consequences of
moral choices to manifest themselves immediately: hence remarkable providences which illustrate his mercy or justice.

For nineteenth century itinerants, therefore, the "way
things are" was providence, and "what to do" was conversion.
The symbols which expressed (at least in part) that world-
view and ethos were the remarkable providence stories.
When an itinerant told a remarkable providence story, he
was expressing a world-view which had been proven true by
the story he was telling, and which moreover, would be true
in the future if the people would experience what the world-
view elicited. Thus the stories at once embodied a world-
view, shaped an ethos, and perpetuated a tradition.

As Geertz suggests, such beliefs are accepted not on
evidence but on faith: credo ut intelligam. In the case of
remarkable providence stories, the weight of faith's authority
is amplified by the anonymity of oral tradition, under which
the stories assume an air of unquestionable general knowledge. Faith and folklore combine, therefore, to make the
stories excellent devices for communicating religious culture.
Moreover, the enormous traditional weight of such stories
makes them resistant to change, both formally and material-
ly. Even today, stories of remarkable providence can be
heard from innumerable pulpits. It may well be that such
relations thrive on social discontent or displacement. The
secular form of the genre--for example, the lurid deaths
and degradations depicted in countless tabloid newspapers,
confidential, romantic, and confessional magazines--appeals
to those who seek the mysterious as a talisman against the
crushing routine of status quo. Readers of such accounts,
like those who search the stars, mitigate the harsh consequences of belief in a fatalistic world by substituting illusory
gnosis for stoic acceptance. Somewhat analogously, the
scrutiny of remarkable providences allows the believer a window into the otherwise baffling decrees of the divine will.

Summary

In short, stories of remarkable providences illustrate
the vitality of Christian belief in God's providence among
Methodist preachers and people in nineteenth century America.
The durability of the belief is traceable not only to literalis-
tic interpretations of the Bible, which helped to validate the
stories, but also to the mode of communication--preaching--
which itself is a traditional art. Moreover, the disordered
frontier provided ready audience for beliefs which emphasized
mysterious disruptions of order rather than routine stasis.
Finally, insofar as they were religious symbols, the stories
occasioned the mutual validation of a traditional metaphysic
and ethic that provided a coherent universe for human religious activity.

Notes

1. The Course of American Democratic Thought: An Intellectual History Since 1815 (New York: The Ronald
   Press Company, 1940), p. 14.
2. Alice Felt Tyler, Freedom's Ferment: Phases of American Social History to 1860 (Minneapolis: University
   of Minnesota Press, 1944), passim.
3. "The Garden of Eden and the Deacon's Meadow," American Heritage, VII (1955), 55.
4. "Folk Beliefs of a Pennsylvania Preacher," Keystone
   Folklore Quarterly, X (1965), 191-93. Barrick illustrates such a tendency in another article: "'All
   Signs in Dry Spells Fails,'" Keystone Folklore Quarterly, IX (1964), 100-10. Vance Randolph has shown the
   extent of fertility rites among fervently religious Holy
   Rollers in the Ozarks: "Nakedness in Ozark Folk Belief," JAF, LXVI (1953), 333-39.
5. See Owst, Literature and Pulpit, pp. 85-87.
6. The New England Mind: The Seventeenth Century (Cambridge, Mass.: Harvard University Press, 1954), pp.
   226-28.
7. Miller, New England, pp. 228-29.
8. In Anthropological Approaches to the Study of Religion,
   ed. by Michael Banton (New York: Frederick A.
   Praeger, 1966), p. 29.
9. Throughout the literature, the itinerants are portrayed
   as opposing Universalists and Calvinists because they
   denied free choice.

PART III

HUMOR AND HEROES

If Methodist preachers reached back to seventeenth century supernaturalistic traditions for their stories of remarkable providences, they drew upon their own experience and upon burgeoning, endemic American folk traditions for the folklore of early Methodism. Fired by unquenchable missionary fervor, Methodist itinerants stalked settlers' wagon tracks in the cold corridors of wilderness forests and in the burning heat of vast prairies. At a time when their countrymen looked for land and a dream the itinerants searched for souls and grace, counting hardship, deprivation, and persecution as nothing for the sake of the Lord. Thus set apart from the people to whom they ministered, itinerants sought consolation in the Lord and companionship in their difficulties from their fellow preachers. Sharing successes and disappointments, joys and sufferings, hopes and weariness as they rode to conference together over the long frontier trails, Methodist ministers provided powerful encouragement to one another in their arduous calling. At conference, preachers traded stories of conversions and judgments; shared dreams; told of prayers answered and deliverances granted; joked about lodgings, food, clothing, characters they had met, and mishaps which had occurred as they preached; boasted about rowdies they had thwarted at camp meetings, Universalists, Deists, Campbellites, Baptists and assorted unbelievers they had verbally demolished; in short, they shared a common life unique to them as a group and in so doing, tightened the bonds of fellowship that welded them together. Stories, carried from the diverse situations of various Methodist preachers to the conference gristmill, were returned to local situations with husks removed and kernels available for further use. Over the years, therefore, lively oral traditions developed which reflected distinctively the Methodist experience, even as it echoes the boasting and yarning of a new America.

Chapter 9

ON THE CIRCUIT

> When notified of their appointments, they went forth
> very much like Abraham, not knowing whither.
> They had never travelled, were ignorant of the ge-
> ography of the country, and had very indefinite
> ideas either of places or routes. With the scanty
> outfit of a Methodist preacher, purses light enough
> to be easily handled, saddened by their first sepa-
> ration from home and friends, embarrassed by
> their ignorance of the world, and oppressed by the
> tremendous responsibility of their mission, they
> wandered on, each to his appointed place. [1]

One itinerant, remembering his exuberant arrival on
a new circuit after an arduous journey, employs an anecdote
to tell how subsequent events shattered his initial optimism:

> I was like a young man when just married. The
> preacher, congratulating him said, 'Now you are
> at the end of your troubles.' Three weeks later
> the young man came back and wanted to whip the
> preacher, saying, 'You told me when I was married
> I was at the end of my troubles.' The preacher
> now said, 'Yes, I told you that, but I did not tell
> you at which end of your troubles you were.' [2]

Like young Spartans sent into battle with the credo that pos-
terior wounds marked a defeat worse than death, youthful
itinerants sallied out into the fray for souls with the words,
"'wearing out is better than rusting out,'" ringing in their
ears. [3] Ideally, no itinerant turned his back on Methodism's
task, no matter what the difficulty. Aged ministers prayed
that they "might cease at once to work and live!,"[4] a wish
that heightened the aphorism above to the loftiest idealism:
itinerants "'must neither wear out nor rust out, but burn
out!'"[5]

Circuit Rider Bids Farewell to His Family

Lore shaped by the experiences of itinerants riding the circuit makes it clear that such ideals were not purchased cheaply. Preachers had to overcome the disappointments of unwelcome or undesirable appointments and of unappreciative people, the discouragements of poor pay, demoralizing accommodations, insufferable travel conditions, and debilitating sicknesses. No one knew better than itinerants that the word of God was carried to frontier folk in vessels of clay on the backs of sweating, fly-plagued horses. Sometimes itinerants quit the ministry, sometimes they located. For those who endured, wry laughter prompted by ironic humor must have made faith's task more human.

The Pork Barrel

Every two years, according to Methodist practice, circuit appointments were made anew. Ultimate responsibility for disposition of preachers rested with the bishop, who usually, however, depended upon the presiding elder of each district for evaluation and advice. Appointments, like lines on the palm or tea leaves in a cup, were the subject of extended exegesis on the part of itinerants. Not only could an appointment be considered an evaluation of the past two years' work, but it would also be regarded as a portent of things to come. Some circuits promised poor pay, hardened people, or wrenching distance from things and persons familiar. Other circuits offered opportunities to shine at less cost, and perhaps a step toward episcopacy. Bishops, who rose from the ranks, took no less seriously than did the circuit riders the business of making appointments; nevertheless, playing God with men's lives must have been troublesome business at best.

According to one account, in the following fashion a Bishop described to his presiding elders the process of making appointments:

> 'Once a western farmer put up his pork in this wise: he put the inferior pieces at the bottom of the barrel, and continued to pack with grades increasing in quality till he reached the top, where he placed the best parts of the hog. He did this because he said that he didn't like to eat the snouts till the last. '

Making the application for his listeners, the Bishop continued:

> 'Brother, you begin. Make two nominations for
> your District of two brethren about whom there can
> be no difficulty and no question; in this way we will
> continue through all the Districts until all such clear
> cases are exhausted; then we will fix the places of
> men about whom there will be trouble and debate. '6

Young itinerants, who were chased to the "starve-out"
circuits to prove themselves, 7 probably felt like "snouts"
when the Bishop packed them away. Numerous accounts record the desolation experienced by young preachers as they
struck off alone from friends, family, and familiarity, beginning to live a strange vocation in unknown country. Frequently they left conference with no blessing, probationers as
well as novices: "'too much top-sail for the hull, '" crusty
old preachers were likely to mutter. 8 No wonder it was that
David Morton, disheartened by his first appointment, came
near to drowning himself in the Ohio River to escape God's
terrible call. 9

The first circuit of a young itinerant frequently tested
his spirit by challenging his ability to survive physically.
Accounts recall how such tender shoots arrived on their circuits penniless, 10 how doors were slammed in their faces
when they looked for lodging after the first day's ride, 11 or
how, after earnest travel to reach their first preaching engagement, they arived in the wrong place at the wrong time.12

Those who weathered "Brush College's" elementary
survival training graduated to more severe spiritual tests,
such as ridicule or untimely advice. The town wag, in one
narrative, after viewing a young itinerant ride into the village, remarked to a friend:

> 'John, I believe I saw yesterday one of the green-
> est things I've yet seen this spring; in fact, it was
> so green that the cows were running after it--it
> was your young Methodist preacher. '13

Waggish jests could be more easily dismissed than snap judgments made by self-styled experts on the subject of ministerial timber. A crass local preacher, called upon to exhort, after the first sermons of a young itinerant on a new
circuit, told the people

"LA, ME! YOU DE PREACHER?—I'SE WERY GLAD. BUT MASSA SAYS YOU NO DO MUCH GOOD DIS YEA', YOU SO YOUNG, AN' NO SPERIENCE. HE SCOLE WERY MUCH, KASE AN OLE MAN WAS NOT SENT."

A Cool Reception for a "Green" Itinerant

that they should try to live humbly, watchfully, and
prayerfully, especially during that year, as they
certainly had a very poor prospect for preaching.

The unfortunate neophyte, continues the narrative, "shrank as
though he would, if possible, have sunk through the floor
.... "14

Such episodes must have been frequent enough to
prompt a counter-offensive in Methodist lore. A very serious story told in various Methodist periodicals encouraged
young circuit riders to persevere. The saga of "The Unwelcome Preacher" recounted how townspeople of Russelville,
Kentucky, believing that they could support a preacher by
themselves, wrote to the Bishop and asked him to make a
separate station of their village. Inasmuch as some ministerial charisma would be necessary for growth, if not per-
durance, of their enterprise, they requested John Johnson
who was "at that time one of the most popular and effective
ministers in the state.... " Instead of sending them Johnson,
the Bishop appointed Rev. E. Stevenson, then a green, un-
tried, and unconfident stripling. Bishop Enoch George accompanied Stevenson to Russelville, where the disappointed
Methodist folk told the Bishop, " 'He will not do at all, sir;
we might as well be left without a preacher altogether.' "
Overhearing this remark, Stevenson resolved to flee; Bishop
George, however, persuaded him to remain in the town, to
fast and pray and perform all pastoral duties for a month,
on the condition that, if he still wished to leave at the end
of that time, he could do so. For three Sundays Stevenson
did as he had agreed, without material change in the situation.
On the last Sabbath, he arose from prayer as the church
bells rang the hour of meeting, went to his window to watch
"the few reluctant hearers" straggle into church,

when, lo! what a sight met his gaze! Group after
group of citizens were flocking toward the Methodist Church! At first a sense of awe came over
him, and then a class of mingled feelings, as if
confidence, and strength, and joy were storming
the heart, while fear, and weakness, and mortifica-
tion still disputed the right of possession.
He hastened to his pulpit, and as he arose
from the first silent prayer, the thought of victory
thrilled through him like the voice of a clarion. 15

Sometimes wise, experienced ministers advised young

men that they " 'had run before they were sent, ' " and that
they ought to pack up and return home before they further embarrassed the church. 16   They were not always, however,
clairvoyant in their counsel.   One story takes grim delight
in lampooning such untimely "wisdom. "   Young Enoch Marvin,
a quixotic figure who, because of his unsightly apparel and
"general awkwardness, " had excited remark and ridicule at
a Conference, was overtaken by three experienced itinerants,
George Smith, Jacob Lannius, and Samuel G. Paterson, as
he rode away from Conference on a bony horse.   The three
"entered into serious conversation with him in regard to his
inexperience and lack of qualification. "   Offering miserable
comfort to this young Job, they

> made known their deep concern for his future wel-
> fare, expressing their surprise that some one had
> not already done him the kindness and justice to
> tell him of his mistake.   Having, in a fatherly way,
> advised him to desist from attempting to preach and
> go home and go to school, and feeling that they had
> fully discharged their duty, they resolved to ride
> on.   From his silence and seeming indifference,
> the three had serious fears that their valuable coun-
> sel was not very highly appreciated.   On leaving
> him to pursue his journey alone, they were thought-
> fully suggested that he should bear in mind that the
> advice given was from men of experience, and if
> not observed he would probably discover his error
> at a time when it would be a source of regret.
> His only reply was: 'Do you think so?'

Marvin's obduracy bore fruit, for he became a distinguished
Bishop of the church.   In following years he preached Lannius' funeral sermon.   Smith "lived to receive an appointment
from him, as Bishop, " and years later, Marvin, after his
reputation was secure, embarrassed Paterson by visiting the
latter on his episcopal round. 17

Despite the encouragement of such lore, many circuit
riders pulled in their horns and went home.   Samuel Clawson anathematized such quitters as " 'sheep in fly-time' ":

> 'You know that a sheep will sometimes get tired
> fighting the flies and jump the fence into an adjoin-
> ing field, but the flies will soon follow.... After
> grazing awhile in the new field, the flies gather
> thicker and bit harder than before, and over the

The Obdurate Enoch Marvin (right) with
his Biographer, Thomas Finney

fence he goes into another field. But some sheep
are worse than others to gather flies, owing to
their being thin skinned. And after going from field
to field, the flies still after him, he concludes there
are flies in all the fields, and he jumps into the
woods, and the wolves catch him and destroy him.'[18]

Landon Taylor, confronting a fellow itinerant who had resolved to go home from a difficult circuit, told him the following tale:

Well, said I, if you will go, I will give you the
benefit of an old fable before you start. 'Very
well, ' said he, 'let me have it. ' I give it here,
in brief: Two friends, setting out together through
a dangerous wood, mutually agreed that in case of
an attack they would assist each other. They had
not proceeded far before they saw a bear making
toward them with great rage. One of them, being
very active, sprang up into a tree; the other threw
himself flat upon the ground, having heard it asserted that a bear would not prey upon a dead car-
cass. The bear came up, and after smelling him
for some time, left him and went on. When he
was fairly out of sight, the man from the tree
cried out: 'Well, my friend, what said the bear?
he seemed to whisper to you very closely. ' 'Yes, '
said the other, 'and he gave me this good piece of
advice, never to associate with a wretch who in the
hour of danger will desert his friend. "[19]

Several accounts tell how doughty wives embolden their
discouraged husbands to return to circuits, [20] or how pious
laymen offer the necessary encouragement to timorous preachers. [21]

Methodist Horses

The early Methodist circuit riders spent more time
with their horses than with any other living being. Together
they shared lonely hours on the trail, plodding up and down
mountain switchbacks, inching across endless prairies, slog-
ging through mud and swamps, swimming innumerable streams
and braving every imaginable kind of weather. A trustworthy
horse could mean the difference between life and death on a

"Brother Van" (William Wesley Van Orsdel)
of Montana on his Faithful Methodist Horse

precipitous mountain trail or in a swift current. It is no
great wonder, then, that over the years individual horses
should have been remembered with special affection and that,
as travel by train and steamer became more convenient and
widespread, the relationship between preachers and horses
should have been exalted as the hallmark of Methodism's
palmy days.

Much of the horse-lore must have been traded, like
horses themselves, at Conference. One itinerant recalls that
at conference preachers whose horses had strayed advertised
for them among their fellows, that they traded remedies for
equine ailments, and that, if a preacher lost his horse, a
collection was taken to replace it, with "the brother who
failed to respond ... regarded as little less than an outlaw."
The same reminiscence continues:

> The close of the Conference, when men who had
> been on stations were assigned to circuits and dis-
> tricts and vice versa, was the signal for a general
> horse-trading. I well remember that just after ad-
> journment at Greenville, in 1855, the street in
> front of a livery stable near the center of the town
> for a square or more was lined with teams and
> traders. Preachers and ponies, women and wagons,
> children and colts were to be seen on all sides.
> There were selling and swapping, and buying and
> bartering, and stripping and saddling. Cash and
> credit and present and future delivery fixed the
> terms of sale, and in a little time the adjustments
> were complete. 22

At such markets the shrewd circuit rider could obtain
a memorable horse, such as Prince, to whom an old Bishop
paid tribute:

> I rode him up hill and down hill, and never knew
> him to tip his toe. He was a great favorite with
> the ladies, to whom I often had to surrender him.
> Only one horse have I seen who would take to the
> water like him. I would put him in any stream
> and with his head piloting above the water, his tail
> spread out like a fan, not more than one-third of
> his body would sink in the water, so that the sad-
> dlebags would never get wet. I afterward sold him
> to Major Hall, of Green County, who used him for
> twenty-five years in the collection of taxes. 23

William Milburn's horse, that had listened to his master practice sermons and sing hymns over miles of lonely travel,
would "prick up his ears and seem to listen with the most
intense attention" at his same voice in a religious service.
He earned the owner's gratitude because "he never went to
sleep while I was discoursing."24   James Erwin boasted that
his steed, "Charley Black," was always ready for an emer-
gency: he "could swim a river, soar over a mountain, skim
the slough-holes, shoot over a 'floating log road,' or distance
a bear, or a pack of hungry wolves on a fair road." So attached were itinerants to their horses, Erwin continues, that
"if we had but twenty-five cents we would spend it cheerfully
for oats, and keep fast day ourselves...."25   Not to be outdone, an unnamed early Methodist Bishop, recalling General
Jackson who bequeathed ten acres to his warhorse in his will,
"pensioned his superannuated itinerant-steed."26

     Enoch Marvin's biographer, Thomas Finney, noted the
contrast between the old days of American Methodism, when
"the horse was an Institution of Methodism," and more recent times, in which "Bishops are dismounted, the Itinerancy
goes by rail, the valise supplants the saddle-bags, pasture
for preachers' horses has dropped out of the accommodations
at conference...." Marvin, says Finney, found sanction for
itinerants' lofty regard for their beasts when he visited a
Coptic Convent in Cairo:

> 'Here we were shown [says Marvin] the figures of
> several of the Apostles carved in wood, in relief,
> on the wall. They were quite like Methodist preach-
> ers in one respect, being on horseback--a decidedly
> apostolic conception.'27

Another eulogist found precedent for the gospel on horseback
not in apostolic practice but in the military campaigns of
conquerors such as Alexander the Great, Cortez and Napole-
on.28

     Less sentiment and more humor marked other horse
reminiscences. William Nast, the premier German Methodist
preacher in America, reportedly was "frequently thrown by
his horse in the mud." The obnoxious animal would then run
from him, and Nast, with saddlebags on arm, would have to
chase him for miles on foot. On one occasion Nast became
so discouraged with his steed that he hitched him to a tree
in the woods, knelt beside him and prayed "earnestly to the
Lord to control the bad disposition of his horse." A story

William Nast.

that Dr. Nast frequently told on himself, "to the amusement
of his friends," related how, after he had been advised to
take good care of his horse by currying and feeding him
daily, he

> went out one morning to feed and curry his horse,
> and when he had gone through the operation system-
> atically, as he thought, a stranger walked into the
> stable and remarked to him, 'Mr. Nast, why did
> you go to the trouble of currying and feeding my
> horse? I could have done it myself.' And not till
> then was he aware that he had curried the wrong
> horse.[29]

Another story recalls the reaction of an elderly German farmer to the sight of itinerants travelling by buggies
to Conference in New York State.

> For the last twenty miles of the distance all the
> roads converged into one. The buggies were placed
> upon elliptic springs. They had as great popularity
> as our modern bikes. As the Conference day ap-
> proached, the ministers came along this common
> highway in their buggies. There seemed no end of
> the long procession. A German and his son were
> working in a field along the pike. The father threw
> down his hoe, and cried out, 'Vel, den, Hance, py
> sure, hell is proke loose.'[30]

E. J. Stanley tells the "One-horse Preacher" story of
an Episcopalian Bishop, D. S. Tuttle, of Salt Lake City.
According to Stanley's account, the Bishop was traveling from
Corvallis to Stevensville, Idaho, one Sunday afternoon for a
preaching engagement, and met two Methodist preachers going
the other way.

> It was a sultry afternoon. Two of the Methodist
> preachers were riding in a brand-new top buggy
> drawn by two horses, and were thus protected from
> the scorching sun and were driving at good speed.
> The Bishop, accompanied by two "other clergy" and
> a boy, was in an open, two seated vehicle drawn
> by one horse that was much jaded and sweating pro-
> fusely under the load that he was drawing. As they
> reined up for a moment's pleasant greeting and chat,
> the Bishop called out in a rather familiar and joking
> way: 'O, you rich Methodist parsons, rushing along

"Perhaps you are one-horse preachers"

here in your two-horse buggy, while we poor Episcopalians have to go plodding along with one horse!
How is it?'

'Perhaps you are one-horse preachers,' rejoined one of the 'parsons' promptly and good-na-
turedly.

'A-a-ah! that's it, is it?' responded the
Bishop, with an air of surprise and a trifle crest-
fallen, followed by a roar of laughter from his
traveling companions, which was kept up, the Bishop joining in frequently the remainder of the journey. 31

Not all itinerants traveled by horse. Some preferred
walking, as did old John Clark, for example. 32 Joseph Willis reputedly walked unshod on his rounds. 33 Bayou preachers poled dugout canoes on portions of their circuits, 34 while
others employed more conventional conveyances, such as the
"iron horse," the steamer, and the stage. Over the years,
tradition clustered anecdotes around such modes of transpor-
tation. McNemee recalls, for example, the steamer to Sehome: "Going to Sehome in 1876 was quite different from
what it is now. Then it was a kind of try-weekly affair.
The steamer went down one week and tried to get back the
next. "35 Such humor, however, signalled the end of certain
romantic characteristics of Methodism on the frontier. No
vehicle could symbolize the virtues and vitality of primitive
American Methodism as aptly as the simple, courageous, and
faithful itinerant pony.

On the Road

Preachers who overcame initial disappointments and
discouragements soon found that annoyance and danger shad-
owed them as they rode frontier trails. Routine as tribula-
tion was, it is a wonder that so few stories record violent
endings for preachers. To be sure, Learner Blackman
drowned while crossing a stream, 36 S. S. Headlee of the
Methodist church, South, was murdered by Federal desperadoes in Missouri during Civil War turmoil, 37 and an unnamed itinerant froze to death in Illinois. 38 A frequently
told story recalls the death of itinerant Richmond Nolley in
a Louisiana swamp. Having been separated from his horse
while crossing a turbulent stream, Nolley attempted to walk
to his destination; fatigue and freezing cold slowed his steps.

He finally fell, to be found dead the next day by a traveler. A favorite detail of the stories is that his knees were muddy, and that kneeprints could be seen in the earth next to the prostrate form, proof that he had prayed to the end. [39] Another twice-told story celebrated the heroic death of itinerants Tucker and Carter at the hands of hostile Indians. [40] Such accounts, however, constitute the exception rather than the rule; circuit riders negotiated innumerable fords, storms, and potentially lethal situations routinely. Memorable incidents, however, entered the lore of Methodism as celebrations of heroic gests, as entertaining comic anecdotes, or as slightly over-wrought memories.

1. "Cooning it." To judge from the literature, streams, creeks, and rivers afforded itinerants considerable experience for the time when they would have to cross the river Jordan. Every preacher had his own style of getting across; where available, of course, ferries furnished transit. In the majority of instances, however, the preacher, not even knowing the disposition of the ford, was left to his own devices. Sometimes, when the body of water permitted, he "cooned it across":

> Jergens Creek was reached. It was swollen, and full from bank to bank, and ten feet deep. We found a foot log, swam the horses across, and carried the saddles, etc., over on the log. Brother Monroe could not walk the log, and got down on his all fours and 'cooned it' with his hands on the log --just jumped along astride like a frog. The scene was rather ludicrous, but it revealed the determined purpose of this man of God to go forward and do the Lord's work. [41]

When the stream was wide, many itinerants simply relied on strong-swimming horses to carry them over with a minimum of wetting. E. C. Gavitt, however, was accustomed to stripping naked, as often as three times a day, tying his clothes with his saddlebags on the pummel of the saddle, and hanging on to his horse's tail as the beast swam the river. [42]

Frequently preachers received unwanted second baptisms as they attempted to traverse wilderness water; in winter such a dip meant riding to a preaching appointment mailed in ice. [43] Such dunkings became the occasion for humor at the expense of Baptists and Campbellites, both groups who believed in immersion as a necessary baptismal ordinance.

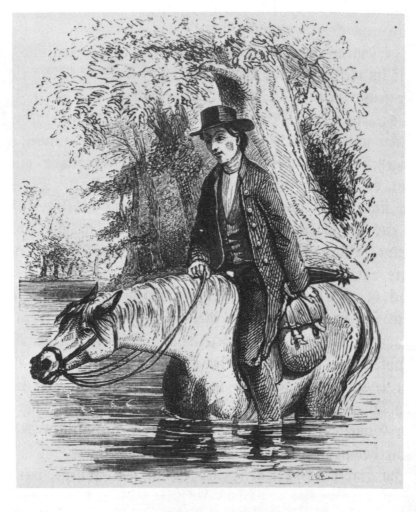

Jacob Gruber Risks a Dunking

One itinerant recalls how his buggy almost foundered in mid-stream, wetting him to the knees.

> The incident was soon reported abroad and a warm friend of mine belonging to the Christian Church approached me thus, 'Ah, lad, they came very near making a Campbellite out of you.' I responded, 'No, my head refused to go under, my feet only got dipped.'44

John Scarlett remembers a swim which the Lord turned to good advantage, somewhat at the former's expense. After wading an icy brook in winter, Scarlett recalls:

> When I arrived at the church, having emptied my boots of the water, it was time to commence service; I was cold, and shivered while preaching.
> After preaching, according to custom, I led class. A good sister remarked 'that the sermon had profited her, for she had been led to pray for the preacher, seeing that he trembled so under the weight of the cross. She thanked the Lord that Brother Scarlett had gracious help to bear it.' I did not think it worth while to explain. 45

Perilous waters, according to one tradition, prompted a circuit to request of a bishop, "'Send us a man who can swim.'"

> 'What do you mean?' inquired the bishop. 'Why, the last man we had, in order to keep an appointment had to cross a fierce, rushing stream, and he was drowned. Send us a man who can swim.'46

In a similar vein, Brother Mack claimed that Gray's River circuit in Oregon needed a man familiar with boats. 47

2. "Oceans of mud."48 Wilderness roads, of dubious merit at their best, became miry nightmares after rainstorms and throughout the spring. One itinerant recalled "deep, black, sticky mud," so viscous that it closed up the spokes of his buggy. 49 In Canada, the muskeg liquified under the summer heat into terrible swamps. According to Rev. Fitch Reed:

> I was told of a traveller who actually lost his horse in the mire. Unable to rescue his beast, he left

him to himself, where two days after he was found,
entirely under the mire except his head. Soon after
the poor animal died. 50

Such incidents gave rise to jests; Thomas Pearne tells
how he came to a slough so formidable that he backtracked a
few miles to ask a settler how to get across. The pioneer
told him:

'It is pretty bad. But you go to the worst-looking
part, and you will see the ears of dead mules stick-
ing up. You follow that sign, and ride over on the
backs of the dead mules, and you can cross that
way. '51

Pearne heard of another man who received similarly doubtful
advice when he got to a tarry slough:

A boy on the hither side was cutting wood. A dialogue ensued. 'Boy, is that a safe slough to cross?'
'O yes. ' 'Has it a good, hard bottom?' 'O yes, '
said the boy. The man essayed to cross. His
horse mired. He had to dismount and wade out.
He was very angry, for he thought the boy had de-
ceived him. He cursed the boy roundly. 'Why did
you lie to me? Didn't you say the slough has a
good, hard, bottom?' 'O yes, ' said the boy, and
then applying his thumb to his nose, with the other
digits erected, he said, 'O yes, the bottom is good
and hard, but you did not get down to it. '52

Stories celebrating escapes from wilderness animals
have been placed elsewhere in these pages. Along with accounts of the annoyance of swarming gnats, mosquitoes, horse-
flies, and greenhead flies, and stories of itinerants iced in
the saddle, such traditions provide impressive evidence of
the incredible difficulties that could erode preachers' dedication.

"Vermin, Filth, Hogs and Hominy"

The preacher who crossed his streams and weathered
his storms safely, might well ask himself, upon arriving at
a frontier cabin, tavern or hotel, at which end (to use an
earlier phrase) of his troubles he stood. Frontier travelers

could presume instant hospitality wherever they stopped, except, wrote Thomas Ware, if you were a Methodist preacher seeking shelter from a deist, Quaker, or infidel. 53   Some preachers displayed wide tolerance of accommodations offered them, but some, such as Jacob Young, avoided unpleasant lodging despite accusations that he favored the rich. 54   Others displayed more delicacy, out of consideration for peoples' feelings:

> And by the way, the old preachers have no fear to mention storms, floods, persecutions; but for the sake of many dear, well-meaning people, they generally keep silent on the subject of vermin, filth, hog, and hominy--often greater ills to bear than storms or winters. 55

Yet bitterness, sometimes tempered with wry laughter, seeps into many memoirs.

Henry Bascom, for example, provides a memorable excoriation of one hostess' breakfast:

> Had a breakfast that might have substituted an emetic, prepared by the 'good wife,' who might, had she floated down the Nile, been safe from molestation by alligators, if filth would frighten them. 56

The Baptist preacher John Mason Peck offers a description of a frontier squatter's cabin at which he was forced to stay; the dirt, deprivation, and listlessness of the inhabitants would have shamed an aborigine, and the instance, says Peck, is "a fair specimen of hundreds of families we found scattered over the extreme frontier settlement in 1818-19. "57

Sleeping arrangements were especially precarious. Although George Gary was moved to tears by the sacrifice of one lay couple who slept in their chairs by the fire while he dozed on the house's only bed, 58 other Methodists wept from frustration when left to shift for themselves.   Corn shuck mattresses or buffalo robes stretched before the fire sufficed for a bed in many lodgings, and sometimes a sleeper had just dozed off when he had to roll over and share his humble portion with a late arrival.   Itinerants who enjoyed the privacy of a cabin loft remember watching the stars through gaps in the roof and waking in the morning with snow drifted over their blankets. 59

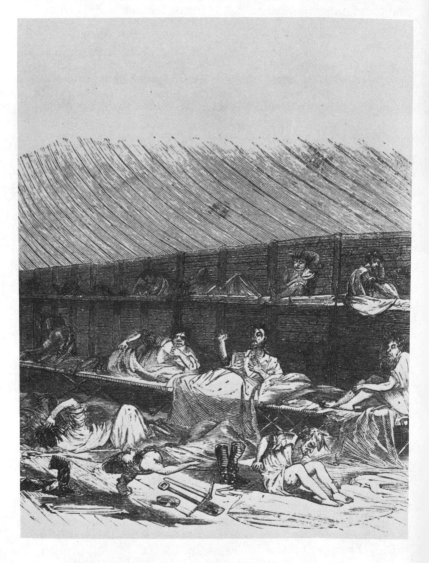

William Taylor's California Boarding-House

Henry Smith, given an old bearskin as his bed before the fire, wrote of how once

> a tribe of busy, hungry insects, who had possession
> of the bear-skins, long before I had, came out upon
> me, and contended earnestly for their rights, and
> annoyed me very much; but they could not disturb
> my peace of mind. 60

William Taylor recalled the ceiling-high bunk-beds of
California boarding houses during the gold rush days. Bare
slats/decorated with wisps of straw served as mattresses;
as for coverings, the penurious proprietors played musical
blankets:

> To the foregoing sleeping arrangements, if you add
> a few coarse grey blankets, you will have an orig-
> inal California lodging house, furnished. I heard
> it positively asserted by many who had been made
> tremblingly sensible of the fact, that in some
> houses a few pairs of blankets supplies a houseful
> of lodgers. As the weary fellows turned in one
> after another, they were comfortably covered till
> they would fall into a sound sleep, and then the
> blankets were removed to cover new recruits, and
> thus they were passed around for the accommoda-
> tion of the whole company. 61

The "topper" to this story is given by William Goff
Caples of Missouri, who narrates that after plunging through
a bitter midwest blizzard one evening, he came to a rude but
welcoming frontier cabin. When both horse and rider had
been fed, Caples looked around, noting that there were only
two beds for himself, the dozen children and their parents.

> Finally his host arose and said, 'Wall, stranger,
> as we gits up in the morning here, I reckon it's
> time we were abed.' So saying he took a light and
> said, 'Come with me.' They went out of the door,
> and round in the rear of the house, where he found
> a shed by the side of the cabin. As they entered
> it a little less than a dozen hounds came sneaking
> out. He was here shown a bed made after the fol-
> lowing fashion: A pole, with one end stuck into a
> crack of the cabin, extended to the centre of the
> room, where it rested on a fork driven into the
> ground. Another pole rested by one end on the

cross-piece of the shed, the other end also in the fork in the centre of the shed. On this frame boards were laid, and the bed made on them--a little shaky, but pretty comfortable. The man remarked as he went out that he must put up the door well or the dogs would get in. But Caples had scarcely begun to get warm in bed when, sure enough, the dogs began to demand entrance, and with very little effort the rickety door was down and they inside. He drove them out, and as well as he could reconstructed the door, but was only snugly tucked in again when the dogs assailed the door, and down it went, and in they came. Finding it impossible to barricade them out he concluded to take the next best chance, which was to let them stay in. They, of course, all piled up under the bed. But just as he was getting into a sweet dream of home and its comforts, a lot of wolves set up a howl near the cabin, and all the hounds rushing out at once, came in collision with the dreamer's centre of support, that is, the fork supporting the poles in the centre, when down came poles, boards, bed, preacher and all.

He stretched his legs out to see if any bones had been broken, and finding them all sound, he quietly adjusted himself to his situation, and was soon sound asleep, from which he did not awake till the full dawn of the following morning. But on awaking he attempted to move his legs, when they utterly refused to obey his will. 'What, ' thought he, 'am I frozen as stiff as a poker? No, that can't be, for I am in general perspiration. It can't be that I am paralyzed?' But drawing the cover a little off his face, what should meet his astonished eyes but the nose of the biggest, ugliest hound in the pack, within three inches of his own nose.

This old fellow had seemingly claimed the distinction of sleeping at the head. On looking down he saw the set had just arranged themselves, ad libitum, literally covering him from head to foot, until he was scarcely able to move a single limb. With a few vehement begones, and sundry, uneasy, spasmodic movements of his lower extremities, however, he soon dislodged his impertinent bed-fellows and rose, congratulating himself that, after all, many a man had slept with meaner dogs than these hounds of the backwoodsman. 62

The unpleasantness of squalid lodgings was compound-
ed by the meanness and ignorance of the primitive settlers.
Bascom described one unhappy visit:

> 'Tried to study, but too much confusion, tried to
> pray in the family, but felt too dull--tried to eat
> breakfast, but the victuals were too dirty for any
> decent man to eat. The old man is an idiot, the
> woman a scold, one son a drunkard, the other a
> sauce-box, and the daughter a mother without a
> husband.'63

J. V. Watson was surprised at the ignorance of people with
whom he lodged. When he asked the mother of the house if
she knew of the death of Jesus, she exclaimed, "'Is he dead?
--Well we had hearn out here of the death of Franklin, and
Washin'ton, and all the great Injun fighters, but never knowed
afore that Jesus was dead!'"64

The food served at frontier lodging frequently was no
better than the mattresses or acumen of the hosts. Rancid
pork and johnny-cake was often the fare. One itinerant's ap-
petite fled when he saw the soap kettle, boiling next to the
dinner kettle over the fire, foam over into the stew.65 Another circuit rider drank water instead of milk for breakfast
when he observed the backwoodsman's son running the fluid
over his fingers as he milked the family cow.66 In a more
elegant setting, William Gurley found a cockroach in his plum
dessert and dismayed his hostess by not finishing,67 while
John Burgess gagged when he found out the ingredients of
"Biestings" he had eaten at a wedding feast.68 The Indian
missionary, E. C. Gavitt, more hardy than his colleague,
learned how to eat savage delicacies such as nearly-hatched
turtle and snake eggs.69

If such reminiscences indicate preachers' discomfiture
at "vermin, filth, hogs, and hominy," other stories disclose
that Methodist itinerants were on occasion themselves offenders against propriety. Peter Cartwright tells the anecdote of
how James Axley, eating a chicken dinner at the elegant home
of Ohio's Governor Tiffin, threw the bones over his shoulder
onto the carpet for the Governor's dog.70

As an earlier chapter has indicated, some folk felt
that preachers were spongers, gobbling up the hard-earned
victuals of the poor while bending not a finger to honest labor. The hefty Jesse Lee (who weighed, by his own account,

259 pounds) recorded an embarrassing situation that occurred
when a company of preachers, including himself, arrived at
a farmhouse at harvest time.

> The gentleman of the house had some of his neigh-
> bors helping him cut wheat that day and a bountiful
> dinner had been prepared for the harvest hands.
> But the hungry preachers were seated at the table
> first, and did full justice to the dinner prepared for
> the harvesters.   When the men from the wheat-
> fields got to the table, there was a look of disap-
> pointment in their faces, but one of them with much
> gravity asked a blessing--
> > Oh Lord, look down on us poor sinners,
> > For the preachers have come and eat up our
> > dinners. 71

Only Lee's hearty laugh at the wit of the blessing relieved the
tension, according to another account of the same incident. 72

Some folk warned that Methodist preachers would eat
you out of house and home. 73   Barton Cartwright had the answer for such accusations:

> He put up over night at the house of the chief man
> of the neighbourhood.   Several politicians--office-
> seekers, we presume--were there for the night also.
> When it became known that they had a preacher in
> their midst, the host walked the floor very gravely
> for a time, and then very gruffly remarked:
> > 'Gentlemen, I once had an uncle worth ten
> > thousand dollars eaten out of house and home by
> > Methodist preachers. '
> > 'They must have had sharp teeth, ' Cartwright
> dryly made answer. 74

As the frontier settled down and circuits stabilized,
certain homes became regular stops for traveling preachers,
and standard "hog and hominy" became "yellow-legged chick-
en. "   The "good sisters, " when they saw the preacher coming, would kill the hen and cook it for him "as the general
belief then was that the Methodist preachers were all passion-
ately fond of chickens. "75   The chickens themselves, according to many accounts, knew their fate when they saw preachers coming.   According to Milburn, "this wise saying has
passed into a saw":

yellow-legged chickens (the largest and finest breed),
know a Methodist preacher as far as they can see
him, and ... they no sooner behold one approaching
than they squeak with terror, and betake themselves
to the timber, knowing their heads are in danger. 76

One wag, when reminded that he had said that the chickens
run when they see a minister coming, asserted: "'That may
have been the case at one time, but in these days the most
of the preachers appear so much like lawyers that the chickens don't know them.'"77

Chicken stories have had a long life among preachers.
Elizabeth Tokar reports interviewing an old Methodist minister in 1967 and hearing the following story:

A preacher was crossing a bridge over a creek.
He looked down at the water and his false teeth
fell out.   He could see them in clear water, so he
asked a boy who was fishing in the stream to go
after them.
        The boy replied, 'It's deeper than you think,
but I can get them.   Where did you eat dinner?'
'At the Jones'.'
        The boy hurried away, returning with a
chicken bone which he tied to the end of his line
and dropped in the water.   When the teeth came in
contact with the bone, they snapped shut and the
boy pulled them up. 78

Popular belief notwithstanding, many preachers must
have shared the reaction of A. D. Field to chicken dinners:

The young preacher was never at home, but always
a visitor; and ever when he came the fat chicken
had to be dressed; so that with chicken three hundred and sixty-five times a year it is no wonder I
came to detest the universal delicacy. 79

"No Foot of Land"

James Quinn, traveling with Francis Asbury, the
"founding father" of American Methodism, recalls how an old
lady asked the Bishop where he lived.   Replied Asbury,

No foot of land do I possess,
No cottage in this wilderness,
    A poor way-faring man.
I lodge awhile in tents below,
Or gladly wander to and fro,
    Till I my Canaan gain.

Nothing on earth I call my own,
A stranger to the world unknown,
    I all their goods despise;
I trample on their whole delight,
And seek a city out of sight,
    A city in the skies. [81]

As an earlier chapter has suggested, the principle of voluntary poverty mistakenly presumed the principle of voluntary contributions on the part of Methodist laymen. As Methodism gradually lost its innocence, ministers were more likely to desire a fixed, dependable income and to complain that the old way was a practice mistakenly elevated to a principle than to sing with light hearts, "No foot of land...."

Preachers were not unable, however, to appreciate the humor of certain situations that emphasized the discrepancy between their own expectations and the doles grudgingly surrendered by laymen.

One such situation involved fees for services performed, such as weddings and funerals. The etiquette of such situations, even today, is delicate: in general, no charge should be made but a fee must be paid.

No charge, however, frequently meant no fee. L. B. Stateler, for example, when asked by a wealthy rancher whom he had just married what the fee was, replied, "'Well, it is not customary for ministers to make charges for such services,'" hoping that the groom would take the hint that he "was at liberty to make as handsome a present as his circumstances and good nature would permit." Instead, the dolt replied, "'I am much obliged to you, Mr. Stateler, though I really did not expect it; I am very much obliged for your trouble, and will try to do as much for you some time.'"[82]

The protocol of the situation, rarely perceived by the layman, forbade asking the question. Samuel Clawson, perhaps more experienced than Stateler, had ready an answer that ensured a fat stipend. When asked by the groom what he charged, Clawson replied,

> 'We don't make a charge ... but allow the groom
> to measure his generosity by the estimate he puts
> on his bride. When I marry such a fine looking
> couple as you are, I always get five or ten dollars,
> but when I marry an indifferent looking couple, I
> don't expect more than two or three dollars.'[83]

The young man, reports the biographer, "was pleased with
the compliment, and handed him a five-dollar bill...."

Most preachers, however, were too diffident to trick
their clients in such a way. Humor arising from the discrepancy between the tacit charge and the niggling contribution was about all that could be salvaged from many episodes.
One groom used pocket change for a stipend, another pump-
kins.[84] At the other end of life's spectrum, a brutish father
paid a circuit rider twenty-five cents for his child's funeral.[85] One groom fumbled so long with a fat bankroll after
the ceremony that his wife became disgusted, jerked the roll
out of his hands, and gave it to the preacher, saying, "'Let
Brother Richardson pay himself.'" The latter took a ten-
dollar bill, noting with satisfaction the look of bereavement
on the face of the man who "evidently [was] looking for a
small bill...."[86] The humor of another episode arises from
more serious embarrassment of the groom. Rev. Davis presided at a wedding for which he received no compensation,
but he said nothing at the time.

> However, not long afterwards, the minister met the
> groom and pleasantly remarked to him: 'You did
> not think to present me with anything for the service
> I rendered you the other day?' The groom replied
> with considerable emotion: 'Mr. Davis, if you will
> only unmarry me, I will pay you both bills.' Poor
> fellow! it is presumable he had a dear bargain, not-
> withstanding the fee was not paid; and it is very
> likely he felt the force of the Scripture: 'It is bet-
> ter to dwell in a corner of the housetop, then with
> a brawling woman, and in a wide house.'[87]

The most pithy appraisal of a miserly groom came from the
lips of an itinerant who, having just presided at an extrava-
gant wedding and having received nothing for his work, said
of the groom: he "is a hog without bristles."[88]

Inability to collect one's salary was a more serious matter than failure to garner stipends. John Burgess recalls an occasion when a preacher borrowed five dollars from a wealthy church member who did not support the church in accord with his means. The minister preached with enthusiasm, and after the service he gave the bill back to the rich man, with thanks, whereupon the latter asked, "'Why brother, you have not used it: why return it so soon?'" The crafty preacher replied, "'you do not know how good it makes a man feel to know he has money in his pocket when he preaches.'" The lesson, says Burgess, "proved effectual."[89]

Even preachers who received their salaries were likely to be disappointed. In Texas, for example, when Confederate money "went down to twenty for one" during the Civil War, a layman consoled himself "that ... it was good for one thing--it would pay the preacher."[90] Hamilton tells the story of the church steward who brought the preacher his Thanksgiving turkey, accepted a polite though not serious invitation to share it with him, arrived on the day of thanks with his wife and numerous children, devoured the meal, and later sent a bill for the bird.[91] Enoch Marvin, however, tells the best anecdote of all, colored perhaps by the character of the land in which it occurred:

> A Steward in one of the best Circuits in the West Texas Conference contributed, as quarterage, one hundred pounds of bacon. Now, bacon was ten cents a pound, but at the quarterly meeting the brother brought in his bill, charging fifteen cents. Objection was made to the price. The brother acknowledged that if he had taken his bacon to town he would not have thought of asking above ten cents for it. Upon being asked why he charged the preacher more than the market price, he gave, in all simplicity and seriousness, this reply--that all he gave to the Church was exactly so much treasure laid up in heaven. It was important to put his bacon at a big price that it might swell that account as much as possible. I gave it up. This exceeded any case I ever heard of in Missouri.[92]

Over the years, Methodist preachers learned to laugh at their financial difficulties. Thomas Pearne remembered, when a man he had married passed by with "nary" a fee, but only the comment, "'Minister, I am ten thousand times obleeged to you,'" that as a boy he had learned "that every

'thank you' was worth eighteen and three-fourths cents." Multiplying that value by ten thousand, he figured that the groom
"had paid me in 'thank you's' eighteen hundred and seventy-
five dollars."[93] Nevertheless the humor, however construc-
tive it might have been, only partially alleviated the itinerants'
bitterness over their people's unwillingness to put their money
where their verbal commitment was.

"'Yis, and Hurra for the Quakers, Too!'"

Frontier preachers, like the people to whom they
preached, had a "'Hobson's choice,'" that is, no choice at
all, over what they would wear: homemade jeans.[94] Increasing prosperity, however, brought options: shad-bellied
or swallow-tailed coats, broad or narrow-brimmed hats, winter and summer models, etc. Like voluntary poverty, however, the early simplicity of dress was exalted by some from
practice to principle, dividing itinerants into two camps.
Rigorists condemned new ministerial fashions as immoral,
while meliorists adjudged old styles unfashionable, and the
question immaterial. Although it is clear that the rigorists'
definition of primitive simplicity changed just one step behind fashionability, the old timers' intransigence kept ministerial styles on the lean side. The following humorous story
recapitulates the problem:

> An incident occurred with these two brethren, dur-
> ing their journey to Pittsburgh, which, as it serves
> to illustrate the different impressions made by the
> appearance of different men on the minds of stran-
> gers, may be related. Mr. Patton dressed well,
> rode well, and, on horseback particularly, was a
> fine-looking man. Mounted, as he generally was,
> on an elegant horse, well caparisoned, and riding
> in his peculiar manner, he presented somewhat a
> majisterial [sic] sort of appearance. On the con-
> trary, Mr. Wilkerson dressed in a remarkably
> plain home-spun material, cut in the real old Meth-
> odist style, with a broad-brimmed, log-crowned hat,
> he presented as plain appearance as was anywhere
> to be found. These two journeyed from East Ten-
> nessee to Pittsburgh on horseback. On their way
> they passed at one place a number of Irish laborers
> at work on a public road. They were separated, in
> companies, a short distance apart. Mr. P. was

riding some distance in advance of his companion.
He passed the first company without remark, but
as he was passing the second, one of the number
looked steadily at him for a moment or two, then
turned and halloed back to the others, 'Hurra for
Gineral Jackson!' Just then Wilkerson was passing
the first company, and one of them replied, 'Yis,
and hurra for the Quakers, too!' This incident
greatly amused Mr. Wilkerson, but his traveling
companion never had much to say on the subject. 95

Summary

Methodist lore about such mundane concerns as appointments, horses, travel, accommodations, and possessions
speaks eloquently and touchingly of the itinerants' humanity.
While the ideals which propelled a young religious enthusiast
into the circuit ministry undoubtedly sustained him, no successful itinerant could forget that human courage and tenacity
were essential ingredients of his vocation.   Too often history
forgets daily life; not so folklore.   The superstitions, jokes,
talismans, taboos, and reminiscences of folk tradition mark
man's immersion in and concern with the ordinary.   In addition, however, such lore through conversation transforms the
ordinary into common experience and hence makes the ordinary endurable.   The folklore of itinerant preachers witnesses, therefore, not only to their humanity but to the
brotherhood that made their humanity endurable.

Notes

1.   Smith, Pierce, p. 20.
2.   McNemee, "Brother Mack, " p. 34.
3.   Scarlett, Itinerant, p. 117.
4.   Field, Worthies, p. 196; also Graves, DeVilbiss, p. 114;
        Fleharty, Phelps, pp. 381-82.
5.   The remark is attributed to Bishop Janes at the Rock
        River Conference of 1848; Field, Worthies, p. 197.
6.   Spottswood, Brief Annals, p. 260.
7.   O. P. Fitzgerald, Dr. Summers: A Life-Study (Nash-
        ville: Southern Methodist Publishing House, 1885),
        pp. 44-45.
8.   Fleharty, Phelps, p. 24; Field, Worthies, p. 152; D.
        Young, Autobiography, p. 69, records the phrase,

"a good deal of sail, but little ballast."

9.   E. R. Wallace, Parson Hanks--Fourteen Years in the
     West. A Story of the Author's Life in the Pan Handle
     of Texas (Arlington, Texas: Journal Print, 1906),
     pp. 30-31.
10. Sullins, Recollections, pp. 102-7.
11. Thomson, Life, pp. 30-31.
12. Smith, Pierce, pp. 20-21.
13. Spottswood, Brief Annals, p. 80. Another itinerant was
     told that he wore the "greenest breeches" a man had
     ever seen: Richardson, Autobiography, p. 42.
14. Patton, Life, p. 68. An old lady told an itinerant who
     stopped for dinner at her house, "'Ah ... Joe, it
     will be a poor preach that you will make.'" Travis,
     Autobiography, p. 33.
15. Watson, Tales and Takings, pp. 167-78. The narrative
     is attributed, in Watson's book, to the editor of The
     Home Circle. Another account quotes from the same
     story, citing its source as the Southern Ladies' Com-
     panion of November and December, 1854; Johnson,
     Recollections, pp. 175-76. Mrs. Johnson, far from
     intending encouragement to young preachers, is anxi-
     ous to point out that her husband was the popular
     preacher first requested by the people of Russelville.
     See J. B. Wakeley, The Bold Frontier Preacher
     (Cincinnati: Hitchcock and Walden, 1869), pp. 158-
     65, for a retelling of the story.
16. Wise, Sketches, p. 105; the advice reportedly was given
     to William McKendree, destined to become one of
     the luminaries of the Methodist episcopacy, by a Mr.
     Epps. Also Wightman, Capers, pp. 94-97, 100-1.
17. Finney, Marvin, pp. 119-20.
18. Robison, Clawson, p. 101.
19. Battlefield, pp. 30-31.
20. Johnson, Recollections, pp. 110-11; Gavitt, Crumbs,
     pp. 285-86.
21. Erastus O. Haven, Autobiography of Erastus O. Haven,
     D.D., LL.D., One of the Bishops of the Methodist
     Episcopal Church, edited by C. C. Stratton (New
     York: Phillips and Hunt, 1883), p. 97; Gavitt,
     Crumbs, pp. 275-76.
22. E. E. Hoss, David Morton: A Biography (Nashville:
     Publishing House of the Methodist Episcopal Church,
     South, 1916), pp. 56-57.
23. Smith, Pierce, pp. 60-61.
24. Milburn, Ten Years, p. 54.
25. Reminiscences, p. 298.

26. Finney, Marvin, p. 134.
27. Finney, Marvin, pp. 133-34.
28. Pearne, Sixty-One Years, p. 481.
29. Adam Miller (comp.), Experience of German Methodist
     Preachers (Cincinnati: Printed at the Methodist Book
     Concern for the Author, 1859), pp. 70-71.
30. Pearne, Sixty-One Years, pp. 482-83.
31. Stanley, Stateler, pp. 280-81. According to Stanley, the
     incident was published widely in area newspapers un-
     der the heading, "How a Methodist parson got away
     with Bishop Tuttle out West." Ibid., pp. 281-82.
          In a Sut Lovingood yarn, "Sut at a Negro Night-
     Meeting," Sut tries to prove that his deviltry at the
     meeting could be called "assistance" by remarking,
     "Ef a wun-hoss preacher sits intu the pulpit while a
     two-hoss one preaches, don't they print hit that he
     'sisted?" George Washington Harris, Sut Lovingood's
     Yarns, ed. by M. Thomas Inge (New Haven, Conn.:
     College and University Press, 1966), p. 128. The
     usage may indicate that the derogatory phrase had
     wider circulation than the incident recorded by Stan-
     ley.
32. Peck, "Father Clark, pp. 268-69.
33. Gorrie, Black River, I, 170.
34. J. O. Andrew, Miscellanies: Comprising Letters, Es-
     says, and Addresses: To Which is Added a Bio-
     graphical Sketch of Mrs. Ann Amelia Andrew (Louis-
     ville: Morton and Griswold, 1854), pp. 61-62.
35. "Brother Mack," p. 17.
36. Johnson, Recollections, p. 109.
37. Finney, Marvin, p. 765.
38. Beard, Sketches, p. 209.
39. Summers, Biographical Sketches, pp. 273-74; Ayres,
     Methodist Heroes, p. 68; Travis, Autobiography, p.
     59.   Motif A972.1.: "Indentions on rocks from im-
     print of gods and saints."
40. Smith, Recollections, p. 38.
41. Stanley, Stateler, p. 56. For similar accounts, see
     Hobart, Recollections, pp. 396-97; Waugh, Autobi-
     ography, p. 109; Graves, DeVilbiss, pp. 20, 38.
42. Crumbs, pp. 150-1. John B. McFerrin recalls an epi-
     sode in which he ended up on the opposite bank of
     a river "half-dressed," his clothing floating down-
     stream on a log. He comments: "This was my first
     and last ride on horse back without 'unmentionables.'"
     Fitzgerald, McFerrin, p. 67.
43. Gaddis, Walker, p. 194, 196-98.

44. B. Franklin Atkinson, The Life Ministry of B. Franklin
     Atkinson (An Autobiographical Sketch) (Louisville:
     The Herald Press, n.d.), p. 50.
              Similar jests are recorded in Graves, Devil-
     biss, p. 38: a horse that goes to the bottom of a
     stream is accused of being a Campbellite; in Chap-
     man, Memoirs, pp. 100-1; dunked in a river with
     his horse, Chapman is jokingly accused of going over
     to the Baptists.
45. Itinerant, p. 115.
46. Sue F. Dromgoole Mooney, My Moving Tent (Nashville:
     Publishing House Methodist Episcopal Church, South,
     1903), p. 255. A Jesse Lee biography, noting Lee's
     near-drowning in the Yadkin River, remarks: "We
     once saw an old call for a preacher 'who is a good
     swimmer, as there are several rivers to cross on
     the round.' Jesse Lee would not have done for that
     circuit." William Henry Meredith, Jesse Lee: A
     Methodist Apostle (New York: Eaton and Mains,
     1909), p. 55.
47. McNemee, "Brother Mack," pp. 66-67.
48. Beard, Sketches, p. 209.
49. Burgess, Pleasant Recollections, p. 328.
50. Carroll, Case, II, 267.
51. Pearne, Sixty-One Years, p. 142. Motif X1655.: "Lies
     about extraordinary mud."
52. Ibid. See also J. L. Dyer's tall tale: "'I was looking
     ahead, and saw a plug hat on the mud, and thought
     I had a prize. As I got nearer, it seemed to have
     a man's head in it, which said, "Let me alone, I
     have a good horse under me!"'" In The Snow-Shoe
     Itinerant (Cincinnati: Cranston and Stowe, 1890),
     p. 27.
53. Ware, Memoir, pp. 144-47.
54. J. Young, Autobiography, p. 262.
55. Field, Worthies, p. 159.
56. Henkle, Bascom, p. 207.
57. Peck, Forty Years, pp. 101-3.
58. Paddock, Memoir, p. 297; "'Never,'" Gary allegedly
     said, "'did a sense of personal unworthiness more
     overwhelm me.'"
59. Carroll, Case, II, 265-66.
60. Smith, Recollections, p. 319.
61. Taylor, Autobiography, p. 90.
62. Marvin, Caples, pp. 152-57.
63. Henkle, Bascom, p. 58.
64. Watson, Tales and Takings, p. 254.

65. Mary O. Tucker, Itinerant Preaching in the Early Days
    of Methodism, ed. by Thomas W. Tucker (Boston:
    B. B. Russell, 1872), pp. 54-55.
66. Burgess, Pleasant Recollections, pp. 288-89.
67. Ibid., p. 198.
68. Burgess defines the dish with a snatch of a boyhood
    song:
           "My father and mother, they killed a black hog
           They made a blood-pudding, which choked our
    black dog." Ibid., pp. 309-10.
69. Gavitt, Crumbs, p. 164.
70. Autobiography, pp. 72-73.
71. Plyler and Plyler, Men, pp. 26-27.
72. Lee, Life, pp. 348-49. In Wise, Sketches, p. 75, the
    first line of the blessing reads, "Please look down
    upon us sinners." Motif J1340.: "Retorts from
    hungry persons."
73. Sullins, Recollections, pp. 44-45.
74. Field, Worthies, pp. 168-69.
75. Waugh, Autobiography, p. 72.
76. Ten Years, p. 57. See also Andrew Manship, History
    of Gospel Tents and Experience (Philadelphia: Pub-
    lished by the Author, 1884), p. 123, for the same
    saying.
77. Wright, Quinn, pp. 183-84. See Erwin, Reminiscences,
    pp. 270-72, for the story of the Ellenburg chickens:
    an immoral old man tried to bribe the preacher with
    a good chicken dinner but was expelled from the
    church anyhow. See also, R. Young, Reminiscences
    (Nashville: Publishing House Methodist Episcopal
    Church, South, 1900), p. 88, for another chicken
    story.
78. Tokar, "Humorous Anecdotes," p. 100. Commenting on
    the story, old Rev. Steinfeldt recapitulated the tradi-
    tion: "'Preachers liked chicken, and this is what
    was served when they were invited out to dinner by
    parishioners. There was so much kidding about chick-
    en, particularly yellow-legged chicken.'"
           Tokar notes other chicken stories in R. M.
    Dorson (ed.), Negro Folktales in Michigan (Cam-
    bridge, Mass.: Harvard University Press, 1956),
    pp. 168-71; and in "Folklore from St. Helena, South
    Carolina," JAF, XXXVIII (1925), 226.
79. Worthies, p. 41.
80. Quinn, p. 103. See Wise, Sketches, p. 48, for another
    account of the episode.
81. Ryder, Superannuate, p. 108; also Graves, DeVilbiss,

p. 91; Patton, <u>Life</u>, p. 44; Camilla Sanderson, <u>John Sanderson the First</u>, or, A Pioneer Preacher at <u>Home</u> (Toronto: William Briggs, 1910), pp. 52-53. Another hymn used by biographers to celebrate itinerant poverty was the familiar "Wayfaring Stranger"; Marine, <u>Hersey</u>, p. 113.

82. Stanley, <u>Stateler</u>, p. 210.
83. Robison, <u>Clawson</u>, pp. 235-36.
84. Brother Mason, pp. 67-68, 152-53.
85. Erwin, <u>Reminiscences</u>, p. 219.
86. Richardson, <u>Sunrise</u>, p. 175.
87. Manship, <u>Thirteen Years</u>', pp. 161-62.
88. Milburn, <u>Ten Years</u>, p. 60.
89. <u>Pleasant Recollections</u>, pp. 379-80; Burgess warns, "'Muzzle not the ox that treadeth out the corn.'"
     In another version of the story, the preacher hands back the borrowed money, and to the rich man's question, replies, "'I had no money, and I can't preach worth a cent unless I have money in my pocket.'" As in the episode above, the lesson was effectual. Robison, <u>Clawson</u>, pp. 236-37.
90. Finney, <u>Marvin</u>, p. 464. Motif K1581.11.: "Prostitute paid with counterfeit money."
91. Hamilton, <u>From the Pulpit to the Poor-house</u>, pp. 19-21.
92. Finney, <u>Marvin</u>, p. 464.
93. Pearne, <u>Sixty-One Years</u>, p. 146.
94. Sullins, <u>Reminiscences</u>, p. 60; Stanley, <u>Stateler</u>, p. 31.
95. Patton, <u>Life</u>, pp. 74-75.

Chapter 10

PREACHING

Methodism was never poverty and rags, nor a
clown's coat and blundering speech, nor an unfur-
nished, half-provisioned house, nor no house at all,
for the preacher; but it was the gospel simply bé-
lieved, and faithfully followed, and earnestly (even
vehemently) insisted on. It was powerful, not because it was poor, but because it was a living,
breathing, active, urgent testimony of the gospel of
the Son of God. It apprehended Christ's presence,
and took hold on his authority to perform its work.
Its every utterance was a 'Thus saith the Lord.'
The Bible, the Bible was ever on its lips. Nothing
but the Bible, and just as the Bible holds it, was
its testimony of truth. [1]

Preachers lived by the Word and taught the Word. As
often as seven days a week they selected a text before a congregation, large or small, indoors or out-of-doors, whatever
the weather or time of day, and delivered the saving news of
God's evangel in accents designed to stir the sleeping, startle
the apathetic, focus the preoccupied and rout the proud. So
incessant was the sermonizing that the negligent though con-
scientious preacher could lose his voice and be forced to retire. [2] Preaching "made" or "broke" reputations; according
to one tradition, William McKendree was elected Bishop in
1808 because of a sermon he preached during conference. [3]
A less fortunate young man, aspiring to the itinerancy against
all advice, learned his lesson when, after he had preached
to a congregation in a little log school-house, he found as
remuneration in a collection plate that was passed around
buttons, chips, pebbles and quids of tobacco. [4]

Preaching was of such importance to circuit riders and
to the salvific work upon which Methodism had embarked that
it must have been, to judge from the literature, a topic of
constant discussion at conference and elsewhere. From these

216

conversations developed a large body of preaching lore, part
of which celebrated the foibles of ministers and people, and
part of which taught, in a more serious vein, what the effective preacher ought to be and do.

"Getting into the Bushes"

The classic situation for "getting into the bushes" was
the young itinerant's first sermon on his first circuit. Frequently, the petrified neophyte would announce his text and
blunder through to the end of his exposition without being able
later to recall anything he had said. [5] If the beginner had
any pretensions about his preaching qualifications, he was
likely to fall the harder when his time came. One itinerant
recalls his first sermon:

> I went through the preliminaries and took my text
> and began operation. It was a text which I have
> since found out that I did not understand, but it af-
> forded me a basis for extended remarks. I used
> it a little like a cowboy uses a stob to which he
> fastens his lariat when he wants his pony to graze.
> It gives him latitude. So I fastened on to that text
> and grazed about it from all points of the compass.
> What I lacked in my knowledge of it I more than
> made up in the length of time I worked at it.

To his horror, just as he was reaching a heated and eloquent
climax, Aunt Rachel Stone, a local eccentric, who "looked
like the tallest woman I had ever seen," arose from her seat,
deliberately strode up to the pulpit, shook her head and said:
"Now, lookie here, my young man, ef you're a goin' to give
it to us in that thar style I'll be switched ef I ain't got 'nuff
of you jest right now."[6]

Older, more experienced preachers were just as likely, when conditions were unpropitious, to have sermon failures as their younger counterparts. One congregation which
had just endured a long-winded, florid preacher, recalls one
itinerant, was "'ready to eat me up without a grain of salt.'"
Not only hostile audiences but also the presence of more il-
lustrious preachers could unhinge speakers: an Iowa itinerant,
under such circumstances, "lost daylight and began to feel
around for thoughts; and as nothing but vacancy appeared, he
sat down," announcing to the people, "'Gentlemen and ladies,

"Ef that's the style you are goin' to give us I've got a nuff of you right now!"

Aunt Rachel Stone interrupts a neophyte's first sermon

there is no use of talking--I have made a failure and you all
know it.'"7 Sometimes the presence of a visiting bishop in
the audience could cramp a preacher's style. Such was the
case with Benjamin Abbott, who began a polished sermon for
the bishop and, when he saw that "no interest was excited,"
paused and said, "'If all the bishops on earth, and the devils
in hell were here, I must preach like Ben Abbott,'" and
went on with a sermon that excited great emotion in the congregation. 8 Similar to Abbott's remarks were those reported
of Peter Cartwright when he succeeded an extremely popular
preacher as presiding elder of the Illinois district; after limp-
ing through part of his first sermon, Cartwright halted and
said: "'I never could preach like any body else; I never did
preach like any body else; I never wanted to preach like any
body else.'"9 Many old preachers, accustomed to speaking
to rural audiences in rough log cabins or under the trees,
found urban, professional audiences suffocating. 10

Frequently laughter was the only antidote for humiliat-
ing sermon embarrassments. Two young preachers remembered long afterward their failures in the same church:

> In after years, when McComb was in the Confer-
> ence, he would recall the fact, and say, 'John, do
> you remember preaching from 'Thou, Solomon my
> son'?' and John would as promptly ask, 'William,
> have you forgotten that 'Charity never faileth'?'
> Like many of our troubles that formerly made us
> weep, they now allow a laugh! 11

Another way of "getting into the bushes" for preachers
both old and young was by pursuing a sermon exemplum to
unedifying lengths. Frontier Methodist preachers, raised up
from among the people, spoke the people's language. They
spiked their sermons with homey examples designed to catch
the ears of weary, often indifferent, farmers and hunters and
to make the drama of salvation as graphic as possible. Such
was the exemplum of Rev. Samuel Clawson, who compared
the unconverted man to a squirrel dangling from the topmost
branch of a tall tree by only one foot, with the huntsman and
the dogs waiting at the base for the fall. 12

Sometimes, however, preachers rode their examples
"into the bushes." One Brother Sprague was assessed by a
colleague as a "pious man" but "not an original thinker or an
easy speaker." The account of his sheep and goats exemplum
illustrates why he was damned with faint praise.

He preached on the 'sheep and the goats.' He had
read Clark's Commentaries closely and undertook
to trace the analogy between the sheep and the Christian and the goat and the sinner. He had a catar-
rhal difficulty that would occasionally affect the
nasal organs, stopping the voice and requiring a
sudden force of the breath to clear it. He became
excited and earnest in showing that the sheep was
useful, and so was the Christian; the sheep was
clean, so was the Christian, etc. Then he took
the other side and stated that the goat was unruly
and so was the sinner; the goat was cross, always
ready to butt anyone that came in his way, so were
sinners. And so he went on until he capped the
climax by announcing that the goat was an offensive
animal, had a bad odor and so had sinners. His
nasal twang threw such emphasis on the latter part
of the sentence as to disturb the gravity of the audience and the younger portion ran from the house in
a burst of laughter. It was considered a moving
sermon. 13

One preacher tried to incorporate a bit of ancient history into his discourse, with disastrous results. Reading
"'Rollin's Ancient History,'" Rev. Samuel Clawson had been
impressed with the heroic exploits of Leonidas at the Battle
of Thermopylae, and determined to use the incident as a sermon illustration. On the Sabbath he took for his text the
passage "'Happy art thou, O Israel: who is like unto thee,
O people saved by the Lord.'" Well into his discourse, he
attempted to introduce his exemplum:

In showing in what respects there was none like
God's Israel, he said there was none like them for
war. He spoke of their numerous and powerful
enemies, and of their coming off 'more than con-
queror.' He said: 'When I think of the Christian
in combat with the great multitudes of his enemies,
I am reminded of--of--" (I [the narrator, who was
listening to the sermon] saw he intended to bring in
Leonidas contending with Xerxes great army, but
he scratched his head so vigorously that I was
filled with laughter, and could not help him).
'Brethren,' he continued, 'I am not good at recol-
lecting proper names, but the battle was fought at--
at I believe-- Pensacola.' At this Brother Reeves
laughed outright, and turned it off with a hearty

amen, which so amused me that I had the greatest
difficulty to suppress my laughter. [14]

Methodist preachers were not the only ones recorded
as confounding themselves with sermon examples. One Baptist preacher, to the disgust of the narrator, made the in-
vidious comparison of grace and lice:

> An old minister named H----, famous for allegor-
> izing, thus noticed the plagues in Egypt, and the
> success of her magicians in imitating some of the
> miracles of Moses, but could not produce the lice.
> 'These lice,' he said, 'signified the grace of God
> in the soul. Now,' he said, 'as you can feel these
> little animals,' suiting the action to the word he
> here scratched his head, 'but cannot see them, so
> you cannot see the grace of God, but you can feel
> it.'[15]

A Presbyterian minister, T. B. Balch, was called to task by
a layman for introducing an anachronism into the story of
the Good Samaritan.

> Once, preaching on the man going down to Jericho
> and falling among thieves, he became very graphic.
> He represented him as waylaid by men who con-
> cealed themselves in 'locks of the fence,' with fire-
> arms ready for the execution of their diabolical pur-
> pose, and when the man came within gunshot, off
> went the weapon of death--representing the sound
> as well as the act. The poor man ran for his life,
> and from another 'lock of the fence' off went an-
> other gun, and so on till, scared almost to death,
> he fell wounded in the way. Then 'they stripped
> and robbed him, and left him half dead.'

After the sermon Irving Spence asked him what came over
him when he was preaching that sermon: "Do you not know
that gunpowder was unknown, and firearms were not invented?"[16] The narrator comments on the incident, providing perhaps the source of the phrase, "getting into the bushes":

> As Solomon Sharp used to say sometimes of him-
> self and of other Methodist preachers, Mr. Balch
> had got into the bushes, and he was very much
> tangled up. [17]

A third source of preaching humor, besides the preacher stammering in discomfiting circumstances and the ill chos-
en exemplum, was the sermon based upon a misquoted scriptural text.

Erwin recalls hearing "ever since I was a boy of
'Father Abbott' taking for his text the words, 'I know thee
to be an oyster man,'" and of the sermon that followed:

> A man went out to the ocean and with a great iron
> rake drew them out. The oyster man represented
> the preacher, the rake the Gospel, the teeth of the
> rake the essential doctrines, the ocean the world.
> And he raked the congregation until he gather sev-
> eral to the 'mourner's bench' and got them soundly
> converted. A friend said to him the next morning:
> 'Father Abbott, you did not read your text right
> last night, it is: "I know thee to be an austere
> man," which means rough, hard, severe.' 'Never
> mind,' said the 'son of thunder,' oyster or austere,
> I got what I was after--souls converted.'18

Sometimes the misquote derived from a lapsus linguae rather
than ignorance. On one occasion, Bishop Marvin inverted the
order of man and angel in a sentence so that he said the opposite of what he intended: "'I am glad,' he asserted, 'I
was born an angel and not a man.'" The young people in
the church laughed and Marvin stopped to rebuke them. Afterwards, the pastor of the church attempted to explain the out-
burst: "'Bishop, I reckon it was thought so near the truth,
that you were more an angel than a man, that they couldn't
help smiling a little.'" Whether or not the pastor assessed
his people's feeling correctly, his remarks mollified the
Bishop.19

On another occasion, a preacher named Barkdull
slipped and inverted "wild ass's colt" to "wild colt's asses."
A friend who told Rev. Barkdull of his blunder reported, "I
never saw or heard any man laugh so heartily as he; and
every few moments he would burst forth in hearty laughter
in his bed...."20

The word "ass," which focused the humor of Barkdull's
mistake, if an excursus may be made, provided considerable
titillation to waggish circuit riders who could excuse the bor-
derline propriety of the term by reference to the Biblical
precedents of Balaam's ass and the ass that Christ rode into
Jerusalem.

One story, noted below in the category of "spontaneous preaching," tells how a Methodist preacher, engaged in a preaching contest with an opponent, received as his text just before he entered the pulpit, "'And Balaam rose in the morning and saddled his ass.'"

William Taylor remembered his sally against a man who attempted to disrupt street preaching in California by riding his donkey through the listening crowd:

> On another occasion a wag, thinking to have a little sport, tried to ride through the crowd on one of the smallest of that small species of animals, the jack. His animal refusing to go through, I said, 'See there; that animal, like Balaam's of the same kind, has more respect for the worship of God than his master, who only lacks the ears of being the greater ass of the two."[21]

A third "ass" story illustrates preacherly antipathy toward the supercilious condescension of the genteel--lawyers, doctors, and magistrates. Rev. John Ray, the story goes, "generally rode a very superior horse."

> Once as he was riding through the town of M____ a group of young lawyers and doctors, seeing him approach, plotted that they would 'stump' him in some way when he came up. On his arrival their chosen spokesman commenced: 'Well, Father Ray, how is it that you are so much better off than your Master? He had to ride on an ass, but you are mounted on a very fine horse; you must be proud. Why don't you ride as did your Master?'
> 'For the simple reason,' said Ray, 'that there are no asses now to be obtained--they turn them all into lawyers and doctors.'
> They said no more.[22]

According to another version of the story, prefaced by the notation that Darius Dunham's "reply to the newly-appointed magistrate's bantering remarks is widely reported," the preacher, questioned by an official, replies that he would ride like his master except that asses are hard to find-- "'the government having made up all the asses into magistrates!'"[13]

On each circuit there were those who watched the

preacher like a hawk and advised him of every mistake after
the sermon. One such critic, an exhorter at the church
where Brother Spottswood preached, told Spottswood that he
should correct the mistake he had made in saying that the
resurrection would come after the judgment. Spottswood said
to him:

> 'O, every body ... knew that I knew better than
> that--that was only a lapsis [sic] linguae, brother;
> however, when I come back, I will rectify my mis-
> take, but I want you to be present also to fix up
> your exhortation.' 'Why?' he asked, in great sur-
> prise. 'Because,' I replied, 'you told us with the
> greatest fervor, if we were faithful to God, we
> would finally get to that house not made by the
> heavens in the sky.' The critic looked crest-fallen.
> He never criticised me again. 24

A fourth way of tangling with the bushes, in the opinion of serious commentators, was to begin there by preaching from a bizarre scriptural text or by sensationally titling
one's sermon. Of the many stories dealing with unusual
texts, the following anecdote, told of Rev. James Jackson,
is perhaps the most amusing:

> He had a great deal of tact in handling a text, and
> frequently preached on very unusual ones, the doc-
> trinal value of which the thoroughly informed would
> be very much inclined to doubt. Here is one of
> his texts, the exposition of which obtained him un-
> bounded eclat among the wondering rustics to whom
> he addressed the sermon: 'There are three-score
> queens, and four-score concubines, and virgins with-
> out number.' (Cant. vi, 8) 25

Sensational sermon topics included titles such as "'Baruch's
Sore Gently Opened and the Salve Skillfully Applied.'" The
disgusted commentator notes that although ministers are
called to be fools for Christ's sake "they are nowhere commanded to make fools of themselves. "26

Interruptions

The preacher who avoided the pitfalls of misquotes,
slips, unfortunate examples, and who preached for God's

approval alone[27] could never be certain that the path from
beginning to end of his discourse would be clear. In the
sermon lore startled sleepers, falling benches, settling foundations, a whole menagerie of animals, bawling children and
unruly drunks, men coming in to hammer and men running
out to shoot turkeys provided the occasion for preachers'
chagrin, sarcasm, and sometimes laughter. Such stories
told among the itinerants must have provided opportunities
for easing the frustration of voicing God's word in a world
often too distracted to pay heed.

      1. Sleepers. Seldom did an itinerant mesmerize an
audience so totally as did the Rev. Isaac Quinn at a preaching appointment on the Tazewell Circuit in southwestern Virginia.

> Here, at one of his appointments, on a hot sum-
> mer's day, the people, most of whom had come on
> foot, were somewhat tired; and, as Isaac was not
> particularly animated, or animating, that day, they
> very quietly, one after another, dropped to sleep,
> until the preacher and one woman were all that
> were not wholly oblivious, for the time, to all ter-
> restrial things. Quinn, casting his eye around, and
> how matters were--that of all his little congregation
> only one remained awake--very quietly raised his
> hands, pronounced the benediction, took up his hat
> and saddle-bags, and left. His passing out at the
> door attracted the attention of the woman awake,
> who, till then, seemed not to have noticed or under-
> stood his movements; and she piteously asked,
> 'Brother Quinn, aint you gwine to leave another
> appintment?' 'No,' said Quinn, turning his head
> and speaking over his shoulder; 'God never called
> me to preach to a people I can not keep awake';
> and kept on. [28]

      Some itinerants, according to another story, accepted
less philosophically than Isaac Quinn their soporific effect
upon weary audiences. Jesse Lee, on one occasion while
preaching, was annoyed not only by sleepers but by people
talking loudly outside the church.

> At another time, while engaged in preaching, he
> was not a little mortified to discover many of the
> congregation taking rest in sleep; and not a little
> annoyed by the loud talking of the people in the yard.

Pausing long enough for the absence of sound to
startle the sleepers, he raised his voice, and cried
out: 'I'll thank the people in the yard not to talk
so loud; they'll wake up the people in the house!'
This was 'killing two birds with one stone,' in a
most adroit and effectual manner. 29

Another preacher, with better temper and perhaps
more tact, watched his entire congregation drift off, on a
warm day, "wholly oblivious to all terrestrial things."

The preacher knew that no benefit would accrue
from preaching to sleepers; yet he did not storm,
or scold, but stopped altogether, till one after another, thinking the service over, aroused himself,
and thought of leaving, when the preacher broke
out with--'When the cradle stops rocking, the baby
wakes up!' and went on and concluded his sermon
to a more wakeful congregation. 30

In one "sleeper" story, a preacher unintentionally
aroused a dozing Frenchman.

At another time, the bold preacher suddenly delivered with considerable emphasis that passage,
'Awake, thou that sleepest.' This aroused a sleepy
old Frenchman, who, overcome by the fatigues of
the week and the warmth of the day, sat nodding in
his pew. He supposing the remark directed particularly at himself, jumped up in great anger, ex-
claiming, 'What you mean, sar? Can't I take von
leetel nap in mine own pew without von insult, sar?
I leaves dis house, sar, an' I comes here no more
sar!' and out marched the irate Frenchman, shaking his cane violently and stamping upon the floor.31

Dozers who nodded while they slept were not always
dealt with as gently as Rev. John Haslam did with a man who,
during a sermon, "began to nod as a sleepy man will do."

Mr. Haslam stopped in the middle of his discourse
and remarked to the man half-asleep, 'You need
not bow to me, sir; I have met you before,' and
then proceeded with his discourse. 32

According to another story, a nodding head invited the
butt of a nearby goat (or lamb, in one version).

At another time, the gravity of the preacher and of
his congregation, was put to a severer trial still.
They were assembled in a grove, or field. During
the progress of the sermon, one of the distant, out-
side hearers, had so far forgotten that it was his
business to listen attentively to the preacher, that
he allowed himself to become quite drowsy. At
length he began to nod. A large surly goat, that
was nibbling grass hard by, happened to notice the
sleeper, and interpreted the nodding of his head as
a challenge for battle. The animal approached and
retired; approached again, and again retired, as
though doubtful whether the gentleman was in earnest. But the sleeper continued to nod, and the animal at length became seriously enraged. He took
a martial position, shook his head in anger, and
then darted forward with fury, and laid the sleeper
low. Many of the congregation smiled; and the
preacher, who was so situated as to be obliged to
witness the whole transaction, could not find it in
his heart to reprove them. There can be no doubt
that the drowsy gentleman was more impressed by
the assault of the goat, than by the sermon of the
preacher. 33

Sometimes sleepers attempted to reproduce dreamed
actions during a sermon, with ludicrous results. During a
sermon by a Presbyterian minister,

My brother-in-law was present, and his colored
man John, who sat on the end of a bench near the
door. The sermon was rather too logical for John,
and falling into a deep sleep, he dreamed that he
was helping to launch a sloop. Considerable effort
seemed necessary to get the vessel started, and
John anxious to show his strength, put, as he
thought, his shoulder to the work, and pushed with
all his might, --in doing so he fell his whole length
upon the floor, to the no small diversion of all the
congregation. 34

Or, sleepers awoke and did not immediately grasp the true
nature of the situation unfolding around them. One such man,
startled into wakefulness by the crash of a bench that had
broken during the sermon, thought the sound was thunder;
leaping up he faced directly into the sunlight streaming through
an unshuttered window,

and the sudden glare of light appeared like lightning.
Still unconscious of what was going on he hurried
to the door, fearing, as he said, that the house was
on fire, and that he must make his escape as quickly as possible. 35

One scheming sleeper, however, knew exactly what
was going on:

> Within the bounds of this work an excellent brother
> was always present at preaching, and took his seat
> in the 'amen corner.' The programme was so well
> laid out and so faithfully kept, that I knew just what
> to expect. About fifteen or twenty minutes of the
> sermon was employed in nodding and snoring, un-
> til the minister became fully engaged, when all at
> once he would awake and begin to praise the Lord
> as if warmed up under the inspiration of divine
> truth. I never blamed him for gratitude to God in
> enjoying a good nap, but for his pretensions of
> getting very happy under the discourse, when every-
> body knew that he had been fast asleep. 36

2. The benches collapse. Needless to say, the sight
of otherwise dignified listeners tumbling helter-skelter over
each other when their seats gave way tempted the risibilities
of grave ministers to the breaking point. As Willian Ryder's
biographer says,

> Religious worship, under any circumstances, is
> peculiarly solemn; and yet instances are upon
> record where grave and devout men have been ir-
> resistibly provoked to smile upon occasions the
> most serious. 37

A slapstick account of such an instance follows:

> He [Ryder] was once at a quarterly meeting held in
> a large barn on the banks of the Hudson. At the
> rear end of the main floor, and directly against the
> folding doors, was erected a temporary rostrum,
> upon which were elevated the presiding elder and
> several preachers, seated upon a rough bench pre-
> pared for the occasion. In the midst of a discourse
> by one of the elders, a rude seat gave way upon
> the barn floor, and the necessary scramble among
> the prostrate occupants occasioned no little mirth

among the younger portion of the congregation,
which was most grotesquely scattered in the bays
and stables, and upon the beams and scaffolds of
the spacious edifice.   To check this ill-timed levity,
the presiding elder rose and said, with great solem-
nity, that 'such conduct was unbecoming in the wor-
shipers of God, and that it was well for such careless sinners that they had not all fallen into hell!'
This dignitary weighed at least tenscore, and as
he resumed his seat the coarse bench crushed beneath its burden, the fastenings of the folding doors,
against which they had unguardedly leaned, gave way
under the united momentum; and bench, presiding
elder, preachers and all, turning ludicrous sum-
mersets, tumbled helter-skelter into the adjoining
barn-yard!38

3.   <u>Animals</u>.   By far the most familiar intruder during sermons was the common dog.   Unlike the itinerant who
believed that, just as the devil had been permitted to enter
into swine in the Gospels, so he was allowed to possess a
dog who disturbed family prayers, most preachers considered

Itinerant Wards Off a Feisty Canine (see note 40)

canine intruders plain nuisances, and not an index of the
devil's presence. [39] The discomfiture of the ministers at
such interruptions increased the merriment of congregations
prone to appreciate low comedy as a means of relieving the
tension of solemn religious worship. According to one such
story, at a camp meeting ground

> the dogs had been troublesome ... and Brother
> Hickey lectured the people on Friday night on the
> necessity of keeping their dogs at home.... The
> dogs became the subject of much merriment in the
> preacher's tent. Monday, as was the custom, I
> had preached a missionary sermon and was sitting
> in the pulpit behind Brother Hickey, who was talk-
> ing to the congregation preparatory to taking a col-
> lection. He and the congregation were intensely in-
> terested in the subject when a dog barked just be-
> hind the pulpit. Hickey turned at once and cried
> out: 'Begone!' 'Ha, ha, ha, !' said I, and the whole
> congregation broke out in a guffaw. [40]

Amusing as these dog stories may have been, they
are not as memorable as anecdotes told of other bestial in-
terlopers. The intrusion of a colt into a meeting, while ludicrous in retrospect, was not considered such by the preacher
and people.

> A colt having lost its dam, came rushing up the
> aisle, put its nose close to the minister's face and
> whinnied; its hot breath nearly suffocated him, and
> started the devout congregation, almost throwing the
> minister off his balance.

But the intent preacher kept on and swept the people with him
in prayer "until the glory cloud burst with benedictions on the
audience and hallelujahs rang through the building. " Later,
a "sneering sceptic, Mr. M. , " asked the minister.

> 'What said the colt to you yesterday as he whinnied
> in your face? Did he not, like Balaam's ass, "for-
> bid the madness of the prophet, " and check your
> burning zeal for us poor sinners?'

But Erwin adroitly turned the tables on his pharasaic questioner:

> 'Oh no, my friend ... as I understand the message,

it was "hold on to God" for the salvation of this
community; especially for that trifler M. for it is
his last call, and if not saved in this revival he
will be damned. '

Chastened out of the horse's mouth, so to speak, "Mr. M. "
became converted before the meeting was over. [41]

In contrast to such seriousness, the story of one un-
popular old preacher's "cackling sermon" afforded much
amusement to Landon Taylor:

Our minister could not bear the least disturbance,
it would totally disconcert him; so about the time
he started out in his sermon, an old hen having a
nest in the porch above, came to the front, assert-
ing her rights, cackling at the top of her voice.
The minister, at the risk of eggs for dinner, bade
Mr. S., the proprietor of the house, 'to drive away
that old hen. ' The mandate was instantly obeyed,
when Mr. S. returned and took his seat; and about
the same time returned the old hen. Louder and
still louder she cackled, when Mr. S. out [sic] and
after her again. This second scare he drove her
some distance away, hoping it would prove effectual;
when he returned to enjoy the sermon. Scarcely
had he resumed his seat, when, lo! here comes the
old hen, reenforced by the old rooster, by the excitement their voices raised to higher notes, when
away went the owner, with raised club, hen and
rooster, who kept guard at a distance until the discourse was finished. I venture to say that Mr. S.
did not get very happy under that gospel sermon,
but it furnished a fine opportunity for amusing history in our winter hours. Many a good laugh have
I enjoyed with Mr. S. over what we called our
'cackling sermons. '[42]

Frogs croaking in a pond behind the meeting house
drowned out the efforts of one weak-voiced preacher, [43] while
a Montana itinerant, L. B. Stateler, was bested by a mimick-
ing parrot:

On one occasion the lady of the house covered the
bird up in a barrel to prevent his interruptions;
but about the middle of the service he escaped, and
perching on a piece of furniture clear out of reach,

A Snake Enlivens the Sermon

was more boisterous than usual, so much as to utterly destroy any chance of further worship. Yield-
ing to the inevitable, he [Stateler] said, 'Friends,
the bird has the advantage of us today; and the service must end. Let us pray.' Poll said: 'Let us
pray.' During the former part of the prayer he
repeated word for word what the preacher was saying, until a general titter went around the whole
room. By this time the bird had become tired and
began to scream at the top of his voice, 'Say amen,
Stateler; say amen,' and continued so to scream
till the grave old preacher was compelled to yield
and close without further ceremony the exercises
of the hour.[44]

Another bird story, however, which relates how a snow
white dove flew through the window of a church at the mention
of the Holy Spirit, must have been told in the awful tones be-
fitting the relation of a remarkable providence.[45]

One cycle of stories played on the humorous sight of
an unwitting minister earnestly preaching with a nest of wasps
behind his head. According to a rendition of the story, one
young itinerant encountered the insects while preaching on his
first circuit:

'The text was taken. The preacher was doing his
best, under the circumstances. But his words
lacked point; his watch chain was pendent; a wasp
warmed out of his nest by the fire had settled upon
the chain, and as the hand touched it that little
creature spent all the power of his single weapon,
and imparted to the preacher a celerity of movement that showed no want of pungency in a wasp's
sting, if there was in a young preacher's words. '46

4. People. On the frontier, practicality sometimes
overruled piety to the extent that a preacher interrupted himself.

The pack-saddle was a invaluable contrivance in the
back-woods, where vehicles were unknown, and
roads were but narrow traces winding through tan-
gled forests. It was merely the limb of a tree,
which forked with the proper angles.... A good
fork was not to be found every day, and the settler
was sure to note any tree that bore so rare a
product. It was with full appreciation of its value
that Joseph Craig, an old pioneer preacher, once
stopped short in his exhortation to a large congregation in the woods, and while his eyes were still
turned devoutly to heaven, suddenly pointed his
finger to a branch of the tree that shaded him, and
exclaimed: 'Brethren, behold up yonder a first-
rate crotch for a pack-saddle. '47

On other occasions pulpit vehemence indirectly provoked dis-
traction, as in the case of the itinerant who, making a grand
flourish, knocked his hymnbook out of the pulpit into the lap
of a girl sitting in the first pew, or in the story of the em-
phatic preacher who whisked his sermon notes off the podium
into the air, causing a dog to bark and running a titter through
the congregation. 48

Probably the most amusing effect of pulpit exuberance
is remembered in the story told of Rev. Samuel Clawson,
who used to leap high in the air while preaching in the pulpit. At a sermon, in Connellsville, Pennsylvania, "a long
time ago, "

an old brother, who was almost deaf, went up to
the top of the winding stairs that led to the pulpit,
and stood near Brother Clawson. I anticipated a

scene, for the old brother was very excitable and
frequently fell down when the Lord blest him. He
listened very attentively till Brother Clawson took
a lofty flight, and leaped so high that some in the
congregation said they saw his feet over the top of
the pulpit. At the same time the old brother shouted, 'Hallelujah, ' and, falling backwards, rolled
down the steps and landed under the altar table,
without receiving the slightest injury, but he did not
go up again. 49

Another preacher was unruffled by a drunkard at a meeting,
who, after interrupting repeatedly with loud groans and amens,
collared the minister and asked: " 'Sir, can you tell me
whether a <u>bumble-bee</u> is a beast or a fowl?' "50

Veteran preachers, hardened by years of front-line
preaching, could handle almost any kind of disturbance by
people of the congregation. In two separate accounts, itinerants simply drowned out the noise of disrupters--in one
case, a man pounding on a door of an adjoining room with a
hatchet, in the other case, a man hammering nails into the
ceiling of the next room. 51

But one story, told of Thomas Morris when he was
not yet a bishop, combined all the typical preaching interruptions by members of the congregation into one classic account, at the end of which the hapless Morris is reduced to
<u>nugatio.</u> The story is presented in its entirety, inasmuch as
it is, according to one account of it, one of "an abundant
store of ... reminiscences and anecdotes" told to pass the
time while riding to conference. 52

In due time, he called at the residence of his hospitable friends in Middletown, on his way home,
and learned that the meeting was appointed to be
held at 'the old Faro-bank room, ' the usual place
for preaching--there being no chapel in the village.
'But, ' added brother Williams, 'there is no
certainty of its being there; for we have a very
singular brother here named Wallace, who assumes
to manage every thing of the sort in his own way,
and that is generally a way the rest of us do not
approve; and I shall not be surprised to find that he
has changed the place. '
After tea they walked up to the faro-bank
room, and found all dark.

THE DOOR FLEW OPEN, AND TWO MEN, WITH FAST HOLD OF EACH
OTHER'S BODIES, FELL THEIR WHOLE LENGTH IN THE AISLE.
THIS PRODUCED GREAT EXCITEMENT AMONG THE PEOPLE
—WOMEN SCREAMED, AND MEN RUSHED TO THE
DOOR, BOTH FROM WITHIN AND WITHOUT.

A Frontier Dispute Interrupts the Service

'Just as I expected, ' said Mr. Williams;
'Wallace has moved the meeting; but, as there is
only one street in the town, we can easily find it. '

They walked on, making inquiry, and learned
that the place was changed to Mr. Blackburn's
school-house. This school-house had been a private
dwelling, and consisted of two rooms and a front
porch. They found the back room full of women,
the other full of men, and the porch full of boys.
The position assigned to the preacher was the door
of the partition between the two rooms, where he
could alternately see both sections of his strange
audience, though the few tallow candles burned but
dimly. Just by the door where he stood was the
teacher's big chair; if placed in the door, it would
have filled it, so that none could pass or repass.
But as that was the only vacant spot, and Mr. Morris wished to occupy it himself, he pushed the chair
to one side in the back room out of his way. The
service commenced. The preacher was fairly
launching out into his subject when a man--after-
ward ascertained to be the officious Mr. Wallace--
pressed through the crowd and through the door,
pushing the preacher aside, and, laying hold of the
big chair, made an attempt to force it through the
crowd to its original place.

'What are you doing, my friend?' inquired
Mr. Morris.

'I am getting this chair round to place before you for a pulpit. '

'Please to desist; I do not need it, and can
do better without than with it. '

After waiting until the brother got out of the
way, the minister proceeded; but he had hardly got
fairly started again, when his attention was attracted
to two men seated near him, engaged in conversation about their private affairs, in tones loud enough
to be heard through the house. Again he desisted
from preaching, and looked steadily at the offenders,
till all eyes were turned toward them, and they at
length became conscious that they were the observed
of all observers.

Perfect stillness being restored, Mr. Morris
quietly remarked, 'We were only waiting for those
two gentlemen to finish their conversation, as that
and preaching at the same time did not harmonize
well together. '

Bishop Thomas Morris, Protagonist of the
Classic "Interrupted Sermon" Story

Again the sermon was resumed. Soon after, however, the boys on the porch commenced an entertainment of their own, of so noisy a character that the voice within could scarcely be heard, and so another pause was necessary. Mr. Wallace made a rush for the porch, where he made more disturbance than the boys had done; but at last the outbreak was quelled, and partial quiet again secured. For the third time the sermon was resumed. A few minutes only had elapsed, when an infant in the back room became restless and noisy; and though the amiable mother resorted to all means usual in such cases to quiet the little one, she failed, and was considerate enough to leave for home. But, as there was no outlet from the back room except through the door where the preacher stood, he must needs stop the flow of his talk again, step aside, and let her pass. When matters again calmed down, he resumed for the fourth time, but whether at the right or wrong place he could not possibly determine.

Shortly after, a small boy in the back room, who was perhaps five or six years old, produced a ludicrous scene. He teased and worried his mother, who used her best endeavors to suppress his rising discontent, but in vain; he whimpered on, waxing worse and worse. She finally shook him angrily, demanding, 'What ails you?' when, in fretful tones, distinctly heard throughout the house, he exclaimed 'Scratch my back!'

The shock was sudden, the effect irresistible; some hung their heads, but the majority broke into a loud laugh. The mortified mother, seizing the urchin, began to drag him toward the door, the preacher making way for her to pass. The enraged child had no notion, however, of leaving on compulsion, and he pulled back with all the strength he had; but his efforts were overcome, and he was dragged through both rooms and across the porch to the street. After order was again restored, Mr. Morris attempted to resume for the fifth time, but could not recall the point at which he had stopped. He then aimed to reach the point by rapidly reviewing the general drift of the subject, but could not strike the trail. Finally, in despair he concluded to go back to the text, but could not even recall that! He could remember neither text nor subject.

> After a long pause, he remarked: 'My
> strange friends, I make no great pretensions as a
> preacher, even under the most favorable circum-
> stances; and under such as now surround me, it is
> utterly impracticable for me to preach at all.
> Please excuse me, and receive the benediction. '53

Unlike Morris, one preacher was reduced to helpless
laughter by a situation that occurred while he was preaching.
According to the story, a husband and wife came late to the
services.   The husband found one vacant seat by the door,
and his wife sat behind him on the door-sill.

> The old lady sat almost behind her husband, and
> had her eyes fixed upon the preacher and her mouth
> wide open.   The old gentleman equally interested,
> had his mouth full of tobacco, which he wished to
> throw out, and putting up his hand, emptied his
> mouth, and forgetting that his wife was behind him,
> threw the whole of it into her mouth.   Almost
> strangled, she sprang up and ran to the spring,
> coughing and spitting as if terribly nauseated.   No
> one saw it but the preacher, who was so excited
> with the occurrence, that he roared out laughing as
> if he would split his sides.   The congregation were
> utterly amazed, and none more so than the old
> gentleman, who looked the very picture of innocence.
> The preacher had lost all control of himself, and
> all his attempts at an explanation only made the
> matter worse.   At last he made out to say, 'Friends,
> go home. '54

People walking out during the sermon sometimes offered annoyance to preachers.   Henry Bascom was only mildly disturbed by the frontiersman who ran out of a cabin with
gun in hand to shoot wild turkeys he had heard gobbling in
the bushes, 55 but another preacher attempted to reprove exit-
ing persons, and received his comeuppance.

> There were a number of overgrown boys here who
> had the disagreeable habit of going out of church in
> the middle of the sermon....   Not long after he
> had begun preaching a young man went out, then
> another, and another.   Just then a tall, handsome
> young fellow sauntered lazily down the aisle.   As
> he neared the door the elder stopped, struck an at-
> titude, and exclaimed: 'Let the next ugliest man

now go out. ' The young man stopped, turned around
in the doorway, and with a genial smile on his frank
face, lifted his arm and beckoned with his hand for
the presiding elder to come.   An audible smile rip-
pled over the congregation, and the elder let it go
at that. 56

In a similar vein, a little old lady, who was "just
deranged enough to make her sharp and witty," turned the
tables on a preacher who ordered her carried out of church
for commenting during the sermon.

Her comments on the sermon disconcerted the
speaker and he asked two of his deacons to remove
her from the house.   Two grave men came and
each taking her by an arm led her slowly through
the broad aisle towards the door.   Everything was
quiet until they reached the middle of the house,
when Mrs. P. said with a resigned, drawling voice:
'O dear me, I never felt so much like my blessed
Master before.   He was crucified between two
thieves.'   This was too much for the gravity of
the congregation; they broke out in a fit of laughter,
and the deacons releasing their hold on the lady
passed through the door, leaving her standing alone
in the aisle. 57

Reactions to Sermons

Not only did preaching mishaps and interruptions enter
into the traditions of early American Methodism, but also
exaggerated and ludicrous responses to and applications of
sermons became part and parcel of Methodist lore as well
as of broader folk traditions.

In the story which tells how Bishop Morris unwittingly
preached the funeral sermon of a living man rather than of
the man's infant child, the puzzled but composed father invited the mortified preacher to dinner. 58   More memorable
and extreme reactions occurred, according to some anecdotes,
when the old time preachers pitched at their hearers the
brimstone of hell or dramatized the damnation of sinners on
the Last Day.   Billy Hibbard preached so graphically of the
lake of hell-fire that his voice was lost in the outcry; "those
in the gallery took fright and ran down stairs so fast, that

many fell at the foot of the stairs, and they lay in quite a
heap; some ran over them, some fell out of doors."[59] Sermons on judgment day provoked similar panics among people.[60] Preachers themselves, even bishops, were susceptible to the imagery of eloquent preachers and exhorters,
evidenced, for example, by the prayer of an old-timer:

> O Lord, have mercy on the wretched, miserable,
> Godforsaken, hell-deserving, heaven-defying, hair-
> hung, and breath-shaken sinner![61]

According to one tradition, old Nicholas Snethen's hell-ser-
mon at a camp meeting caused Bishop Enoch George to attempt to scale a tree.[62] According to another tradition,
Henry Bascom's oratory caused Snethen himself to scream
his fear of the devil during a sermon.[63]

Another cycle of stories links hellfire and judgment
sermons to terrifying thunderstorms concurrent with the discourse. In one account, the coincidence offered an occasion
for a leather-lunged preacher to out-shout the crashing thunder.[64] But in other accounts, lightning was regarded a
divine communication,[65] and the frenzy of the storm outside
the church seemed to be heavenly confirmation of impending
doom.[66]

Such hellfire and brimstone discourses, with or without the assistance of nature, reportedly brought frightened
sinners by the score to the mourner's bench. In one story,
originally told of Lorenzo Dow and later appropriated by
other itinerants, a trick was employed to inspire Judgment
Day fear in the people.

A biographer of Dow regards the story as "clearly
apocryphal" but includes it anyhow:

> He intended to preach a sermon at a camp-meeting
> on 'The Judgment Day.' But beforehand he sent a
> negro boy up into a nearby tree to blow a horn in
> response to his call upon Gabriel to announce that
> time should be no more. In the midst of an im-
> passioned description of the judgment the preacher
> called upon the great archangel to blow, and in re-
> sponse to the call Gabriel blew, and the people
> shouted and shrieked and cried for mercy. But
> when the fake was discovered only the intercession
> of Lorenzo Dow could save the defenseless negro
> from the hands of the mob.[67]

People who mistook the preacher's lesson, or applied it too literally, gave rise to humorous anecdotes such as the one about the ignorant Dutchman and his scolding wife who took to heart the preaching of a Rev. Lee on the subject of taking up one's cross and carrying it. After his sermon, Lee was riding to his next appointment when he saw in the distance, "a man trudging along, carrying a woman on his back." When he got closer, Lee saw that it was the ignorant Dutchman carrying his wife. The itinerant dismounted and asked the man if he could be of assistance. The Dutchman replied:

> 'Besure you did tell us in your sarmon dat we must take up de cross and follow de Saviour, or dat we could not be saved or go to heaven, and I does desire to go to heaven so much as any pody; and dish vife is so pad, she scold and scold all de time, and dish woman is de createst cross I have in de whole world, and I does take her up and pare her, for I must save my soul.'

The nonplussed preacher sat down with them alongside the road, got out his Bible and instructed them in the lessons of the cross; soon enough reports Cartwright, the Dutchman "got clear of his cross."[68]

Some preachers achieved reputations for jocosity, such as did Peter Cartwright. Others were famous for lachrymose effects. Peter Borein, of Southern Illinois, could melt the most hardened sinners, and it was said that when "Augustus Garrett, the auctioneer, would be selling a handkerchief, he would exclaim: 'You will want this if you go to hear Borein preach.'"[69]

"'Bench 'em, Sir! Bench 'em, Sir!'"[70]

If the preceding stories functioned to relieve tension and frustration by laughter and to consolidate preacherly communion by sharing experiences, the following stories preserve and transmit preaching ideals by illustrating desirable and undesirable pulpit tactics.

To judge from some accounts, young itinerants, like young men about to be married receiving parting advice from their fathers, must have heard much about pulpit modes and

"Vy" He Called My Daughter Sal. a Sow.

A Dutchman Misinterprets the Preacher

manners from wise old preachers whose experience warranted
cautions in apodictic form. George Gary, about to ride to
his first circuit, was told by a preacher: " 'Never pretend
that you know much, or the people will soon find that you are
sadly mistaken; neither tell them how little you know, for
this they will find out soon enough.' "[71] Landon Taylor remembered the advice that "Uncle Dan" Young had given him
when he began his ministerial career; besides the cautions to
be "kind and pleasant always to the children," and not to
"abuse the dogs, lest you might insult the owner," Taylor
was told

> Be yourself, i.e., be natural. Some young minis-
> ters seem to think they must assume a kind of
> preaching tone, which is unnatural, and thereby in-
> jure themselves and destroy their usefulness during
> life.... Be short. Never tell all you know in one
> sermon.... Spare the Bible. Do not pound it, for
> it is God's book; in this way you will show your
> reverence for his word, and your good sense...
> Quit when you are done, and don't annoy your con-
> gregation with useless repetitions.[72]

Such admonitions indicate that preaching styles must
have varied widely in delivery and effectiveness. Over the
years Methodist tradition sifted out those characteristics which
constituted the best preaching and presented them to succeed-
ing generations as ideals.

1. Preaching should be plain. According to one very
strong tradition, Anglo-Saxon language is preferable to words
"from foreign sources"[73] by reason of its familiarity and di-
rectness:

> The words earliest used, and most familiar, the
> names which are dearest to us, our household
> words, and the language of the counting house, the
> shop, the market, the street, the farm, are all
> for the most part, of the Anglo-Saxon stamp....[74]

Orators such as Henry Bascom gained reluctant approval in the traditions of Methodist preaching. Of his early
preaching efforts, "old men [Methodist ministers] with gray
hairs and round coats looked sad, and said, 'He would make
a fine lawyer or statesman, but he is not the stuff of which
to make a Methodist preacher....' "[75] Men of less genius
and learning than Bascom were likely to lapse into gaucheries

such as that of a young itinerant "lately returned from a high
school, " who, when he saw that his magniloquence had little
effect,

> started suddenly back, showing a fearful counte-
> nance, looked down, and pointing with his hand to-
> ward the floor, as if he saw a trap door opened
> leading to the pit of wo; and, at the same time,
> with a swelling voice cried out, saying, 'Sinner, if
> you don't repent you will be precipitated down the
> lubricated steep of the opake profundity of damna-
> tion!'76

One preacher, given to lofty rhetorical flights, was advised
by a colleague:

> 'When I saw you making your lofty flights, I thought
> if you could only have a few feathers plucked from
> the wings of your imagination and placed in the tail
> of your judgment, you would make a grand flyer.'77

Methodist preaching lore regarded preaching popularity
in the same light as rhetorical ability, that is, as being
slightly beside the point, if not positively misleading. 78   Andrew Manship, after delivering a particularly moving funeral
sermon, was told by an old layman, "'Brother Manship, you
did well at the funeral, but I think it is likely the devil has
told you so before this. '"79

2.   Preaching should be extemporaneous.   Not all
Methodist preachers were as quick-witted as the one who
earned the hatred of a local Calvinist minister by preaching
clearly, fervently, and without notes.   The Calvinist claimed
that the Methodist committed his sermons to memory and
could not preach extemporaneously.   To prove his contention,
he devised a test by which he would give the Methodist his
sermon text on a piece of paper just before he went into the
pulpit.   The itinerant agreed to the proposal.   Word of the
test excited great curiosity among the people, and on the appointed day, they filled the church.   As the Methodist preacher made his way to the pulpit, his opponent handed him a
slip of paper, on which the text, "'And Balaam saddled his
ass, '" was written.   The cool Methodist, unruffled by the
titillating subject, divided the text into three heads, and proceeded immediately to the application.   Balaam, he said
represented hireling priests who attempt to prophesy falsely
and mislead the people; the saddle, he continued, "represented

the doctrinal system of Calvinism and the legal taxes with
which the hireling priests contrived to saddle the people"; and
the ass, he concluded, represented the people who submit to
heavy and unreasonable burdens, and who allow themselves
to be instructed by a hireling ministry. But before the Methodist preacher finished,

> the reverend gentleman and a few of his more an-
> cient friends had departed. They could not stay to
> hear him through, but remained long enough to be
> fully convinced that Methodist preachers can preach,
> not only without notes, but without committing their
> sermons to memory. 80

Other anecdotes emphasized the point that good Methodist preaching is neither read, memorized, nor from notes.
At a camp meeting, a minister with a written sermon preached
after an extemporaneous sermon by John B. McFerrin which
exemplified "the sweep and freedom of the hustings, the wild
energy of the West"; one listener sniffed at the reader's effort: "'A minnow wiggling along in the wake of a whale!'"81
According to another story, a preacher who read his sermon
from "full notes" was embarrassed when a layman sitting in
the front pew fell asleep, had a dream and awoke with a
start, shouting, "'There! there! he is turning over another
leaf!'"82 A similar anecdote recalls how an old layman,
scrutinizing a new preacher with sermon notes in his hand,
told him he was unwelcome if he read his sermons: "'no
'Piscopalians here--nor Pruspatarans nother.'" When the
minister protested that he did not read his sermons but only
used written notes,

> the old brother looked very grave, and said; 'that
> war' not the way the preachers did in old times;
> they jist went into the stand, and opened the Bible
> any hwar', and tuck the fust text they found, and
> jist banged away. Then we had sich good old fash-
> ioned times. '83

If the tradition disapproved of sermons read from text
or notes, it anathematized plagiarized sermons. Severe embarrassment or disgusted listeners, according to various
stories, result from such borrowing. One young itinerant,
not yet confident of his extemporaneous powers, memorized
a sermon of John Wesley's for delivery at a camp meeting.
When his time came, he arose, announced his text, and "on
the instant his mind became completely inactive. " So shocked

and mortified was the young man that he fell unconscious,
and only the brotherly solicitude of his presiding elder kept
him in the ministry. [84] Listeners dubbed the sermon of a
preoccupied young itinerant (which they recognized as a "re-
hash of Watson's First Part") "as dry as Sahara, and as
long as a Puritan's face. "[85]

The warnings of such stories notwithstanding, borrowing must have been fairly common, especially when itinerants
were collared for a discourse on short notice or when they
were preaching for an "impressive" audience and wanted to
speak in style. Humorous stories about such episodes must
have been common as well. One itinerant in Virginia, around
1878, asked to preach on short notice, remembered hearing
as a boy the story "of one of our preachers who used Bishop
Early's sermon in the Bishop's presence at a camp-meeting
.... "[86] Invariably, the borrower botched the sermon he
plagiarized, as in the story of a man who lifted a sermon
from William Burkitt:

> This pious expositor [William Burkitt] going one
> Sunday to church from the parsonage-house, met
> an old college friend who was purposely coming to
> give him a call before sermon. After the accus-
> tomed salutation, Burkitt told his friend that, as
> he had intended him the favor of a visit, his parish-
> ioners would expect the favor of a sermon. The
> other excused himself by saying that he had no ser-
> mon with him; but on looking at Burkitt's pocket,
> and perceiving his sermon-case, he drew it gently
> out and put it into his own pocket. He then said
> smilingly, 'Mr. Burkitt, I agree to preach for
> you. ' He did so; and he preached Burkitt's ser-
> mon. But he appeared to great disadvantage after
> Burkitt, for he had a voice rough and untuneful,
> whereas Burkitt's was remarkably melodious. 'Ah, '
> said Burkitt to him after sermon, in the vestry,
> 'you was but half a rogue; you stole my fiddle, but
> you could not steal my fiddle-stick. '[87]

A similar story illustrates at once the fruitlessness
of borrowing, the value of prestige, and the credulity of laymen. According to this anecdote an itinerant named S. J.
Catlin, anxious to impress a new congregation in Montana,
memorized a sermon of Bishop Bascom's and delivered it
"in the most impressive manner possible, " but critics pronounced the sermon "a very ordinary affair. " Later, Catlin

preached a sermon on the " 'Ten Virgins' " from elaborate
notes which he inadvertently left in the pulpit. A church
official who was an ardent friend of Bishop Marvin (who had
visited that same week and preached on the same subject)
discovered the notes, thought they were Marvin's, and but-
tonholed the unfortunate Catlin to show him the "souvenir."
Catlin listened patiently while the layman extolled his [Cat-
lin's] sermon sketch as if it were Marvin's: " 'Now, that is
perfect; no man except Marvin would ever had thought of
that, or said so much in a few words.' " The narrator noticed the irony of the situation:

> Thus a sermon produced by a bishop and accredited
> to a humble preacher out West is considered quite
> inferior, while the production of the same humble
> itinerant accredited to a bishop is lauded to the
> skies and pronounced incapable of improvement.

The tendency of the people, he continued, to judge preaching
by glitter rather than substance is exemplified in another
anecdote that the Catlin-Marvin story resembles. According
to the second story, a Negro, Jim, went with his master to
hear a famous bishop preach. Unknown to Jim, another
preacher substituted for the tardy celebrity. During the sermon, the master discovered the slave shouting and rolling
on the ground in ecstasy, praising the preaching of the great
bishop. When informed that the switch had been made, and
that this preacher was only an ordinary circuit rider, Jim
exclaimed: " 'Well, please help me bresh dis dirt off. Jim
hab all dis trouble for nuffin'.' "[88]

The burden of tradition's demand that preaching be
extemporaneous was augmented by the insistence that some
variety be maintained. Circuit riders, preaching at different locations every week and on different circuits every two
years, could get by, if they were of the mind, with only a
few sermons, made new by new listeners. Against accusations that such a possibility was the rule among itinerants,
Mr. Griffith of the Baltimore Conference, a pioneer preacher,
testified before God that, "although he had traveled for forty
years, he had never preached the same sermon twice. He
had preached from the same text, but never preached twice
the same sermon."[89] Obnoxious laymen, such as Brother
Sealy, who, when a preacher announced his text, cried out,
"That text was preached from two weeks ago, by brother
White," encouraged fresh thinking among stagnant preachers.
According to some clergymen, however, excessive variety
signalled banality:

The great Dr. Hall, when asked how many sermons
a preacher could make in a week, made this reply:
'If he is an extraordinary man, he can make one;
if he is a mediocre, he can make two; but if he
is an ass, he can make a dozen. '90

Repetitious preachers became the object of snide humor
among their colleagues. Bishop Fowler, "whose humor had
an acid touch in it, " when asked if it were "true that Bishop _____ has only two sermons" replied: " 'Two? ... Is
there really a second one?' "91

Along with extemporaneity, originality, and variety,
tradition demanded that preaching be fervid. Such a require-
ment expressed itself by the metaphor of "fire. " In one
church an old layman would call out to stilted preachers,
" 'Put on a little more fire, brother. ' "92 In another locale,
Uncle Jack Walker would admonish preachers "rather slow
in warming up, " by slapping his thigh and shouting, " 'Fire
up ... fire up!' "93 Rev. William Caples, at a service
where the sluggishness and hesitation of a young preacher
caused people to begin filtering out, shouted out:

> 'Fire, brother, fire quick! Don't wait to take a
> rest. Fire off-hand, the people here are all in a
> hurry. They won't stand for you. Fire quick, or
> that last one of them will be gone. '94

According to one tradition, fever literally enhanced
fervidity. Chills and sweats were accompanied by shakes so
violent that, according to one of many tall tales, a little boy
at the dinner table shook off all his buttons and then his
pants. 95 Fever frequently afflicted frontier folk and especially weather-beaten circuit riders. Henry Smith testified
that it helped him preach better:

> I had long rides over bad roads, in the midst of
> much rain, and I repeatedly got wet, and the ague
> returned upon me. One day, while I was preach-
> ing on Mad River, shaking from head to foot with
> the ague, I requested the people to bear with me,
> and went on as well as I could till the fever came
> on, and then I had great liberty of speech.... I
> left them with a high fever, but a glad heart. 96

According to Billy Hibbard, "Some said I preached better in
my delirium, than when I had my senses. "97 One itinerant

attributed the heat of preachers' discourses to the red hot
potash cauldron placed at the front of little churches for
heat: "I have heard of late years of 'a pulpit sweat, ' and
think it must have originated over that red hot potash kettle. "98

     Despite the emphasis upon fire in Methodist preaching
lore, cooler traditions warned that "empty wagons often make
more noise than loaded ones, " and that "shallow waters sometimes make more foam than deep waters. "99   According to
one anecdote in this counter-tradition, an old-time Methodist
who at first demanded of Thomas Morris a shouting style of
preaching, tempered his expectation when he discovered that
the patient soft-sell had equally effective results. 100

     The final stricture of the lore has to do with the ap-
propriate length of sermons.   No rigid time limit is set;
one receives the impression that spellbinding preachers could
continue at any length: A. E. Phelps reportedly preached so
powerfully that when he had finished, after two and a half
hours, people swore that only a half-hour had elapsed. 101
Preachers with ambition but less talent than Phelps, however,
were advised how to shorten their sermons: "'Cut a piece
off from both ends ... and it will be long enough then. '"102
Whatever the preacher's merits, a sermon of only a half-
hour was too short, as one laywoman told a young circuit
rider. 103   When young Peter Doub was informed that some
objected to his preaching because it was too short, he replied, that "he said all he knew, and did not like to repeat. "
An old preacher advised him: "'Brother Doub, read more,
study more, pray more, and you will be able to preach
more. '"104

     3.   Preaching should be democratic.   Democratic
preaching does not refer to explicit advocacy of a political
philosophy but to the belief of the Methodist lore that the
same Word of God should be addressed to the high and the
low, to the many and to the few, without regard for conse-
quence.

     The perfect exemplar of this tradition is the story
told of Peter Cartwright and General Jackson. 105   Shortly
after the Battle of New Orleans, the story runs, Cartwright
was visiting preacher in a Nashville church.   As he announced his text,

          there was a stir in the crowded congregation; he

[Cartwright] paused until the excitement should subside. The pastor of the church took advantage of
the opportunity to pull the shirt of the preacher's
coat and admonish him in a whisper, 'Brother Cartwright, you must be careful how you preach to-
night, General Jackson has just come in. ' In a
loud tone, Cartwright replied, 'what do you suppose
I care for General Jackson; if he don't repent of
his sins and believe on the Lord Jesus Christ, he
will die and be damned like any other sinner, ' and
then proceeded with his sermon. The next morning
(both rose with the lark), as the preacher passed
the general's quarters in his morning stroll, a servant ran after him with the message that General
Jackson wished to speak with him. Turning, his
hand was grasped by the hero, who shook it heartily, saying, 'Sir, you are a man after my own heart;
if I had a regiment of men as brave as you, and
you for the chaplain, I'd agree to conquer any
country on earth. ' A strong friendship sprang up
between these men, in whom were many points of
resemblance. 106

Other anecdotes taught disregard for numbers, rather
than class distinctions, for the sake of the gospel. An old
preacher, questioned by one of his rural constituents as to
why his preaching was so eloquent in the villages and so thin
"'in our school-house appointments, '" replied: "'The experienced hunter adapts the load of his rifle to the size of his
game; a bear-charge for a bear, and a squirrel-charge for
a squirrel. '" A few weeks later the circuit rider received
his comeuppance:

the preacher came round again, and put up for the
night at the same farm-house [of his questioner].
'Have you fed my horse any oats, brother?' said
he to the proprietor of the establishment. 'I have
fed him a gill, ' said the yeoman with the utmost
nonchalance. 'A gill!' cried the astonished preacher, 'what do you mean?' 'A bear-charge for a
bear, and a squirrel-charge for a squirrel!' re-
torted the imperturbable Scotchman; 'I only imitate
the example of a preacher who regulates his efforts
for the salvation of men by the size of his congregations rather than by a proper regard for the
priceless value of the souls he professes to be
striving to save!'107

Numerous other anecdotes conjoin the pastoral duty of
never missing an appointment to that of preaching at an appointment regardless of how many people arrive.   George
Washington Ivey, after laboring through mud and slush on a
"cold, rainy, disagreeable day, " found nobody at the church
where he was appointed to preach.   Duty overruled conven-
ience; the old itinerant unlocked the door, went into the building, and after prayer, began to preach the sermon he had
prepared.   In a short time "a man with his rifle, passing
by and hearing the preaching, went in and remained through
the service. " Recounting the episode later, Ivey remarked:
"The congregation was not large, but it was very orderly
and attentive, and on the whole we had a pretty good service. "[108] In similar anecdotes, the preacher, after laboring
through most unpleasant weather, arrives at the appointment,
preaches to a few people, and converts one of them, a widely known unbeliever, whose testimony precipitates a great
revival in the immediate locale.[109]

Besides indifference to class distinction or numbers
in a congregation, the lore enjoined preachers to present
the unalloyed Word without regard for the domesticated sins
of their listeners, who tended to consider their peccadilloes
as unassailable.   In one such story, Samuel Clawson sketched
certain professors of religion by using the homey exemplum
of a lazy farmer, whose incompetence and sloppiness was described graphically and in detail.   After the sermon,

> One man ... thought Clawson was personal in his
> description of the slovenly, lazy farmer, and got
> fighting mad, and blamed the brother, with whom
> Clawson staid, with telling Clawson about his farm-
> ing, etc.   When meeting was over, the angry farm-
> er accused this brother of having acted meanly in
> getting him exposed before the whole community, as
> Clawson had done.   The brother declared his inno-
> cence, but the farmer insisted that he must have
> done it, or Clawson could not have given such a
> description without a knowledge of the facts.   The
> neighbors interfered and prevented a hostile colli-
> sion.   All agreed, however, that, though the bow
> was drawn at a venture, the arrow certainly found
> its mark.[110]

Sermon Boasts

The exploits of the giants among Methodist preachers

"Ef I thawt yo'd never be back no more I'd have you preach my funeral 'fore you leave."

High Praise for a Departing Preacher

often picked up accretions by oral transmission until they matched the stature of their subjects. In some accounts hundreds of people literally fall under the influence of heady preaching, and elsewhere, biographers enumerate incredible mass conversions. [111]

Other stories tell of the not improbable but unlikely distance at which bellowing itinerants could be heard. Andrew Manship, the all-time champion, was heard two miles away while preaching on a quiet night. [112] Henry Ryan and George Bowman both projected their voices a mile, [113] and alas, Billy Hibbard could be heard only half a mile. [114] Jesse Lee reportedly thundered in such tones that the women of one place complained that his preaching made their heads ache. [115]

Other reports, presuming the stentorian voice of their subjects, tell of unusually large congregations listening to speakers. None among the ministers could match the booming reach of Henry Clay's oratory on the occasion when he reportedly spoke to 120,000 people. [116] Taking their cue from such accounts, however, Methodist storytellers attributed audiences of five to six thousand to Giles, McKendree, and Healey, [117] and a crowd of twelve thousand to Rev. Joshua Thomas. [118]

Under some spellbinders, time passed unnoticed (see supra, p. 250), or audiences spontaneously arose and, unaware of their disposition, stood listening. [119] The atmosphere was so intense at early camp meetings that people forgot to eat. [120] At an unsuccessful meeting, the older preachers allowed John Johnson, a beardless boy, to preach just as the people were packing their belongings to go home; the neophyte, however, discoursed with such power that the people unpacked their goods and stayed for two more weeks. [121]

Summary

Holding before themselves the ideals of simplicity, spontaneity, and spirituality, zealous itinerants found themselves relieved of their failures, in part at least, by sharing stories which attributed sermon difficulties to unnerving circumstances, tactical miscalculations, and interruptions by man and beast.

The laughter that circuit riders traded over their own

and their congregations' foibles does not obscure the seriousness with which itinerants approached the responsibility of
the Gospel and the effectiveness with which they did, in fact,
preach it. That preaching, in the half century from 1800 to
1850, helped to people the American countryside with Methodists and made the followers of Wesley the major American
denomination. It was no small wonder that itinerants' memories of their efforts frequently became boasts!

<h2 style="text-align:center">Notes</h2>

1. Wightman, Capers, pp. 205-6.
2. Rodney Cline, Asbury Wilkinson: Pioneer Preacher
   (New York: Vantage Press, 1956), p. 91.
3. J. B. Wakeley, The Heroes of Methodism, containing
   Sketches of Eminent Methodist Ministers and Characteristic Anecdotes of their Personal History (11th
   ed. ; Toronto: William Briggs, 1855), p. 109.
4. Taylor, Battlefield, pp. 104-5.
5. Fitzgerald, McFerrin, pp. 55-56. Sometimes the aspiring preacher would freeze, after announcing his
   text, and be unable to continue, to the great discomfiture of the congregation; Marlay, Morris, pp.
   25-26.
6. Rankin, Story, p. 177.
7. Taylor, Battlefield, pp. 287-88. Such manliness con-
   trasts favorably with the behavior of an itinerant
   who, after he had "gotten into the bushes" during a
   sermon at a camp meeting, hid underneath the
   benches in the preachers' tent. Richardson, Autobiography, p. 41. Sometimes the preacher was more
   aware of his failure than his listeners however.
   Travis records, for the benefit of discouraged young
   preachers, meeting a young man who was converted
   by one of his sermons which he had judged to be a
   perfect failure. Autobiography, p. 132.
8. D. Young, Autobiography, pp. 216-17. A similar story
   is told of a Billy Hibbard sermon, called his "half
   and half" sermon: half in polished style and half in
   Hibbard style. Ayres, Methodist Heroes, p. 140.
9. Fleharty, Phelps, p. 27.
10. Watson, Tales and Takings, pp. 284-85.
11. Roche, Autobiography, pp. 78-80.
12. Robison, Clawson, pp. 170-71. Clawson's exemplum
    can be traced to a famous humorous sermon, "The
    Harp of a Thousand Strings, " allegedly recorded by

Rev. Henry T. Lewis from a "Hardshell" Baptist
preacher in the 1820's or 1830's at Waterproof,
Louisiana. Long in oral circulation by Lewis' preaching, it finally appeared in print, also at his instiga-
tion, in the Brandon (Mississippi) Republican newspaper in 1854, and since then has been reprinted
hundreds of times. Arthur Palmer Hudson (ed.),
Humor of the Old Deep South (New York: The Macmillan Co. , 1936), pp. 233-34. In the version presented by Hudson, the preacher compares the various denominations to animals; Episcopalians are like
turkey buzzards, a "high salin' and a highfalutin' set";
Methodists are like squirrels running up a tree,
from one degree of grace to another, jumping from
limb to limb until they fall from grace; but Baptists
are like the oppossum on a persimmon tree: "you
may shake one foot loose, and the other's thar; and
you may shake all feet loose, and he laps his tail
around the lim', and he clings fur-ever." Ibid. , pp.
235-36. In the Robison account, Clawson was told
by a fellow preacher that no good would come of
that example; years later, however, a man revealed
he had been converted by it.

James B. Finley, describing the oppossum in
his frontier bestiary, notes that "a Hard-shell Baptist preacher once introduced this animal into his discourse, to illustrate the doctrine of final perseverance." Autobiography, p. 96. If "The Harp of a
Thousand Strings" was published in 1854, as Hudson
asserts, then Finley's Autobiography (published in
1853) witnesses to widespread oral circulation of the
sermon.

13. Erwin, Reminiscences, p. 105. Robert Perry, an itin-
     erant of the Niagara Circuit, is recorded as preach-
     ing a sermon on the same subject "a little too alle-
     gorical, which diverted the less reverential, and of-
     fended the taste of the more grave and discerning."
     A hired man, reporting on the sermon to the family
     he lived with, said: "'The minister preached all
     about sheep, and all the people laughed, except Hugh
     Wilson, and he looked as mad!'" Carroll, Case,
     I, 131.

14. Robison, Clawson, pp. 142-45. For a ludicrous ex-
     ample of an illustration memorized from another
     preacher going astray, see Spottswood, Brief Annals,
     p. 338.

15. Peck, Forty Years, p. 198.

16. Roche, Autobiography, p. 88.
17. Ibid., pp. 88-89. Stories about such mishaps must
     have been told often, if the commentary is any indi-
     cation. "Many stories," notes Roche, "were told
     of him [Balch] illustrating the latter's characteristic
     eccentricity...." The anecdote of Balch's anachron-
     istic exemplum "lacks its full force till heard through
     the lips of the naturally witty and sometimes waggish
     George Hudson." Ibid., pp. 88, 89.
18. Erwin, Reminiscences, p. 109. Benjamin Abbott's mis-
     quotes are mentioned in another instance; D. Young,
     Autobiography, p. 216. In both instances the moral
     is to eschew Abbott's ignorance but to retain his
     spirit.
          Other instances of misquotes include "hearsay"
     for "heresy" (Green, Life, p. 74); "snach crab" for
     "Sennacherib" (Erwin, Reminiscences, p. 109); "lines"
     for "loins" (Hatcher, Jeter, p. 27); "vicarious" for
     "precarious" (Robison, Clawson, p. 42); "molasses"
     for "kolasis" (E. Thomson, Sketches, Biographical
     and Incidental [Cincinnati: L. Swormstedt & A. Poe,
     1856], pp. 158-59). Motif J1823.: "Misunderstand-
     ing of church customs or ceremonies causes inap-
     propriate action." See also Jan Brunvand, "Jokes
     About Misunderstood Religious Texts," Western Folk-
     lore, XXIV (1965), 199-200.
19. Finney, Marvin, p. 551.
20. Burgess, Pleasant Recollections, p. 370.
21. Taylor, Autobiography, pp. 122-23. Motif J1352.:
     "Person calls another an ass." A similar jest oc-
     curs in a seventeenth century English jestbook: see
     Robert Chamberlain, Conceits, Clinches, Flashes and
     Whimzies Newly Studied (London, 1639), p. 260.
22. Ayres, Methodist Heroes, pp. 133-34. Motif H571.1.:
     "Counterquestion: 'What is the difference between
     you and an ass?'"
23. Carroll, Case, I, 38. A similar jest occurs in the
     facetiae of Poggio; see Poggio-Bracciolini, The
     Facetiae of Poggio and Other Medieval Story-Tellers,
     tr. by Edward Storer (London: G. Routledge & Sons,
     1928), p. 64.
24. Spottswood, Brief Annals, pp. 71-72.
25. Carroll, Case, II, 98-99. See Watson, Tales and Tak-
     ings, pp. 243-44, for the odd topics of another
     preacher with unusual tastes, including "'Woe to the
     women that sew pillows to all armholes.'" For oth-
     er examples see Fleharty, Phelps, p. 337; Wise,

          Sketches, pp. 53-54, for an ironic text chosen by
          Bishop Asbury when forced to preach unexpectedly.

26.   Finney, Marvin, p. 316. Among other topics, Finney
          lists the following: "'Some Biscuits Baked in the
          Oven of Charity, Carefully Conserved for the Chick-
          ens of the Church, the Sparrows of the Spirit and
          the Sweet Swallows of Salvation'"; "'A Pack of Cards
          to Win Christ.'" The latter topic is a stock-in-
          trade of contemporary Negro preachers; see Rosen-
          berg, Folk Preacher, p. 29. It was also employed
          by medieval preachers; see Owst, Literature and
          Pulpit, p. 99.

27.   One humble preacher, asked if he feared preaching after
          the great, eloquent Bascom, said, "I have preached
          in the presence of Bascom's God." Spottswood,
          Brief Annals, p. 327.

28.   Patton, Life, pp. 29-30. The sequel to the story is
          that the people awoke, and highly embarrassed at
          their discourteous treatment of the minister, prayed
          that God would bless them; a great revival followed.

29.   Lee, Life, p. 397. Another account of the episode is
          told in Ayres, Methodist Heroes, pp. 44-45.
               The same story is told of Henry Bascom;
          Henkle, Bascom, pp. 102-3. See also Randolph,
          Hot Springs, p. 110: "The Preacher Hollered Fire,"
          for a common ploy, in many stories, to wake sleep-
          ing congregations.

30.   Carroll, "Father Corson," pp. 107-8. Another anec-
          dote recalls how a preacher, noting his congregation
          asleep, changed the order of the service and "lined
          out" the following hymn:
               'My drowsy powers, why sleep ye so?
                   Awake, my sluggish soul!
               Nothing hath half they work to do,
                   Yet nothing's half so dull.'
          Taylor, Battlefield, pp. 84-85.

31.   Tucker, Itinerant Preaching, pp. 26-27.
               Another story records the reaction of a French-
          man to boisterous Methodist preaching: "On one oc-
          casion, a Frenchman, using broken English, who was
          a member of the Presbyterian Church, said, 'Me go
          to my church, me go to sleep; me go to hear you,
          me no sleep; you make too much noise!'" Mathews,
          Peeps, p. 17. As a rule in the literature, French-
          men make rare appearances as comic stereotypes,
          that honor being reserved for Dutchmen.

32.   Ayres, Methodist Heroes, p. 144.

33. Charles D. Mallary, Memoirs of Elder Edmund Bots-
     ford (Charleston: W. Riley, 1832), pp. 54-55. This
     Baptist account is the best version of the story. A
     longer version, in which a pet lamb fells a nodding
     blacksmith, occurs in Ryder, Superannuate, pp. 98-
     99, and a condensed version of the latter account
     (although an ordinary man, not a blacksmith, is the
     victim) is found in Cartwright, Autobiography, p. 40.
     The two Methodist accounts locate the scene indoors;
     both claim personal witness to the incident.
34. Coles, My First Seven Years, p. 194.
35. Ibid., p. 193.
36. Taylor, Battlefield, p. 84.
37. Ryder, Superannuate, p. 98.
38. Ibid., p. 100. One minister, after witnessing the col-
     lapse of benches holding portly matrons at a meeting,
     condoned the laughter of his people by saying: "I
     do not know who could avoid it, [laughter]--a long
     bench, containing nine women rather above the ordi-
     nary size, breaking suddenly in the middle, and
     letting them all down at once, was rather a ludicrous
     affair. " Coles, My First Seven Years, p. 193.
     For other accounts of collapsing benches: McNemee,
     "Brother Mack, " p. 53; Watson, Tales and Takings,
     p. 269. For the account of the floor of a church
     sinking during the sermon: Spottswood, Brief Annals,
     pp. 292-93.
39. Manship, Thirteen Years', pp. 32-33.
40. Richardson, Sunrise, p. 116. For similar preaching in-
     cidents see Mathews, Peeps, p. 55; Erwin, Reminis-
     cences, pp. 197-98.
         For anecdotes of dogs disturbing family prayer
     see Plyler and Plyler, Men, p. 64; Manship, Thir-
     teen Years', pp. 32-33; for an account of the "bench-
     legged fice" attacking an Elder of the church, see
     Rankin, Story, pp. 185-87; for stories of hounds tree-
     ing the young preacher who goes out in back of the
     house to pray after supper, see Richardson, Autobi-
     ography, p. 6; for a story of hounds treeing Lorenzo
     Dow see Plyler and Plyler, Men, pp. 177-78; for a
     similar story told of Robert Sheffey, see Barbery,
     Sheffey, p. 98.
41. Erwin, Reminiscences, pp. 198-99.
42. Taylor, Battlefield, p. 41.
43. Godbey, Seventy Years, p. 124.
44. Stanley, Stateler, pp. 349-50. Motif J1118. 1.: "Clever
     parrot. "

45. Sims, Eddy, p. 184. See Brewer, Dictionary, p. 107;
    "Doves." A white pigeon reportedly flew into the
    window of the church during the funeral sermon of a
    beloved Pennsylvania Dutch minister, Preacher Henry,
    in 1897; Korson, Black Rock, p. 295. Motif X418.:
    "Parson is to let a dove fly in the church."
46. Roche, Autobiography, p. 76. For similar stories see
    Waugh, Autobiography, pp. 77-78; Ware, Memoir,
    pp. 158-59. In the latter account, the humor is
    turned against a Baptist minister who tried to prosely-
    tize a Methodist congregation (which had allowed him
    to exhort at its meetings) by prearranging a scene
    in which a woman arises with a child and asks for
    its baptism, whereat he discourses at length upon
    the evils of "baby-sprinkling." But the trick back-
    fired: a hornet stung him on the eye just after he
    began his polemic; the woman who presented her
    child told him she knew of a remedy for the bite,
    and they went off together, never again to be seen
    in those parts. Motif X411.: "Parson put to flight
    during his sermon"; X411.3.: "Sexton arranges wasp-
    nest so that parson sits on it."
47. Williams, Smith, p. 30. For a similar story, see
    Field, Worthies, p. 224.
        Another practical function performed by travel-
    ing ministers was conveyance of news, in lieu of
    newspapers, on the outposts of the frontier. W. H.
    Withrow, Neville Trueman, The Pioneer Preacher:
    A Tale of the War of 1812 (4th ed.; Toronto: Wil-
    lian Briggs, 1900), p. 30. According to Yarbrough,
    Boyhood, pp. 20-21, primitive Baptist itinerants
    would relate scraps of news during low emotional
    cycles of sermons.
48. Gaddis, Walker, pp. 572-73; Mathews, Peeps, p. 55.
49. Robison, Clawson, pp. 108-9.
50. Smith, Recollections, p. 91. See also D. Young, Auto-
    biography, pp. 228-29, for skillful handling of a drunk
    at a meeting.
51. Green, A. L. P. Green, p. 99; Ryder, Superannuate,
    pp. 62-63. Dan Young continued preaching without
    a flinch as a heavy gun was fired off at his feet in
    a private house. Autobiography, p. 106.
52. William Henry Milburn, Ten Years, p. 73; the entire
    anecdote pp. 71-73. The account reproduced in these
    pages is from Marlay, Morris, pp. 98-101. The ver-
    sions differ slightly in details and sequence.
53. Marlay, Morris, pp. 98-101.

54. Robison, Clawson, pp. 183-84.
       The anecdote, which borders perilously close
    to poor taste, illustrates why some Methodists re-
    garded storytellers with a jaundiced eye.
55. Henkle, Bascom, p. 128.
56. Wilding, Memories, pp. 54-55.
57. Erwin, Reminiscences, pp. 99-100. See also Wakeley,
    Bold Preacher, pp. 46-47.   Motif J1261.1.5.: "Wo-
    man causes disturbance in church, is carried out
    forcibly." In this account, the lady remarks: "'Well
    I am more favored than my Lord. He had but one
    ass to ride, while I have two.'" See motif X313.:
    "Dying like Christ--between two thieves."
       A related story is told in Green, Life, p. 37;
    when a Methodist minister attempted to exhort at a
    silent Quaker meeting, "an old man cried out, 'A
    wolf! a wolf!' At this a few youngsters caught up
    the preacher and carried him outdoors. 'Well,' says
    the minister, 'this is reversing the usual order. I
    have often heard of the wolf carrying off the sheep,
    but this is the first time I ever heard of the sheep
    carrying off the wolf.'"
58. Marlay, Morris, pp. 69-73.
59. Hibbard, Memoirs, p. 229. For another hellfire ser-
    mon couched in terms of a burning lake, see Roche,
    Autobiography, pp. 104-5.
60. Peck, Luther Peck, pp. 131-32; Field, Worthies, pp.
    156-57.
61. Fleharty, Phelps, p. 349.
62. Henkle, Bascom, p. 152.
63. Burgess, Pleasant Recollections, pp. 450-51.
64. Peck, Luther Peck, p. 156.
65. New Jersey Conference Memorial, p. 89.
66. D. Young, Autobiography, p. 217; Erwin, Reminiscences,
    pp. 64-66; Fleharty, Phelps, pp. 132-33.
67. Plyler and Plyler, Men, pp. 180-1. In a similar ac-
    count, told of Rev. J. G. Sansom, Gabriel speaks
    in reply to the preacher's call; Chapman, Memoirs,
    pp. 66-67.
       For parallel accounts in secular folklore, see
    Hudson, Humor, pp. 224-26; George Kummer, "Speci-
    mens of Ante-Bellum Buckeye Humor," Ohio Histori-
    cal Quarterly, LXVI (1955), 426; Mody C. Boatright,
    "Comic Exempla," p. 164; Randolph, Hot Springs,
    pp. 53-54.
68. Cartwright, Autobiography, pp. 40-1. Motif J2495.:
    "Religious words or exercises interpreted with absurd

literalness. " The story has a long lineage. According to one version, the captain of a storm-tossed
ship commanded every man to throw into the sea the
heaviest thing he could spare; one man tried to jet-
tison his wife, claiming she was his heaviest burden.
See A Banquet of Jests; or, Change of Cheare (London, 1633), pp. 132-33); also Poggio, Facetiae, pp.
49-50.

69. Field, Worthies, p. 129.
70. The quotation is the punch line of an anecdote illustrating Bishop Marvin's style of preaching: "His
[Marvin's] method and its value are illustrated in an
anecdote of a New York City Methodist pastor, in the
succession of Captain Webb's pulpit, but setting aside
the mourner's bench, in receiving members. He
soon found that the world was running away with his
Church. He carried his trouble to one of the old
Bishops, Hedding or Waugh, who replied: 'Bench
'em, Sir! Bench 'em, sir!'" Finney, Marvin, p.
599.
71. Paddock, Memoir, p. 296.
72. Taylor, Battlefield, p. 28.
73. Thomson, Sketches, p. 87.
74. Carroll, Sketches, p. 260. The most effective American speakers and writers, such as Brougham, Webster, and Irving, Carroll asserts, "cultivate the
Anglo-Saxon." Ibid., p. 262.
75. Henkle, Bascom, p. 44. For a description of Bascom's
preaching at its best, see Fitzgerald, Sunset Views,
p. 171.
76. Giles, Pioneer, p. 154.
77. Miller, Thirty Years, p. 101.
78. Smith, Recollections, pp. 157-58.
79. Manship, Thirteen Years', p. 62. The warning is a
traditional cliche; see Wakeley, Whitefield, pp. 137-
38.
80. Spicer, Autobiography, pp. 222-23. Motif D1719.1.1.:
"Contest in magic between druid and saint." The
anecdote, titled "Balaam Saddling the Ass," is introduced as a story "told of one of our preachers, that
is a little amusing." The same story is told in Erwin, Reminiscences, pp. 312-15. In the Erwin version, the opponent has agreed to match his spontaneous ability against that of the Methodist; he receives,
after the Methodist has successfully preached on the
Balaam text, the verse, "'Am I not thine ass?'"
Confused and embarrassed, he mumbles the phrase

over and over again until an irritated member of the
congregation arises and agrees, "'Yes, you are a
real Methodist ass!'"

81. Fitzgerald, McFerrin, p. 311.
82. Scarlett, Itinerant, p. 144.
83. Brother Mason, pp. 16-17.
84. Marvin, Caples, p. 105. See Spottswood, Brief Annals,
p. 338, for the ludicrous account of an itinerant attempting to reproduce a memorized passage and ending up with a howl.
85. Field, Worthies, p. 218.
86. D. Gregory Claiborne Butts, From Saddle to City by
Buggy, Boat and Railway (Hilton Village, Va.: n.p.,
1922 [date from preface]), p. 106.
87. Carroll, Sketches, p. 278.
88. Stanley, Stateler, pp. 234-37. For a similar misjudg-
ment told of fashionable Baltimore Methodists, see
Smith, Recollections, pp. 157-58. The same story
is told of a man who went to hear the eighteenth
century itinerant, George Whitefield: Wakeley,
Whitefield, pp. 327-28.
89. Gavitt, Crumbs, p. 15.
90. Morrison, Autobiography, p. 56.
91. E. E. Hoss, William McKendree; A Biographical Study
(Nashville: Publishing House of the M. E. Church,
South, 1916), p. 125.
92. Coles, My First Seven Years, p. 68.
93. Wilding, Memories, p. 62.
94. Marvin, Caples, p. 162. Such sluggards were remembered as lacking that "peculiar 'snap'" necessary
for a good Methodist preacher. Field, Worthies,
pp. 253-54.
95. Dorson, American Folklore, p. 53.
96. Recollections, pp. 69-70. According to Erwin, the ex-
ertion of preaching brought on copious perspiration,
known as "pulpit sweat," that temporarily broke the
fever and loosened the preacher's tongue: "A pulpit sweat and God's blessing have saved me from
many a fit of sickness." Reminiscences, p. 123.
97. Memoir, p. 223. Thomas H. Pearne, however, under
the influence of fever, rambled so incoherently from
the pulpit that his people had to remove him to his
bed, where his fever was diagnosed as typhoid.
Sixty-One Years, pp. 73-74.
98. Erwin, Reminiscences, p. 114.
99. Spicer, Autobiography, p. 311.
100. Marlay, Morris, pp. 61-63.

101. Fleharty, Phelps, pp. 353-54. Motif D2011. 1. 2.:
      "Three days and three nights seem one hour as
      saint preaches."
102. Taylor, Battlefield, p. 75.
103. Spottswood, Brief Annals, pp. 24-25.
104. Plyler and Plyler, Men, p. 207.
105. Cartwright, Autobiography, pp. 133-34; Milburn, Ten
      Years, pp. 179-80. Although details vary slightly
      between the two stories, the substance is similar.
106. Milburn, Ten Years, pp. 179-80. In both accounts an
      anecdote follows which relates how Jackson, having
      invited Cartwright to an elegant dinner at the Her-
      mitage, defends him from a sneering young Nash-
      ville lawyer who had come to ridicule the preacher.
107. Ryder, Superannuate, pp. 128-29.
108. Plyler and Plyler, Men, p. 69. The same story is
      told of Lyman Beecher in Hood, World of Anecdote,
      pp. 208-9. Other humorous remarks include the
      one by Enoch Marvin, after converting the one un-
      converted person of a congregation of three: it
      was the only occasion in his ministry, he said,
      when "'he had swept the platter.'" Finney, Mar-
      vin, p. 109. For a similar remark, see Lee,
      Life, p. 358.
109. Patton, Life, pp. 47-48; Johnson, Recollections, pp.
      58-61; Smith, Pierce, pp. 61-62.
110. Robison, Clawson, pp. 127-28.
          The phrase recurs frequently as explanation
      for such incidents: when Billy Hibbard preached
      against drunkenness and offended a minister, Mem-
      oir, pp. 206-7; when Spottswood preached against
      general sinfulness, Brief Annals, p. 163.
          When one preacher offended a Calvinist in
      his congregation, he said to the injured party,
      "'Can't I throw a stone at the devil without hitting
      you?'" Gorrie, Black River, I, 174.
          Using another analogy, a cool preacher told
      an enraged listener who felt singled out: "'I have
      cut out the garment and thrown it down; if any one
      picks it up, tries it on, and finds that it fits him,
      let him wear it.'" Tucker, Itinerant Preaching,
      p. 26. Hibbard uses the garment metaphor as
      well, Memoirs, p. 177.
          In another account, as a sinner leapt up and
      ran out of the meeting-house, an old Brother cried
      out, "'The wicked flee when no man pursueth!'"
      D. Young, Autobiography, p. 37.

For similar "singling out" episodes: Hobart, Recollections, pp. 350-52; Spottswood, Brief Annals, pp. 74-75. In the latter account the itinerant barely averts a duel with the offended man, a Virginia "gentleman."

111. Cartwright, Autobiography, p. 72. J. Young, Autobiography, p. 139; five hundred people reportedly got "the jerks" at once. Brewer, Dictionary, p. 68: "Conversions in large numbers."

112. Manship, Thirteen Years', p. 109. Brewer, Dictionary, p. 474: "The sermon of St. Antony of Padua heard three miles off."

113. Carroll, Case, II, 314; Taylor, Battlefield, p. 75.

114. Hibbard, Memoirs, p. 230.

115. Lee, Life, p. 234.

116. Burgess, Pleasant Recollections, p. 197.

117. Giles, Pioneer, p. 279; Hoss, McKendree, pp. 197-98, when the Bishop was an old man!; Carroll, Case, II, 425.

118. Manship, Thirteen Years', p. 245.

119. Malmsbury, Pitman, p. 73.

120. Stanley, Stateler, p. 280.

121. Johnson, Recollections, pp. 64-67.

Chapter 11

CONTROVERSY

Ye different sects, who all declare,
'Lo! here is Christ, or Christ is there,'
Your stronger proofs divinely give,
And show me where the Christians live. [1]

Frontier religion, taking its cue from the raw, boisterous, eye-gouging, ear-biting, self-aggrandizing, individual-
istic milieu in which it found itself, [2] hurled itself into the struggle for souls with the same pioneering spirit that kept the frontier
moving westward and consolidating behind. The struggle for
souls, however, quickly became competition for converts,
and denominational warfare triumphed over Christian unity.

Every preacher, therefore, went to battle armed not
only with Bible and sometimes doctrine but also with a quiver
full of the arrows of ridicule, rebuttal, caricature, and
mockery. Pioneer Methodism, in particular, found itself opposed by Baptists and Campbellites on the western frontier
and Calvinism on the New England frontier. The stories that
follow point up representative examples of the lore that enabled preachers to deal with their Baptist and Campbellite
adversaries.

Methodists versus Baptists

'You needn't think that you can make goslings out
of my chickens. '[3]

The lore of Methodist-Baptist jousting revolves around
the material and proper administration of the sacrament of
Baptism. Disputes over such questions involve profound and
age-old differences in conceptions of the nature of grace and
of faith, but in the lore, for the most part, theological distinctions are masked by slurs, jests, and caricatures slanted

ad hominem to illustrate the absurdity, insincerity, or incon-
sistency of proponents of the variant belief.

The Baptist belief in immersion as the only mode of
administering the Gospel ordinance was characterized as absurd formalism in stories which illustrate the debilitating results of such insistence under unfavorable circumstances.
According to one account, a Baptist preacher named Billy
Wood had to cut a hole in creek ice with an axe to immerse
converts during the winter.

> When Mr. Wood came out of the water with the
> last one, he was asked if the water was not cold.
> 'Cold, ' said he, 'not at all.   The temperature de-
> pends on the warmth of the heart. '   This was
> thought singular, when those who had been baptized
> were trembling with the chilling effect produced by
> their immersion.   But the people did not know that
> Brother Wood was provided with an undersuit of
> gum elastic clothing that protected him so thorough-
> ly that not a drop of water touched his skin.   The
> next day Clawson had to immerse six or seven at
> the same place, and when he came out of the water
> trembling, he said: 'It is awfully cold, and if
> Billy Wood says it ain't cold, he lies. '   Poor man,
> he had as warm a heart as ever throbbed in a hu-
> man bosom, but he had no gum elastic undersuit. [4]

Methodists ridiculed what they considered the inconsistencies of the Calvinistic theological background of their
Baptist opponents.   Brother Mings, a " 'forty gallon Baptist, ' "
according to a Methodist account, believed that

> 'when you found religion, you didn't want it.   When
> you had it, you didn't know it.   If you had it, you
> couldn't lose it.   And if you lost it, you never had
> it. ' [5]

By contrast Methodism, according to another narrative, taught
that

> 'if you have been converted you know it; and if you
> know it you have got it; if you have got it you may
> lose it; and if you lose it you must have had it. ' [6]

Baptist preachers, according to the Methodists, were
likely to be ignorant or immoral.   In a debate with the Meth-

odist George Harmon, a Baptist took his stand on the propo-
sition that no one "'was authorized to baptize who had not
been baptized himself.'" Harmon took him to task:

> Mr. Harmon asked if he might ask a question,
>   'Certainly,' was the reply.
>   'Who baptized the apostles?'
>   'John the Baptist,' was the answer.
>   'And who baptized John the Baptist?'
> No answer was given, and the Baptist brother left,
> 'highly excited.'7

O. P. Fitzgerald notes the absurd results of ignorant Biblical literalism with a sermon reportedly preached by a Baptist:

> 'You are a sinful set up here, and you commit al-
> most all sorts of sins and abominations. But, my
> brethren some things is sins, and some isn't. As
> for pitchin' dollars, fightin' chickens, playin' cards,
> shootin' for beef, and drinkin' whisky, them things
> may be sins, or they may not: the Scripter do not
> say. But, my brethring, this thing of playin' mar-
> vels is all wrong--for the Scripter says emphatical-
> ly, "Marvel not!"'8

One Baptist preacher pretended that he was quoting the original Greek to refute a Methodist itinerant; the latter, who
understood the "low Dutch" in which the imposter was really
speaking, exposed the sham and refuted him.9

> Rev. Joseph Travis characterized Baptists as "ig-
norant and superstitious, believing in witches, wizards, hob-
goblins, bloody bones, etc." Furthermore, they were "great
advocates for water, but loving it still better when well
mixed with whisky."10 A Baptist preacher, Alfred Ross, reportedly gave an ignorant sermon on the question of whether
or not it is right to prohibit the liquor traffic:

> 'Fellow citizens, I am an uneducated man; but I
> have been studying dis here question by night, by
> fire knots; I am not a hired preacher, and I have
> to work for my living. Dis Methodist preacher,
> who has been trying to take your liberties away,
> has a wagin load of books, and has nothing to do
> but read 'em. But I am opposed to dist question
> because it has sprung up in de dark; I am opposed

to it because it is de tail of de dragon spoke on in de vevulation dat will drag down a third of de stars, ah.'[11]

As for immorality, the story of the Baptist preacher who was stung by a hornet at a Methodist meeting and ran away with a woman who knew a cure for such stings has already been told in another context.[12]

Water, as earlier allusions indicate, constituted the heart of many humorous anecdotes. Simon Peter Richardson recalls, while preaching in a Baptist stronghold, comparing the local religion to "some coffee--it had too much water in it." The next day, while dining at a Baptist house,

> the old lady showed me a cup of coffee, and asked me to try that, saying she reckoned I would find it Methodist enough for me. It was strong as coffee could make it.[13]

Peter Cartwright records the repartee that occurred between himself and Mr. Roads, a "New Light preacher" who was "a very great stickler for immersion";

> That afternoon there arose a dark cloud, and presently the rain fell in torrents, and continued almost all night; nearly the whole face of the earth was covered with water; the streams rose suddenly and overflowed their banks. A little brook near the house rose so rapidly that it swept away the spring house and some of the fences. Next morning I was riding up the grove to see an old acquaintance. I met Mr. Roads, my New light preacher, and said, 'Good morning, sir,'
> 'Good morning,' he replied.
> Said I, 'We have had a tremendous rain.'
> 'Yes sir,' said he; 'the Lord sent that rain to convince you of your error.'
> 'Ah!' said I, 'what error?'
> 'Why, about baptism. The Lord sent this flood to convince you that much water was necessary.'
> 'Very good, sir,' said I; 'and he in like manner sent this flood to convince you of your error.'
> 'What error?' said he.
> 'Why,' said I, 'to show you that water comes by pouring and not by immersion.'[14]

That Baptists were not prone to receive such jabs
supinely is illustrated by the same anecdote, told in Baptist
biography, with the last laugh ridiculing the Methodists. After
noting the terrific rainfall, the story goes on to say that a
Methodist preacher accosted the Baptist, Elder Arnold, and

> charged him with intruding on his territory. When
> asked in what way, said that he (alluding to Elder
> Arnold) was taking water by pouring.
>   Elder Arnold replied by saying, that Baptist
> preachers were some times like Methodist babies,
> had to take water contrary to their choice![15]

G. C. Rankin, a Methodist itinerant, records the following
attack made by a "Hardshell" Baptist preacher on Methodist
baptism:

> 'The Methodists remind me, ah, of a old nigger
> whose moster's old goose died, ah. He tole old
> Zeak to take'er out, ah, behine the crib and bury
> 'er, ah. The next mornin' the ole moster was out
> thar, ah, and seed the ole goose a layin' thar with
> some dirt sprinkled on 'er head, ah. He went
> back and jumped on Zeak, ah, and axed him why he
> did not bury that goose, ah? Zeak said, ah, that
> he had sprinkled some dirt, ah, on 'er head, and
> that accordin' to Methodist baptism that was bein'
> buried, ah.'[16]

Such satirical exchanges between pugnacious Methodist
and Baptist preachers must have occurred frequently enough
to excite considerable interest among frontier folk. [17] In
Methodist tradition, however, Methodists always carried off
the spoils. After a sermon in which James Erwin passion-
ately refuted the Baptist position, he recalls that the class
leader got up and exultantly led the song:

> 'The world, John Calvin, and Tom Paine,
> May hate the Methodists in vain.
> I know the Lord will them increase,
> And fill the world with Methodists. '

"'There go the pond-lilies,'" a wag called after the departing Baptists. [18]

Methodists versus Campbellites

Methodist laughter at the Campbellite belief that baptismal immersion itself effects regeneration has been noted above. If immersion alone saved a man, Methodists joked, then dipping in a river, for example, could make even a horse or saddlebags Campbellite: as Peter Cartwright remarked after an unplanned swim, "my books and clothes had all turned Campbellite."[19] If a man could keep his head above water, however, no one could accuse him of leaving Methodist ranks for the opposition. With such thrusts Methodists lampooned what they considered ex opere operato sacramentality.

Methodist attacks on the Campbellites were similar to those on the Baptists. Campbellite preaching, according to one account, was like a certain kind of "hog slop": the hog "drinks lots of slop, but don't get fat."[20] According to Clawson, Campbellites cry

> 'Come, father, mother, son and daughter,
> Here's the Gospel in the water.'

But their mode of making Christians is like the lady who, making candles, first dipped the wicks in water: "when she came to light them, they would hiss and spit, and sputter and flash, and go out." In a similar fashion, Campbellites

> get hold of a sinner, and the first thing they do with him is to dip him in the water and pronounce him a Christian. But this process does not make him a burning and shining light. He may, like the old lady's candle, hiss and flash, but is sure to go out. Water in the heart is the difficulty. They will all go out.[21]

Burgess, after watching a preacher of that denomination baptize people in a "dead, stale, and low pond of water, all covered with a thick and green scum of accumulated filth," adjudged that Campbellites "strain at a gnat and swallow a camel."[22]

Campbellites were represented as absurd Scriptural literalists; a Methodist named Mitchell

> had a three-days' hitch [debate] with a noted Campbellite who made the assertion that every mention

of water in the Scriptures was literal, and was
never used to represent spirit or spiritual operation.

Mitchell in reply asked the gentleman a few
questions which led to a colloquy to this effect:
' "Ho, every one that thirsteth, come ye to
the waters. " Is that "literal?"'
'Yes, most assuredly. '
' "Whosoever will, let him take of the water
of life freely. " Is that "literal?"'
'Yes, certainly; any child can see that. '
' "Whosoever drinketh of this water shall
thirst again: but whosoever drinketh of the water
that I shall give him shall never thirst; but the water that I shall give him shall be in him a well of
water springing up into everlasting life. " Is that
"literal?"'
'Yes, yes, all literal. '
' "He that believeth on Me, out of his belly
shall flow rivers of living water. " Is that "literal?"'
'All literal, all literal. '
'Well, then, I have only to say that in western Kansas, where water is so scarce, such a man
would be a great blessing to that country as a mill
seat and water supply!'
The mill-seat man seized his hat and ran![23]

In Methodist tradition, Methodist champions of Davidic
stature defeated Campbellites in public debate. According to
Thomas Finney, "the current reformation [Campbellite] got
such an airing from this young David [Enoch Marvin] of the
Methodist Israel as, I presume, it seldom, if ever, received."[24] Or, as Simon P. Richardson told a Campbellite
preacher, "I would take him out of the water, hang him on
the fence to dry, then set him afire, and take him into the
Methodist Church."[25]

Methodists versus Other Denominations

Upholders of other traditions fell prey to Methodist
champions of valor equal to those who vindicated that tradition against Baptists and Campbellites. Not fatalistic Calvinism, superstitious Romanism, formalistic Anglicanism or
fanatic " Dunkerdism, " simplistic Universalism, or quietistic

Quakerism could meet the standards of religion as perceived
in Scriptures by the Methodists. While it valued its superior
and timely organization as a means of frontier conquest,
Methodist tradition remembered even more vividly that it
succeeded because it was true. The cohesiveness fashioned
by such memories could be and was a valuable asset in times
less competitive and absolutistic.

Notes

1. D. Young, Autobiography, p. 3 34.
2. Thomas D. Clark, The Rampaging Frontier; Manners
   and Humors of Pioneer Days in the South and the
   Middle West (Indianapolis: The Bobbs-Merrill Co.,
   1939).
3. Ayres, Methodist Heroes, p. 145. Rev. John Haslam
   reportedly made the remark to a Baptist preacher
   who attempted to proselytize newly-made Methodist
   converts in his absence. Motif V350.: "Conflicts
   between religions."
4. Robison, Clawson, pp. 131-32.
5. Hobart, Recollections, p. 138.
6. Erwin, Reminiscences, p. 95. In this account, the
   characterization of Calvinism is: "'If you seek religion you can't find it. If you find it you won't
   know it. If you don't know it you have got it; and
   if you have got it you can't lose it; and if you lose
   it you never had it.'" Lorenzo Dow's recension of
   the caricature was succinct: "'You can and you
   can't; you will and you won't; you shall and you
   shan't; you'll be damned if you do, and you'll be
   damned if you don't.'" Ibid.
7. Ayres, Methodist Heroes, p. 73.
8. Fifty Years: Observations--Opinions--Experiences
   (Nashville: Publishing House of the M. E. Church,
   South, 1903), pp. 129-30.
9. Ware, Memoir, p. 188.
10. Autobiography, p. 139. Some Baptists shared a similar
    evaluation of Baptist intemperance. Elder Joseph
    Hicks "used sometimes to reprimand the church and
    congregation, but more especially on the vice of in-
    temperance. Upon one occasion, when some of the
    members of one of his congregations had been indulg-
    ing too freely in the ardent, he exclaimed: 'The
    Methodists cry Fire, fire! The Presbyterians cry,
    Order, order! The Baptists cry, Water, water! but mix

a little whiskey with it. Shame, shame, upon the
Baptists.'" Borum, Biographical Sketches, p. 540.

11. Nash, Recollections, p. 32.
12. Ware, Memoir, pp. 158-59; supra, pp. 232-33.
13. Autobiography, p. 233.
14. Autobiography, p. 169.
15. Borum, Biographical Sketches, p. 20. Motif J1262.:
    "Repartee based on doctrinal discussions."
16. Rankin, Story, p. 181.
17. See Johnson, Recollections, pp. 150-53, for the account
    of how John Johnson hounded the Baptist controver-
    sialist Vardiman across the width of middle Tennes-
    see.
18. Erwin, Reminiscences, pp. 30, 29.
19. Autobiography, p. 221.
20. Godbey, Seventy Years, p. 134.
21. Robison, Clawson, pp. 133-34.
22. Pleasant Recollections, pp. 156-57.
23. Taylor, Autobiography, p. 151. See also Gavitt, Crumbs,
    p. 120, for an instance of Methodist superiority in
    Scriptural repartee.
24. Finney, Marvin, p. 239.
25. Autobiography, p. 254.

Chapter 12

GIANTS AND HEROES

This great and good man cannot easily be assigned
to his true position in Methodistic history. The
remoteness of the period in which he lived--that
fact that he left but few private papers, and kept
no journal--the absorbed and uncommunicative nature of the man, the disappearance in death of his
contemporaries both in the ministry and society,
make it impossible to collect the facts which alone,
could do justice to the man. Yet, living at a period when the name of Methodist was a synonym for
all that was romantic, perilous, and self-sacrificing
in religion, and being of a stern, determined, and
energetic character, it is certain that his life was
full of incidents, noble sacrifices, and glorious successes, and his status is rightly given as among
the giants of those days. [1]

Just as the prophet Hosea appealed to Israel's forty-
year "honeymoon" with Yahweh in the desert as the Golden
Age to which his people should return in spirit, so American
Methodist tradition hearkened to the frontier era which forged
heroes and giants on the anvil of the deprivation and inse-
curity as the spiritual headwaters of the denomination. "At
the call of the Master," E. J. Stanley notes in the introduction to his biography of Stateler, early itinerants

> forsook all and went forth into the wilderness, per-
> forming heroic tasks and enduring untold privations,
> not a few laying down their lives in the noble work,
> and without thought of compensation except that
> which comes from a sense of duty performed, the
> joy of ministering to the spiritual welfare of their
> fellow-men, and the promise of a crown of life in
> the world to come. [2]

Admiration of such courage and dedication, warned Thomas

275

The Heroism of Brother Van, Beloved Montana Itinerant, Memorialized in a Painting by the Famous Western Artist, Charles Russell

Summers, is not enough:

> It is hoped that the record of their labors will
> quicken the zeal of those who have entered into
> them; and the memorial of their godly lives will
> induce many of their spiritual descendants to 'ad-
> mire' the portraits, 'nor stop to admire, but imi-
> tate and live.'[3]

Raw human potential, other biographers assert, flow-
ered in frontier times and places. To put it another way:
circumstances that demanded heroic actions nurtured heroes.
Ignited by the individualism, aggressiveness, and courage of
the Revolutionary spirit, "Methodist preachers of that day
reflected in their character and methods the very genius of
that heroic time." They carried westward the torch of a
nation "born into freedom amid blood and flame" kindling it
anew and refining it "into a holier flame" to effect a second
rebirth under God.[4] The Western wilderness, in turn, tempered Revolutionary idealism in the cold bath of discipline:

> He [Matthew Simpson] lacked the physical robust-
> ness that seemed necessary to one destined to take
> such an important part in the affairs of church and
> state, but his lot was cast with what was then the
> West--the Far West. Methods of living were sim-
> pler and more natural, and this tougher and coarser
> life proved health-producing. He soon became
> strong and robust. The forest school made of him
> an intellectual and physical giant, and helped him
> to bear up under the strain of his later work, which
> extended somewhat beyond the allotted three-score
> years and ten.[5]

Enthusiastic raconteurs were quick to point up the
frontier virtues as well as the Christian virtues of early
preachers. Gigantic in physical as well as spiritual stature,[6]
Methodist heroes could out-shoot, out-work, out-fight, and
out-wit their contemporaries. "'That boy will do for Texas!'" by-standers huzzahed after John Wesley DeVilbiss won
a shooting match.[7] "'Wonder if a great logroller like you
can be the preacher?'" awed mountaineers asked the virile
William Taylor. "'Come and see,'" he replied.[8] John Burgess' father had told him "'to keep on the good side, even of
a dog, and you won't be bitten.'" Young Burgess became so
proficient with the bow and arrow that savage Indians exclaimed, "'He half Injun--he half Injun!'"[9] In Texas, the

tough Josiah Whipple "had the respect of every one, gangs of
rowdy rangers at times riding with him to his appointments
to protect him from the Indians. "10

Methodist preachers got stronger the harder they
worked. 11   When old Father Corson was urged to retire at
a Conference on the grounds that he was no longer physically
equal to the demands of the itinerancy, he lost his patience
and

> stepped out into the aisle, sprang into the air, as
> in the days of his boyhood, and rapped his feet
> three times together before he returned to the floor.
> 'There!' said he with a look of scorn and defiance,
> 'Are there any of you here that can do that?'12

McKendree preached to six thousand people in his old age,
according to William Hoss. 13   One amusing story tells how
the vital James McCourt (not a preacher but a Methodist of
old-time flavor), converted at age ninety-eight, was promised
a hundred-dollar purse by friends if he could run one hundred
yards in five minutes on his hundredth birthday.   When the
time came the old man covered the distance in three minutes
instead of five. 14

In certain biographies the heroic aura of the age suf-
fused the nativity and youth of the subjects.   John B. McFerrin, whose life-principle was "sanctified pugnacity, " was
"'Born in a cane-brake and cardled in a sugar trough. '"
The prodigy began to walk when only seven months old--"a
sort of prophecy of his itinerant career."15   Erastus Haven's
mother, converted shortly before her accouchement, gave
birth to him without pain. 16   Joseph Travis recalls his miraculous salvation from a fire as an infant, while James
Quinn was providentially spared from death when a gun burst
while he was shooting. 17

Lineage as well as life, in some narratives, deter-
mines the heroic outlines of a subject.   Thomas Pearne, who
began his biography with the assertion "I was well born ...
the tradition runs that on mother's side there was a dash of
the Wesley blood in our veins,"18 was the exception in appeal-
ing to British antecedents; most heroes were content to trace
their vigor to patriots of the Revolutionary era and to pioneers of the early frontier days.   William Patton's father,
Henry, came from stock that "had borne an active part in
her [the United States'] struggles for political freedom, as

well as helped to clear the then Western forests, and form
settlements in their hitherto unbroken wilds.... "19 Benjamin
Paddock's father "belonged to a physical stock remarkable
for manly proportions and uncommon strength, " and some
members of the lineage "were scarcely less distinguished for
mental capacity and general culture."10 Moral character as
well as physical could be transmitted; William Goff Caples
"was possessed of that sort of deep, unassailable principle
that is apt to be hereditary. " Enoch Marvin, his biographer,
continues: "my observation is that where there is very high
moral tone it may be traced to an honorable line of ances-
try. "21

        The heroic age of Methodism, it is clear, is closely
linked with the heroic exigencies created by an advancing and
sometimes chaotic frontier civilization. Some narratives
contrast the exuberant vigor of the "noble savages" molded
in the West with the parlor virtues of Easterners. The itinerant Henry Smith, returning from Kentucky to his home in
Virginia for a visit, intimidated local rowdies who had threatened to "funnel" him (to pour whiskey down his throat); when
they saw him they became "absolutely afraid of me, and said,
'He has been to the west, where he learned the art of knocking them down; for until he came home there was none of
it.'"22

        Bascom's biographer, Henkle, takes great pains to
illustrate how the orator of the West bearded the Eastern
champion imported from England (David Summerville) in his
own den by out-preaching him. 13 A. E. Phelps, in a similar saga, made such an impression in Boston that years later
he was spoken of in Boston "as the greatest pulpit orator
that has appeared there for years."24 Peter Cartwright remembers how, when he was riding the "iron horse" to Boston, the train stopped at the Massachusetts state line for
some reason and Cartwright dashed out without his hat for a
drink of water. When he returned, he saw that his traveling companions were laughing "at my expense. "

                Said I, 'Gentlemen, what are you laughing
        at?'
                One, somewhat composing his risibilities,
        answered,
                'How dare you enter the sacred, classic
        land of the pilgrims bareheaded?'
                'My dear sir, ' said I, 'God Almighty crowd-
        ed me into the world bareheaded, and I think it no

Henry Smith, Who Knew "the Art of Knocking Them Down"

more harm to enter Massachusetts bareheaded than
for the Lord to bring me into the world without a
hat. '25

The faceless David Bartine, of whom the initial quotation of this section said in effect that, since he lived in heroic times, he must have been a hero, begins to acquire fea-
tures as the lineaments of more specific heroes emerge in
the literature. Some preachers entered tradition renowned
for ebullience, others for diffidence; some for wit and others
for eccentricity; some as holy men or as muscle men, and
others as cranks or as geniuses; and some for clairvoyance,
asceticism, or prescience.

Perhaps the most characteristic hero of frontier Methodism, however, was the strong man, more lion than lamb,
who muscled the Gospel into the craws of tough frontiersmen.
Before turning to the exploits of such heroes, the present
section considers characteristic anecdotes of other early heroes.

Jesse Walker

Tradition remembers Jesse Walker as the Methodist
"scout" par excellence. Called in many accounts Methodism's
"Daniel Boone, " he was "always first, always ahead of everybody else, preceding all others long enough to be the pilot of
the newcomer. "26 His wilderness expertise was legendary,
and tradition credited him with almost mystical intimacy with
Nature. According to one story, when a young preacher ex-
plained to Walker that, unless he read more, he would not
be able to preach well, Walker patiently replied:

'You little fellows cannot learn any thing until some-
body else finds it out first and puts it in a book;
then you can learn it. But I know it before it goes
in a book: I know what they make books out of. '

Editorializing on the anecdote, the narrator continues:

He took lessons from rocks and trees, mountains
and rivers; he held Nature's keys, and forced her,
secretive as she is, to divulge her secrets. He
lived in the antechamber of Wisdom's storehouse.
He slaked his thirst from the mountain brook at its

source, plucked flowers from stalks that had never
been transplanted, and read the volume of nature
in the first edition, without note or comment.   He
was one of nature's great men. [27]

Such intuition would have made Thoreau envious, and such a
rhapsody echoes James Fenimore Cooper's paeans to his heroic scouts.   The ideal of the noble savage, self-reliant and
without need of formal learning, recurs again and again in
Methodist biography.   Ability to read the book of nature, or
to read men, is attributed to Francis Asbury, James Gwin,
William Caples, Hope Hull, Dan Young, and A. E. Phelps,
to mention a few.   To Walker, however, belong the laurels.

According to Pennewell, the dauntless Walker preached
on the gospel frontiers of nine different states--Virginia,
North Carolina, Tennessee, Kentucky, Indiana, Illinois, Missouri, Arkansas, and Wisconsin--and is said to have founded
the Methodist church in numerous towns, including St. Louis,
Peoria, Bloomington, Indiana, Chicago, and Racine, Wisconsin. [28]   The most characteristic Walker anecdote, however,
is the story of how he founded the church in St. Louis.   As
told by A. D. Field, Walker and two other itinerants agreed
to "invade" St. Louis together.

After establishing themselves in their own circuits,
the two preachers met Jesse Walker, according to
appointment, to join him on his entry into the then
Capital City of the West.   When they reached St.
Louis, the Territorial Legislature was in session,
and every public place was full.   When it became
known who they were, they received ridicule and
curses.   There seemed to be no opening for meetings, or for even lodging for the preachers.   Hin-
dered at every point, they rode into the public
square, and held a consultation on their horses.
The young preachers concluded that, had the Master
work for them, a door would be opened; and by this
token they concluded the Lord had no work for them
to do there.   Their leader tried to rally them, but
in vain.   The West had almost everywhere received
the preachers with gladness, but here were only in-
sults.   They deliverately brushed the dust from
their feet, and rode off, leaving the disconsolate
Walker sitting on his horse alone.   Perhaps that
hour had more of despondency than any other Jesse
Walker ever suffered.   In the midst of his disap-

pointment he said: 'I will go to the State of Mississippi, and look up the desolate places there.'
Turning his horse to the south, he rode away. He
rode as far as eighteen miles, with anguish of
spirit, and yet all the time praying, thus seeking
to know the will of the Master. The early itinerants had a wonderful trust in the guiding of Providence. At length he broke into the following solilo-
quy: 'Was I ever defeated before? Never! Did
ever any one trust in the Lord Jesus Christ and
get confounded? No! And by the grace of God I
will go back and take St. Louis!'

The story goes on to tell how Walker turned back to the city,
and, under almost impossible conditions, founded Methodism
there. 29

Jesse Lee

If Jesse Walker was Methodism's harbinger on the
Western frontier, another Jesse was its apostle on the New
England frontier. While the former Jesse carried Methodism
to a traditionless wilderness, Jesse Lee blazed the gospel
trail in what, to Methodist eyes, was a jungle glutted with
baneful Calvinistic and Deistic traditions. Walker's task demanded physical courage and endurance, but Lee's required
wit and common sense. The one was a pioneer grappling
with the frontier on its own terms; the other a frontiersman
returning to beard the Genteel Tradition in its lair.

"Do you have a liberal education?" cynical Yankees
were likely to ask Lee, baiting him and his religion for its
reportedly humble origins and its enthusiasm. With "characteristic shrewdness," Lee would reply that he had nothing
to boast of, though "he believed he had enough to carry him
through the country!"30

Most characteristic of Lee in New England is the story
of Lee and the lawyers. Repeated with zest in Lee biogra-
phics, the story also finds its way, often in truncated form,
into other memoirs as an illustration of how native shrewdness (Lee) confounds cultivated ignorance (lawyers).

The oft-told anecdote of Lee and the Lawyers, has
its location between Boston and Lynn. (The location

and genuineness of this anecdote are derived from
a contemporary and intimate friend of Mr. Lee,
who received it from himself.) Mr. Lee was riding leisurely along the road to Lynn, on one occasion, when he was overtaken by two sprigs of the
law, who knew him to be a Methodist Preacher,
but of whom he knew nothing. Full of life and
good humour, they determined on a little innocent
amusement with the parson; and after a friendly
salutation, one riding on either side of him, something like the following pass-at-arms occurred between them:

    1st Lawyer. 'I believe you are a Preacher,
sir?'

    Mr. Lee. 'Yes; I generally pass for one.'

    1st Law. 'You preach very often, I suppose?'

    Lee. 'Generally every day; frequently twice,
or more.'

    2d Law. 'How do you find time to study,
when you preach so often?'

    Lee. 'I study when riding, and read when
resting.'

    1st Law. 'But do you not write your ser-
mons?'

    Lee. 'No; not very often, at least.'

    2d Law. 'Do you not often make mistakes in
preaching extemporaneously?'

    Lee. 'I do sometimes.'

    2d Law. 'How do you do then? Do you cor-
rect them?'

    Lee. 'That depends upon the character of
the mistake. I was preaching the other day, and
I went to quote the text, '"All liars shall have their
part in the lake that burneth with fire and brimstone"; and, by mistake, I said "All lawyers shall
have their part--"'

    2d Law. (interrupting him.) 'What did you
do with that? Did you correct it?'

    Lee. 'O, no, indeed! It was so nearly
true, I didn't think it worth while to correct it.'

    'Humph!' said one of them (with a hasty and
impatient glance at the other), 'I don't know whether
you are the more a knave or a fool!'

    'Neither,' he quietly replied, turning at the
same time his mischievous eyes from one to the
other; 'I believe I am just between the two!'

    Finding they were measuring wit with one of

its masters, and excessively mortified at their discomfiture, the knights of the green bag drove ahead,
leaving the victor to solitude and his own reflections.
The echoing of a merry laugh that chased their
steeds, added very little comfort to the self-esteem
of their riders. 31

Some reminiscences join the lawyer-liar or knave-fool
repartee, or both, to another Lee anecdote:

On a certain occasion a young lawyer, with a view
to puzzle Mr. Lee, addressed him in Latin; to
whom he replied in German--a language not understood either by the speaker or his friends, who
were anxiously listening to the conversation. 'There, '
said a gentleman, who was in the secret of the lawyer's intentions, 'the preacher has answered you
in Hebrew, and therefore he must be a learned
man. '32

Andrew Manship joins the story to the lawyer-liar repartee,
as does W. H. Withrow. 33 Ayres, however, joins the Latin-
German anecdote to the knave-fool repartee, omitting the
lawyer-liar portion of the story. 34 Other accounts relate the
Latin-German anecdote separately, portraying the questioner
as a condescending clergyman35 or as a college student,
rather than as a lawyer. 36

Methodist tradition found the humor of the anecdote so
delicious that it could not resist spreading the charisma of
Lee's wit. Dr. Shadrach Bostwick, reportedly a "Professor
in Brush College" and a graduate of "Swamp University, "
confounded a "learned doctor of divinity" who questioned him
by replying not only in German but in Latin, French, and
Hebrew as well. Bostwick's astounded opponent remarked:
" 'I never saw such a man!' "37 Such a recension of the
story loses the deft touch of the original; not so Peter Cartwright's version. While the incident may not have originated
with Cartwright, he nevertheless was a good enough story-
teller and teacher to use it for his purposes, namely, to dis-
prove the opinion of "literary gentlemen" that Methodist
preachers were "illiterate, ignorant babblers. "38 Finally,
Thomas Pearne attributes all three stories, told as if they
occurred on the same ride, to the eccentric Jacob Gruber. 39

Lee's effectiveness in New England, according to Methodist lore, emerges in a story which relates the impression
of his preaching upon the people.

A tinker came to Weston in search of work; and,
on inquiring into the probability of finding employ-
ment in the place, was told that the Methodists
were likely to beat a hole through the Saybrook
Platform, and if he could mend that, and could
stay long enough, he might be employed. 40

Lorenzo Dow

According to a description of Dow by Dan Young, Dow
was "rather quick and active in his motions; his complexion
was light, with intelligent blue eyes...."41   Another description, by a Mr. McCorkle, relates that Dow's appearance was
"somewhat remarkable.   His eyes were the most striking
feature of his face, being very dark and piercing...."42

If eyes are truly the windows of the soul, the dis-
parate memories of Lorenzo Dow's eyes by Young and Mc-
Corkle illuminate the complexities of this self-styled "Citizen
of the World."43   Without formal education, Dow nevertheless possessed intelligence so sharp that its edge became
ragged.   In the estimation of many observers, Dow was certainly eccentric, probably a crank, and possibly insane. 44
Yet, although he stood in a long line of noted itinerant "ec-
centrics," such as Wilson Pitner, Billy Hibbard, Shadrach
Bostwick, John Hersey, and Robert Sayers Sheffey, Dow's
unusual perspicuity earned him the respect due one who, the
stories asserted, was clairvoyant and prophetic.   He relied
on dreams, visions, and inward impressions rather than on
doctrines, rules, and regulations. 45   He foretold futures,
such as the impending death of a giddy girl laughing during
the sermon, 46 or the future ministerial vocation of young
Joseph Travis. 47   When asked how he could predict people's
futures with such confidence, he said "that things came to his
mind with such light and power, that if he did not speak of
them he felt guilty."48

The most widely-told Dow anecdote recalls one of his
many sermon tricks: before a discourse on the Last Judgment, he hired a boy to climb to the top of a tree and blow
a trumpet at the appropriate moment. 49   Most characteristic
of Dow's clairvoyant reputation, however, is the story of
how he found a stolen purse.

After a long and tiresome journey he stopped about

"Crazy" Dow Leading "The Jerks" at a Camp Meeting

nightfall at the door of a country tavern in Western
Virginia. He retired to his apartment, but was
much disturbed by a party of revelers who sat at
their cups and cards till a late hour. Near midnight one of their company discovered that he had
lost his pocketbook, and a search was proposed.
The landlord here remarked that Lorenzo Dow was
in the house, and that if the money had been lost
there he could certainly find it. The suggestion
was adopted at once, and Dow was aroused and requested to find the rogue. As he entered the room
he glanced searchingly around, but could see no
signs of guilt on any face. The loser was in great
trouble and begged Dow to find his money.

'Have you left the room since you lost your
money,' asked Dow.

'Nein, nein,' replied the man.

'Then,' said Dow, turning to the landlady,
'go and bring me your large dinner pot.'

This excited not little astonishment, but as
they accorded to him supernatural power, the order
was promptly obeyed, and the pot was placed in
the center of the room.

'Now,' said Dow, 'go and bring the old
chicken cock from the roost.'

The amazement grew apace; however, the
old rooster was brought in, placed in the pot, and
securely covered.

'Let the doors be now fastened, and all the
lights put out,' said Dow. This was done.

'Now,' said he, 'every person in the room
must rub his hand hard against the pot, and when
the guilty hand touches it the cock will crow.'

All then came forward and rubbed or pretended to rub against the pot, but the cock did not
crow.

'Let the candles be now lighted; there is no
guilty person here; if the man ever had any money,
he must have left it in some other place,' said
Dow.

'But stop,' he exclaimed suddenly, 'let us
now examine the hands.' This was, of course, the
main point in the whole affair. It was found upon
examination that one man had not rubbed against
the pot. 'There,' said Dow, pointing to the man
with clean hands, 'there is the man who picked your
pocket.' The thief at once confessed and gave up
the money. 150

Of note in the anecdote is the fact that Dow's reputation for
clairvoyance, not actual clairvoyant power, precipitates exposure of the thief.

Dow's reputation grew, in the sight of his contemporaries, until the use of his name was sufficient excuse for
many a twice-told tale. Of the Methodist itinerants, Dow
reverberates most of all not only within the folklore of the
brotherhood, but in American "secular" folklore as well. 51
He must have remained an enigma to his more prosaic and
stable colleagues who recognized, even as they regretted his
sensationalism, the good that the man did:

> A good man he was, no doubt; and, as we have al-
> ready said, useful in his widely eccentric orbit,
> yet one such character in half a century is enough.52

Robert R. Roberts

One man's pathway into legend is not another's. If
Lorenzo Dow entered folk history because of aggressive eccentricity, Robert R. Roberts, the "Log Cabin Bishop, " was
hypostasized because of reticence. The characteristic Roberts
anecdote tells how the bishop arrives at a place, on his episcopal travels, is unrecognized and remains incognito until
puzzled questioners, seeking his identity, find to their amazement that they are in the presence of a bishop. Such stories,
which echo Motif K1812 ("King in disguise"), indicate that
Roberts entered tradition not only because of extreme diffidence but because the latter quality appealed to one side of
early Methodism's ambivalence toward the episcopacy itself.
The "offense" of the hierarchy would be mitigated if bishops
were in fact indistinguishable from laity.

Another reason for Roberts' appeal to folk memory
arises from his identification, not only with the laity, but
with the common man. Set aside by their vocation, many
preachers were humanly eager to brush aside stereotypes of
themselves as hypocrites, charlatans, ignoramuses, or prigs
and to be regarded simply as men. 53 " 'If I had been out
with a rifle to shoot parsons, I should never have pulled the
trigger at you, ' " a southern plantation owner told William Milburn as they rode together on a stagecoach. 54 Roberts epito-
mized such yearning for preachers sensitive to the biases
with which common folk approach them. Needless to say, the

"My Name is Roberts"--Bishop Robert R. Roberts

fact that a man of humble origins could rise to the episcopacy was an ecclesiastical version of the rags-to-riches motif.

One of the most commonly told tales of Bishop Roberts relates how both the bishop and a gay young preacher stopped at the same house for lodging on their way home from conference. His host thought him a "rustic traveler," and offered him little more than basic hospitality. The neophyte preacher, "young, frivolous, and foppish," monopolized the attentions of the family during dinner and afterwards, joking and laughing especially with the daughters of the family, frequently at the expense of the "rustic traveler." When bedtime came, the young preacher and Roberts were quartered in the same room. The former climbed into bed without prayers, but the latter poured out his soul to God. After Roberts had gotten into bed, the young man asked,

> 'Do you happen to know anything of Bishop Roberts?'
> 'Yes.'
> 'Are you personally acquainted with him?'
> 'Yes, I know him well.'
> 'What is your name.'
> 'My name is Roberts.'
> 'Roberts? Not Bishop Roberts?'
> 'They sometimes call me Bishop Roberts.'
> 'Bishop Roberts! Bishop Roberts!' shouted
> the young man, leaping out of bed, astonished beyond measure.[55]

The young preacher, mortified by his unbecoming conduct, apologized to the humble Roberts and learned a lesson in ministerial decorum.

Jesse Walker, Jesse Lee, Lorenzo Dow, and Robert Roberts are only a few of the heroic figures of early Methodism. Of course, no full account of Methodist heroes could omit the exploits of Bishop Francis Asbury, American Methodism's "Founding Father." His unwavering self-discipline, uncanny administrative ability, and prodigious travels inspired countless anecdotes which convey the awe and even fear with which men regarded him. Peter Cartwright, too, deserves treatment more exhaustive than can be given him here. His own Autobiography, which is full of Methodist folklore, paints him as an ebullient, cocky, tough frontiersman, always ready to fight fire with fire, to trade story for story and trick for

trick. Another remembrance, however, depicts him as a
bully and shyster, unscrupulous in his tactics and goals. 56
Methodist heroes--scout, pioneer, clever man, eccentric,
common man, founding father, and trickster--echo the acclaim
tendered by Americans to their secular heroes. 57

Legends about such religious heroes, therefore, indicate the pervasive acculturation between folk and religious belief. Nowhere is such acculturation more evident, however,
than in the one heroic figure remaining to be considered: the
strong man.

The Strong Man

Camp meetings, developed after 1799 by frontier evan-
gelists of many denominations as a response to wilderness religious exigencies, became by 1825 the almost exclusive property of the Methodists. 58 Because such revival meetings
were social as well as religious occasions they invariably attracted persons with motives other than religious. At the
dark perimeters of these woodland gatherings people seeking
non-religious stimulation met those who would vend it, and,
emboldened by their new-found courage, hot-blooded youth,
old drunks, and assorted ne'er-do-wells banded together in
precarious associations to assail the sobriety and moral fervor that tacitly condemned their own dissipations and purpose-
lessness. Such groups frequently butted into the turmoil of
preaching, shouting and singing that especially characterized
the early camp meetings, with the intent of amplifying the
hubbub to the point of chaos. Met with equivalent and demoralizing physical resistance, rowdies resorted to more
subtle interruptions, frequently in the form of practical jokes.
Such an expediency is recounted in the story of the man who
"gathered and strung ... a batch of frogs" which he intended
to slip over Peter Cartwright's head while the latter was
stooping and praying for mourners. 59

As Methodism's reputation for moral rigor spread on
the frontier, Methodist preachers became fair game for bullies
and toughs in or out of camp meetings. Stories tell how jokers dropped a halloween pumpkin over the head of a preacher
during a sermon, 60 or how they coaxed a flock of geese up
the aisle of the church during a service;61 how buffoons
shaved the tail of old Father Owen's horse (appropriately
named Samson), 62 or how they hoisted A. E. Phelps' buggy
to the roof of a barn. 63

Denominational extinction or retreat was the price of submission to the chaos fomented by frontier rowdies and practical jokers. Methodist lore recalls that early itinerants gained respect on the frontier by appeal to legal processes, where possible, but most frequently by trickery, by moral or physical intimidation, or by sheer physical force. In only a few anecdotes do rowdies prove susceptible to sweet remonstrance, and never does suffering gain their respect.

Some anecdotes recall tricks that backfired. One tippler, having resolved to trim the preacher's coattails, crept up while the latter prayed, and, to avoid detection, "knelt back to back with his victim" while slitting off the skirt. When the trickster returned to his saloon with the trophy, he was chagrined to hear the bartender exclaim, "'C_____, they have docked you!'" Taking off his coat, he found his own tails neatly trimmed. 64

Another backfire involving the skirts of a rowdy's coat is recorded by James Erwin. Near the end of a camp-meeting "fellows of the baser sort" determined to mock the mourners at a prayer meeting. The Methodists, however, learned of their plan, and when the ringleader, "a stalwart man with a slouching hat drawn down over his eyes, and a long over-coat buttoned to his neck and reaching nearly to his feet," entered and knelt down to pray in apparent earnestness, "two heavy brethren knelt by his side ... drew out the skirts of his strong overcoat and knelt upon them."

> They began to pray for this heaven-daring, God-provoking sinner who, adding to an ungodly life, was now mocking God and insulting the people by palming himself off as a seeker of His mercy. They prayed that God would not strike him dead as He did the men in the camp of Israel who offered strange fire, but show him his sins and shake him over hell until he felt the scorching of the flames. He began to feel uneasy and tried to rise, his wicked comrades enjoying the scene. Just then the strong-lunged Scotchman shouted with a trumpet voice that went ringing above everything else: 'Power of the Lord, seize him! Nail him to the ground!'
> The terrified man attempted to spring to his feet, found himself fastened to the ground, roared in frightened anguish and begun in earnest to cry for mercy, confessing his sins with real penitence. His friends, hearing his piteous cries, fled from the ground amazed and confounded. 65

Other stories recount how itinerants outwit foolish
rowdies. John Haslam reportedly quieted noisy persons at
a camp meeting by having them engage in a contest to see
who could climb to the top of a large tree first, and then by
offering a quarter to the one who could keep still the longest
in his lofty perch. 66

Dan Young, on one occasion, tricked disrupters into
becoming sentinels for a camp meeting; on another occasion,
in a neighborhood where hog-stealing had incensed the people
to the point of mayhem, he got up at the beginning of the
meeting and implied that there would be no trouble unless it
were caused by the same people who were stealing hogs. Of
course no one wanted to be thought a hog-stealer, so the
meeting transpired smoothly. 67 Peter Cartwright tells how
rowdies threatened to stone the preachers' tent at a camp
meeting one night after Cartwright had preempted their barrel of whiskey; Cartwright dressed in old clothes, mingled
with the ruffians and learned their plans, then went down to
the river, filled his pockets with stones, and just as the disrupters were about to begin their deviltry, he rushed among
them, throwing handfuls of stones in every direction and
shouting "'Here they are! here they are! take them! take
them!'" The startled rowdies, imagining they were besieged
by a superior force, ran helter-skelter for their lives. 68

Besides trickery, another tactic recounted in anecdotes
was sheer moral courage. A. C. Morehouse, for example,
refused to step aside when a crowd of bullies tried to gain
entrance to a meeting, whereat

one of the ring-leaders turned, and facing the crowd,
rolled up his sleeves, and doubling up his fists,
said, 'He is a good fellow, and I will defend him
.... '69

Other itinerants, in good frontier fashion, "stared down"
those who would do them harm. Riding over a narrow wilderness pass, Henry Bascom was beset by three toughs whose
sensibilities he had offended the day before in a sermon.
Undaunted by the threat of a beating, Bascom rode right by
his would-be assailants:

His dark brow was knit, his lips strongly com-
pressed, every muscle seemed tense with concen-
trated resolve and courage, and his keen, penetrat-
ing eye, kindling to its intensest severity, seemed

almost to shoot out arrows of flame. In this state,
with an aspect terribly defiant, he rode forward,
and as he approached, cast at each of the ruffians
in turn, such a piercing glance, as seemed to penetrate them through, and caused them to quail and
cower. Not one of the three dared to meet his
scathing look; not one dared attack him; not one had
even the courage to speak, and Bascom rode on un-
molested. 70

Moral integrity, in a story told of Peter/Doub, gave him
power even over ferocious animals. On one occasion, when
Doub was confronted by a vicious dog, the preacher

looked at him straight and asked, 'Are you not
ashamed to want to bite a poor Methodist preacher?'
The brute dropped his bristles, licked the preacher's hands, and walked by his side till he reached
the farmhouse door, much to the consternation of
the family within. 71

Certain preachers with no less moral integrity but with
considerably greater physical endowment gained a place in
tradition by real or reputed manifestations of physical prowess
by which they defended Methodism from its attackers.   The
most famous among these Methodist strongarms was James
Gilruth, whom Jacob Young remembers as a "man of uncommon muscular power ... almost everybody in the county was
afraid of him. "72   According to one report, Gilruth was "the
largest minister I ever saw.... I stood beside him once in
a pulpit, and the contrast was interesting, as I came only
within three hundred pounds of his weight; yet I was a young
man grown to my highest reach. "73   As a member of a regiment in the War of 1812, Gilruth "could outrun or throw
down any man in the army, seemingly with the greatest ease, "
and on one occasion,

a large iron which two men had carried out into the
yard on a bet, Brother G. , wishing to hitch his
horse, with one hand set up against a stump and
made it a hitching-post. 74

The young Gilruth was wild, brawling and afraid of
neither man nor beast; but after being wrestled to a draw by
Mr. Webb, Gilruth began to learn the lesson of true strength:

'He then thought it was the thunder that split the

tree, but he had since learned that it was the lightning that did the execution. '75

Around Gilruth tradition clustered many stories told of other
muscular circuit riders as well: Henry Ryan, Zane Bland,
Isaac Collins, and Jesse Walker, to mention a few. Gilruth,
however, loomed largest in the lore.

While travelling to a meeting, according to one narrator, Gilruth followed people through a private field to avoid
a swampy place in a road. When he was almost through the
field, the owner intercepted him, "mad and raving, " and
ordered him to go back. Gilruth attempted to reason with
the angry man, but to no avail; the man insisted, " 'You shall,
you must return. ' "

> Gilruth looked at him with a stern eye, lifted his
> great half-bared muscular arm, and said, 'My
> friend, do you see this arm?' The man stood in
> silence for a moment, then looked at the minister's
> determined face and said, in a subdued manner,
> 'Well, you can pass this time. ' The itinerant
> thanked him, and went through in peace. 76

In another story, reported by Thomas Hall Pearne,
Gilruth, "the Hercules of the Ohio Conference, "

> seized an antagonist around the waist, and lifted
> him off the ground; then raising the bottom rail of
> the fence with one of his hands, he pushed the man's
> head under and dropped the rails over his neck,
> and left him thus in limbo, while Gilruth began to
> ride off with the honors. The man cried after him
> for mercy, and was released. He was afterwards
> converted under Mr. Gilruth's preaching. 77

In similar stories told of other Methodist strongmen,
the preacher simply hurls the bully over the fence. While
traveling to a camp-meeting one day, Joseph Collins met with
a stranger, who, after pleasantries were exchanged, asserted
that he was on his way to a camp meeting to give Joseph Collins a licking. Collins asked the stranger whether Mr. Collins had ever done him harm, and when the man replied nega-
tively, Collins warned, " 'If I were you, and Collins had never
done you any harm, I would let him alone. ' " When they
drew near to the camp meeting, several miles later, Collins
dismounted and said to the bully:

'My name is Collins. I am the man you want to
lick. We are near the camp-ground, and we may
as well have the trial of strength here, and now. '
When the man had alighted and hitched his horse,
Mr. Collins seized him by the collar and the slack
of his trousers, and flung him over the fence. The
stranger, picking himself up and rubbing the part
on which he had fallen, is reported to have said,
'Mr. Collins, if you will kindly hand my horse over,
we will call it quits. '[78]

A third Gilruth story describes how the giant regularly
defended himself and his people at camp meetings, in this
case, by legal prosecution:

This prompt action in defense of himself or of his
right was shown in his admonition to the impertinent lawyer who, in defending an important case,
had made sport of him as a witness, and ridiculed
him as a Methodist minister; and finally asked him
to state to the jury about how hard he supposed his
client in the case had struck the plaintiff, Mr. Gilruth. Having obtained permission of the judge to
show the jury, he knocked the lawyer half way
across the Court Room, and said it was something
like that. The reply appeared to be satisfactory to
the judge and jury, if not to the lawyer. [79]

To judge by some accounts, legal redress frequently failed
to protect Methodists in their camp-meetings and churches.
John Lenhart, during a service interrupted by noisy coster-
mongers, waited until the ringleader's back was turned, then
"suddenly descended from the pulpit, twisted his fingers in
the neck-band of the ruffian's shirt, tightening it till he
choked him, then ran him down the aisle, through the door,
out upon the platform, and, administering a farewell kick,
re-entered the church...." The ejected man took Lenhart to
court for assault, and while in the court, the man and his
companions began to assault the minister, to the dismay of
the incompetent magistrate. Lenhart said, addressing the
magistrate,

'Since you cannot protect me, I will protect myself...' Then, grasping his heavy cane in the middle of his length, he brought it on a level with the
eyes and noses of his assailants as they stood on
either side of him, when whirling it rapidly, it

became a matter of necessity if they would preserve
those useful appurtenances that they should 'fall
back.... '80

According to another Gilruth story, a dandy "smart
aleck" repeatedly interrupted Gilruth's preaching.   When the
insolent fellow refused to desist, Gilruth took him by the coat-
collar, carried him at arm's length to a stream and walked
him back and forth in the water until "he was wet as a rat
from head to foot. "81

A story that had Gilruth in mind is the anecdote of
the blacksmith, Ned Forgron, and the preacher, Mr. Nobleworth.   Forgron, an infidel who read Tom Paine regularly,
had vowed to beat every Methodist preacher who was appointed to his circuit the first time he rode by the smithy.   When
Mr. Nobleworth rode by, the burly Forgron strode from his
shop, grabbed the preacher's horse by its bridle, and told
Nobleworth to descend for his beating.   The courageous circuit rider dismounted, dropped Forgron with a single blow,
then sat on his chest and "commenced his devotional exercise, where he left off as he approached the blacksmith
shop. "   That exercise was a lively hymn, and the itinerant
pounded out the time upon the blacksmith's head.   Finally
Forgron cried quarter, but the preacher had requests to make
before he let the prostrate man arise.   Between blows, Nobleworth made the blacksmith repeat hymns and prayers after
him, promise to read the Bible, burn his Tom Paine, and
come to meeting.   Nobleworth later told a congregation,
"'my brethren, I do really believe I did pound the grace of
God into his infidel soul.' "82

Few voices questioned such muscular Christianity, although other tactics were recognized.   In one anecdote, old
Rev. John Forbes had been told by "'lewd fellows of the
baser sort'" whom he offended by his preaching that they
would ship him the next chance they got.   The fearless
Forbes ascended the platform and began to preach on divine
punishment and forgiveness.   As he went on, he "'got happy'" and shouted:

'Where are those fellows who came here to-day to
whip me?...   Why, He would not let a thousand
such harm me.   Where are they?' he repeated;
and as he spoke, with his eyes shut and his rugged
face shining, he left the preaching stand and made
his way up and down the aisles, exhorting as he

> moved. 'My God, ' he exclaimed, 'wouldn't let fifty
> thousand sinners whip me to-day!--but boys, ' he
> continued with a sudden overflow of tenderness, 'he
> is able to forgive and save you all this day, ' placing
> his hand upon the head of one of the opposing party
> as he spoke. The effect was indescribable. A
> mighty wave of feeling swept over the entire assem-
> bly ... the preacher got no whipping that day. 83

To judge by the literature, however, Methodist adapted itself
to frontier militancy, gaining respect by inspiring fear. To
repeat the reminiscence of a western itinerant:

> In this place, and in several other places, Satan
> was dreadfully enraged, and I was often threatened
> by the wicked. Here they threatened to bring whis-
> key, and, if I would not drink, they would funnel
> me, and make me drunk, &c; but none of their
> threats were ever executed. Some were absolutely
> afraid of me, and said, 'He has been to the west,
> where he learned the art of knocking them down;
> for until he came home there was none of it. '84

Summary and Conclusions

Nineteenth century Methodist folklore of the circuit
life, preaching, controversy, and heroism reflects the mutual
conditioning of Methodist idealism and American experience.
Sustained by evangelical pietism and articulated by the itinerant system, American Methodism adapted itself to the exigencies and vagaries of American life, and in particular to
the chaotic culture of the expanding frontier. The raw vitality, religious apathy, and social disintegration endemic to
frontier life affected Methodist preachers at every point, im-
parting to their oral traditions a shape not easily altered.
The pages of Part III have noted such religious folklore, both
folktale and legend, marking where possible the sharing of
themes between religious and secular lore.

As previous pages have shown, oral traditions (especially in Chapters 9-11) functioned as entertainments which
socialized individual experience through conversation, indirectly conveyed ideals, and relieved the tensions of inadequate
performance through laughter. Such benefits inevitably enhanced group solidarity.

An Itinerant's "Foot of Land"--Montana Grave of L. B. Stateler

Group solidarity was reinforced, in another way, by legends of living and dead heroes, who concretized Methodist idealism in their exploits. No itinerant could claim that his vocational burden was too heavy if he knew that the likes of Asbury, Walker, Lee, Cartwright, Dow, and Roberts had triumphed under the same load. The centripetal force of heroic legends must have kept many a discouraged foot-soldier in the ranks. Moreover, the delineation of the heroic Methodists presents a fascinating opportunity for study of itinerant self-conception: such communal representations present the past in terms of what the present ought to be. The latter-day itinerant who traded stories of early heroes, therefore, said what he himself wished to be: as courageous as Jesse Walker, as resourceful as Jesse Lee, as disciplined and tireless as Asbury, as shrewd as Cartwright, as successful as Roberts, and as tough as Gilruth. Study of the shifting configuration of the hero, in Methodist hagiography, could indicate fundamental changes within Methodism itself; for example, the transition from Methodism's frontier phase to its increasing identification with settled urban life could be documented by noting how the figure of the preacher as orator supplants the figure of the preacher as tough circuit rider.

The lore of early Methodism, incorporated in the biographies, autobiographies, and reminiscences of the second half of the nineteenth century for the digestion of a wider Methodist reading public, not only satisfied and titillated romantic tastes but also allowed that clientele to participate in and recapitulate primitive ideals for present and future purposes.

Notes

1. New Jersey Conference Memorial, p. 183, makes the statement of Rev. David Bartine.
2. Stateler, pp. iii-iv. Speaking of early Tennessee Methodist preachers, O. P. Fitzgerald exclaims: "Grand, gifted, holy men! Heroes, saints, martyrs, each one is worthy of a volume to himself...." McFerrin, p. 83. See also Watson, Tales and Takings, pp. 371-73; Ayres, Methodist Heroes, pp. 9-11; Carroll, "Father Corson," p. 143; Beard, Sketches, I, 116, for a similar appraisal of early Cumberland Presbyterian ministers.
3. Biographical Sketches, p. viii. Similar sentiments are expressed in the "Advertisement to the Memoir of

Rev. Thomas Ware," Ware, Memoir, pp. 3-4. See
Paddock, Memoir, pp. 245-48, for an eloquent tribute to the legacy of the heroes.

4. Fitzgerald, McFerrin, p. 40.

5. Clarence True Wilson, Matthew Simpson: Patriot,
   Preacher, Prophet (New York: The Methodist Book
   Concern, 1929), p. 18. For a similar, more detailed statement of the salubrious effects of life in
   the wilderness, see Stanley, Stateler, pp. 6-11; the
   account concludes: "It is easy to see how such a
   mode of life develops habits of industry, economy,
   self-reliance, patience, and perseverance and pre-
   pares the way for success in after life." Ibid.,
   p. 11. See Pearne, Sixty-One Years, pp. 7-8, for
   the assertion that Methodism was the major factor
   in the civilizing of the Western frontier.

6. Wise, Sketches, p. 301; Carroll, "Father Corson," p.
   27: at the 1824 Canadian Annual Conference, "I can
   remember that there were several rather undersized
   preachers (dwarfed all the more by contrast with such
   almost gigantic persons as Elijah Hedding, Nathan
   Bangs, William Slater, William Ryerson, not to mention David Calp and John Ryerson, who were sizable
   men)...."

7. Graves, DeVilbiss, pp. 30-31. See also the story of
   Bishop Roberts beating soldiers at a shooting match:
   Worth Tippy, Frontier Bishop: The Life and Times
   of Robert Richford Roberts (New York: Abingdon
   Press, 1958), p. 102; Gorrie, Lives, p. 325.

8. Taylor, Autobiography, p. 27.

9. Burgess, Pleasant Recollections, p. 132.

10. Field, Worthies, p. 271.

11. Smith, Recollections, p. 98.

12. Carroll, "Father Corson," pp. 161-62.

13. McKendree, pp. 197-98.

14. Taylor, Autobiography, pp. 27-28.

15. Fitzgerald, McFerrin, pp. 43, 11, 33. See also
    Charles B. Galloway, The Editor-Bishop: Linus
    Parker, His Life and Writings (Nashville: Southern
    Methodist Publishing House, 1886), pp. 17-19, for
    another account of prophetic childhood.

16. Haven, Autobiography, pp. 25-26. Loomis, White Mag-
    ic, p. 16: painless births are common in hagiogra-
    phy.

17. Travis, Autobiography, pp. 13-14; Wright, Quinn, p. 22.

18. Sixty-One Years, p. 21.

19. Patton, Life, p. 7. See Frank C. Haddock, The Life

of Rev. George C. Haddock (2nd ed.; New York: Funk and Wagnalls, 1887), pp. 28-39, 39-40, for a panegyric to fine American blood.

20. Paddock, Memoir, p. 17.
21. Marvin, Caples, p. 8.
22. Smith, Recollections, pp. 100-1.
23. Bascom, pp. 137-54, 150-60. For another account of a Westerner bearding the Easterners, see Fitzgerald, McFerrin, pp. 317-20.
24. Field, Worthies, pp. 161-62.
25. Autobiography, p. 307.
26. Summers, Biographical Sketches, p. 53. In other narratives Walker is called "Pioneer Preacher," "A Church Extension Society," "trailblazer," "explorer," "Pathfinder," "horseman of God." Field, Worthies, p. 53; Almer Pennewell, A Voice in the Wilderness: Jesse Walker, "The Daniel Boone of Methodism" (Nashville: The Parthenon Press, n.d.), p. 11.
27. Summers, Biographical Sketches, p. 56.
28. Walker, p. 11.
29. Field, Worthies, pp. 65-68. Slightly different versions of the story are told in Summers, Biographical Sketches, pp. 54-55, and in Pennewell, Walker, pp. 99-101, quoting an account by Thomas Morris.
    Pennewell regards the anecdote as spurious, especially its militaristic overtones.
    See Francis Emmett Williams, Centenary Methodist Church of St. Louis: The First Hundred Years, 1839-1939 (St. Louis: Mound City Press, Inc., 1939), pp. 2-4, for two versions of the story.
30. Lee, Life, p. 222; also in Minton Thrift, Memoir of the Rev. Jesse Lee, with Extracts from his Journals (New York: Published by N. Bangs and T. Mason, for the Methodist Episcopal Church, 1823), p. 147.
31. Lee, Life, pp. 455-56; Meredith, Lee, pp. 88-89; Wise, Sketches, pp. 73-74. All three sketches repeat the story, with minor variations, in the same fashion.
    In Peck, Sketches, pp. 64-65, the incident is repeated, with a different scriptural text and without the knave-fool repartee. The knave-fool repartee is traditional; see Banquet of Jests (1633), p. 142.
32. Manship, Thirteen Years', p. 234.
33. Ibid., p. 235; Withrow, Makers of Methodism (New York: Eaton and Mains, 1898), pp. 294-96.
34. Methodist Heroes, p. 44.
35. Lee, Life, p. 242; Erwin, Reminiscences, pp. 317-18.
36. D. Young, Autobiography, pp. 109-10.

37. Ayres, Methodist Heroes, pp. 57-58.
38. Autobiography, p. 64. Wise, Sketches, parrots Cart-
    wright's version of the anecdote, p. 278.
39. Sixty-One Years, p. 484.
40. Lee, Life, p. 229; the Saybrook Platform, 1708, founded
    Congregational Puritan orthodoxy.
41. Autobiography, p. 95.
42. Ewing, Historical Memoirs, p. 154.
43. Lorenzo Dow, History of Cosmopolite, or The Four Vol-
    umes of Lorenzo's Journal, Concentrated into One
    (3rd ed.; Philadelphia, Ratestraw, 1816).
44. Plyler and Plyler, Men, p. 108; a common sobriquet
    for the man was "crazy Dow."
45. Plyler and Plyler, Men, p. 90.
46. Woolsey, Supernumerary, pp. 123-24.
47. Autobiography, p. 30.
48. Woolsey, Supernumerary, p. 124.
49. Supra, p. 241.
50. Plyler and Plyler, Men, pp. 179-80, quoting an uniden-
    tified source. Motif J1140.: "Cleverness in the de-
    tection of truth." According to a variation of the
    story, Dow finds a stolen axe: see Vaughan, Gem
    Cyclopedia, p. 142.
51. Gardner, Schoharie Hills, pp. 36-37, 314-17; Hudson,
    Humor, pp. 222-26; Puckett, Folk Beliefs, pp. 281-
    82.
52. John W. Grant (ed.), Salvation! O the Joyful Sound:
    The Selected Writings of John Carroll (Toronto: Ox-
    ford University Press, 1967), p. 222.
53. Penrod, "Teachers and Preachers," p. 96, for the line-
    aments of the preacher in early southern yarns.
54. Ten Years, p. 304; the same story is told of Henry
    Bascom; Henkle, Bascom, pp. 123-25.
55. Wise, Sketches, pp. 201-2; also Benjamin St. James
    Fry, The Life of Robert R. Roberts (New York:
    Carlton and Porter, 1856), pp. 71-75; Travis, Auto-
    biography, pp. 133-34; Peck, Sketches, pp. 152-54;
    Gorrie, Lives, pp. 327-28. The latter two accounts
    insist that the story has circulated in the religious
    press with the protagonist incorrectly identified as
    Bishop George.
56. Johnson, Recollections, pp. 31-33, 104-5, 117, 142,
    199-202, 302.
57. Dixon Wector, The Hero in America; A Chronicle of
    Hero-Worship (New York: Charles Scribner's Sons,
    1941); Kent Steckmesser, The Western Hero in His-
    tory and Legend (Norman, Okla.: University of

Oklahoma Press, 1965).
58. See ch. 1, "The Frontier's Religious Challenge," ch.
     2, "Seed Time," and ch. 4, "Camp Meetings Gain
     New Sponsors," in Charles A. Johnson, The Frontier
     Camp Meeting; Religion's Harvest Time (Dallas:
     Southern Methodist University Press, 1955), for back-
     ground.
59. Cartwright, Autobiography, p. 102. According to Sut
     Lovingood's yarn, "Parson John Bullen's Lizards,"
     slimy reptiles introduced to the pants-legs of a
     preacher discoursing about "hell-sarpints" effected
     amazing contortions that were mistaken by preachers
     and believers to the delight of the practical joker, as
     manifestations of a religious struggle: in Harris,
     Lovingood, pp. 51-58.
          Vance Randolph relates the story of the young
     man who slipped a snake up the pant leg of a friend
     who had fallen prostrate at a revival; the victim
     "give a big jump and started to run, and it just hap-
     pened he was headed towards the pulpit." His ex-
     ample "helped them other folks that was too bashful
     to go forward." Hot Springs, pp. 86-87.
          The Cartwright story constitutes an effective
     refutation of such shenanigans, however, for before
     the trickster could slip the frogs around Cartwright's
     neck, he was felled by preaching and truly converted;
     thus ended, Cartwright concludes, the "Frog Cam-
     paign." Autobiography, p. 103.
60. Paddock, Memoir, p. 336.
61. Spottswood, Brief Annals, p. 23.
62. Ayres, Methodist Heroes, p. 35.
63. Fleharty, Phelps, p. 128.
64. Hall, "Father Clark," p. 64. A successful "skirt" hunt
     is recorded in Carl Wittke, William Nast; Patriarch
     of German Methodism (Detroit: Wayne State Univer-
     sity Press, 1959), p. 43.
65. Reminiscences, pp. 85-86.
66. Ayres, Methodist Heroes, p. 144.
67. Autobiography, pp. 203-5.
68. Autobiography, p. 182.
69. Autobiography, p. 68.
70. Henkle, Bascom, pp. 104-5. For a parallel account
     see Gorrie, Lives, pp. 367-68: (Fisk stares down
     insane woman brandishing knife).
71. Plyler and Plyler, Men, p. 210.
72. Autobiography, p. 343.
73. Burgess, Pleasant Recollections, p. 438. On another

page Burgess states flatly that Gilruth weighed four
hundred pounds: p. 121.

74. Taylor, Battlefield, p. 335.

75. Taylor, Battlefield, pp. 332, 334.

76. Burgess, Pleasant Recollections, pp. 438-39. Henry
Ryan told an opponent, "'See here; God did not give
me this arm for nothing!'"; Spicer, Autobiography,
p. 232; in another account, Ryan says, "'Take care,
my friend: God did not give me this arm for nothing; and if you come very near me, I cannot promise
that you will not be hurt.'" Carroll, Case, II, 313;
Joseph Everett, another strong man, told an attacker,
"'Do you think that God ever made this arm to be
whipped by a sinner? No, no!'" Travis, Autobiography, p. 36.

In parallel accounts, Isaac Collins intimidated
a ruffian by holding his fist under his nose; Spottswood, Brief Annals, p. 338; a man who threatened
to cane an itinerant backed off in fear, saying, "'he
would not leave a grease spot of me.'" Nash, Recollections, p. 46.

According to one story, Rev. John Schrock,
warned not to come back to a town where he had in-
sulted rowdies, rode boldly to the meeting house,
dismounted, and with horsewhip in hand, walked into
the building, and began services with his horsewhip
in easy reach. After the hymn and prayer, "he
drew up his sleeve and showed them the size of his
arm, saying 'I was brought up a blacksmith, and
know the strength of that arm.' Then unbuttoning
his collar, he exhibited his short, thick, Dutch neck,
and asked the congregation if they thought that God
had given him such muscular powers to let a set of
ruffians run over him in a free country for simply
doing his duty as a minister....'" John G. Jones,
A Complete History of Methodism As Connected with
the Mississippi Conference of the Methodist Episcopal Church, South (2 vols.; Nashville: Publishing
House of the M. E. Church, South, 1908), I, 335-
38. The account goes on to note how Schrock,
bragging at Conference about his exploits, was reproved by Bishop Robert R. Roberts: "'Put up thy
sword, Peter!'" Ibid., p. 359. The remark is
misquoted and the protagonist's name spelled "Shrook"
in Worth Tippy's account of the episode, taken from
the Jones account; in Roberts, p. 117.

Roberts' reproof might have been delivered as

well to a tough young preacher who tamed the town
of "Sinful Bend" in the Ozarks by preaching with a
Bible, hymn book, and pistol on the desk before him:
Godbey, Seventy Years, pp. 126-29.

77. Sixty-One Years, p. 486.

78. Pearne, Sixty-One Years, pp. 485-86. The same story
is told of Jesse Walker in Pennewell, Walker, p. 36,
of William Cravens in Wakeley, Bold Preacher, pp.
29-31. When the story is told of Henry Ryan throwing a blacksmith over the fence, the humble request
is omitted: Case, Carroll, II, 314.

In a variation of the story, Zane Bland throws
a disrupter out of church; the man knocks on the door
and meekly asks for his hat; Taylor, Autobiography,
p. 26.

79. Gavitt, Crumbs, pp. 246-47.

80. New Jersey Conference Memorial, p. 450. Peter Cartwright had to beat up an unwilling magistrate as well
as rowdies in one story; Autobiography, pp. 70-72;
ibid., pp. 212, 248-49, for accounts of successful
prosecutions. See also Hibbard, Memoirs, pp. 295-
96, and Brother Mason, pp. 89-94, for accounts of
rum sellers and miscreants successfully prosecuted
by local justice.

See Spicer, Autobiography, for the story of
how a man approached Henry Ryan while the latter
was preaching. Intending violence, the man was intimidated by the gestures of Ryan's brawny arm; p.
233.

81. Burgess, Pleasant Recollections, p. 121. See Cartwright, Autobiography, pp. 95-96, for another "duck-
ing" story.

82. Gavitt, Crumbs, pp. 236-46. Gavitt identifies Nobleworth as a member of the Ohio Conference "for many
years" who emigrated to and died in Iowa. The details of James Gilruth's career are the same--see
Taylor, Battlefield, pp. 333-34--and hence it seems
likely that the real protagonist of Gavitt's story was
Gilruth.

The account is repeated in Buoy, Representative Women, p. 300, and in Wakeley, Bold Preacher,
pp. 80-82, 103-5. Spicer tells the story of Henry
Ryan, Autobiography, pp. 232-33, without the actual
beating, as does Carroll, Case, II, 313-14.

Different accounts of Ryan exploits by Carroll
and Spicer provide a case study of the manner in
which oral tradition mixes and combines details.

Carroll tells the "Intimidation by brawny arm" anecdote in the setting of a religious service; Spicer in
the setting of a tavern.   Carroll relates the "Blacksmith" story with the ending of another story, that
is, Ryan throws the surly smith over a fence.   Spicer, on the other hand, tells the "Blacksmith" story
with an "Intimidation by brawny arm" ending.   The
remark attributed to Ryan in Spicer's "Blacksmith"
account closely resembled that attributed to him in
Carroll's "Intimidation" story.

The preacher versus blacksmith story circu-
lated widely in yarns of the old Southwest.   James
Penrod, in "Teachers and Preachers in Old South-
western Yarns," Tennessee Folklore Society Bulletin,
XVIII (1952), 96, refers to a preacher-blacksmith
story in which the adversaries are named Ned For-
gerson and Rev. Stubbleworth: taken from John B.
Lamar, "The Blacksmith of the Mountain Pass,"
Polly Peablossoms' Wedding, and Other Tales, ed.
T. A. Burke (Philadelphia: T. B. Peterson and
Bros., 1851), pp. 76-88.

83.   Fitzgerald, Sunset Views, pp. 49-51.

For similar accounts; Smith, Recollections,
pp. 308-9; Wright, Quinn, pp. 225-26; Lowry, Donnell, p. 207.

84.   Smith, Recollections, pp. 100-1.

CONCLUSION

This book has used the methods of folklore to illuminate an aspect of the history of American religion, and in so doing, to suggest the possibility and profitability of using folklore as an historical source.

Essential to the enterprise has been the ability to recognize and classify oral traditions in written materials. Such recognition has been aided by criteria noted in Part I: 1) traditionality--established by the use of folklore collections and folkloristic classificatory tools; 2) recurrence of themes, narratives, or structures in formularized cliches; 3) variation; 4) anonymity; 5) explicit references in the material to oral transmission; 6) reference in the material to situations in which folklore is likely to have circulated.

Folklore culled, according to the above criteria, from the autobiographies, biographies, and reminiscences of nineteenth century Methodist itinerant ministers, has constituted the core data used in this volume. Equally important, for both folklore and history, is classification of the data. Rather than group the stories by folk genre (such as legend, proverb, folk narrative, etc.), I have opted for a functional grouping, and within that, a topical grouping. Hence, didactic stories are in Part II, folk narratives in Part III. In my opinion, such grouping not only points up the meaning of the lore for the folk group itself, but clarifies its meaning for the historian. The didactic tales, or stories of remarkable providences, illustrate the connection of nineteenth century religion with Old World traditions; the folk narratives illustrate the interplay of tradition and circumstance (construed in the widest possible sense), or past and present.

Part II shows how nineteenth century Methodism continued the tradition of remarkable providences, primarily in didactic contexts such as preaching. Operating, like their colonial forebears, against the backdrop of a wilderness both wonderful and chaotic, Methodist divines appealed to traditional

309

stories, rooted in Old World hagiographic traditions and ultimately in biblical precedents, in order to illustrate the nature
of God's divine guidance.   The stories, as do their hagiographic and biblical precedents, vacillate between religious
folklore and folk religion (as defined in the Introduction), and
offer a case study of the tension between official religion on
the one hand and unofficial religion on the other, between orthodoxy and heterodoxy, between creed and belief.   The occasional biography that escapes the tacit censorship of sentire cum ecclesia and that points to the unnoticed reservoir
of folk religion also indicates the tension between official and
unofficial religion.

Part II suggests that the frontier situation--itself a
standing disruption of order--weighed heavily in favor of remarkable providences, which emphasize the unusual and startling interventions of God, rather than in favor of a doctrine
which stressed the ordinary habitual governance of the cosmos.
Finally, Part II indicates that the stories of remarkable providences, insofar as they were employed as preaching exempla,
are also religious symbols which occasioned mutual validation
of world-view and ethos, thereby providing for congregations
a coherent and compelling world.

Stories of remarkable providences offer fresh grounds
for reassessment of the role of traditional beliefs in the Second Great Awakening, and beyond that historical phenomenon,
in American religion as a whole.   According to the folklorist
Richard Dorson, "By the time of the Revolution ... the force
and zeal of supernatural Calvinism spent itself, fading in the
sober climate of the Enlightenment ... so the providences
and wonders passed from general attention."[1]   The persistence
and vitality, however, of such stories--stock-in-trade of
preachers from the medieval friars to modern television and
radio religious entrepreneurs--indicates the popularity and
even propriety of the tradition.   Surely such stories fulfill
a religious need not satisfied by creeds, theologies, social
involvement or withdrawal.   Perhaps men need to believe that
the mysterious element experienced at the core of daily living
--in birth and death, suffering and bafflement, beauty and
squalor, in short, in the thousands of situations of a lifetime
which bear home to man the full burden of the contingency of
his being and destiny--has a reason beyond that assigned to
it by the certainties of science and the mechanics of tech-
nology.   In short, notwithstanding religionless Christianity,
the secular city, and the death of God,[2] the persistence of
such stories suggests that man needs the supernatural, that

he needs a belief which removes the onus of contingency from
his own back and places it on shoulders more suited to the
task. If official religion does not answer the need, man
searches elsewhere--witness the current renascence of interest in astrology, parapsychology, the occult, witchcraft,
transcendental meditation, drugs, the Jesus Movement, and
neo-Pentecostalism. Each in distinctive ways allows man to
confront the mystery he experiences at the heart of his life
by giving him means by which to fashion a universe in which
ultimate reality and expected behavior complement one another.
Stories of remarkable providences deserve study, in American
church history, because they express and satisfy needs too
often ignored by the creeds of churchmen and the theologies
of academics.

Part III presents folklore arising from the confronta-
tion between Methodist preachers' ideals and American en-
vironment. While it is true the social and denominational
histories have utilized segments of such material to add color
and vividness to their narratives, [3] no study, to my knowledge,
has recognized it as folklore or has used it as a means to
understand the corporate cultural life of a religious group.
I have simply attempted to document certain traditional elements of that corporate life and to suggest in a tentative way
the direction further historical elucidation might follow.

Another service performed by this volume is to enun-
ciate questions, crucial to the understanding of the human,
incarnational aspect of religious life, which have become
clear in the writing of the work. Such questions indicate not
only the complexity of the historical phenomenon of religion
but also the trans-historical significance of the problems
raised by the study of one group.

First of all, to what extent does the secular environ-
ment condition religion? For example, on what level does
the muscular frontier idealism represented by the burly hero
James Gilruth meet the idealism embodied in the image of
Jesus as the suffering servant? Or, at what point can the
doctrine of providence be reconciled with the ideal of aggressive, militant Christianity? What is the nexus between belief in Christian unity and denominational competition? At
a more fundamental level, what transformations of Christianity
occur when it opens itself to an alternate, essentially supernaturalistic worldview, such as that of folk religion? Dreams
and portents lean toward divination; healings, providences and

prayers transmogrify into magic; the sovereign God becomes
a manipulable power. Is religious man often, or always, in
his existential state, not only acculturated but also syncretis-
tic--or even tacitly polytheistic? At what level would such
complexity achieve existential coherence? Could such coherence, if achieved, be effected in the face of rational contra-
dictions between belief-systems, or between religion and culture? Should the term "religion," in the study of the history
of Christianity, be construed more broadly?

Secondly, what role does humor play in the on-going
life of a religious group? Part III indicates that itinerants
told jokes on themselves, on their people, and on their adversaries. What different role, in each case, did the humor
play? Is such jesting dysfunctional? Does humor directed
at another religion serve any useful purpose?

Thirdly, what are the dynamics of group memory--
the search for a useable past? Why does oral tradition cull
certain facts from the kaleidoscope of daily and yearly life
and canonize them? Furthermore, what is the relationship
of oral and written traditions within a group? Do priorities
exist between the two? Can one correct the other?

Full answers to such questions would involve excur-
sions, beyond the scope of this book, into the disciplines of
sociology, anthropology, and psychology. This work tenta-
tively proposes that reminiscences and jokes functioned primarily to enhance group solidarity by socializing individual
experience, and that legends functioned in the same fashion
by offering concrete examples which reduced the terrors of
the future for young itinerants. Further exploration of the
role of humor and heroes in group religious life would reveal
not only the complexities of American Methodist history but
the complexity of the religious situation of man--caught between an heroic God and godly heroes, struggling between
primeval group instincts and idealistic brotherhood, chagrined
at the discrepancy of ideal and fact.

When such questions have been raised, and to some
degree, explored, there still remains before the eyes of history a group of men--Methodist itinerants--unique both for
their dedication and their humanness. Fired white-hot by
their enthusiasm for the Word they preached, they nevertheless found time to laugh, commiserate, boast of their accom-
plishments, and beat their breasts. They were flexible
enough to call their own prudes and giants, intellectuals and

dolts, bullies, busybodies, moaners, primadonnas, ascetics, mystics, cranks, geniuses, and administrators. They knew their fellows to be fat and lean, ugly and handsome, fervid and tepid, mediocre and exceptional. Such a baptism of common humanity commends them to the respect and gratitude of history.

Notes

1. American Folklore, pp. 39-40.
2. For the idea of religionless Christianity, see Dietrich Bonhoeffer, Letters and Papers from Prison, ed. by Eberhard Bethge, tr. by Reginald Fuller, rev. by Frank Clarke et al. (3rd ed. rev. and enl.; London: S. C. M. Press, 1967); for the idea of the secular city, see Harvey Cox, The Secular City; Secularization and Urbanization in Theological Perspective (rev. ed.; New York: Macmillan, 1966) for the idea of the death of God, see Gabriel Vahanian, The Death of God: The Culture of our Post-Christian Era (New York: G. Braziller, 1961).
3. Johnson, Camp Meeting, pp. 170-91; W. W. Sweet, Methodism in American History (New York: The Methodist Book Concern, 1933), pp. 143-206; Theodore L. Agnew, "Methodism on the Frontier," in The History of American Methodism, ed. by Emory S. Bucke et al. (3 vols.; Nashville: Abingdon Press, 1964), I, 488-545.

SELECTED BIBLIOGRAPHY

I. Autobiographies, biographies, and reminiscences

Alexander, James W. The Life of Archibald Alexander. New York: Charles Scribner, 1854.

Anderson, J., and S. B. Howard. Memoirs of Rev. Laban Jones and Rev. John H. Irvine, Late Ministers in the Cumberland Presbyterian Church and Members of the Kentucky Presbytery. Louisville: Morton and Griswold, 1850.

Andrew, J. O. Miscellanies: Comprising Letters, Essays, and Addresses; to Which is Added a Biographical Sketch of Mrs. Ann Amelia Andrew. Louisville: Morton and Griswold, 1854.

Atkinson, B. Franklin. The Life Ministry of B. Franklin Atkinson (An Autobiographical Sketch). Louisville: The Herald Press, n. d.

Ayres, Samuel G. Methodist Heroes of Other Days. New York: The Methodist Book Concern, 1916.

Bangs, Heman. Autobiography and Journal of Rev. Heman Bangs, with an Introduction by Rev. Bishop Janes, D. D. Edited by Bangs' daughters. New York: N. Tibbals and Son, 1872.

Barbery, Willard S. Story of the Life of Robert Sayers Sheffey: A Courier of the Long Trail--God's Gentleman-- A Man of Prayer and Unbroken Faith. Bluefield, Va.: n. p., n. d.

Beard, Richard. Brief Biographical Sketches of Some of the Early Ministers of the Cumberland Presbyterian Church. Nashville: Southern Methodist Publishing House, 1867.

314

_____. Brief Biographical Sketches of Some of the Early
Ministers of the Cumberland Presbyterian Church. Second Series. Nashville: Cumberland Presbyterian Board
of Publication, 1874.

Bird, Milton. The Life of Rev. Alexander Chapman. Nashville: W. E. Dunaway, 1872.

Blackman, W. S. The Boy of Battle Ford and the Man.
Marion, Ill.: The Egyptian Press Printing Co., 1906.

Borum, Joseph H. Biographical Sketches of Tennessee Baptist Ministers. Memphis: Rogers and Co., 1880.

Brother Mason, the Circuit Rider; or Ten Years a Methodist
Preacher. Cincinnati: H. M. Rulison, Queen City Publishing House, 1856.

Brown, George. Recollections of Itinerant Life: Including
Early Reminiscences. Cincinnati: R. W. Carroll and
Co., 1868.

Buoy, Charles Wesley. Representative Women of Methodism.
New York: Hunt and Eaton, 1893.

Burgess, John. Pleasant Recollections of Characters and
Works of Noble Men, with Old Scenes and Merry Times
of Long, Long, Ago. Cincinnati: Cranston and Stowe,
1887.

Butts, D. Gregory Claiborne. From Saddle to City by Buggy,
Boat, and Railway. Hilton Village, Va.: n. p., n. d.

Candler, Warren A. Life of Thomas Coke. Nashville: Publishing House M. E. Church, South, 1923.

Carhart, J. Wesley. Four Years on Wheels: or Life as a
Presiding Elder. Oshkosh, Wis.: Allen and Hicks,
1880.

Carroll, Andrew. Moral and Religious Sketches and Collections, with Incidents of Ten Years' Itinerancy in the
West. Vol. I. Cincinnati: Methodist Book Concern,
1857.

Carroll, John. Case, and His Cotemporaries; or, The Canadian Itinerants' Memorial: Constituting a Biographical

History of Methodism, from its Introduction into the
Province Till the Death of the Rev. William Case, in
1855. 5 vols. Toronto: Published at the Wesleyan
Conference Office, 1867-1877.

_____ . "Father Corson"; or, The Old Style Canadian Itinerant: Embracing the Life and Gospel Labours of the
Rev. Robert Corson, Fifty-Six Years a Minister in Connection with the Central Methodism of Upper Canada.
Toronto: Published by the Rev. Samuel Rose, D.D.,
at the Methodist Book Room, 1879.

_____ . My Boy Life, Presented in a Succession of True
Stories. Toronto: William Briggs, 1882.

Cartwright, Peter. Autobiography of Peter Cartwright.
Edited by Charles L. Wallis. New York: Abingdon
Press, 1956.

_____ . Fifty Years as a Presiding Elder. Edited by
W. S. Hooper. Cincinnati: Hitchcock and Walden, 1871.

Caruthers, E. W. A Sketch of the Life and Character of the
Rev. David Caldwell, D.D. Greensborough, N.C.:
Swaim and Sherwood, 1842.

Chapman, H. L. Memoirs of an Itinerant: An Autobiography.
N. p., n. d.

Cline, Rodney. Asbury Wilkinson: Pioneer Preacher. New
York: Vantage Press, 1956.

Coles, George. Heroines of Methodism; or Pen and Ink
Sketches of the Mothers and Daughters of the Church.
New York: Carlton and Porter, 1857.

_____ . My First Seven Years in America. Edited by
D. P. Kidder. New York: Carlton and Phillips, 1852.

Compton, Lucius B. Life of Lucius B. Compton, the Mountain Evangelist; or From the Depths of Sin to the
Heights of Holiness. Cincinnati: Office of God's Re-
vivalist, 1903.

Cotton, A. J. Cotton's Sketch-Book. Portland, Me.:
Printed by B. Thurston and Co., 1874.

Daniels, W. H., ed. Memorials of Gilbert Haven, Bishop of
    the Methodist Episcopal Church. Boston: B. B. Rus-
    sell and Co., 1880.

Dow, Lorenzo. History of Cosmopolite, or The Four Volumes
    of Lorenzo's Journal, Concentrated into One. 3rd ed.
    Philadelphia: Ratestraw, 1816.

Drake, B. M. A Sketch of the Life of Rev. Elijah Steele.
    Cincinnati: Printed for the author, at the Methodist
    Book Concern, 1843.

Du Bose, Horace M. Life and Memories of Rev. J. D.
    Barbee (Doctor in Divinity). Nashville: Publishing
    House of the Methodist Episcopal Church, South, 1906.

_____. Life of Joshua Soule. Nashville: Publishing
    House of the M. E. Church, South, 1911.

Duren, William L. The Top Sergeant of the Pioneers; The
    Story of a Lifelong Battle for an Ideal. Emory Univer-
    sity, Ga.: Banner Press, 1930.

Dyer, J. L. The Snow-Shoe Itinerant. Cincinnati: Cranston
    and Stowe, 1890.

Edwards, John Ellis. Life of Rev. John Wesley Childs: for
    Twenty-Three Years an Itinerant Methodist Minister.
    Richmond, Va.: John Early, 1852.

Erwin, James. Reminiscences of Early Circuit Life. Toledo:
    Spear, Johnson, and Co., 1884.

Ewing, R. C. Historical Memoirs: Containing a Brief His-
    tory of the Cumberland Presbyterian Church in Missouri,
    and Biographical Sketches of a Number of Those Minis-
    ters Who Contributed to the Organization and the Es-
    tablishment of that Church, in the Country West of the
    Mississippi River. Nashville: Cumberland Presbyterian
    Board of Publication, 1874.

Ffirth, John. Experience and Gospel Labours of the Rev.
    Benjamin Abbott; to Which is Annexed a Narrative of
    his Life and Death. New York: B. Waugh and T.
    Mason, 1833.

Field, A. D. Worthies and Workers, Both Ministers and

Laymen, of the Rock River Conference.   Cincinnati:
Cranston and Curts, 1896.

Finley, James B.   Autobiography of Rev. James B. Finley;
or Pioneer Life in the West.   Edited by W. P. Strickland.   Cincinnati: Jennings and Pye, 1853.

_____.   Sketches of Western Methodism: Biographical,
Historical and Miscellaneous, Illustrative of Pioneer
Life.   Edited by W. P. Strickland.   Cincinnati: Printed
at the Methodist Book Concern, for the Author, 1855.

Finney, Thomas M.   The Life and Labors of Enoch Mather
Marvin, Late Bishop of the Methodist Episcopal Church,
South.   St. Louis: James H. Chambers, 1881.

Fitzgerald, O. P.   Centenary Cameos.   Nashville: Publishing House of the M. E. Church, South, 1893.

_____.   Dr. Summers: A Life-Study.   Nashville: South-
ern Methodist Publishing House, 1885.

_____.   Fifty Years: Observations--Opinions--Experiences.
Nashville: Publishing House of the M. E. Church,
South, 1903.

_____.   John B. McFerrin: A Biography.   Nashville:
Publishing House of the M. E. Church, South, 1888.

_____.   Sunset Views.   Nashville: Publishing House of
the M. E. Church, South, 1906.

Fleharty, J. J.   Glimpses of the Life of Rev. A. E. Phelps
and His Co-Laborers; or, Twenty-Five Years in the
Methodist Itinerancy.   Cincinnati: Hitchcock and Walden,
1878.

Fry, Benjamin St. James.   The Life of Robert R. Roberts,
One of the Bishops of the Methodist Episcopal Church.
New York: Carlton and Porter, 1856.

Gaddis, Maxwell.   Brief Recollections of the Late Rev.
George Walker.   Cincinnati: Published by Swormstedt
and Poe, for the Author, 1857.

Galloway, Charles B.   The Editor-Bishop: Linus Parker,
His Life and Writings.   Nashville: Southern Methodist

Publishing House, 1886.

Gavitt, Elnathan C.   Crumbs from my Saddle Bags or, Reminiscences of Pioneer Life and Biographical Sketches.
Toledo: Blade Printing and Paper Co., 1884.

Giles, Charles.   Pioneer: A Narrative of the Nativity, Experience, Travels, and Ministerial Labours of Rev.
Charles Giles, Author of the "Triumph of Truth," etc.,
with Incidents, Observations and Reflections.   New York:
G. Lane and P. P. Sandford, 1844.

Goben, Jesse J.   The Writings of Jesse J. Goben, to Which
Are Added the Letters of Willis E. Moore and William
H. Darnall.   Middletown, N. Y.:   G. Beebe's Sons,
n. d.

Godbey, J. E.   Lights and Shadows of Seventy Years.   St.
Louis: Nixon-Jones Printing Co., 1913.

Gorrie, P. Douglas.   Black River and Northern New York
Conference Memorial, Second Series.   Watertown, N. Y.:
Charles E. Holbrook, Printer, 1881.

_____.   The Black River Conference Memorial: Contain-
ing Sketches of the Life and Character of the Deceased
Members of the Black River Conference of the M. E.
Church.   New York: Carlton and Phillips, 1852.

_____.   The Lives of Eminent Methodist Ministers; Con-
taining Biographical Sketches, Incidents, Anecdotes,
Records of Travel, Reflections, &c., &c.   New York:
R. Worthington, 1881.

Grant, John W., ed.   Salvation! O The Joyful Sound.   The
Selected Writings of John Carroll.   Toronto: Oxford
University Press, 1967.

Graves, H. A., compiler.   Reminiscences and Events in the
Ministerial Life of Rev. John Wesley DeVilbiss.   Gal-
veston, Tex.:   W. A. Shaw and Co., 1886.

Green, Anson.   The Life and Times of the Rev. Anson Green,
D. D., Written by Himself, at the Request of the Toronto Conference, and Presented to the Church for the
Benefit of the Superannuation Fund.   Toronto: Published
at the Methodist Book Room, 1877.

Green, William M. Life and Papers of A. L. P. Green,
    D. D. Edited by T. O. Summers. Nashville: Southern
    Methodist Publishing House, 1877.

Gurley, L. B. Memoir of Rev. William Gurley, Late of
    Milan, Ohio, A Local Minister of the Methodist Episco-
    pal Church; Including a Sketch of the Irish Insurrection
    and Martyrs of 1798. Cincinnati: Printed for the
    Author, at the Methodist Book Concern, 1858.

Haddock, Frank C. The Life of Rev. George C. Haddock.
    2nd ed. New York: Funk and Wagnalls, 1887.

Hall, B. M. The Life of Rev. John Clark. New York:
    Carlton and Porter, 1857.

Hamilton, Jay Benson. From the Pulpit to the Poorhouse and
    Other Romances of the Methodist Itinerancy. New York:
    Hunt and Eaton, 1892.

Hatcher, William. Life of J. B. Jeter, D. D. Baltimore:
    H. M. Wharton and Co., 1887.

Haven, Erastus O. Autobiography of Erastus O. Haven,
    D. D., LL. D., One of the Bishops of the Methodist
    Episcopal Church. Edited by C. C. Stratton. New
    York: Phillips and Hunt, 1883.

Haven, Gilbert, and Thomas Russell. Incidents and Anec-
    dotes of Rev. Edward Taylor, For Over Forty Years
    Pastor of the Seaman's Bethel, Boston. New York:
    Hunt and Eaton, 1871.

Hawkins, William George. Life of John H. W. Hawkins.
    Boston: John P. Jewett and Co., 1859.

Henkle, M. M. The Life of Henry Biddleman Bascom, D. D.,
    LL. D., Late Bishop of the Methodist Episcopal Church,
    South. Louisville: Morton and Griswold, 1854.

Hibbard, Billy. Memoirs of the Life and Travels of B. Hib-
    bard, Minister of the Gospel, Containing an Account of
    His Experience of Religion; and of His Call to and La-
    bors in the Ministry, for Nearly Fifty Years: in Which
    are Recorded Many Important, Curious, and Interesting
    Events, Illustrative of the Providence and Grace of God.
    New York: Printed for and Published by the Author,
    1843.

Hibbard, F. G. Biography of Leonidas L. Hamline, D. D.,
    Late One of the Bishops of the Methodist Episcopal
    Church. Cincinnati: Walden and Stowe, 1881.

Hobart, Chauncey. Recollections of My Life: Fifty Years of
    Itinerancy in the Northwest. Red Wing, Minn.: Red
    Wing Printing Co., 1885.

Holdich, Joseph. The Wesleyan Student; or, Memoirs of
    Aaron Haynes Hurd, Late a Member of the Wesleyan
    University, Middletown, Conn. New York: Published
    by George Lane for the Methodist Episcopal Church,
    1841.

Hoss, Elijah E. David Morton: A Biography. Nashville:
    Publishing House of the Methodist Episcopal Church
    South, 1916.

_____. William McKendree: A Biographical Study. Nash-
    ville: Publishing House of the Methodist Episcopal
    Church South, 1916.

Howell, Peter. The Life and Travels of Peter Howell, Writ-
    ten by Himself; in Which Will Be Seen Some Marvelous
    Instances of the Gracious Providence of God. New
    Bern, N. C.: Published by W. H. Mayhew, for the
    Author, 1849.

Jackson, Green P. Sunshine and Shade in a Happy Itinerant's
    Life. Nashville: Publishing House of the M. E.
    Church, South, 1904.

James, John T. Four Years of Methodist Ministry, 1865-
    1869. Staunton, Va.: Stoneburner and Prufer, Steam
    Printers, 1894.

Johnson, Susannah. Recollections of the Rev. John Johnson
    and His Home: An Autobiography. Nashville: South-
    ern Methodist Publishing House, 1869.

Jones, John G. A Complete History of Methodism As Con-
    nected with the Mississippi Conference of the Methodist
    Episcopal Church, South. 2 vols. Nashville: Publish-
    ing House of the M. E. Church, South, 1908.

Kay, John. Biography of the Rev. William Gundy, for Twen-
    ty Years a Minister of the Methodist New Connexion

Church in Canada. Toronto: James Campbell and Son, 1871.

Lee, Jesse. A Short Account of the Life and Death of the Rev. John Lee, a Methodist Minister in the United States of America. Baltimore: John West Butler, 1805.

Lee, Leroy. The Life and Times of the Rev. Jesse Lee. Charleston, S. C.: Published by John Early, for the Methodist Episcopal Church, South, 1848.

Leming, John L. Experiences of the Circuit Rider. New York: Methodist Book Concern, 1932.

Life and Times of William Patton. N. p., n. d.

Lockwood, John P. The Western Pioneers; or, Memorials of the Lives and Labours of the Rev. Richard Boardman and the Rev. Joseph Pilmoor, the First Preachers Appointed by John Wesley to Labour in North America; with Brief Notices of Contemporary Persons and Events. London: Wesleyan Conference Office, 1881.

Lowry, David. Life and Labors of the Late Rev. Robert Donnell, of Alabama, Minister of the Gospel in the Cumberland Presbyterian Church. Alton, Ill.: S. V. Crossman, 1867.

McConnell, Francis John. Borden Parker Bowne: His Life and Philosophy. New York: The Abingdon Press, 1929.

MacLean, John. William Black: The Apostle of Methodism in the Maritime Provinces of Canada. Halifax, Nova Scotia: The Methodist Book Room, 1907.

McNemee, A. J. "Brother Mack": The Frontier Preacher; A Brief Record of the Difficulties and Hardships of a Pioneer Itinerant. Portland, Ore.: T. G. Robison, 1924.

Mains, George. James Monroe Buckly. New York: The Methodist Book Concern, 1917.

Mallary, Charles D. Memoirs of Elder Edmund Botsford. Charleston: W. Riley, 1832.

Malmsbury, C. A. The Life, Labors, and Sermons of Rev.
Charles Pitman, D. D., of the New Jersey Conference.
Philadelphia: Methodist Episcopal Book Room, 1887.

Manship, Andrew. History of Gospel Tents and Experience.
Philadelphia: Published by the Author, 1884.

_____. Thirteen Years' Experience in the Itinerancy; with
Observations on the Old Country. Philadelphia: Methodist Episcopal Book and Publishing House, 1881.

Marine, F. E. Sketch of Rev. John Hersey, Minister of the
Gospel of the M. E. Church. Baltimore: Hoffman and
Co., 1879.

Marlay, John F. The Life of Rev. Thomas A. Morris, D. D.,
Late Senior Bishop of the Methodist Episcopal Church.
Cincinnati: Hitchcock and Walden, 1875.

Marshall, A. J. The Autobiography of Mrs. A. J. Marshall,
Age, 84 Years. Pine Bluff, Ark.: Adams-Wilson
Printing Co., 1897.

Marvin, E. M. The Life of Rev. William Goff Caples, of
the Missouri Conference of the Methodist Episcopal
Church, South. St. Louis: Southwestern Book and Publishing Co., 1871.

Mathews, John. Peeps into Life: Autobiography of Rev.
John Mathews, D. D., a Minister of the Gospel for
Sixty Years. N. p.: Published by Request of the Ten-
nessee Annual Conference of the Methodist Episcopal
Church South, 1904.

Meredith, William H. Jesse Lee: A Methodist Apostle.
New York: Eaton and Mains, 1909.

Milburn, William H. The Pioneer Preacher; or, Rifle, Axe,
and Saddle-Bags, and Other Lectures. New York:
Derby and Jackson, 1858.

_____. Ten Years of Preacher-Life: Chapters from an
Autobiography. New York: Derby and Jackson, 1859.

Miller, Adam, collector and arranger. Experience of German Methodist Preachers. Edited by D. W. Clark,
Cincinnati: Printed at the Methodist Book Concern, for
the Author, 1859.

Miller, W. G. Thirty Years in the Itinerancy. Milwaukee:
    I. L. Hauser and Co., 1875.

Mooney, Sue F. Dromgoole. My Moving Tent. Nashville:
    Publishing House Methodist Episcopal Church, South,
    1903.

Morehouse, A. C. Autobiography of A. C. Morehouse, an
    Itinerant Minister of the New York and New York East
    Conferences of the Methodist Episcopal Church. New
    York: Tibbals Book Company, 1895.

Morrison, H. C. Autobiography of Bishop Henry Clay Mor-
    rison. Edited by George Means. Nashville: Publish-
    ing House of the M. E. Church, South, 1917.

Nash, L. L. Recollections and Observations During a Min-
    istry in the North Carolina Conference, Methodist Epis-
    copal Church, South, of Forty-Three Years. Raleigh:
    Mutual Publishing Co., Printers, 1916.

Newell, E. F. Life and Observations of Rev. E. F. Newell,
    Who Has Been More Than Forty Years an Itinerant
    Minister in the Methodist Episcopal Church. Worces-
    ter, Mass.: C. W. Ainsworth, 1847.

The New Jersey Conference Memorial, Containing Biograph-
    ical Sketches of All Its Deceased Members, Including
    Those Who Have Died in the Newark Conference. Phila-
    delphia: Perkinpine and Higgins, 1865.

Olive, Johnson. One of the Wonders of the Age; or, the
    Life and Times of Rev. Johnson Olive, Wake County,
    North Carolina, Written by Himself, at the Solicitation
    of Friends, and for the Benefit of All Who Read It.
    Raleigh: Edwards, Broughton, and Co., 1886.

Osborn, Elbert. Autobiography of Elbert Osborn, an Itiner-
    ant Minister of the Methodist Episcopal Church. New
    York: Published for the Author, 1868.

Paddock, Z. Memoir of Rev. Benjamin Paddock, with Brief
    Notices of Early Ministerial Associates. New York:
    Nelson and Phillips, 1875.

Palmer, Walter C. Life and Letters of Leonidas L. Ham-
    line, D.D., Late One of the Bishops of the Methodist

Episcopal Church. New York: Nelson and Phillips, 1877.

Pearne, Thomas H. Sixty-One Years of Itinerant Christian Life in Church and State. Cincinnati: Curts and Jennings, 1898.

Peck, George. Sketches and Incidents; or, a Budget from the Saddle-Bags of a Superannuated Itinerant. 2 vols. Cincinnati: Swormstedt and Mitchell, 1848.

Peck, J. K. Luther Peck and His Five Sons. New York: Eaton and Mains, 1897.

Peck, John M. "Father Clark," or, the Pioneer Preacher: Sketches and Incidents of Rev. John Clark, by an Old Pioneer. New York: Sheldon, Lamport, and Blakeman, 1855.

_____. Forty Years of Pioneer Life: Memoir of John Mason Peck. Edited by Rufus Babcock. Philadelphia: American Baptist Society, 1864.

Pennewell, Almer. A Voice in the Wilderness: Jesse Walker, "The Daniel Boone of Methodism." Nashville: The Parthenon Press, n. d.

Pinson, W. W. George R. Stuart: Life and Work. Nashville: Cokesbury Press, 1927.

Plyler, Alva W. The Iron Duke of the Methodist Itinerancy: an Account of the Life and Labors of Reverend John Tillett of North Carolina. Nashville: Cokesbury Press, 1925.

Plyler, Marion T., and Alva W. Men of the Burning Heart: Ivey--Dow--Doub. Raleigh, N. C.: Commercial Printing Co., 1918.

Prentice, George. The Life of Gilbert Haven, Bishop of the Methodist Episcopal Church. New York: Phillips and Hunt, 1884.

Rankin, G. C. The Story of My Life, or More Than a Half Century as I Have Lived It and Seen It Lived. Nashville: Smith and Lamar, 1912.

Rice, M. S. William Alfred Quayle: the Skylark of Metho-
    dism. New York: The Abingdon Press, 1928.

Richardson, Frank. From Sunrise to Sunset. Bristol, Tenn.:
    The King Printing Co., 1910.

Richardson, Simon P. The Lights and Shadows of Itinerant
    Life: an Autobiography. Nashville: Publishing House
    Methodist Episcopal Church, South, 1901.

Ridgeway, Henry B. The Life of the Rev. Alfred Cookman,
    with Some Account of His Father, the Rev. George
    Gromston Cookman. New York: Harper and Bros.,
    1873.

Robison, James. Recollections of Rev. Samuel Clawson.
    Pittsburgh: Charles A. Scott, 1883.

Roche, John A. Autobiography and Sermons, Together with
    the Expressions Elicited by His Death. N. p.: Print-
    ed by Eaton and Mains, n. d.

Rogers, J. P. Life of Rev. James Needham, the Oldest
    Methodist Preacher. Pilot Mountain, N. C.: The
    Surry Printing House, 1899.

Ryder, William. The Superannuate: or Anecdotes, Incidents,
    and Sketches of the Life and Experience of William Ry-
    der, a "Worn-out" Preacher of the Troy Conference of
    the M. E. Church. Edited by George Peck. New York:
    G. Lane and C. B. Tippett, 1845.

Sanderson, Camilla. John Sanderson the First, or, a Pio-
    neer Preacher at Home. Toronto: William Briggs,
    1910.

Scarlett, John. The Itinerant on Foot; or, Life-Scenes Re-
    called. New York: W. C. Palmer, 1882.

Sims, Charles. The Life of Rev. Thomas M. Eddy. New
    York: Phillips and Hunt, 1880.

Smith, Ernest Ashton. Martin Ruter. New York: The
    Methodist Book Concern, 1915.

Smith, George C. The Life and Times of George Foster
    Pierce, D. D., LL. D., Bishop of the Methodist Episco-

pal Church, South, with His Sketch of Lovick Pierce, D.D., His Father. Sparta, Ga.: Hancock Publishing Co., 1888.

Smith, Henry. Recollections and Reflections of an Old Itinerant. Edited by George Peck. New York: Carlton and Phillips, 1854.

Spicer, Tobias. Autobiography of Rev. Tobias Spicer: Containing Incidents and Observations; also, Some Account of His Visit to England. New York: Lane and Scott, 1852.

Spottswood, W. Lee. Brief Annals. Harrisburg, Pa.: Publishing Department M. E. Book Room, 1888.

Stanley, E. J. Life of Rev. L. B. Stateler; a Story of Life on the Old Frontier, Containing Incidents, Anecdotes, and Sketches of Methodist History in the West and Northwest. Revised edition. Nashville: Publishing House of the M. E. Church, South, 1916.

Sullins, D. Recollections of an Old Man; Seventy Years in Dixie, 1827-1897. Bristol, Tenn.: The King Printing Co., 1910.

Summers, Thomas O., ed. Biographical Sketches of Eminent Itinerant Ministers Distinguished, for the Most Part, as Pioneers of Methodism Within the Bounds of the Methodist Episcopal Church, South. Nashville: Southern Methodist Publishing House, 1859.

Taylor, Landon. The Battlefield Reviewed, Narrow Escape from Massacre by the Indians of Spirit Lake, when Presiding Elder of Sioux City District. Chicago: Published for the Author, 1881.

Taylor, William. William Taylor of California, Bishop of Africa: An Autobiography. Revised edition, with a preface by G. C. Moore. London: Hodder and Stoughton, 1897.

Thomson, Edward. Life of Edward Thomson, D.D., LL.D., Late a Bishop of the Methodist Episcopal Church. Cincinnati: Cranston and Stowe, 1885.

_____. Sketches, Biographical and Incidental. Edited by

D. W. Clarke. Cincinnati: L. Swormstedt and A. Poe,
    1856.

Thrift, Minton. Memoir of the Rev. Jesse Lee, with Ex-
    tracts from His Journals. New York: Published by N.
    Bangs and T. Mason, for the Methodist Episcopal
    Church, 1823.

Tippy, Worth Marion. Frontier Bishop: The Life and Times
    of Robert Richford Roberts. New York: Abingdon
    Press, 1958.

Travis, Joseph. Autobiography of the Rev. Joseph Travis,
    A. M., a Member of the Memphis Annual Conference.
    Edited by Thomas O. Summers. Nashville: E. Steven-
    son and F. A. Owen, 1856.

Tucker, Mary O. Itinerant Preaching in the Early Days of
    Methodism. Edited by Thomas W. Tucker. Boston:
    B. B. Russell, 1872.

Tuttle, A. H. Nathan Bangs. New York: Eaton and Mains,
    1909.

Vansant, Nicholas. Sunset Memories. New York: Eaton
    and Mains, 1896.

Vernon, Walter A. William Stevenson: Riding Preacher.
    Dallas: Southern Methodist University Press, 1964.

Wakeley, J. B. The Bold Frontier Preacher. Cincinnati:
    Hitchcock and Walden, 1869.

_____. The Heroes of Methodism: Containing Sketches
    of Eminent Methodist Ministers, and Characteristic
    Anecdotes of Their Personal History. 11th ed. Toron-
    to: William Briggs, 1855.

Wallace, E. R. Parson Hanks--Fourteen Years in the West.
    Arlington, Tex.: Journal Print, 1906.

[Ware, Thomas]. Memoir of Thomas Ware. N. p., n. d.

Watson, J. V. Tales and Takings, Sketches and Incidents,
    from the Itinerant and Editorial Budget of Rev. J. V.
    Watson, D. D., Editor of the Northwestern Christian Ad-
    vocate. New York: Published by Carlton and Porter,
    1856.

Waugh, Lorenzo. Autobiography of Lorenzo Waugh.   San
    Francisco: Methodist Book Concern, 1896.

Wightman, William. Life of William Capers, D. D. , One of
    the Bishops of the Methodist Episcopal Church, South;
    Including an Autobiography. Nashville: Southern Meth-
    odist Publishing House, 1859.

Wilding, George C. Memories of a Mountain Circuit.   Rich-
    wood, W. Va.: Published by the Nicholas News Co.,
    n. d.

Williams, Francis Emmett. Centenary Methodist Church of
    St. Louis: The First Hundred Years, 1839-1939.   St.
    Louis: Mound City Press, Inc. , 1939.

Williams, John A. Life of Elder John Smith; with Some Ac-
    count of the Rise and Progress of the Current Reforma-
    tion. Cincinnati: R. W. Carroll and Co. , 1870.

Wilson, Clarence T. Matthew Simpson: Patriot, Preacher,
    Prophet. New York: The Methodist Book Concern,
    1929.

Wise, Daniel. Sketches and Anecdotes of American Metho-
    dists of "The Days That Are No More." New York:
    Phillips and Hunt, 1886.

Withrow, W. H. Barbara Heck: A Tale of Early Methodism.
    Toronto: William Briggs, 1895.

_____. Makers of Methodism. New York: Eaton and
    Mains, 1898.

_____. Neville Trueman, the Pioneer Preacher: a Tale
    of the War of 1812. 4th ed. Toronto: William Briggs,
    1900.

Wittke, Carl. William Nast: Patriarch of German Metho-
    dism. Detroit: Wayne State University Press, 1959.

Woolsey, Elijah. The Supernumerary; or Lights and Shadows
    of Itinerancy. Compiled by George Coles. New York:
    Published by Lane and Scott, 1852.

Wright, John F. Sketches of the Life and Labors of James
    Quinn, Who Was Nearly Half a Century a Minister of

the Gospel in the Methodist Episcopal Church. Cincinnati: Methodist Book Concern, 1851.

Yarbrough, George W. Boyhood and Other Days in Georgia.
Edited by H. M. DuBose. Nashville: Publishing House
of the M. E. Church, South, 1917.

Young, Dan. Autobiography of Dan Young, a New England
Preacher of the Olden Time. Edited by W. P. Strickland. New York: Carlton and Porter, 1860.

Young, Jacob. Autobiography of a Pioneer; or the Nativity,
Experience, Travels, and Ministerial Labors of Rev.
Jacob Young, with Incidents, Observations, and Reflec-
tions. Cincinnati: Cranston and Curts, 1857.

Young, R. A. Reminiscences. Nashville: Publishing House
Methodist Episcopal Church, South, 1900.

II.   Folklore

A.   Introductions

Bascom, William. "Folklore and Anthropology." Journal of
American Folklore, LXVI (1953), 283-90.

_____. "Four Functions of Folklore." Journal of Ameri-
can Folklore, LXVII (1954), 333-49.

_____. "Verbal Art." Journal of American Folklore,
LXVIII (1955), 245-52.

Baumann, Richard. "Towards a Behavioral Theory of Folklore. A Reply to Roger Welsch." Journal of American Folklore, LXXXII (1969), 167-70.

Bayard, Samuel P. "The Materials of Folklore." Journal
of American Folklore, LXVI (1953), 1-17.

Brunvand, Jan H. The Study of American Folklore: An Introduction. New York: W. W. Norton Co., 1968.

Coffin, Tristram P. "Folklore in the American Twentieth
Century." American Quarterly, XIII (1961), 526-33.

"Conference on the Character and State of Studies in Folklore." Journal of American Folklore, XLIX (1946), 495-527.

Dorson, Richard M. American Folklore. Chicago and London: University of Chicago Press, 1959.

_____. "The American Folklore Scene, 1963." Folk-Lore, LXXIV (1963), 433-49.

_____. "Current Folklore Theories." Current Anthropology, IV (1963), 93-112.

_____. Folklore and Folklife: An Introduction. Chicago: University of Chicago Press, 1972.

_____. Folklore Research Around the World: A North American Point of View. Bloomington, Ind.: Indiana University Press, 1961.

_____. Folklore: Selected Essays. Bloomington, Ind.: Indiana University Press, 1972.

_____. "Techniques of the Folklorist." Louisiana Folklore Miscellany, II (1968), 1-23.

Dundes, Alan. "The American Concept of Folklore." Journal of the Folklore Institute, III (1966), 226-49.

_____. The Study of Folklore. Englewood Cliffs, N.J.: Prentice-Hall, Inc., 1965.

"Folklore Research in North America." Journal of American Folklore, LX (1947), 350-416.

Funk and Wagnalls Standard Dictionary of Folklore, Mythology, and Legend. Edited by Maria Leach and Jerome Fried. 2 vols. New York: Funk and Wagnalls Co., 1949.

Halpert, Herbert. "Folklore: Breadth vs. Depth." Journal of American Folklore, LXXI (1958), 97-103.

_____. "Some Underdeveloped Areas in American Folklore." Journal of American Folklore, LXX (1957), 299-305.

Hand, Wayland. "American Folklore After Seventy Years: Survey and Prospect." Journal of American Folklore, LXXIII (1960), 1-11.

Haywood, Charles. A Bibliography of North American Folklore and Folksong. New York: Greenburg, 1951.

Herskovits, Melville J. "Folklore after a Hundred Years: A Problem in Redefinition." Journal of American Folklore, LIX (1946), 89-100.

Newell, W. W. "Review." Journal of American Folklore, XI (1898), 302-4.

Thompson, Stith, ed. Four Symposia on Folklore. Bloomington, Ind.: Indiana University Press, 1953.

Welsch, Roger. "A Note on Definitions." Journal of American Folklore, LXXXI (1968), 262-64.

Yoder, Don. "The Folklife Studies Movement." Pennsylvania Folklife, XIII (1963), 43-56.

Zanger, Jules, ed. "A Report of the Eleventh Newberry Library Conference on American Studies." Newberry Library Bulletin, V (1961), 227-39.

B.   Indices

Aarne, Antti A. The Types of the Folktale; A Classification and Bibliography. 2nd revision. Translated and enlarged by Stith Thompson. Folklore Fellows Communications, V. 75, no. 184. Helsinki: Soumalainen Tiedeakatemia, 1961.

Coffin, Tristram P. The British Traditional Ballad in America. Rev. ed. Philadelphia: American Folklore Society, 1963.

Laws, G. Malcolm. American Balladry from British Broadsides; A Guide for Students and Collectors of Traditional Song. Philadelphia: American Folklore Society, 1957.

_____. Native American Balladry: A Descriptive Study and Bibliographical Syllabus. Rev. ed. Philadelphia: American Folklore Society, 1964.

Nettl, Bruno. Folk and Traditional Music of the Western Continents. Englewood Cliffs, N.J.: Prentice-Hall, Inc., 1965.

Taylor, Archer. English Riddles from Oral Tradition.
Berkeley, Cal.: University of California Press, 1951.

_____ and Bartlett Whiting. A Dictionary of American
Proverbs and Proverbial Phrases, 1820-1880. Cambridge, Mass.: Harvard University Press, 1958.

Thompson, Stith. Motif-Index of Folk-Literature; A Classification of Narrative Elements in Folktales, Ballads,
Myths, Fables, Medieval Romances, Exempla, Fabliaux,
Jest-Books and Local Legends. Revised and enlarged
edition. Vols. 1-6. Bloomington, Ind.: Indiana University Press, 1955-58.

C. Collections and Monographs

Abrahams, Roger. Deep Down in the Jungle ... Negro Narrative Folklore from the Streets of Philadelphia. Hatboro, Pa.: Folklore Associates, 1964.

Boatright, Mody. Folklore of the Oil Industry. Dallas:
Southern Methodist University Press, 1963.

Chase, Richard, ed. Grandfather Tales. Boston: Houghton-
Mifflin Co., 1948.

Dorson, Richard. Buying the Wind. Chicago and London:
University of Chicago Press, 1964.

Ericson, Eston. "Folklore and Folkway in the Tarboro
(N.C.) Free Press (1824-1850)." Southern Folklore
Quarterly, V (1941), 107-25.

Fife, Austin E. and Alta S. Saints of Sage and Saddle.
Bloomington, Ind.: Indiana University Press, 1956.

The Frank C. Brown Collection of North Carolina Folklore.
Edited by Newman Ivey White, et al. 7 vols. Durham,
N.C.: Duke University Press, 1952-1964.

Gardner, Emelyn. Folklore from the Schoharie Hills, New
York. Ann Arbor, Mich.: University of Michigan
Press, 1937.

Harris, George Washington. Sut Lovingood's Yarns. Edited
by M. Thomas Inge. New Haven, Conn.: College and
University Press, 1966.

Hudson, Arthur. Humor of the Old Deep South. New York: The Macmillan Co., 1936.

Jones, Ora L. Peculiarities of the Appalachian Mountaineers; A Summary of Legends, Traditions, Signs and Superstitions That Are Almost Forgotten. Detroit: Harlo Press, 1967.

Jordan, Philip. "Humor of the Backwoods, 1820-1840." Mississippi Valley Historical Review, XXV (1938), 25-38.

Korson, George. Black Rock: Mining Folklore of the Pennsylvania Dutch. Baltimore: The Johns Hopkins Press, 1960.

Kummer, George. "Specimens of Ante-Bellum Buckeye Humor." Ohio Historical Quarterly, LXIV (1955), 424-37.

Legman, Gershon. Rationale of the Dirty Joke. New York: Grove Press, 1968.

Montell, William L. The Saga of Coe Ridge: A Study in Oral History. Knoxville: University of Tennessee Press, 1970.

Pound, Louise. Nebraska Folklore. Lincoln, Nebraska: University of Nebraska Press, 1959.

Price, William B. Tales and Lore of the Mountaineers. Salem, W. Va.: Quest Publishing Company, 1963.

Puckett, Newbell N. Folk Beliefs of the Southern Negro. Chapel Hill, N.C.: University of North Carolina Press, 1926.

Randolph, Vance. Hot Springs and Hell, and Other Folk Jests and Anecdotes from the Ozarks. Hatboro, Pa.: Folklore Associates, 1965.

Sackett, S. J., and William E. Koch. Kansas Folklore. Lincoln, Nebraska: University of Nebraska Press, 1961.

Williams, Phyllis. South Italian Folkways in Europe and America. New Haven, Conn.: Yale University Press, 1938.

III.   Folklore and History

Blegen, Theodore. Grass Roots History. Minneapolis: University of Minnesota Press, 1947.

Campa, Arthur L. "Folklore and History." Western Folklore, XXIV (1965), 1-5.

Carlson, Signe. "An Interdisciplinary Approach to Folklore Study." Journal of the Ohio Folklore Society, II (1967), 149-65.

Davidson, H. R. Ellis. "Folklore and Man's Past." Folk-Lore, LXXIV (1963), 527-44.

Davidson, Levette. "Folklore as a Supplement to Western History." Nebraska History, XXIX (1948), 3-15.

Dorson, Richard. American Folklore and the Historian. Chicago: University of Chicago Press, 1971.

_____. "Ethnohistory and Ethnic Folklore." Ethnohistory, VIII (1961), 12-27.

_____. "Folklore and Cultural History." In Research Opportunities in American Cultural History. Edited by John F. McDermott. Lexington, Ky.: University of Kentucky Press, 1961.

_____. "Folklore in Relation to American Studies." In Frontiers of American Culture. Edited by Ray Browne. West Lafayette, Ind.: Purdue University Studies, 1968.

_____. "Historical Method and American Folklore." Indiana History Bulletin, XXIII (1946), 84-99.

_____. "Oral Tradition and Written History: The Case for the United States." Journal of the Folklore Institute, I (1964), 220-34.

_____. "A Theory for American Folklore." Journal of American Folklore, LXXII (1959), 197-215.

_____. "A Theory for American Folklore Reviewed." Journal of American Folklore, LXXXII (1969), 226-44.

Elliot, John. "Folksong and Its Use as Evidence in the

Humanities." Issued as an insert in English Song and
Dance, XXX (1968).

Fife, Austin E. "Folklore and Local History." Utah Historical Quarterly, XXXI (1963), 315-23.

Hurst, Richard M. "History and Folklore." New York Folklore Quarterly, XXV (1969), 243-61.

_____. "On the Relationship of Folklore and History."
Journal of the Ohio Folklore Society, I (1966), 63-74.

Jones, Louis C. "Folk Culture and the Historical Society."
Minnesota History, XXXI (1950), 11-17.

_____. "Three Eyes on the Past: A New Triangulation
for Local Studies." New York Folklore Quarterly, XII
(1956), 3-13, 143-49.

Jordan, Philip D. "History and Folklore." Missouri Historical Review, XLIV (1950), 119-29.

Kramer, Frank. Voices in the Valley: Myth-Making and
Folk Beliefs in the Shaping of the Middle West. Madison, Wisc.: University of Wisconsin Press, 1964.

McCoy, Donald R. "Underdeveloped Sources of Understanding in American History." Journal of American History,
LIV (1967), 255-70.

Opie, Peter. "The Tentacles of Tradition." Folk-Lore,
LXXIV (1963), 507-26.

Pilis, Mario de. "Folklore and the American West." Arizona and the West, IV (1963), 291-314.

Thompson, Stith. "Folklore and Minnesota History." Minnesota History, XXVI (1945), 97-105.

Vansina, Jan. Oral Tradition. Translated by H. M. Wright.
Chicago: University of Chicago Press, 1965.

Wells, Merle. "History and Folklore: A Suggestion for Cooperation." Journal of the West, IV (1965), 95-97.

IV. Folklore and Religion

Angles, Higini. "Relations of Spanish Folk Song to Gregorian Chant." Journal of the International Folk Music Council, XVI (1964), 54-56.

Barrick, Mac. "'All Signs in Dry Spells Fails.'" Keystone Folklore Quarterly, IX (1964), 23-28.

_____. "Folk Beliefs of a Pennsylvania Preacher." Keystone Folklore Quarterly, X (1965), 191-93.

_____. "Folk Medicine in Cumberland County." Keystone Folklore Quarterly, IX (1964), 100-110.

Boatright, Mody C. "Comic Exempla of the Pioneer Pulpit." In Coyote Wisdom, edited by J. Frank Dobie, Mody Boatright, and Harry H. Ransom. Texas Folklore Society Publications No. XIV. Austin, Tex.: Texas Folklore Society, 1938, pp. 155-68.

Bonser, Wilfred. "The Cult of Relics in the Middle Ages." Folk-Lore, LXXXIII (1962), 234-57.

Bousett, Wilhelm. The AntiChrist Legend; A Chapter in Christian and Jewish Folklore. London: Hutchinson and Co., 1896.

Bratcher, James T. "Religion-Centered Anecdotes of Fort Sill." Western Folklore, XXIII (1964), 265-67.

Bruce, Dickson D. And They All Sang Hallelujah: Plainfolk Camp-Meeting Religion, 1800-1845. University of Pennsylvania: Unpublished Doctoral Dissertation, 1971.

Brückner, Wolfgang. "Popular Piety in Central Europe." Journal of the Folklore Institute, V (1968), 158-74.

_____. "Rulle und der marianische Umkreis der Bienenlegende." Rheinisch-Westfälische Zeitschrift für Volkskunde, IX (1962), 28-39.

Brunvand, Jan. "Jokes About Misunderstood Religious Texts." Western Folklore, XXIV (1965), 199-200.

Dietz, Josef. "Vom Brot im kirchlichen Brauch des Bonner Landes." Rheinisch-Westfälische Zeitschrift für Volkskunde, IX (1962), 18-27.

Dowling, Alfred E. "A Study in the Flora of the Holy Church."
    American Catholic Quarterly Review, XXVII (1902), 452-
    75.

Downey, James C. "Revivalism, the Gospel Songs, and So-
    cial Reform." Ethnomusicology, VIII (1965), 115-25.

Englekirk, John E. "The Passion Play in New Mexico."
    Western Folklore, XXV (1966), 17-33.

Ettlinger, Ellen. "Folklore in Oxfordshire Churches." Folk-
    Lore, LXXIII (1962), 160-78.

Field, Jerome. "Folk Tales from North Dakota." Western
    Folklore, XVII (1958), 29-33.

Fife, Austin E. "Christian Swarm Charms from the Ninth
    to the Nineteenth Centuries." Journal of American
    Folklore, LXXVII (1964), 154-59.

Gerrard, Nathan L. "The Serpent-Handling Religions of West
    Virginia." Trans-Action, V (1968), 22-28.

Groot, Adrian de. Saint Nicholas; A Psychoanalytic Study of
    His History and Myth. The Hague: Mouton and Co.,
    1965.

Hackwood, Frederick W. Christ Lore; Being the Legends,
    Traditions, Myths, Symbols, Customs, and Superstitions
    of the Christian Church. London: Elliot Stock, 1902.

Heilbut, Tony. The Gospel Sound: Good News and Bad
    Times. New York: Simon and Schuster, 1971.

Horn, Dorothy. Sing to Me of Heaven: A Study of Folk and
    Early American Materials in Three Old Harp Books.
    Gainesville: University of Florida Press, 1970.

Hsu, Francis L. K. "A Neglected Aspect of Witchcraft
    Studies." Journal of American Folklore, LXXIII (1960),
    35-38.

Huguenin, Charles A. "A Prayer for Examinations." New
    York Folklore Quarterly, XVIII (1962), 145-48.

Jackson, George P. "The Old Time Religion as a Folk Re-
    ligion." Tennessee Folklore Society Bulletin, VII (1941),
    30-39.

_____. White Spirituals in the Southern Uplands. Chapel Hill, N.C.: University of North Carolina Press, 1933.

Kring, Hilda. The Harmonists: A Folk Cultural Approach. Metuchen, N.J.: Scarecrow Press, 1973.

Lagarde, Marie-Louise. "A South Louisiana Negro Baptizing." Louisiana Folklore Quarterly, II (1968), 45-55.

Lee, J. Frank. "The Informal Organization of White Southern Protestant Funerals: The Role of the Arranger." Tennessee Folklore Society Bulletin, XXXIII (1967), 36-40.

Loomis, C. Grant. "The American Tall Tale and the Miraculous." California Folklore Quarterly, IV (1945), 109-28.

_____. "Legend and Folklore." California Folklore Quarterly, II (1943), 279-97.

_____. White Magic: An Introduction to the Folklore of Christian Legend. Cambridge, Mass.: The Medieval Academy of America, 1948.

Lowe, Cosette Chaves. "A Lash for the Grace of God." New Mexico Folklore Record, XI (1963-64), 18-20.

Marchand, James. "A Note on the Sunday Letter." Tennessee Folklore Society Bulletin, XXIX (1963), 4-9.

Monteiro, George. "Parodies of Scripture, Prayer, and Hymn." Journal of American Folklore, LXXVII (1964), 45-52.

Neal, Julia. "Shaker Festival." Kentucky Folklore Record, VIII (1962), 127-35.

Patai, R. and Francis L. Utley. Studies in Biblical and Jewish Folklore. Indiana University Folklore Series, No. 13. Bloomington, Ind.: Indiana University Press, 1960.

Penrod, James. "Teachers and Preachers in Old Southwestern Yarns." Tennessee Folklore Society Bulletin, XVIII (1952), 91-96.

Phares, Ross. Bible in Pocket, Gun in Hand: The Story of
     Frontier Religion. Lincoln: University of Nebraska
     Press, 1971.

Popescu, Mircea. "Eliade and Folklore." In Myths and
     Symbols: Studies in Honor of Mircea Eliade. Edited
     by Joseph Kitagawa and Charles Long. Chicago: Uni-
     versity of Chicago Press, 1969, pp. 81-90.

Puckett, Newbell N. "Religious Folk Beliefs of Whites and
     Negroes." Journal of Negro History, XVI (1931), 9-
     35.

Randolph, Vance. "Nakedness in Ozark Folk Belief." Jour-
     nal of American Folklore, LXVI (1953), 333-39.

Rickels, Patricia. "The Folklore of Sacraments and Sacra-
     mentals in South Louisiana." Louisiana Folklore Miscel-
     lany, II (1965), 27-44.

Rosenberg, Bruce. The Art of the American Folk Preacher.
     New York: Oxford University Press, 1970.

Simon, Irmgard. Die Gemeinschaft der Siebenten-Tags Ad-
     ventisten in volkskundliches Sicht. Münster: Aschen-
     dorf, 1965.

Stekert, Ellen. "The Snake Handling Sect of Harlan County,
     Kentucky: Its Influence on Folk Tradition." Southern
     Folklore Quarterly, XXVII (1963), 316-22.

Sugg, Redding. "Heaven Bound." Southern Folklore Quar-
     terly, XXVII (1963), 249-66.

Swetnam, George. "The Church Hymn as a Folklore Form."
     Keystone Folklore Quarterly, IX (1964), 144-53.

Szoverfty, Joseph. "Some Notes on Medieval Studies and
     Folklore." Journal of American Folklore, LXXIII
     (1960), 239-43.

Tallmadge, William. "The Responsorial and Antiphonal Prac-
     tice in Gospel Song." Ethnomusicology, XII (1968),
     219-38.

Tokar, Elizabeth. "Humorous Anecdotes Collected from a
     Methodist Minister." Western Folklore, XXVI (1967),
     89-100.

Utley, Francis L. "The Bible of the Folk." California Folklore Quarterly, IV (1945), 1-17.

Wenzel, Marian. "Graveside Feasts and Dances in Yugoslavia." Folk-Lore, LXXIII (1962), 1-13.

Whitney, Stephen. "The Church with the Hand on Top."
Yankee, XXX (1966), 48-50.

Wilder, Mitchell A. "Santos (Religious Folk Art of New
Mexico)." American West, II (1965), 37-46.

Winner, Julia Hall. "Some Religious Humor from the Past."
New York Folklore Quarterly, XXI (1965), 58-62.

Wood, R. C. "Life, Death, and Poetry as Seen by the Pennsylvania Dutch." Monats-hefte für Deutschen Unterricht,
XXXVII (1945), 453-65.

Yoder, Don. "Organized Religion versus Folk Religion."
Pennsylvania Folklife, XV (1965), 36-52.

_____. Pennsylvania Spirituals. Lancaster: Pennsyl-
vania Folklife Society, 1961.

V. Miscellaneous

Adams, Percy G. Travelers and Travel Liars, 1660-1800.
Berkeley, Cal.: University of California Press, 1962.

Agnew, Theodore L. "Methodism on the Frontier." In The
History of American Methodism. Edited by Emory S.
Bucke et al. 3 vols. Nashville: Abingdon Press,
1964.

Aubrey, John. Miscellanies. London, 1696.

A Banquet of Jests: or, Change of Cheare. London, 1633.

Beard, Thomas. The Theatre of Gods Iudgements: or, A
Collection of Histories out of Sacred, Ecclesiasticall,
and Prophane Authours, Concerning the Admirable Iudgements of God Upon the Transgressions of His Commandments. London, 1597.

Beverley, Robert. The History and Present State of Virginia.

Edited with an introduction by Louis B. Wright. Chapel
Hill, N.C.: University of North Carolina Press, 1947.

Bonhoeffer, Dietrich. Letters and Papers from Prison.
Edited by Eberhard Bethge. Translated by Reginald
Fuller. Revised by Frank Clarke et al. 3rd ed., rev.
and enl. London: S. C. M. Press, 1957.

Brand, John. Observations on the Popular Antiquities of
Great Britain. Revised by Henry Ellis. London:
H. G. Bohn, 1853.

Brewer, E. Cobham. A Dictionary of Miracles, Imitative,
Realistic, and Dogmatic, with Illustrations. Philadel-
phia: J. B. Lippincott Co., n. d. Republished by
Gale Research Co., Book Tower, Detroit, 1966.

Brinckmair, L. The Warnings of Germany, by Wonderfull
Signes, and Strange Prodigies Seene in Divers Parts
of that Countrey of Germany, Betweene the Yeare 1618
and 1638. London, 1638.

Buell, L. H. "Elizabethan Portents: Superstition or Doc-
trine?" In Essays Critical and Historical Dedicated to
Lily B. Campbell. Berkeley: University of California
Press, 1950, pp. 27-41.

Bunyan, John. The Pilgrim's Progress from This World to
That Which Is to Come Delivered Under the Similitude
of a Dream; Wherein Is Discovered the Manner of His
Setting Out; His Dangerous Journey; and Safe Arrival at
the Desired Country. New York: Rae D. Henkle Co.,
n. d.

Burton, Henry. A Divine Tragedie Lately Acted, or A Collection of Sundry Memorable Examples of Gods Judgments upon Sabbath-Breakers, and Other Libertines, in
their Unlawfull Spirits.... London, 1636.

Campbell, Joseph, ed. Myths, Dreams, and Religion. New
York: E. P. Dutton & Co., Inc., 1970.

Chamberlain, Robert. Conceits, Clinches, Flashes and
Whimzies Newly Studied. London, 1639.

Clark, Thomas D. The Rampaging Frontier: Manners and
Humors of Pioneer Days in the South and Middle West.

Indianapolis, Ind.: The Bobbs-Merrill Co., 1939.

Cleveland, Catherine. The Great Revival in the West, 1797-
1805. Chicago: University of Chicago Press, 1916.

Cox, Harvey. The Secular City: Secularization and Urbanization in Theological Perspective. Rev. ed. New York:
MacMillan, 1966.

Crane, Thomas, ed. The Exempla or Illustrative Stories
from the Sermon Vulgares of Jacques de Vitry. London: The Folklore Society, 1890.

Dorson, Richard M., ed. America Begins: Early American
Writing. New York: Pantheon Books, Inc., 1950.

Fishwick, Marshall. The American Hero: Myth and Reality.
Washington, D.C.: Public Affairs Press, 1954.

Gabriel, Ralph. The Course of American Democratic Thought:
An Intellectual History Since 1815. New York: The
Ronald Press Co., 1940.

Geertz, Clifford. "Religion as a Cultural System." In An-
thropological Approaches to the Study of Religion.
Edited by Michael Banton. New York: Frederick A.
Praeger, 1966.

Gesta Romanorum, or Entertaining Moral Stories, Invented
by the Monks as a Fireside Recreation, and Commonly
Applied in their Discourses from the Pulpit. Edited by
Charles Swan and Wynnard Hooper. London: George
Bell & Sons, 1877.

Hall, Clayton Colman. Narratives of Early Maryland 1633-
1684. New York: Charles Scribner's Sons, 1910.

Hansen, Chadwick. Witchcraft at Salem. New York: G.
Braziller, 1969.

Henry, Stuart. "Puritan Character in the Witchcraft Episode
of Salem." In A Miscellany of American Christianity;
Essays in Honor of H. Shelton Smith. Edited by Stuart
C. Henry. Durham, N.C.: Duke University Press,
1963.

Hood, Edwin Paxton, ed. The World of Anecdote. Philadelphia: J. B. Lippincott Company, 1887.

Hudson, Charles. "The Structure of a Fundamentalist Christian Belief-System." In Religion and the Solid South. Edited by Samuel S. Hill, Jr. Nashville: Abingdon Press, 1972, pp. 122-42.

James, Bartlett B. and J. Franklin Jamison, eds. The Journal of Jasper Danckaerts 1679-1680. New York: Charles Scribner's Sons, 1913.

Jessey, Henry. The Lords Loud Call to England: Being a True Relation of Some Late, Various, and Wonderful Judgments, or Handy-Works of God, by Earthquake, Lightening, Whirlewind, Great Multitude of Toads and Flyes; and also the Striking of Divers Persons with Sudden Death, in Several Places.... London, 1660.

Johnson, Charles. The Frontier Camp-Meeting; Religion's Harvest Time. Dallas: Southern Methodist University Press, 1955.

Josephus, Flavius. The Genuine Works of Flavius Josephus. Translated by William Whiston. 5 vols. Edinburgh: Printed for Thomas Brown, 1793.

Kelsey, Morton. Dreams: The Dark Speech of the Spirit; A Christian Interpretation. Garden City, N.Y.: Doubleday, 1968.

Kittredge, George L. Witchcraft in Old and New England. Cambridge, Mass.: Harvard University Press, 1939.

Lawson, John. Lawson's History of North Carolina; Containing the Exact Description, and Natural History of That Country, Together with the Present State Thereof and a Journal of a Thousand Miles Traveled Through Several Nations of Indians, Giving a Particular Account of Their Customs, Manners, Etc. Etc. (London, 1714) Richmond, Va.: Garrett and Massie, 1951.

Lord, Albert B. The Singer of Tales. Cambridge, Mass.: Harvard University Press, 1960.

Masterson, James R. "Traveler's Tales of Colonial Natural History." Journal of American Folklore, LIX (1946), 51-67, 174-88.

Mather, Cotton. Magnalia Christi Americana: or, The Ecclesiastical History of New England, From its First
Planting in the Year 1620, Unto the Year of our Lord,
1698. Hartford, Conn.: Silas Andrus and Son, 1852.

Meyers, Marvin. The Jacksonian Persuasion: Politics and
Belief. Palo Alto, Cal.: Stanford University Press,
1957.

Miller, Perry. Errand Into the Wilderness. Cambridge,
Mass.: Harvard University Press, 1956.

_____. "The Garden of Eden and the Deacon's Meadow."
American Heritage, VII (1955), 54-61, 102.

_____. The New England Mind: The Seventeenth Century.
Cambridge, Mass.: Harvard University Press, 1954.

_____. "The Religious Impulse in the Founding of Virginia:
Religion and Society in the Early Literature." William
and Mary Quarterly, Ser. III, V (1948), 492-522.

Moore, Arthur. The Frontier Mind: A Cultural Analysis of
the Kentucky Frontiersman. Lexington, Ky.: University of Kentucky Press, 1957.

Mosher, J. A. The Exemplum in the Early Religious and
Didactic Literature of England. New York: Columbia
University Press, 1911.

Murdock, Kenneth. "William Hubbard and the Providential
Interpretation of History," Proceedings of the American
Antiquarian Society, LII, pt. 1 (1942), 15-37.

Owst, G. R. Literature and Pulpit in Medieval England; A
Neglected Chapter in the History of English Letters and
of the English People. Oxford: Basil Blackwell, 1966.

_____. Preaching in Medieval England; An Introduction to
Sermon Manuscripts of the Period c. 1350-1450. New
York: Russell and Russell, 1965.

Parry, Milman. "Studies in the Epic Technique of Oral
Verse-Making. I: Homer and Homeric Style." Harvard Studies in Classical Philosophy, XLI (1930), 73-
147.

Peckham, Howard H. Captured by Indians: True Tales of
    Pioneer Survivors. New Brunswick, N. J.: Rutgers
    University Press, 1954.

Poggio-Bracciolini. The Facetiae of Poggio and Other Medi-
    eval Story-Tellers. Trans. by Edward Storer. Lon-
    don: G. Routledge & Sons, 1928.

Rowe, Kenneth E. "New Light on Early Methodist Theological
    Education." Methodist History, X (1971), 58-62.

Sam Jones' Anecdotes and Illustrations, Related by Him in
    His Revival Work. Chicago: Rhodes and McClure Pub-
    lishing House, 1889.

Spelman, Henry. The History and Fate of Sacrilege, Dis-
    covered by Examples of Scripture, of Heathens and of
    Christians; from the Beginning of the World Continually
    to this Day. London, 1698.

Steckmesser, Kent L. The Western Hero in History and
    Legend. Norman, Okla.: University of Oklahoma
    Press, 1965.

Stidger, William L. Sermon Nuggets in Stories. New York:
    Abingdon-Cokesbury Press, 1964.

Stuart, George R. Stories and Parables to Illustrate Gospel
    Truths. Nashville: Publishing House of the Methodist
    Episcopal Church South, 1920.

Sweet, William W. Methodism in American History. New
    York: The Methodist Book Concern, 1933.

Turner, William. A Compleat History of the Most Remark-
    able Providences, Both of Judgements and Mercy, Which
    Have Happened in this Present Age. London: J. Dun-
    ton, 1697.

Tyler, Alice Felt. Freedom's Ferment; Phases of American
    Social History to 1860. Minneapolis: University of
    Minnesota Press, 1944.

Vahanian, Gabriel. The Death of God; The Culture of Our
    Post-Christian Era. New York: G. Braziller, 1961.

Vaughan, J. G. The Gem Cyclopedia of Illustrations. Cincinnati: Cranston & Stowe, 1889.

Wakeley, J. B. , ed. Anecdotes of the Rev. George Whitefield, M. A. , with Biographical Sketch. 3rd edition.
London: Hodder and Stoughton, 1875.

_____. Anecdotes of the Wesleys: Illustrations of their
Character and Personal History. New York: Carlton
and Lanahan, 1869.

Wallace, A. F. C. "Revitalization Movements. " In Reader
in Comparative Religion. 3rd edition. Edited by W. A.
Lessa and Evon Z. Vogt. New York: Harper and Row,
1972, pp. 504-12.

Wanley, Nathaniel. The Wonders of the Little World: or,
A General History of Man in Six Books. London, 1678.

Ware, Caroline, ed. The Cultural Approach to History.
New York: Columbia University Press, 1940.

Wector, Dixon. The Hero In America; A Chronicle of Hero-
Worship. New York: Charles Scribner's Sons, 1941.

Woodrow, Robert. Analecta: or, Materials for a History
of Remarkable Providences; Mostly Relating to Scotch
Ministers and Christians. 4 volumes. Edinburgh:
Printed for the Maitland Club, 1842-43.

Wright, Thomas. The Glory of Gods Revenge Against the
Bloody and Detestable Sins of Murther and Adultery,
Expressed in Thirty Modern Tragical Histories. Lon-
don, 1685.

Wright, Thomas, ed. A Selection of Latin Stories, from
Manuscripts of the Thirteenth and Fourteenth Centuries:
A Contribution to the History of Fiction During the Mid-
dle Ages. London, 1842.

INDEX

Abbott, Benjamin 57, 115, 116, 219, 222
Alabama 152
American Folklore Society 1
American Historical Association 6
Ancient of Days 57
Appleseed, Johnny 21
Arkansas 282
Asbury, Francis 28, 64, 107, 205, 282, 291, 301
atheism 84
Axley, James 203
Ayres, Samuel 28, 285

backslider 44, 88, 90, 110, 115
Balch, T. B. 221
Bangs, Nathan 65-6
Baptists 18, 28, 58, 70, 71, 99, 116, 118, 122, 127, 137, 178, 195, 221, 256, 260, 266-70, 272, 273
Bartine, David 281
Bascom, Henry 129-30, 153, 199, 203, 239, 241, 244, 247, 279, 294
Beecher, Lyman 264
Berryman, John 159
Bible 13, 56, 85, 117, 123, 134, 139, 168, 171-2, 177, 216, 246, 266, 298
Bidlack, Benjamin 142
Bland, Zane 296
Blegen, Theodore 7
Boone, Daniel 281
Borein, Peter 242

Bostwick, Shadrach 285, 286
Bowman, George 254
Bray, Henry 155
Brewer, E. Cobham 44
British see England
Brunvand, Jan H. 2, 3
"Brush College" 182
bundling 21
Bunyan, John 75-6
Bunyan, Paul 3
Buoy, Charles 110
Burgess, John 21, 203, 208, 271, 277
Burkitt, William 247

Calhoun, John 21
California 201
Calvinism 58, 177, 245-6, 266, 267, 270, 283, 310
Campbellites 28, 178, 195, 197, 266, 271-2
camp-meeting 13, 28, 65, 91, 92, 95, 118, 124, 159, 161, 254, 292, 296
Canada 197
Capers, William 48, 140
Caples, William G. 23-4, 201-2, 249, 279, 282
Carroll, Andrew 90
Cartwright, Barton 204
Cartwright, Peter 12, 25, 27, 56, 164, 203, 219, 242, 250-1, 269, 271, 279-80, 285, 291-2, 294, 301
Catlin, S. J. 247-8

349